First World War
and Army of Occupation
War Diary
France, Belgium and Germany

41 DIVISION
Headquarters, Branches and Services
Commander Royal Artillery
1 March 1918 - 31 March 1919

WO95/2621/2

The Naval & Military Press Ltd
www.nmarchive.com
Published in association with The National Archives

Published by

The Naval & Military Press Ltd

Unit 10 Ridgewood Industrial Park,

Uckfield, East Sussex,

TN22 5QE England

Tel: +44 (0) 1825 749494

www.naval-military-press.com

www.nmarchive.com

This diary has been reprinted in facsimile from the original. Any imperfections are inevitably reproduced and the quality may fall short of modern type and cartographic standards.

© **Crown Copyright**
Images reproduced by permission of The National Archives, London, England, 2015.

Contents

Document type	Place/Title	Date From	Date To
Heading	WO95/2621 41 Div Commander R.A. Mar 18-Mar 19		
Heading	Returned from Italy 7/13.3.18 War Diary Headquarters, 41st Divisional Artillery. March 1918		
War Diary	Italy Riese	01/03/1918	05/03/1918
War Diary	Sovernigo	05/03/1918	06/03/1918
War Diary	Treviso	07/03/1918	07/03/1918
War Diary	France Doullens	10/03/1918	14/03/1918
War Diary	Contay	21/03/1918	21/03/1918
War Diary	Favreuil & Grevillers	22/03/1918	22/03/1918
War Diary	Grevillers	23/03/1918	23/03/1918
War Diary	Achiet Le Petit	24/03/1918	24/03/1918
War Diary	France Achiet-Le Petit	24/03/1918	24/03/1918
War Diary	Bucquoy & Fonquevillers	25/03/1918	25/03/1918
War Diary	Fonquevillers & Bailleuval	26/03/1918	26/03/1918
War Diary	Bailleuval	27/03/1918	27/03/1918
War Diary	Souastre	28/03/1918	31/03/1918
Heading	Appendices A, B and C.		
Operation(al) Order(s)	41st Divisional Artillery Order No. 156	04/03/1918	04/03/1918
Miscellaneous	March Table	04/03/1918	04/03/1918
Miscellaneous	Amendment to 41st. Divisional Arty. Instruction No. 1	07/03/1918	07/03/1918
Miscellaneous	41st Divisional Artillery. Instruction No. 1	06/03/1918	06/03/1918
Miscellaneous	Entraining Table 41st Divisional Artillery Instruction No. 1	06/03/1918	06/03/1918
Miscellaneous	Pro-Forma Vide-Para. 6		
Miscellaneous	Medical Arrangements	06/03/1918	06/03/1918
Diagram etc	Sketch Shewing Treviso Central Station and the Approach Thereto		
Operation(al) Order(s)	41st Divisional Artillery Order 157 App C	20/03/1918	20/03/1918
Miscellaneous	March Table issued with 41st Divisional Artillery Order No. 157		
Heading	41st Division. C.R.A. 41st Division April 1918		
War Diary	Souastre	01/04/1918	17/04/1918
War Diary	Pas-En-Artois	18/04/1918	30/04/1918
Miscellaneous	Headquarters, 62nd. Division "G" IVth. Corps, R.A. Appendix A	05/04/1918	05/04/1918
Miscellaneous	Table "A" Approximate Areas for 18 Brigades R.F.A., to cover the Red Line (i.e., Line Willow Patch-Coigneux-Louvencourt-Lealvillers.)		
Miscellaneous	Table "B" Approximate areas for 18 Brigades R.F.A., to cover the Red Line from Lealvillers to BOIS du Warnimont and the "Pas Switch" through St. Leger to C. 17 (Central)		
Miscellaneous	41st Divisional Artillery Instruction No. 4 Appendix B	18/04/1918	18/04/1918
Miscellaneous	1st Addendum to 41st Divisional Artillery Instructions No. 4 Appendix "C"	21/04/1918	21/04/1918
Heading	HQ Ra 41 D Vol 24 May		
Heading	Officer F/c A. G's Office G.H.2 3rd Echelon		
War Diary	France Pas-En-Artois	01/05/1918	05/05/1918
War Diary	Couin	06/05/1918	13/05/1918
War Diary	France Couin & Doullens	14/05/1918	14/05/1918

Type	Description	From	To
War Diary	Belgium La Lovie	15/05/1918	31/05/1918
War Diary	France Pas-En-Artois	01/05/1918	05/05/1918
War Diary	Couin	06/05/1918	13/05/1918
War Diary	France Couin & Doullens	14/05/1918	14/05/1918
War Diary	Belgium La Lovie	15/05/1918	31/05/1918
Miscellaneous	41st Divisional Artillery Instructions No 5 Appendix "A"		
Miscellaneous	41st Divisional Artillery Instructions No 6 Appendix "B"	05/05/1918	05/05/1918
Miscellaneous	42nd Divisional Artillery Defence Scheme. Centre Division-IV Corps Appendix "C"	02/05/1918	02/05/1918
Miscellaneous	Instructions Regarding Ammunition Supply Appendix 'C'		
Miscellaneous	List of O.PS. of 42nd Division (Centre Division) Appendix 'A'	02/05/1918	02/05/1918
Miscellaneous	42nd D.A. No. B.M. 296	02/05/1918	02/05/1918
Miscellaneous	Reference 42nd Divisional Artillery Defence Scheme issued under this office No. B.M. 296	02/05/1918	02/05/1918
Miscellaneous	Positions to Cover Purple Line System		
Miscellaneous	1st Amendment to 42nd D.A. Defence Scheme. Appendix "D"	07/05/1918	07/05/1918
Miscellaneous	Appendix "D" to 42nd D.A. Defence Scheme.	07/05/1918	07/05/1918
Miscellaneous	2nd Amendment to 42nd D.A. Defence Scheme Appendix "E"	10/05/1918	10/05/1918
Miscellaneous	41st D.A. No. S628	11/05/1918	11/05/1918
Miscellaneous	Corrigenda to 1st Amendments 42nd D.A. Defence Scheme.		
Miscellaneous	41st Divisional Artillery Instruction No. 1 Appendix "F"		
Miscellaneous	Table "A"		
Miscellaneous	Pro-Forma "B"		
Miscellaneous	Rear Lines of Defence. Appendix "G"	15/05/1918	15/05/1918
Miscellaneous	41" O.A. No. S654 Appendix "H"	17/05/1918	17/05/1918
Miscellaneous	41st Divisional Artillery Instructions No 2 Appendix "1"	18/05/1918	18/05/1918
Miscellaneous	Amendment No. 1 to 41st D.A. Instructions No. 2	19/05/1918	19/05/1918
Miscellaneous	41st Divisional Artillery Instructions No. 3 Appendix "J"	19/05/1918	19/05/1918
Miscellaneous	Reference 41st D.A. Instructions No. 4 of date. Appendix "K"	21/05/1918	21/05/1918
Miscellaneous	41st Divisional Artillery Instructions No 4	21/05/1918	21/05/1918
Miscellaneous	41st Divisional Artillery Defence Scheme No. 1. Appendix "L"	19/05/1918	19/05/1918
Miscellaneous	Appendix "A" Issued with 41st. D.A. Defence Scheme No. 1	17/05/1918	17/05/1918
Miscellaneous	Appendix "B" Issued with 41st. D.A. Defence Scheme No. 1	20/05/1918	20/05/1918
Miscellaneous	41st Divisional Artillery Instructions No 5 "C"	30/04/1918	30/04/1918
Miscellaneous	Appendix "D". Issued with 41st D.A. Defence Scheme No. 1	20/05/1918	20/05/1918
Miscellaneous	Appendix "E". Issued with 41st D.A. Defence Scheme No. 1	20/05/1918	20/05/1918
Miscellaneous	Appendix "F" Issued with 41st D.A. Defence Scheme No. 1	20/05/1918	20/05/1918
Miscellaneous	Appendix "G" Issued with 41st D.A. Defence Scheme No. 1	21/05/1918	21/05/1918

Type	Description	Date From	Date To
Diagram etc	Signal Communications Issued with 41st. D.A. Defence Scheme No. 1		
Miscellaneous	41st D.A. No. S 671 Appendix "M"	21/05/1918	21/05/1918
Miscellaneous	41st Divisional Artillery Instructions No 6 Appendix "N"	24/05/1918	24/05/1918
Miscellaneous	Amendment No. to 41st. D.A. Defence Scheme No. 1 Appendix "O"	25/05/1918	25/05/1918
Miscellaneous	Programme for Visit of G.C.C. to Wagon Lines. 25-5-18 Appendix "P"	25/05/1918	25/05/1918
Miscellaneous	1st. Amendment to Appendix "F" 41st. D.A. Defence Scheme No. 1 Appendix "Q"	25/05/1918	25/05/1918
Miscellaneous	Amendment No. 2 to 41st, D.A. Defence Scheme No. 1 Appendix "R"	27/05/1918	27/05/1918
Miscellaneous	41st Divisional Artillery Instructions No 7 Appendix "S"	29/05/1918	29/05/1918
War Diary	La Lovie (Belgium)	01/06/1918	05/06/1918
War Diary	Bambecque (France)	06/06/1918	06/06/1918
War Diary	Zeggers-Cappel	07/06/1918	07/06/1918
War Diary	Polincove	08/06/1918	24/06/1918
War Diary	Zeggers-Cappel	25/06/1918	25/06/1918
War Diary	Abeele area. (Belgium)	26/06/1918	30/06/1918
Miscellaneous	41st D.A. No. S. 737 Appendix "A"	31/05/1918	31/05/1918
Miscellaneous	41st D.A. No. S. 746. Appendix "B"	02/06/1918	02/06/1918
Operation(al) Order(s)	41st Divisional Artillery Order No. 4 Appendix "C"	03/06/1918	03/06/1918
Miscellaneous	41st Divisional Artillery Administrative Instruction No. 4, issued in connection with 41st. D.A. Order No. 5 Appendix "D"		
Miscellaneous	Schedule "A" Accommodation Night 6/7th June 1918	06/06/1918	06/06/1918
Miscellaneous	Schedule "B" Accommodation Night 7/8th June 1918	07/06/1918	07/06/1918
Operation(al) Order(s)	41st Divisional Artillery Order No. 6 Appendix "E"	05/06/1918	05/06/1918
Miscellaneous	41st Divisional Artillery Administrative Instructions No. 5 Appendix F	06/06/1918	06/06/1918
Miscellaneous	Appendix "A"		
Miscellaneous	Schedule "C"		
Miscellaneous	Addendum to 41st Divisional Artillery Instruction No. 9 Appendix C	14/06/1918	14/06/1918
Miscellaneous	41st Divisional Artillery Instructions No 9	14/06/1918	14/06/1918
Miscellaneous	Outline of Field Firing Operation to be carried out by 41st Divisional Artillery in conjunction with 39th Division (Training Division with American Army) on 15-6-18	15/06/1918	15/06/1918
Miscellaneous	41st D.A. Administrative Instruction issued in connection with 41st D.A. Instructions, No. 10	15/06/1918	15/06/1918
Miscellaneous	41st Divisional Artillery Instructions No 10 Appendix H	15/06/1918	15/06/1918
Miscellaneous	18-Pdr. Task and Time Table		
Miscellaneous	4.5" How. Task and Time Table.		
Map			
Operation(al) Order(s)	41st Divisional Artillery Order No. 7. Appendix "1"	24/06/1918	24/06/1918
Operation(al) Order(s)	41st Divisional Artillery Order No. 8	24/06/1918	24/06/1918
Miscellaneous	Officer Commanding, 187th. Brigade, R.F.A.	24/06/1918	24/06/1918
Operation(al) Order(s)	41st Divisional Artillery Order No. 9 Appendix "J"	25/06/1918	25/06/1918
Miscellaneous	March Table Issued with 41st Divisional Artillery Order No. 9	25/06/1918	25/06/1918
Miscellaneous	41st Divisional Artillery Instructions No. 12 Appendix "K"	27/06/1918	27/06/1918

Miscellaneous	Appendix issued with 41st Divisional Arty. Instructions No. 12	27/06/1918	27/06/1918
Miscellaneous	1st Amendment to 41st Divisional Artillery Instruction No. 12	29/06/1918	29/06/1918
Miscellaneous	41st. Divisional Artillery Administrative Instructions No. 12 issued in connection with 41st D.A. Instructions No. 12, dated 28th June 1918	29/06/1918	29/06/1918
Miscellaneous	Table "A" Accommodation of 41st. Divisional Artillery		
Miscellaneous	41st Divisional Artillery Instructions No. 13 Appendix "L"	30/06/1918	30/06/1918
Heading	HQ RA 41 D Vol 27		
Miscellaneous	A.G. Office Base		
War Diary	Belgium Abeele Area	01/07/1918	18/07/1918
War Diary	Belgium Area of Abeele	19/07/1918	30/07/1918
Miscellaneous	41st Divisional Artillery Instructions No. 12 Appendix "A"	27/06/1918	27/06/1918
Miscellaneous	Appendix issued with 41st Divisional Arty Instructions No. 12	27/06/1918	27/06/1918
Miscellaneous	41st Divisional Artillery Defence Scheme Appendix "B"	03/07/1918	03/07/1918
Miscellaneous	Appendix "A" issued with 41st Divisional Artillery Defence Scheme	03/07/1918	03/07/1918
Miscellaneous	Addendum No. 1 to 41st D.A. Defence Scheme (Temporary) dated 3rd July 1918	06/07/1918	06/07/1918
Miscellaneous	41st. Divisional Artillery Defence Scheme No. 2 Appendix "C"		
Miscellaneous	41st D.A. Defence Scheme No. 2		
Miscellaneous	41st. Divisional Artillery Defence Scheme No. 2	09/07/1918	09/07/1918
Miscellaneous	Addendum to 41st D.A. Defence Scheme No. 2	11/07/1918	11/07/1918
Miscellaneous	Addendum to 41st D.A. Defence Scheme No. 2	15/07/1918	15/07/1918
Miscellaneous	Appendix "A" issued with 41st D.A. Defence Scheme No. 2	09/07/1918	09/07/1918
Miscellaneous	Amendment to Appendix "B" 41st D.A. Defence Scheme No. 2 Appendix "C"	12/07/1918	12/07/1918
Miscellaneous	Addendum to Appendix "B" 41st D.A. Defence Scheme No. 2	19/07/1918	19/07/1918
Miscellaneous	Appendix "B" issued with 41st D.A. Defence Scheme No. 2		
Miscellaneous	Appendix "C" issued with 41st. D.A. Defence Scheme No. 2	09/07/1918	09/07/1918
Miscellaneous	41st. Divisional Artillery Instruction No. 5	30/04/1918	30/04/1918
Miscellaneous	2nd Amendment to Appendix "E" 41st D.A. Defence Scheme No. 2	20/07/1918	20/07/1918
Miscellaneous	Amendment to 41st D.A. Defence Scheme No. 2 Appendix "E"	17/07/1918	17/07/1918
Miscellaneous	Appendix "E" issued with 41st D.A. Defence Scheme No. 2	09/07/1918	09/07/1918
Diagram etc	Counter-Preparation		
Miscellaneous	To all recipients of 41st D.A. Defence Scheme No. 2	31/07/1918	31/07/1918
Miscellaneous	S.O.S. Tasks Barrage I (covering Front Line).	31/07/1918	31/07/1918
Miscellaneous	S.O.S. Tasks. Barrage II (Covering Scherpenberg-La Clytte Line).	31/07/1918	31/07/1918
Miscellaneous	Appendix "F" issued with 41st D.A. Defence Scheme No. 2	10/07/1918	10/07/1918
Miscellaneous	Amendment No. 2 to Appendix "H" 41st D.A. Defence Scheme No. 2	26/07/1918	26/07/1918

Miscellaneous	Appendix "H" to 41st D.A. Defence Scheme No. 2	17/07/1918	17/07/1918
Miscellaneous	Addendum to Appendix "H" 41st D.A. Defence Scheme No. 2	20/07/1918	20/07/1918
Miscellaneous	Amendment to Appendix "H" of 41st D.A. Defence Scheme No. 2	18/07/1918	18/07/1918
Miscellaneous	Addendum No. 2 to Appendix "H" 41st D.A. Defence Scheme No. 2	25/07/1918	25/07/1918
Diagram etc	Appendix "I" issued with 45 D.M. Defence Scheme No. 2		
Miscellaneous	Appendix "J" Administrative Arrangements		
Miscellaneous	41st D.A. No. S. 1023	25/07/1918	25/07/1918
Miscellaneous	Amendments to Appendices 41st D.A. Defence Scheme No. 2		
Miscellaneous	S.O.S. Tasks Barrage I (covering outpost line)		
Miscellaneous	S.O.S. Tasks Barrage II (Covering Scherpenberg La Clytte Line).		
Miscellaneous	41st. Divisional Artillery Instructions No. 14 (Appendix "D")		
Miscellaneous	Addendum to 41st D.A. Instructions No. 14	13/07/1918	13/07/1918
Miscellaneous	41st. Division Instruction No. 5 Appendix "E"	16/07/1918	16/07/1918
Miscellaneous	41st D.A. No. S. 953 Appendix "F"	17/07/1918	17/07/1918
Miscellaneous	Bombardment Table.		
Miscellaneous	41st D.A. Instruction No. 15 Appendix "G"	18/07/1918	18/07/1918
Miscellaneous	Table "A" issued with 41st D.A. Instructions No. 15	18/07/1918	18/07/1918
Operation(al) Order(s)	41st. Divisional Artillery Order No. 10 Appendix "H"	21/07/1918	21/07/1918
Miscellaneous	41st. Divisional Artillery Instructions No. 16 Appendix "1"	21/07/1918	21/07/1918
Miscellaneous	Addendum No. 1 to 41st D.A. Instructions No. 16	22/07/1918	22/07/1918
Miscellaneous	41st D.A. No. S. 1017 (Appendix "J")	25/07/1918	25/07/1918
Miscellaneous	41st D.A Instructions No. 17 Appendix K	27/06/1918	27/06/1918
Miscellaneous	Table issued with 41st D.A. Instructions No. 17	27/07/1918	27/07/1918
Miscellaneous	41st. Divisional Artillery Instructions No. 19 Appendix "I"	30/07/1918	30/07/1918
Heading	Operation Orders Minor operation 8/9 Aug 18 (War Diary) With Map Vol 28		
War Diary	(Belgium) Abeele Area	01/08/1918	18/08/1918
War Diary	France St. Laurent	19/08/1918	27/08/1918
War Diary	Belgium Abeele Area	28/08/1918	30/08/1918
War Diary	Scherpenberg Area	31/08/1918	31/08/1918
Miscellaneous	41st. Divisional Artillery Instructions No. 20 Appendix A	01/08/1918	01/08/1918
Miscellaneous	To all recipients of 41st D.A. Instructions No. 20 Appendix "B"	02/08/1918	02/08/1918
Miscellaneous	To all recipients of 41st D.A. Instructions No. 20 Appendix C	05/08/1918	05/08/1918
Miscellaneous	Second Amendment to 41st D.A. Operation Order No. 11	07/08/1918	07/08/1918
Miscellaneous	41st D.A. No. S. 1149	07/08/1918	07/08/1918
Miscellaneous	41st D.A. No. S. 1150	07/08/1918	07/08/1918
Miscellaneous	First Amendment to 41st D.A. Operation Order No. 11	07/08/1918	07/08/1918
Miscellaneous	41st D.A. No. S. 1156	08/08/1918	08/08/1918
Miscellaneous	41st D.A. No. S. 1155	08/08/1918	08/08/1918
Miscellaneous	First Addendum to 41st D.A. Operation Order No. 11	07/08/1918	07/08/1918
Miscellaneous	41st. Divisional Artillery Instructions No. 21	08/08/1918	08/08/1918
Miscellaneous	Movement Table issued with 41st D.A. Instructions No. 21	08/08/1918	08/08/1918

Type	Description	Date From	Date To
Operation(al) Order(s)	41st. Divisional Artillery Operation Order No. 11 Appendix "D"	05/08/1918	05/08/1918
Map	Reference Letter For Map Squared N.		
Miscellaneous	Appendix "B" issued with 41st D.A. Operation Order No. 11	05/08/1918	05/08/1918
Miscellaneous	Appendix "C" Issued with 41st D.A. Operation Order No. 11	05/08/1918	05/08/1918
Operation(al) Order(s)	Appendix "D" Issued with 41st D.A. Operation Order No. 11	05/08/1918	05/08/1918
Miscellaneous	41st. Divisional Artillery Instructions No. 22 Appendix E	11/08/1918	11/08/1918
Miscellaneous	Counter Preparation Table issued with 41st D.A. Instructions No. 22	11/08/1918	11/08/1918
Miscellaneous	41st. Divisional Artillery Instructions No. 24 Appendix "F"	12/08/1918	12/08/1918
Miscellaneous	Addendum to 41st D.A. Instructions No. 22 Appendix E	11/08/1918	11/08/1918
Miscellaneous	41st. Divisional Artillery Instructions No. 23 Appendix G	12/08/1918	12/08/1918
Miscellaneous	41st. Divisional Artillery Instructions No. 26 Appendix H	14/08/1918	14/08/1918
Miscellaneous	41st D.A. No. S. 1198 Appendix I	14/08/1918	14/08/1918
Operation(al) Order(s)	41st. Divisional Artillery Order No. 12 Appendix J	15/08/1918	15/08/1918
Miscellaneous	41st. Divisional Artillery Instructions No. 27	15/08/1918	15/08/1918
Operation(al) Order(s)	41st. Divisional Artillery Order No. 13 Appendix L	17/08/1918	17/08/1918
Operation(al) Order(s)	Administrative Instruction Issued With 41st D.A. Order No. 13 dated 17th. Aug 18 App "L"	17/08/1918	17/08/1918
Miscellaneous	Locations of Wagon Lines to be Occupied by 41st. Div Arty. on & from 19th. Aug. 1918	19/08/1918	19/08/1918
Operation(al) Order(s)	41st. Divisional Artillery Order No. 14 Appendix M	25/08/1918	25/08/1918
War Diary	Belgium Scherpenberg Area	01/09/1918	07/09/1918
War Diary	Abeele Area	08/09/1918	13/09/1918
War Diary	Belgium Abeele Area	14/09/1918	26/09/1918
War Diary	Busseboom Area	27/09/1918	28/09/1918
War Diary	Belgium Mersey Camp (Busseboom Area)	28/09/1918	29/09/1918
War Diary	Belgium Mersey Camp (Busseboom Area) & Lankhof Fm. Nr. Ypres Comines Canal	29/09/1918	30/09/1918
Operation(al) Order(s)	41st. Divisional Artillery Order No. 15 Appendix A	02/09/1918	02/09/1918
Operation(al) Order(s)	41st. Divisional Artillery Order No. 16 Appendix B	05/09/1918	05/09/1918
Miscellaneous	Appendix "A" to 41st D.A. Order No. 16	05/09/1918	05/09/1918
Miscellaneous	41st D.A. No. S. 1314	06/09/1918	06/09/1918
Miscellaneous	41st. Divisional Artillery Instructions No. 30	05/09/1918	05/09/1918
Miscellaneous	41st. Divisional Artillery Instruction No. 31 Appendix C	05/09/1918	05/09/1918
Miscellaneous	41st. Divisional Artillery Instructions No. 32 Appendix D	07/09/1918	07/09/1918
Miscellaneous	41st Divisional Artillery Instructions No. 33 Appendix E	07/09/1918	07/09/1918
Miscellaneous	Not to be Taken Beyond Main Battery Positions Appendix F	13/09/1918	13/09/1918
Miscellaneous	Appendix A To Dickebusch Sector Provisional Artillery Defence Scheme Artillery Dispositions.	13/09/1918	13/09/1918
Miscellaneous	Appendix B. To Vierstraat Sector Provisional Artillery Defence Scheme	18/09/1918	18/09/1918
Miscellaneous	Appendix C. To Vierstraat Sector Provisional Artillery Defence Scheme	18/09/1918	18/09/1918

Miscellaneous	41st Divisional Artillery Instructions No. 35 Appendix G	26/09/1918	26/09/1918
Miscellaneous	Appendix "A" Issued with 41st D.A. Instructions No. 35 Signalling Arrangements.	26/09/1918	26/09/1918
Diagram etc	Diagram of Communications		
Miscellaneous Map	41st D.A. No. S. 117 Appendix "H"	28/09/1918	28/09/1918
Miscellaneous Map	41st D.A. No. S. 122 Appendix "1"	28/09/1918	28/09/1918
Heading	41st D.A. Oct. 18		
War Diary	Belgium Lankhof Farm (Ypres Comines Canal)	01/10/1918	04/10/1918
War Diary	Gheluvelt & Fort Garry.	04/10/1918	04/10/1918
War Diary	Fort Garry	05/10/1918	15/10/1918
War Diary	Ashmore Fm. Moorseele Area	16/10/1918	19/10/1918
War Diary	Poeselhoek (nr. Gulleghem)	20/10/1918	20/10/1918
War Diary	T'Hooghe (nr. Courtrai)	21/10/1918	31/10/1918
Miscellaneous	41st Divisional Artillery Preliminary Instructions No. 36 App A	08/10/1918	08/10/1918
Miscellaneous	1st Addendum to 41st Divisional Artillery Preliminary Instructions No. 36	09/10/1918	09/10/1918
Miscellaneous	Appendix A. 41st Divisional Artillery		
Miscellaneous	Second Addendum to 41st D.A. Preliminary Instructions No. 36	12/10/1918	12/10/1918
Miscellaneous	Appendix B. To 2nd Addendum to 41st D.A. Preliminary Instructions No. 36	12/10/1918	12/10/1918
Diagram etc	Diagram of Lines after move of Bde Hqrs.		
Miscellaneous	41st D.A. No. S. 203	12/10/1918	12/10/1918
Miscellaneous	Third Addendum to 41st D.A. Instructions No. 36 (in accordance with 41st Divn. Order No. 275	12/10/1918	12/10/1918
Miscellaneous	Reference Map Sheet 28 1/40,000	16/10/1918	16/10/1918
Miscellaneous	March Table		
Operation(al) Order(s)	41st Divisional Artillery Order No. 17 App C	19/10/1918	19/10/1918
Miscellaneous	March Table to Accompany 41st Division Order No. 286	19/10/1918	19/10/1918
Operation(al) Order(s)	41st. Divisional Artillery Order No. 18 App E	23/10/1918	23/10/1918
Operation(al) Order(s)	41st. Divisional Artillery Order No. 19 App F	23/10/1918	23/10/1918
Miscellaneous	Reference Para 11 (b) 41st D.A. Order No. 20 App Y	24/10/1918	24/10/1918
Operation(al) Order(s) Diagram etc	41st Divisional Artillery Order No. 20	24/10/1918	24/10/1918
Operation(al) Order(s)	41st Divisional Artillery Order No. 21 App H	25/10/1918	25/10/1918
Miscellaneous Diagram etc	41st D.A. No. S. 242	26/10/1918	26/10/1918
Miscellaneous	A Form. Messages And Signals.		
Operation(al) Order(s)	41st Divisional Artillery Order No. 22 App I	29/10/1918	29/10/1918
Miscellaneous	41st D.A. No. S. 257	30/10/1918	30/10/1918
Miscellaneous	41st D.A. No. S. 266 App J	31/10/1918	31/10/1918
War Diary	T'Hooge Courtrai	01/11/1918	01/11/1918
War Diary	St. Louis	02/11/1918	06/11/1918
War Diary	Vichte	07/11/1918	09/11/1918
War Diary	Caster	10/11/1918	10/11/1918
War Diary	Belgium Schoorisse	11/11/1918	11/11/1918
War Diary	Nederbrakel	12/11/1918	17/11/1918
War Diary	Sant Bergen	18/11/1918	19/11/1918
War Diary	Grammont	21/11/1918	30/11/1918
Operation(al) Order(s)	41st Divisional Artillery Order No. 23 Appendix "A"	01/11/1918	01/11/1918

Miscellaneous	41st Divisional Artillery Instructions No. 37 Appendix B	04/11/1918	04/11/1918
Operation(al) Order(s)	41st Divisional Artillery Order No. 28 Appendix C	09/11/1918	09/11/1918
Operation(al) Order(s)	41st Divisional Artillery Order No. 26 Appendix "D"	10/11/1918	10/11/1918
Operation(al) Order(s)	41st Divisional Artillery Order No. 27 Appendix "E"	12/11/1918	12/11/1918
Miscellaneous	March Table.		
Operation(al) Order(s)	41st Divisional Artillery Order No. 28 Appendix "F"	17/11/1918	17/11/1918
Miscellaneous	March Table		
Miscellaneous	Presentation of Medal Ribbons Appendix G	25/11/1918	25/11/1918
War Diary	Belgium Grammont	01/12/1918	10/12/1918
War Diary	Tubize	12/12/1918	12/12/1918
War Diary	Braine Le Chateau	13/12/1918	13/12/1918
War Diary	Mont St. Jean	15/12/1918	15/12/1918
War Diary	Sart-Dame-Avelines.	16/12/1918	16/12/1918
War Diary	St. Martin	17/12/1918	17/12/1918
War Diary	Noville-Les-Bois	18/12/1918	18/12/1918
War Diary	Oteppe	19/12/1918	20/12/1918
War Diary	Belgium Oteppe	31/12/1918	31/12/1918
Operation(al) Order(s)	41st Divisional Artillery Order No. 28 Appendix "A"	10/12/1918	10/12/1918
Miscellaneous	March Table to accompany 41st D.A. Order No. 28		
Operation(al) Order(s)	To all recipients of 41st D.A. Order No. 28	11/12/1918	11/12/1918
Miscellaneous	11th Army Bde. R.F.A.	13/12/1918	13/12/1918
Miscellaneous	March Table to accompany 41st D.A. Order No. 28	17/12/1918	17/12/1918
War Diary	Belgium Oteppe	05/01/1919	12/01/1919
War Diary	Germany Cologne (Bayenthal)	13/01/1919	31/03/1919

WO95/2621 (2)

41 Div

Commander R.A
Mar '18 — Mar '19

Returned from Italy 7/13.3.18.

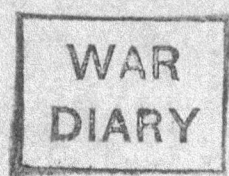

Headquarters,

41st DIVISIONAL ARTILLERY.

M A R C H

1 9 1 8

Attached:-

Appendices A, B & C.

Army Form C. 2118.

WAR DIARY
or
INTELLIGENCE SUMMARY

Headquarters, 41st. Divisional Artillery

(Erase heading not required.)

Instructions regarding War Diaries and Intelligence Summaries are contained in F.S. Regs., Part II. and the Staff Manual respectively. Title Pages will be prepared in manuscript.

Place	Date	Hour	Summary of Events and Information	Remarks and references to Appendices
ITALY	1918			
RIESE	March 1st.		A and B/187th.Brigade, A, B, and C/190th.Brigade, R.F.A., having been placed at the disposal of XI Corps, went into action in 5th.Division Area.	
"	" 2nd		D/187 and D/190 Batteries went into action in 7th.Divisional Area, but under orders of 5th. Divisional Artillery.	
"	" 4th.		On night 4/5th.March all guns, 41st.Divisional Artillery, were withdrawn from action.	
"	" 5th.		41st.Divisional Artillery concentrated in entraining area, West of TREVISO, in accordance with 41st.D.A.,Order No.156 (App: A). C/187 Battery, and all guns, and 190th.Brigade H.Q., rejoined there from 5th. & 7th.Divisional Areas.	App: A
SOVERNIGO	" "		Lieut.Col. G.A.Cardew, C.M.G.,D.S.O., on reporting from leave in England assumed command of the 41st.Divisional Artillery, vice Lieut.Col. A.R.Hurst,D.S.O. a/Lieut.Colonel C.D.G.Lyon, D.S.O., reported his arrival, and assumed command of 187th. Brigade, R.F.A., vice Lieut.Col. G.Symonds, D.S.O., employed with Ministry of Munitions.	
"	" 6th.		Under instructions from XIV Corps Q., the 41st.D.A.G., was reorganized on the lower establishment; all surplus being handed over to the 48th.Division.	
TREVISO	" 7th.		Entrainment commenced at TREVISO Central Station in accordance with 41st.D.A.,Administrative Instructions (attached App: B) Progress of entrainment throughout Normal	App: B
FRANCE DOULLENS	" 10th.		Detrainment commenced at DOULLENS Station. Progress of detrainment - normal.	
"	" 13th.		Detrainment of 41st.Divl: Artillery completed. 41st.Divl: Artillery concentrated in the vicinity of DOULLENS. Brigadier General A.S. Gotton, D.S.O., R.F.A., on returning from leave in England, assumed command of 41st.Divisional Artillery, vice Lieut.Col. G.A.Cardew,C.M.G., D.S.O.,	

-1-

Army Form C. 2118.

WAR DIARY
or
INTELLIGENCE-SUMMARY

(Erase heading not required.)

Headquarters, 41st. Divisional Artillery

Instructions regarding War Diaries and Intelligence Summaries are contained in F.S. Regs., Part II. and the Staff Manual respectively. Title Pages will be prepared in manuscript.

Place	Date	Hour	Summary of Events and Information	Remarks and references to Appendices
FRANCE DOULLENS.	March 14th.		41st. Division in G.H.Q. Reserve.	
CONTAY	" 21st.		41st. Divisional Artillery moved to CONTAY Area.	
FAVREUIL.& GREVILLERS	" 22nd.		On the morning of the 22nd., march of the 41st. Division to BUIRE-RIBEMONT Area was cancelled, the Division being directed to proceed to ACHIET-LE-PETIT Area. En route further orders were received for the Artillery to proceed forthwith to take up positions in action East of FAVREUIL to cover the Green Line. These positions were occupied at about 5 p.m., and the Divisional Artillery passed under the command of the 6th. Division. 41st.D.A., Headquarters opened at FAVREUIL at 3 p.m. At 6 p.m., 41st.D.A.Headquarters moved back to GREVILLERS.	(App:G)
GREVILLERS	" 23rd.		During the night 22/23rd., 41st.Division Infantry relieved 6th.Divisional Infantry. Consequent to the withdrawal of the Right flank in the vicinity of BEUGNY it became necessary on the afternoon of the 23rd. to draw back 187th. and 190th.Brigades,R.F.A., from their present positions East of FAVREUIL to positions West of SAPIGNIES - BAPAUME Road in the vicinity of the MONUMENT and SAPIGNIES.	
ACHIET LE PETIT.	" 24th		At 10 a.m., B.G.,R.A.,41st.Division, assumed command of the Artillery covering the Divisional front. At that time it was organized as follows:- Right Group covering front of Right Inf.Brigade (123rd.Inf.Bde) 187th.Brigade, 2nd.Brigade, 236th.Brigade, R.F.A. Left Group (covering front of 122nd.Inf.Brigade) 190th.Brigade,/93rd.(Army) Brigade, 110th.Brigade, R.F.A. Two heavy Brigades were also attached, and placed under the command of the G.R.A., namely, 48th. Brigade, and 90th.Brigade,R.G.A. During the afternoon it became apparent that, owing to the withdrawal of the Infantry of the Divisions on the Right, that the positions of the artillery in the vicinity of BAPAUME would become untenable. The 236th.Brigade,R.F.A., was therefore ordered to withdraw to positions that had been reconnoitred S. of BIHUCOURT. The 90th.Brigade,R.G.A., was also directed to withdraw to positions S.W. of ACHIET-le-GRAND.	

Army Form C. 2118.

WAR DIARY
or
INTELLIGENCE-SUMMARY

(Erase heading not required.) Headquarters, 41st. Divisional Artillery

Instructions regarding War Diaries and Intelligence Summaries are contained in F.S. Regs., Part II. and the Staff Manual respectively. Title Pages will be prepared in manuscript.

Place	Date	Hour	Summary of Events and Information	Remarks and references to Appendices
FRANCE ACHIET - LE PETIT.	March 24th.		(Contd). At about 7 p.m., orders were issued for the withdrawal of the Infantry during the night of the 24/25th. to the line, approximately, SAPIGNIES - BIENVILLERS. The Artillery were ordered to cover this withdrawal, and to withdraw to positions in the vicinity of ACHIET LE GRAND. This operation was successfully carried out, the last batteries withdrawing from the SAPIGNIES - BAPAUME Line at 1 a.m, on the 25th. At 6 p.m., Divisional Headquarters moved from GREVILLERS to ACHIET LE PETIT. At 6 p.m., the 48th. and 90th.Brigades,R.G.A., were transferred to another Division, and the 87th. and 92nd.Brigades,R.G.A., were allotted to 41st.Division instead, and were ordered into positions in action between ESSARTS and BUCQUOY.	
BUCQUOY & FONQUEVILLERS	"	25th.	At 5 a.m., Divisional Headquarters moved from ACHIET LE PETIT to BUCQUOY, and shortly afterwards orders were issued for the withdrawal of the Infantry to the LOGEAST WOOD, E. of ACHIET LE PETIT, Line. The Artillery were ordered to fall back, covering the withdrawal, to positions, which had previously been reconnoitred, E. of BUCQUOY. This operation was completed by mid-day. During the afternoon the 62nd.Division arrived, and its Infantry moved up to relieve the 41st. Division. One Artillery Brigade, 62nd.Division, moved up into action to relieve 2nd.Brigade R.F.A.,(6th.Division), which was withdrawn to rest. At 8 p.m., the B.G.,R.A., 41st.Division, handed over the command of the Artillery covering the front to the B.G.,R.A., 62nd.Division, and 41st.D.A.,Headquarters moved to FONQUEVILLERS.	
FONQUEVILLERS & BAILLEUVAL	"	26th.	Brigades withdrew to positions in action between ESSARTS and HANNESCAMPS owing to the infantry coming back to the ABLAINZEVELLE, E. of BUCQUOY, Line. 41st.D.A.,Headquarters moved to BAILLEUVAL. 41st.D.A.C. moved to SOUASTRE.	
BAILLEUVAL	"	27th.	Situation and positions remained unchanged.	
SOUASTRE	"	28th.	41st.D.A.,Headquarters moved to SOUASTRE.	
"	"	29th. 30th. 31st.	No change.	

A. J. Orton
Brigadier General,
41st.Divisional Artillery.

A P P E N D I C E S

A, B and C .

SECRET

A

Copy No. 12

41st. DIVISIONAL ARTILLERY ORDER No.156

Reference Map 1/100,000
(Sheets CONEGLIANO & VENEZIA)

4th. March 1918

1. On the 5th. March the 41st. Divisional Artillery will concentrate in their entraining area West of TREVISO.

    Billeting area for night 5/6th. March PAESE - CASTAGNOLE - Via DI VILIA.

2. The following parties will meet the Staff Captain, R.A., 41st. Division at the CHURCH, CASTAGNOLE at 10 a.m.

    (a) Usual Billeting parties under command of Lieutenants Gray and Penney respectively from 187th. and 190th. Brigades present Wagon Lines.

    (b) Billeting parties from 41st. D.A.C., and No.1 Company 41st. Divisional Train.

    (c) Billeting party from C/187 Battery.

    (d) Guides only from all Gun lines (less C/187).

3. Brigade Wagon Lines in RIESE Area, 41st. D.A.C., and No.1 Company Train will march under Brigade, etc., arrangements in accordance with March Table attached.

4. (a) Rations for consumption on 6th. inst. will be drawn on 5th. inst. as heretofore.

    (b) Refilling point on 6th. inst. for consumption 7th. will be notified later.

5. Orders for entrainment will be issued later, but units will probably entrain in the following order:-
    Commencing on 6th. March
            41st. D.A.C.,
            "A" & "B" 190th. Brigade,
            D.A., H.Q., with H.Q., 190th. Brigade,
            Remainder 190th. Brigade,
            "A" & "D" 187th. Brigade,
            H.Q., 187th. Brigade with No.1 Coy. Divl: Train,
            Remainder 187th. Brigade

6. D.A., H.Q., will be at SOVERNIGO.

7. Brigade Wagon Lines, D.A.C., and No.1 Company, Divl: Train please acknowledge.

                                            Hugh Walker.
                                            Brigade Major,
                                         41st. Divisional Artillery.

Copy No. 1 XIVth. Corps, R.A.,
"   "   2 XIth. Corps, R.A.,
"   "   3 H.Q., 187th. Bde, R.F.A. (4 spare)
"   "   4 H.Q., 190th. Bde, R.F.A. (4 spare)
"   "   5 41st. D.A.C.
"   "   6 No.1 Coy. Divl Train,
"   "   7 7th. Divl: Artillery,
"   "   8 5th. Divl: Artillery,
"   "   9 A.P.M., 14th. Corps,
"   "   10 A.P.M., 11th. Corps,
"   "   11-13 War Diary and file.

MARCH TABLE

Serial No.	Date	Unit	From	To probably	Starting Point & hour of passing	REMARKS
1.	5th.March	41st. D.A.C.	VEDELAGO	CASTAGNOLE	"	To be clear of VEDELAGO by 10 a.m.
2.	5th.March	190th.Brigade, R.A.A. Wagon Lines	CASELLE area.	PAESE	VEDELAGO Cr: Roads 10.15 a.m.	
3.	5th.March	187th.Brigade, R.A.A. Wagon Lines (less C/187)	RAMON area	Vl. DI VILLA	VEDELAGO Cr: Roads 10.45 a.m.	
4.	5th.March	No.1 Company, Divl:Train.	VAILA.	PAESE	"	Not to reach VEDELAGO before 11.15 a.m.

4th. March.1918.

"B"

AMENDMENT TO 41st. DIVISIONAL ARTY. INSTRUCTION No.1.

para.
(11)
      x   x   x

(4) for "seven days rations" read "eight days rations".

(5) for "remaining six days rations" read "remaining seven days rations". and in the remainder of this para. read "eight" days for "seven days" in each case where it occurs.

In the Entraining Table, Train "X" serial 4144, for "PORTA CAVOUR" read "TREVISO Central".

Captain,
Staff Captain, 41st. Divisional Artillery.

7-3-18.

"B"

SECRET.

41st. DIVISIONAL ARTILLERY INSTRUCTION No.1

Move to FRANCE.

(1) The 41st. Divisional Artillery will entrain in accordance with Table attached.

(2) Captain G. WOODWARD R.F.A. will be entraining Officer with H.Q. c/o R.T.O. TREVISO Central.
Lieut: A.W.PENTRESS R.F.A. will assist him.
These Officers will entrain on the last train from TREVISO Central.

(3) All transport will report at entraining station 3 hours before advertised time of departure of train.

(4) Seven days rations will be delivered and issued at entraining station. An issuing Officer and supply details will be provided by G.H.Q. but O.C. No.1 Coy. will detail one Officer to assist him in checking indents. This Officer will report at TREVISO Central Station on evening of to-day (6th.inst).
O.C.No.1 Coy.41st.Divnl.Train will arrange to draw bread for 3 days consumption for 100% of total strength from Field Bakery TREVISO (near PORTA CAVOUR Station) and to deliver to TREVISO Central.

(5) Units will be rationed in this area for the last time for consumption on day of entrainment. Supply wagons will march with units and refill before entraining. The remaining 6 days rations will be loaded on the train.
Officers Commanding Trains will indent in bulk for the 7 days rations for the Officers, Men and Horses travelling on their train.
They will have their indents ready to hand over to Supply Officer at entraining station 3 hours before departure of train.
It must be clearly impressed upon all Commanding Officers that of the seven days rations accompanying units, a complete days rations must be handed over on detraining for each day less than 7 days which the journey may occupy. Units will be held responsible for any shortage on this quantity.

(6) A State and Certificate on pro-forma attached will be handed to Entraining Officer, who will deliver it to representative of XLth.Corps at the Station.

(7) All units will reconnoitre approaches to the entraining stations.

(8) Harness and Saddlery will be taken off before entrainment and if possible placed in a truck other than that used for horses. Complete sets of saddlery should be tied together so that each set is kept separate and is readily available on detrainment. Buckets will be taken in the truck with the horses.

Sheet 2.

(9) The Senior Officer in each train will be O.C., Train.
He will be responsible for the discipline of the troops on his train and that the wishes of the railway authorities are carried out.
No men are permitted to travel on open trucks, or the top of carriages.
Men are to be specially warned regarding the danger of the electrified portion of the line. Once personnel are entrained no man will leave his carriage or truck except with the permission of an Officer.
In order to prevent men being left behind at Halts, when men are permitted to alight, a bugle should be sounded five minutes before the departure of the train.
In cases where there is no R.T.O. it is suggested that Liaison be established with the engine-driver.
Latrine accommodation provided is to be used and indiscriminate fouling of the ground to be avoided as far as possible.
At Halts, regimental police should patrol the train.
All possible precautions must be taken to prevent an outbreak of fire, and fire orders will be issued by Officers Commanding trains.

(10) Units are reminded that lights are not provided in first or third class carriages and only one lantern per covered truck.

(11) No oats will be fed for the first twenty-four hours of the journey and after that half feeds only.

(12) Instructions regarding Medical arrangements are attached.

J.W.Mitchell
Captain,
Staff Captain, 41st. Divl: Artillery.

6th. March 1918.

187th. Brigade, R.F.A. (5 copies)
190th. Brigade, R.F.A., (5 copies)
41st. D.A.C., (4 copies)
No.1 Company, Divl Train (2 copies)
4 Spare.

SECRET

ENTRAINING TABLE

41st. DIVISIONAL ARTILLERY INSTRUCTION No.1

MOVE to TRAMES

Train	Serial	Unit	Station	Time depart.
(a)	4171 4174	(1/3rd.No.1Section,D.A.C.) (4 G.S.Wagons & teams No.3 Section)	Treviso (Central)	3.50 March 7.
(b)	4171a. 4174c.	-do-	Treviso (Central)	6.50 March 7.
(c)	4171b. 4174b.	-do-	Treviso (Central)	9.20 March 7.
(d)	4172 4170	(1/3rd.No.2 Sec.D.A.C.) (H.C.,D.A.C.)	Treviso (Central)	11.20 March 7.
(e)	4172a. 4174c.	(1/3rd.No.2 Section,D.A.C) (4 G.S.Wagons & teams No.3 Section)	Treviso (Central)	13.50 March 7.
(f)	4172b. 4174d.	(1/3rd.No.2 Section,D.A.C) (4 G.S.Wagons & teams No.3 Section)	Treviso (Central)	16.20 March 7.
(g)	4173 4192	(Pt.No.3 Section,D.A.C.) ("X" T.M.B.)	Treviso (Central)	18.50 March 7.
(h)	4173a. 4193 4194	(Pt.No.3 Section,D.A.C.) ("Y" T.M.B.) ("Z" T.M.B.)	Treviso (Central)	23.50 March 7.
(i)	4196G.	Remainder of M.T.Company	Padova (Central)	17.25 March 7.

ENTRAINING TABLE (Cont'd)

Train	Serial	Unit	Station	Time d'part	March
(j)	4151	(2/3rd. "A" Battery.190 (Brigade,R.F.A.)	Treviso (Central)	3.50 March 8th.	
(k)	4151a.	(1/3rd. "A" Battery 190th. (Brigade,R.F.A.)	Treviso (Central)	6.50 March 8th.	
	4152a.	(1/3rd. "B" Battery 190th. (Brigade,R.F.A.)			
(l)	4152	(2/3rd. "B" Battery 190th. (Brigade,R.F.A.)	Treviso (Central)	9.20 March 8th.	
(m)	4102 4150	(H.Q.,Divl.Artillery) (H.Q.,190th.Brigade,R.F.A.)	Treviso (Central)	11.20 March 8th.	
(n)	4155	(2/3rd. "C" Battery,190th. (Brigade,R.F.A.)	Treviso (Central)	13.50 March 8th.	
(o)	4153a. 4154a.	(1/3rd. "C" Battery,R.F.A.) (1/3rd. "D" Battery,190th. (Brigade,R.F.A.)	Treviso (Central)	16.20 March 8th.	
(p)	4154	(2/3rd. "D" Battery,190th. (Brigade,R.F.A.)	Treviso (Central)	18.50 March 8th.	
(q)	4141	(2/3rd. "A" Battery,187th. (Brigade,R.F.A.)	Treviso (Central)	23.50 March 8th.	
(r)	4196e	(½ remainder of M.T.Company	Padova (Central)	17.25 March 8th.	

ENTRAINING TABLE (Continued)

Train	Serial	Unit	Station	Time depart.	March
(s)	4141a.	1/3rd. "A" Battery, 187th. Brigade R.F.A.	Treviso (Central)	6.50	March 9th.
	4142a.	1/3rd. "B" Battery, 187th. Brigade, R.F.A.	---	---	---
(t)	4142	2/3rd. "B" Battery, 187th. Brigade, R.F.A.	Treviso (Central)	9.20	March 9th.
(u)	4140 4175a.	H.Q., 187th. Brigade, R.F.A. No.1 Company, Train.	Treviso (Central)	11.20	March 9th.
(v)	4143	2/3rd. "C" Battery, 187th. Brigade, R.F.A.	Treviso (Central)	16.20	March 9th.
(w)	4143a.	1/3rd. "C" Battery, 187th. Brigade, R.F.A.	Treviso (Central)	18.50	March 9th.
	4144a.	1/3rd. "D" Battery, 187th. Brigade, R.F.A.			
(x)	4144.	2/3rd. "D" Battery, 187th. Brigade, R.F.A.	Porta Cavour	9.20	March 10th.

8th. March 1918.

Staff Captain, 41st. Divl: Artillery.

PRO - FORMA
vide - Para.6.

ENTRAINING STRENGTH			HORSES		HORSE DRAWN VEHICLES		MECHANICAL VEHICLES			
Officers	O.R.	Riders	H.D.	L.D.	4-Wheeled	2-Wheeled	Motor Cars	Motor Ambulances	Lorries	Stm.Lorries

I hereby certify that my unit is complete in equipment, and in the Rations,

Commanding..........................

MEDICAL ARRANGEMENTS

(1) Medical Officers in charge of units will distribute their medical personnel to the best advantage.

(2) Cases of serious sudden illness which cannot be treated in the train will be handed over with written instructions to the French or Italian authorities at the first important station.

(3) Each O.C., Train will detail a sanitary squad on his train. Each sanitary squad will be provided with sufficient picks, shovels, brooms and if possible a few sandbags.
At all halts where latrines do not exist sanitary squads will prepare trench latrines and urinals which will be carefully filled in before departure.

(4) At all fixed halts the railway vehicles will be vacated and swept out by the Sanitary squad.

(5) To expedite work of sanitary squads, one of the sandbags mentioned in para.3 will be placed in each covered vehicle, and used for reception of rubbish.

(6) Spitting in all vehicles will be made the subject of disciplinary action.

6th.March 1918.

Captain,
Staff Captain, 41st. Divl: Artillery

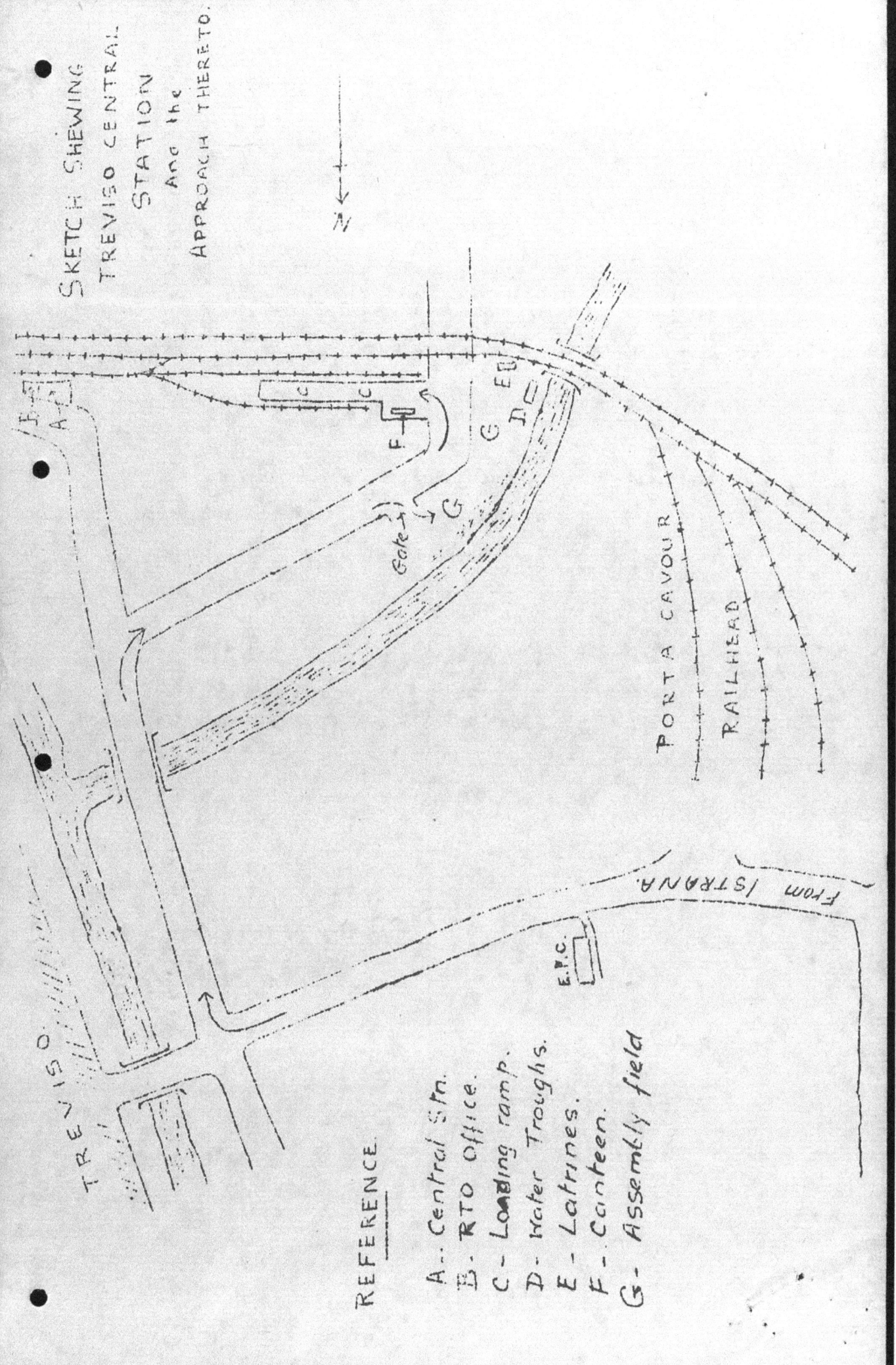

SECRET   App: C.   Copy No. 23

War Diary

41st. DIVISIONAL ARTILLERY ORDER 157

Reference Map 1/100,000 LENS & AMIENS Sheets

20th. March 1918

1. The 41st. Divisional Artillery will march to MERICOURT - BUIRE Area on the 21st and 22nd. March in accordance with March Table attached. Staging Area night of 21st/22nd. March, CONTAY Area.

2. 41st. Division (less Artillery) are proceeding to BAIZIEUX Area on March 21st, by Tactical trains.

3. The Division will continue to be in G.H.Q. Reserve. Entraining stations if required, on and after 22nd. March:-
    AVELUY - ALBERT - EDGEHILL.

4. Following distances will be maintained on the March:-
    Between Sections of Batteries & subsections D.A.C.   50 yards
    Between Batteries and Sections D.A.C.   100 yards.

5. Usual Billeting parties will report to the Billet Wardens in their respective villages for billets.
    Orders regarding Billeting parties for the 22nd. will be notified later.

6. Refilling Point will be notified later. On 21st. instant units will send guides to collect supply wagons from BAVELINCOURT at 5 p.m.

7. (a) Divisional H.Q. will open at BAIZIEUX at 12 noon on 21st. March.

    (b) Divisional Artillery H.Q., will close at GEZAINCOURT at 8 a.m., on 21st.instant, and will open on completion of march each day.
         21st. March   CONTAY.
         22nd. March   Probably TREUX.

8. Lorry to convey Trench Mortar equipment will be at D.A.,H.Q., GEZAINCOURT 7 a.m. D.T.M.O. will send a guide to fetch it.

9. ACKNOWLEDGE.

                                           Brigade Major,
                                   41st. Divisional Artillery.

```
Copy No.1       41st. Division G.
  "   2 - 6    187th. Brigade, R.F.A.
  "   7 -11    190th. Brigade, R.F.A.
  "  12 -16    41st. D.A.C. (1 copy for D.T.M.O.)
  "   17       41st. Division Q.
  "   18       41st. Artillery Signals
  "   19       S.C.,R.A.,41st. Division.
  "   20       H.Q.,41st. Divl:Train.
  "   21       No.1 Coy. Divl:Train
  "   22       A.P.M.,41st. Division.
  "  23 - 25   War Diary & File.
```

MARCH TABLE

Issued with 41st. Divisional Artillery Order No.157.

Serial No.	Date	Unit	From	To	Route	Starting Point & hour of passing	Remarks
1.	21st.March	187th.Bde.	GEZAINCOURT	BEAUCOURT	BEAUVAL-TALMAS-VILLERS-BOCAGE-MOLLIENS	Cross Roads LENS 5D 96 8.55 am.	To be clear of Starting Point by 8.45 a.m.
2.	"	Dvl:Art: H.Q.	"	CONTAY	BEAUQUESNE-PUCHVILLERS-TOUTENCOURT -do-	9.15 am.	
3.	"	HQ & 2 Btys 190th.Bde.	"	) CONTAY	-do-		
4.	"	2 Batteries 190th.Bde.	GROUCHES	-do-	-do-	Rd.Junction LENS 5 E 1860 at 9.30 am.	
5.	"	41st.D.A.C.	GROUCHES-RILLY Area	MOLLIENS-AU-BOIS		as above 10 a.m.	Will march independently but must not interfere with the march of 190.Bde.
6.	"	No.1 Coy. Dvl:Train	BEAUREPAIRE	BAVELINCOURT		-	
7.	22nd.March	190th.Bde.	CONTAY	VILLE (1 bty in BUIRE)	FRANVILLERS-RIBEMONT.	Road Junction FRANVILLERS 10.15am.	
8.	"	Dvl:Arty H.Q.	CONTAY	TREUX	-do-	10.45 am.	
9.	"	187th.Bde.	BEAUCOURT	MERICOURT (2 btys in TREUX)	-do-	11.0 am.	
10.	"	41st.D.A.C.	MOLLIENS	BUIRE	do	Cross Roads N.of MONTIGNY 10.0 a.m.	To follow 187th.Brigade.
11.	"	No.1 Coy, Dvl:Train.	BAVELINCOURT	BUIRE	-do-	-	March independently.

41st Division.

C. R. A.

41st DIVISION

APRIL 1918

Army Form C. 2118.

WAR DIARY
or
INTELLIGENCE SUMMARY.
(Erase heading not required.) Headquarters, 41st. Divisional Artillery

Vol 24

Place	Date	Hour	Summary of Events and Information	Remarks and references to Appendices
SOUASTRE	1918 April 1st.		41st.D.A.,H.Q., at SOUASTRE. Artillery Brigades of 41st.Divisional Artillery under C.R.A., 62nd.Division, formed Left Group under Command of Lieut.Col.G.A.CARDEW,C.M.G.,D.S.O.,covering Infantry of 37th.Division. MM	
	2nd.		Lieut.Col.CARDEW relieved by Brigadier-General A.S.COTTON, D.S.O.,C.R.A., 41st.Division. Lieut. Col. CARDEW came to 41st.D.A.,H.Q., for two days rest. MM	
	4th.		Brigadier-General COTTON returned to SOUASTRE. C.R.A., and Brigade Major carried-out reconnaissance of Artillery positions to cover Reserve Lines (Appendix "A" attached) MM	App: "A"
	5th.		Attack on ROSSIGNOL WOOD carried out by 37th.Division at 5.30 a.m.,with Artillery and Tank support; the enemy attacked BUCQUOY about the same hour. All batteries of the 187th. and 190th.Brigades were heavily shelled throughout the morning, gas shell being largely used. C/187 suffered most severely. Enemy gained part of BUCQUOY; our attack on ROSSIGNOL WOOD was partially successful. MM H.W.	
	7th.		Major E.L.WALTER,M.C.,Brigade Major, 41st.D.A., wounded while visiting batteries in the vicinity of ESSARTS. He was evacuated to No.3 Canadian Stationary Hospital, DOULLENS. MM	
	10th.		Lieut.Col.C.D.G.LYON,D.S.O.,Commanding 187th.Brigade,R.F.A.,and Staff relieved by Brigadier-General A.S.COTTON and Staff. Lieut.Col.LYON came to SOUASTRE for two days rest. MM	
	12th.		187th. and 190th.Brigades, forming one Group under command of Lieut.Col.G.A.CARDEW, C.M.G.,D.S.O. came under Command of C.R.A.,37th.Division. MM	
	15th.		Infantry of 42nd.Division relieved infantry of 37th.Division. MM	
	17th.		187th.Brigade and No.1 Section, 41st.D.A.C., came under Command of C.R.A.,62nd.Division, 190th. Brigade, and No.2 Section, 41st.D.A.C. under Command of C.R.A.,42nd.Division. MM	

1.1

Army Form C. 2118.

WAR DIARY
or
INTELLIGENCE-SUMMARY.

(Erase heading not required.) Headquarters, 41st. Divisional Artillery

Instructions regarding War Diaries and Intelligence Summaries are contained in F.S. Regs., Part II. and the Staff Manual respectively. Title pages will be prepared in manuscript.

Place	Date	Hour	Summary of Events and Information	Remarks and references to Appendices
PAS-en-ARTOIS	April 18th		41st.D.A.,H.Q., moved to PAS-en-ARTOIS. Brigadier-General A.S.COTTON,D.S.O., assumed Command of R.A., to the 57th.Division, which was in Army Reserve. The Artillery under the C.R.A., consisted of 315th.(Army) Brigade,R.F.A. Orders regarding battery positions for reserve lines were issued (Appendix "B" attached)	App: "B"
"	21st		Orders regarding Visual Signalling and O.Ps for Artillery covering the Reserve lines were issued. (Appendix "C")	App: "C"
"	22nd		315th.(Army) Brigade, R.F.A., relieved a New Zealand Artillery Brigade in action with 1st. N.Z.Division under orders from IVth.Corps. 187th.Brigade,R.F.A., and No.1 Section, 41st.D.A.C. came under the Command of C.R.A.,42nd.Division.	
"	23rd		187th.Brigade, R.F.A., replaced 315th.(Army) Brigade, R.F.A., in Corps Reserve.	
"	30th		187th.Brigade, R.F.A., relieved 190th.Brigade,R.F.A., in action under 42nd.D.A.; 190th.Brigade replaced 187th.Brigade,R.F.A., in Corps Reserve on completion of relief.	
	1st.May 1918.			

A.S. Cotton, Brigadier General,
Commanding 41st.Divisional Artillery.

SECRET   41st.D.A., S.No.497

War Diary Appendix A

Headquarters,
 62nd. Division "G"
 IVth. Corps, R.A.
----

1. Reconnaissance of Artillery Brigade Positions to cover:-

Table "A" Red Line (i.e., WILLOW PATCH - East of COIGNEUX -
    BOIS du WARNIMONT - East of LOUVENCOURT - LEALVILLERS)

Table "B" PAS SWITCH (BOIS du CHATELET - ST. LEGER les AUTHIE -
    BOIS du WARNIMONT) and thence to LEALVILLERS as for
    Table "A" above.

2. The country is for the most part open and undulating, and under cultivation, which renders the going very heavy in wet weather.

  Artillery positions can be found almost everywhere in the valleys, but the area between PAS - GRENAS - HALLOY - THIEVRES is for the most part high ground and slopes gradually Eastwards rendering positions in this area difficult.

  The valley of R. QUILIENNS is very steep on both sides and careful reconnaissance will be necessary to get Brigade "M" in.

  The valley E. and W. of THIEVRES is wooded and unsuitable.

3. The system adopted has been as far as possible to have two Brigades forward at a range of between 3,000 and 4,000 yards and a supporting Brigade further in rear.

  To cover the line S. and E. of SOUASTRE it has been necessary to select positions outside the CORPS BOUNDARY.

          (Sgd) A.S. COTTON, Brigadier General,
5th. April 1918.   Commanding 41st. Divisional Artillery.

TABLE "A"

Approximate Areas for 18 Brigades R.F.A., to cover the Red Line (i.e., Line WILLOW PATCH - COIGNEUX - LOUVENCOURT - LEALVILLERS.)

Reference Map - 1/40,000 - Sheet 57 D.

Serial No.	Brigade	Approximate Area	Approx. Zone for which selected	REMARKS
1	A	O.14.c.& d. O.20.a.	O.24.b.central	Open country - Plough - Road ARQUEVES to O.19 central is in a cutting with steep sides.
2	B	O.13.c. O.19.a. to		Open country - Plough
3	C	O.7.a. and c.	O.11 central	Open country - Plough
4	D	O.1.b. and d.	O.11 central to	Open country - Plough - South end of valley in which F Brigade are.
5	E	I.31.a. and c.		Long valley - Some trees
6	F	I.31.b. & d.	I.30.c.O.O.	Long valley - Some scrub - Good positions.
7	G	I.26.b. and c.	I.30.c.O.O. to	Open country,but good positions. Position available for more than one Brigade is required.
8	H	I.13.d. I.19.b.		Open country - certain amount of new trenches & wire
9	I	I.20.a.& c. I.26.a.	I.24.b.central	Open country - some plough.
10	J	I.14.b., 15 a.	Junction with	Open country - 1 Battery North of road.
11	K	I.3.d., I.4.a.	PAS SWITCH to	Open country in plough
12	L	C.29.b. C.24.c.	J.15.a.central	Open country - Position in valley astride Road
13	M	C.24.d. D.19.c.	J.15 a central	Open country
14	N	C.17.d. C.18.c.	to	Along the south edge of wood.
15	O	D.14.a.	D.28/central	Open country
16	P	D.8.d. D.9.c.	D.28.d.central	Open country - Position South of BEAUCAMP Rav.
17	Q	D.2.c. and d.	to	Open country - Covered by trees
18	R	D.10.b.	WILLOW PATCH	Open country - No cover

Approximate areas for 18 Brigades R.F.A., to cover the Red line from LEAUVILLERS to BOIS du WARNIMONT and the "PAS SWITCH" through ST.LEGER to C.17 (Central)

TABLE "B"

Reference Map - 1/40,000 - Sheet 57 D.

Serial No.	Brigade	Approximate Area	Approx Zone for which selected.	REMARKS
1 - 9	A - I (inclusive)	As shown in Table "A"	As shown in Table "A"	
10	J'	As shown in Table "A"	PAS SWITCH I.24.d.central	This is the Pivot Brigade and need not move
11	K'	2 Batteries - I.13.a. 2 Batteries - I. 8.c.	ST. LEGER (inclusive)	Behind Crest E. of MARIEUX-THIEVRES Road In valley - astride Road - South of AUTHIE River
12	L'	I.1.a. and c.		Open country - approach by track commencing I.1.d.0.4.
13	M'	C.26.c.	ST.LEGER (inclusive) - C.29.d. central	Along N. side of Road; Positions require careful selection owing to trees.
14	N'	B.24.d. B.30.b.		In the open - South side of Road.
15	O'	C.19.c. C.25.a.		Open country - astride Road - covered by HURTEBISE FMF.
16	P'	2 Batteries - B.18.b. 2 Batteries - C.7.d.	C.29.d.central Road Junction G.17.b.	In a depression - Bare flash cover Same valley as R Brigade,but on N. side of Rd.
17	Q'	B.18.a.		Open country - Plough - Bare flash cover
18	R'	C.14.a. and c.		Open country - Batteries willhve to be echeloned in depth.

Appendix B
32

SECRET.

41st DIVISIONAL ARTILLERY INSTRUCTION No.4.

Reference Map 18-4-18
57 D 1/40,000.

The following instructions are issued with reference to IV Corps No. 67/3/34 G. dated 17-4-18.

1. In the event of its being necessary to fall back from covering the PURPLE LINE to cover the RED LINE the Field Artillery covering the LEFT SECTOR front (J.14.Central - WILLOW PATCH 'A' E.13.c.) passes under the command of C.R.A. 41st Division, whose Headquarters will be with 57th Division at the MAIRIE, HENU.

Orders for the retirement will be issued by Headquarters of Centre and Left Divisions.

2. The following areas are allotted to Brigades after consultation with C.R.A's 42nd and 62nd Divisions:-

	Serial Letter.	Area	Allotted to		Wagon Line Areas
	J.	I.14.b.,15.a.	211th Bde.	42nd D.A.	H.12.central.
	K.	I.3.d.,4.a.	210th "	"	H.11.central.
	L.	C.29.b.,24.c.	190th "	41st D.A.	C.26.c.
Serial letters as referred to in IV Corps R.A 1941/44 Table A.	M.	C.24.d.) D.19.c.)	187th "	"	I.2.a.
	N.	C.17.d.,18.c.	314th "	62nd D.A.	C.27.a.
	O.	D.14.a.	310th "	"	C.21.central
	P.	D.8.d,9.c.	26th A.F.A. Bde.		C.16.b.
	Q.	D.2.c. & d.	295th Bde. 59th D.A.		C.16.a.
	R.	D.10.b.	296th "	"	C.15.b.

315th A.F.A. Brigade will be kept as Mobile Reserve at C.27.b.

D.A.Cs. will occupy the following areas:-

42nd D.A.C.	H.4.d.
41st D.A.C.	BOIS BRULE B.25 N.W.Portion.
62nd D.A.C.	BOIS BRULE B.25 S.E.Portion.
59th D.A.C.	D.16.d.
26th D.A.C.	C.16.b. BOIS de CHATEAU.
315th D.A.C.	C.27.b.

Immediately Brigades occupy the positions indicated above an Officer will be sent to report to 41st D.A.H.Q. HENU for instructions, and to inform D.A. or H.Q. selected by Brigade Commanders with approximate positions of batteries.
A mounted or cyclist orderly per Brigade will be detailed, with rations for 24 hours, to remain at 41st D.A.H.Q. These

P.T.O.

orderlies will be relieved daily under Brigade arrangements at 10 a.m. On arrival they will report to R.S.M. 41st D.A. They will be rationed by their own Brigades.

3. The Field Artillery as detailed in para. 2 will be divided into three groups.

   Right Group Serial letters J.K.L.
   Centre Group   " " M.N.O.
   Left Group   " " P.Q.R.

The senior Lieutenant Colonel in each Group will act as Group Commander.

The zones for which Groups will be responsible are as follows:-

 Right Group Red Line from J.14.c.0.5. - Road Junction J.10.c. inclusive.

 Centre Group " from Road Junction J.10.c. exclusive - SOUASTRE - SAILLY Road D.29.c. inclusive.

 Left Group " from Road D.29.c. exclusive - Road Junction about E.13. central inclus.

4. <u>AMMUNITION</u> Dumps exist at the following places:-

   Corps Dumps I.14.d. I.12.a. C.23.b.
   Divl. Dumps D.26.d. L.15.d.

Batteries will refill at Divisional Dumps until these are exhausted.
Ammunition Railheads are at St.LEGER I.12. and MONDICOURT C.2. from which ammunition may be drawn.
A Corps Dump is under construction at AMPLIER, H.3.a.

Ammunition will probably be delivered by rail at the following sidings:-
  AUTHIE, I.15.a.
  ORVILLE, H.10.a. & b.
  AUTHIEULE, H.30.b.
  AMPLIER, H.3.a.

5. ACKNOWLEDGE.

             Major R.F.A.,
             Ag. D.H.R.A.
Issued at:- 9.30 p.m. 41st Divisional Artillery.

Copy No.1-2 IVth Corps
   3 IVth Corps R.A.
  4-5 57th Division.
  13-23 62nd Divn R.A.
  6-12 42nd Divn R.A.
  24-25 59th Divn. R.A.
  26   37th Divn. R.A.
  27-28 315 Army Bde.
  29   S.C.R.A. 41st Divn.
  30   S.O. 41st Divn. R.A.
  31-33 War Diary and File.

War Diary

Appendix "C"

SECRET.

21st April 1918.

1st ADDENDUM to 41st Divisional Artillery
Instructions No.4.

VISUAL SIGNALLING and O.P's.

A D.A.H.Q. Central Visual Station has been established at D.19.d.7.0. and will be used in the initial stages of the occupation of the RED LINE for communication between advanced D.A.H.Q. at HENU and Groups.

Brigades should make themselves acquainted with this station with a view to establishment of communication with it when necessary.

The following suggestions for O.P's, based on reconnaissance of the RED LINE, are forwarded in the hope that they may be of use to Brigades in the reconnaissance and establishment of their O.P's and the communications from them to Batteries.

RIGHT GROUP SECTOR.

    Right portion.   O.P. in front line.
        Visual station at Reservoir near point 152 (J.20.a
        Visual station on Ridge in I.6.a.&.b.

    Centre Portion.   O.P. in front line.
        Telephone line to Visual station near point 152.
        Visual station on Ridge in I.6.a.&.b.

    Left Portion.   O.P. in Support Line S.E. of ROSSIGNOL FARM about
        J.9.b.0.8.
        Telephone Line to Visual Station about 300 yards
        E of ROSSIGNOL FARM.
        Visual Station on Ridge in D.25.b. &.d.

    NOTE:-

    210th and 211th Brigades will probably occupy positions in the vicinity of C.30.central and not in areas J and K. Instructions on this point will be issued when the matter has been settled.

CENTRE GROUP SECTOR.

    Right Portion.   O.P. in front line.
        Telephone Line to Visual Station about 300 yards
        E of ROSSIGNOL FARM.
        Visual Station either on Ridge in D.25.b. & d.
        or on Ridge S. of HENU - SOUASTRE Road.

    Centre Portion.   O.P. on Ridge S. of HENU - SOUASTRE Road.
        Thence by telephone or visual to batteries.

    Left Portion.   O.P. in front line near SOUASTRE - BAYENCOURT
        Road.
        Telephone Line to Visual Station in Support Line.
        Visual Station either on Ridge in D.25.b. &.d. or
        on Ridge S. of HENU - SOUASTRE Road.

P. T. O.

LEFT GROUP SECTOR.

 Right Portion.) O.P's in Front Line.
 Centre Portion.) Telephone Lines to Visual Stations in Support
 Left Portion.) Line.
         Visual Stations on Ridge S. and E. of ST.AMAND.
         Thence to batteries by telephone or visual
          probably through area R.

                 Major R.F.A.,
Issued at:- / /6. M.   Ag. Brigade Major,
              41st Divisional Artillery.

To all recipients of 41st Divisional Artillery Instructions
  No. 4.

On His Majesty's Service.

Registered

Officer I/c
A G's Office
G.H.Q.
3rd Echelon

Army Form C. 2118.

WAR DIARY
or
INTELLIGENCE SUMMARY.
(Erase heading not required.)   Headquarters, 41st. Divisional Artillery

Instructions regarding War Diaries and Intelligence Summaries are contained in F. S. Regs., Part II. and the Staff Manual respectively. Title pages will be prepared in manuscript.

Place	Date	Hour	Summary of Events and Information	Remarks and references to Appendices
FRANCE	1918			
PAS – en ARTOIS	May 1st.		Warning Order received from IVth.Corps, R.A., to the effect that 57th.Division (less Artillery) would relieve 42nd.Division (less Artillery) in the Centre Sector of the IVth.Corps front in a few days time.	App: "A"
"	3rd.		41st.Divisional Artillery Instructions regarding Liaison with Infantry issued. (App:"A")	App: "B"
"	5th.		Orders regarding artillery defence for the Red Line issued. Cancelled previous instructions (App:"B")	
COUIN	6th.		57th.Divisional Headquarters moved to COUIN and took over from 42nd.Divisional Headquarters. 41st.D.A., Headquarters moved to COUIN and took over from 42nd.D.A., Headquarters, Brigadier General A.S.COTTON, D.S.O., acting as C.R.A., to 57th.Division. The artillery covering the front consisted of the following:-
211th.Brigade, R.F.A.,)
210th.Brigade, R.F.A.,) 42nd. D.A.
312th.Brigade, R.F.A.,)
310th.Brigade, R.F.A.,) 62nd. D.A.
X/41st.T.M.Battery relieved Y/42nd.T.M.Battery in the GOMMECOURT Area.	
"	7th.		42nd.Divl: Artillery Defence Scheme amended (App:"C") (App:"D")	App: "C" App: "D"
"	10th.		57th.D.A., Headquarters arrived at COUIN. Further amendments to 42nd.D.A., Defence Scheme issued (App:"E")	App: "E"
"	12th.		C.R.A.,57th.Division took over command of Artillery covering 57th.Division from C.R.A., 41st. Division. 187th.Brigade, R.F.A., (41st.D.A.) relieved by 285th.Brigade, R.F.A., (57th.D.A.) covering the New Zealand Division on the right sector, IVth.Corps. On completion of relief 187th.Brigade was concentrated in the vicinity of COUIN.	
"	13th.		Orders for Entrainment of 41st.D.A., to proceed to Second Army Area issued (App:"F")	App: "F"

-1-

Army Form C. 2118.

WAR DIARY
INTELLIGENCE SUMMARY.
(Erase heading not required.)

Headquarters, 41st. Divisional Artillery

Instructions regarding War Diaries and Intelligence Summaries are contained in F. S. Regs., Part II. and the Staff Manual respectively. Title pages will be prepared in manuscript.

Place	Date	Hour	Summary of Events and Information	Remarks and references to Appendices
FRANCE COUIN & DOULLENS	1918 May 14th		Entrainment of 41st.D.A. commenced at DOULLENS. Progress of entrainment normal throughout. MWM	
BELGIUM LA LOVIE	" 15th		Detrainment commenced at HEYDEBEEK and WAAYENBURG. 41st.D.A., Headquarters established at LA LOVIE CHATEAU. Brigadier-General A.S.COTTON, D.S.O., took over command of the Artillery covering the 41st.Division at 4 p.m., from C.R.A., 29th.Division. Night of 15/16th.May 190th.Brigade,R.F.A., relieved 15th.Brigade,R.H.A., covering the Left Sector, 41st.Divisional Front. Orders regarding rear lines of Defence issued (App:"G") MWM	App: "G"
"	" 16th		187th.Brigade,R.F.A., relieved 162nd.Brigade, R.F.A., covering the Right sector,41st.Divisional Front on night 16th/17th.May. MWM	
"	" 17th		Counter Preparation ordered at 5 p.m., and also at 3.10 a.m., on the 18th., as an attack was expected. Owing to the large front covered by each gun in S.O.S. tasks, it was found necessary to thicken up the barrage at certain points where the enemy might assemble or advance, and make the barrage thin at other points xxxx where the enemy would be dealt with easily by small arms and Trench Mortars. (App:"H") MWM	App:"H"
"	" 18th		In order that batteries might be distributed in greater depth, it was found necessary to move two sections each of two 18pdr.Batteries,187th.Brigade, R.F.A., and two Sections of "C" Battery, 190th.Brigade,R.F.A., the remaining section of each battery remained in action at its position for ordinary harassing fire. (App:"I") MWM	App:"I"
"	" 19th		On account of information received from Infantry patrols that no enemy was encountered 1,000 yards from our own front line, it was decided in future to have harassing fire carried out according to Appendix "J". The ammunition expenditure was also reduced. MWM	App:"J"
"	" 20th		Nothing to report. MWM	
"	" 21st		Arrangements were made for 41st.D.A., to assist in the artillery support of a raid to be carried out by two Companies of the D.L.I., of the 6th.Division on the Right.(App:K) MWM	App:"K"

Army Form C. 2118

WAR DIARY
— or —
INTELLIGENCE SUMMARY

(Erase heading not required.) Headquarters, 41st. Divisional Artillery

Instructions regarding War Diaries and Intelligence Summaries are contained in F.S. Regs., Part II. and the Staff Manual respectively. Title Pages will be prepared in manuscript.

Place	Date	Hour	Summary of Events and Information	Remarks and references to Appendices
BELGIUM LA LOVIE	May	22nd	The raid was successfully carried out, at midnight 21st/22nd.May - 16 prisoners being taken. 41st.Divisional Artillery Defence Scheme issued (App:"L"). The S.O.S. lines as laid down in this Defence Scheme came into operation at 12 noon, 22nd.May (App:"M")	App:"L" App:"M"
"	"	23rd.	Nothing to record.	
"	"	24th.	Programme of harassing fire shoots in conjunction with Heavy Artillery and 41st. Machine Gun Battalion were issued. (App:"N")	App:"N"
"	"	25th.	Amendment to 41st.D.A., Defence Scheme issued (App:"O") regarding positions for 6" Newton Trench Mortars; positions for four Trench Mortars were chosen to cover the present line of resistance; four positions were already dug for the defence of the YPRES DEFENCES, and four were chosen for defence of the Purple line. G.O.C., 41st.Division inspected Wagon Lines of 41st.D.A., Owing to lack of time only Wagon lines of 187th.Brigade and 41st.D.A.C. were inspected (App:"P") Amendment to 41st.D.A., Defence Scheme issued regarding rear lines of defence (App;"Q")	App:"O" App:"P" App:"Q"
"	"	26th.	At 1 a.m., a heavy bombardment was opened in the vicinity of DICKEBUSCH on our Right. All the area occupied by 187th.Brigade, R.F.A., and 190th.Brigade, R.F.A., batteries was heavily shelled, mustard gas being largely used. Counter preparation was ordered and was carried out by all batteries between 4 a.m., and 4.15 a.m. The enemy attacked the French and succeeded in gaining some ground in the vicinity of VIERSTRAAT & SCOTTISH WOOD.	
"	"	27th.	G.O.C., 41st.Division completed his inspection of Wagon Lines of 41st.D.A. Orders regarding Counter preparation to be given by Brigade Commanders in the event of all wires being cut were issued. (App:"R")	App:"R"
"	"	28th.	French regained practically all the ground near VIERSTRAAT & RIDGE WOOD lost on the morning of the 26th.	
"	"	29th.	Orders regarding alternative positions issued (App:"S")	App:"S"
"	"	31st.	187th.Brigade Headquarters moved to MACHINE GUN FARM at H.5.b.10.20.(Sheet 28 NW 1/20,000) where the Brigade Headquarters of the Infantry they were covering was situated.	

1st. June 1918.

C.J.C.
Brigadier General,
Commanding 41st. Divisional Artillery

Army Form C. 2118.

WAR DIARY
INTELLIGENCE SUMMARY.
(Erase heading not required.)

Headquarters, 41st. Divisional Artillery

Instructions regarding War Diaries and Intelligence Summaries are contained in F.S. Regs., Part II. and the Staff Manual respectively. Title pages will be prepared in manuscript.

Place	Date	Hour	Summary of Events and Information	Remarks and references to Appendices
FRANCE PAS - en - ARTOIS	1918 May 1st.		Warning Order received from IVth.Corps, R.A., to the effect that 57th.Division (less Artillery) would relieve 42nd.Division (less Artillery) in the Centre Sector of the IVth.Corps front in a few days time.	
"	3rd.		41st.Divisional Artillery Instructions regarding Liaison with Infantry issued. (App:"A")	App: "A"
"	5th.		Orders regarding artillery defence for the Red Line issued. Cancelled previous instructions (App:"B")	App: "B"
COUIN	6th.		57th.Divisional Headquarters moved to COUIN and took over from 42nd.Divisional Headquarters. 41st.D.A., Headquarters moved to COUIN and took over from 42nd.D.A., Headquarters, Brigadier General A.S.COTTON, D.S.O., acting as C.R.A., to 57th.Division. The artillery covering the front consisted of the following:- 211th.Brigade,R.F.A.;) 210th.Brigade,R.F.A.;) 42nd. D.A. 312th.Brigade,R.F.A.;) 310th.Brigade,R.F.A.;) 62nd. D.A. X/41st.T.M.Battery relieved V/42nd.T.M.Battery in the GOMMECOURT Area.	
"	7th.		42nd.Divl: Artillery Defence Scheme amended (App:"C") (App:"D")	App: "C" App: "D"
"	10th.		57th.D.A., Headquarters arrived at COUIN. Further amendments to 42nd.D.A., Defence Scheme issued (App:"E")	App: "E"
"	12th.		C.R.A., 57th.Division took over command of Artillery covering 57th.Division from C.R.A. 41st. Division. 187th.Brigade,R.F.A.,(41st.D.A.) relieved by 285th.Brigade,R.F.A.,(57th.D.A.) covering the New Zealand Division on the right sector,IVth.Corps. On completion of relief 187th.Brigade was concentrated in the vicinity of COUIN.	
"	13th.		Orders for Entrainment of 41st.D.A., to proceed to Second Army Area issued (App:"F")	App: "F"

-1-

Army Form C. 2118.

WAR DIARY
—or—
INTELLIGENCE-SUMMARY.

Headquarters, 41st. Divisional Artillery

(Erase heading not required.)

* Instructions regarding War Diaries and Intelligence Summaries are contained in F. S. Regs., Part II. and the Staff Manual respectively. Title pages will be prepared in manuscript.

Place	Date	Hour	Summary of Events and Information	Remarks and references to Appendices
FRANCE COUIN & DOULLENS	May 1918 14th		Entrainment of 41st.D.A. commenced at DOULLENS. Progress of entrainment normal throughout.	
BELGIUM LA LOVIE	" 15th		Detrainment commenced at HEYDEBEEK and WAAYEBURG. 41st.D.A., Headquarters established at LA LOVIE CHATEAU. Brigadier-General A.S.COTTON, D.S.O., took over command of the Artillery covering the 41st.Division at 4 p.m., from C.R.A., 29th.Division. Night of 15/16th.May 190th.Brigade,R.F.A.,relieved 15th.Brigade,R.H.A., covering the Left Sector, 41st.Divisional Front. Orders regarding rear lines of Defence issued (App:"G")	App: "G"
"	" 16th		187th.Brigade,R.F.A., relieved 162nd.Brigade, R.F.A., covering the Right sector,41st.Divisional Front on night 16th/17th.May.	
"	" 17th		Counter Preparation ordered at 5 p.m., and also at 3.10 a.m., on the 18th., as an attack was expected. Owing to the large front covered by each gun in S.O.S. tasks, it was found necessary to thicken up the barrage at certain points where the enemy might assemble or advance, and make the barrage thin at other points where the enemy would be dealt with easily by small arms and Trench Mortars. (App:"H")	App:"H"
"	" 18th		In order that batteries might be distributed in greater depth, it was found necessary to move two sections each of two 18pdr.Batteries,187th.Brigade, R.F.A., and two Sections of "C" Battery, 190th.Brigade,R.F.A.,the remaining section of each battery remained in action at its position for ordinary harassing fire. (App:"I")	App:"I"
"	" 19th		On account of information received from Infantry patrols that no enemy was encountered 1,000 yards from our own front line, it was decided in future to have harassing fire carried out according to Appendix "J". The ammunition expenditure was also reduced.	App:"J"
"	" 20th		Nothing to report.	
"	" 21st		Arrangements were made for 41st.D.A., to assist in the artillery support of a raid to be carried out by two Companies of the D.L.I., of the 6th.Division on the Right.(App:K)	App:"K"

.2.

Army Form C. 2118

WAR DIARY
INTELLIGENCE SUMMARY

(Erase heading not required.) Headquarters, 41st. Divisional Artillery

Instructions regarding War Diaries and Intelligence Summaries are contained in F.S. Regs., Part II and the Staff Manual respectively. Title Pages will be prepared in manuscript.

Place	Date	Hour	Summary of Events and Information	Remarks and references to Appendices
BELGIUM LA LOVIE	May 22nd		The raid was successfully carried out, at midnight 21st/22nd.May - 16 prisoners being taken. 41st.Divisional Artillery Defence Scheme issued (App:"L"). The S.O.S.Lines as laid down in this Defence Scheme came into operation at 12 noon,22nd.May (App:"M")	App:"L" App:"M"
"	23rd.		Nothing to record.	
"	24th.		Programme of harassing fire shoots in conjunction with Heavy Artillery and 41st.Machine Gun Battalion were issued. (App:"N")	App:"N"
"	25th.		Amendment to 41st.D.A.,Defence Scheme issued (App:"O") regarding positions for 6" Newton Trench Mortars; positions for four Trench Mortars were chosen to cover the present line of resistance; four positions were already dug for the defence of the YPRES DEFENCES, and four were chosen for defence of the Purple line. G.O.C.,41st.Division inspected Wagon Lines of 41st.D.A.; Owing to lack of time only Wagon lines of 187th.Brigade and 41st.D.A.C. were inspected (App:"P") Amendment to 41st.D.A.,Defence Scheme issued regarding rear lines of defence (App;"Q")	App:"O" App:"P" App:"Q"
"	26th.		At 1 a.m., a heavy bombardment was opened in the vicinity of DICKEBUSCH on our Right. All the area occupied by 187th.Brigade, R.F.A., and 190th.Brigade, R.F.A., batteries was heavily shelled, mustard gas being largely used. Counter preparation was ordered and was carried out by all batteries between 4 a.m., and 4.15 a.m. The enemy attacked the French and succeeded in gaining some ground in the vicinity of VIERSTRAAT & SCOTTISH WOOD.	
"	27th.		G.O.C.,41st.Division completed his inspection of Wagon Lines of 41st.D.A. Orders regarding Counter preparation to be given by Brigade Commanders in the event of all wires being cut were issued. (App:"R")	App:"R"
"	28th.		French regained practically all the ground near VIERSTRAAT & RIDGE WOOD lost on the morning of the 26th.	
"	29th.		Orders regarding alternative positions issued (App:"S")	App:"S"
"	31st.		187th.Brigade Headquarters moved to MACHINE GUN FARM at H.5.b.10.20.(Sheet 28 NW 1/20,000) where the Brigade Headquarters of the Infantry they were covering was situated.	

1st.June 1918.

Brigadier General,
Commanding 41st.Divisional Artillery

SECRET   *Appendix 'A'*

War Diary   Copy No. 26

41st DIVISIONAL ARTILLERY INSTRUCTIONS No. 5

Liaison between Artillery and Infantry.

On the 57th Division taking over the Centre Sector of IV Corps front the following procedure will be adopted regarding Liaison with and visiting of Infantry in the line.

1. A specially selected senior Liaison Officer, who may be one of the Lieutenant Colonels other than the Group Commander, will be detailed for duty with each Infantry Brigade in the line when any active operations either defensive or offensive are in prospect; this Officer will remain with the Infantry Brigadier for the whole period of these operations. In normal circumstances a senior Liaison Officer will be told off for a tour of duty with Infantry Brigade and this Officer should be changed as seldom as possible having due regard to the efficiency of his unit; if possible he should remain during the whole tour of the Infantry Brigade.

Should Group Headquarters and Infantry Brigade Headquarters be adjacent, which is the ideal arrangement, the above does not apply.

2. Liaison Officers will be detailed with Battalions on either of the following principles:-

(a). For a period of 3 or 4 days: which duty does not necessitate his sitting at Battalion Headquarters for the whole period. This officer should be responsible for all R.A. Signalling communications with Battalion Headquarters and should work with the Battalion Signal Officer; he should know all O.P's in his area, his way about all trenches, the whereabouts of Company and Platoon Headquarters and be personally acquainted with the Commanders themselves; he should be prepared to accompany the Battalion Commander on his rounds if required and able to furnish information as to what batteries cover the front, and their respective zones, and generally to advise the Battalion Commander on any Artillery points which may arise.

(b). For a night only, in which case an Officer who has done a tour by day at an O.P. will proceed at dusk to Battalion Headquarters and stay there the night, returning to his Battery next morning; his duty being to advise the Battalion Commander on Artillery matters and acquaint the Group Commander with the situation.

Method (a) will be adopted as soon as possible; arrangements are being made for accommodation for the Liaison Officer to be provided where this does not already exist. This Officer should not be relieved at the same time as the Infantry Battalion.

It is obvious that the value of a Battalion Liaison Officer is much reduced without direct communication with the Artillery covering the Sector, but this cannot always be provided at present owing to shortage of wire.

3. Each Group Commander will arrange that not only Infantry Brigade Headquarters is visited by him or his representative daily but that each Battalion Headquarters is similarly visited by the O.C.Brigade covering it and if possible Company Commanders also.

Each Battalion will be visited daily by at least one of the Battery Commanders covering it and whenever possible Company and Platoon Commanders also will be visited by this Officer. A roster of Battery Commanders will be kept for this purpose, but this does not mean that no Battery Commander is to go near his Battalion except when detailed.

4. Battalion Commanders should be provided with a sketch shewing Artillery dispositions of all guns covering their front.

5. All Artillery Officers should know their sectors intimately; complaints have been made that Liaison Officers with Battalions are not fully acquainted with the Sectors they cover: this is perhaps unavoidable with the large number of young Officers who have recently joined the Artillery but it should be a matter of personal pride that all Artillery Officers know at least as much of the sectors as the Infantry holding them. This can be arranged by Officers not actually required for duty with the guns visiting the trenches and becoming acquainted as much as possible with all O.P's, Battalion, Company and Platoon Headquarters &c. &c.

6. The object aimed at in the foregoing instructions is the closest possible touch with the Infantry; the moral support afforded to the latter by the constant and daily presence of Artillery Officers amongst them is very great. This is particularly so in times of stress when all Artillery Officers are needed with their batteries and the Inf. then realize that it is not want of will that prevents the daily visits of their comrades in the Artillery, which will be resumed at the earliest possible moment.

It is fully understood that the procedure outlined above is carried out already to a very great extent and attention is only drawn to these points on a fresh Division coming into the line with Artillery from various other Divisions covering it.

Major; R.F.A.
Ag. Brigade Major,
41st Divisional Artillery.

Issued at:- 5/p.m. to

R.A. IV Corps (2 copies)
57th Division (15 Cops).
41st Division (2 ")
190th Bde. R.F.A.(5 copies)
War Diary & File (3 copies)
Spare copies (30).

War Diary   Appendix 'B'

SECRET.   Copy No. 27

41st DIVISIONAL ARTILLERY INSTRUCTIONS No.6.

Field Artillery Defence of the RED LINE.

Reference Maps 57 D,N.E.) 1/20,000.
               57 D,N.W.)

                                        5th May 1918.

COMMAND.   1. 41st Divisional Artillery Instructions No.4 are cancelled.

                2. In the event of its being necessary to defend the RED LINE the Field Artillery covering the LEFT SECTOR of that line (J.9.d.4.0. to IV Corps Boundary near WILLOW PATCH "A", about E.3.d.3.4.) will be under command of C.R.A. of the Division in Army Reserve, whose Battle Headquarters will be at HENU.
At present C.R.A. 41st Division is C.R.A. of the Division in Army Reserve.

ORDERS FOR WITHDRAWAL.   Orders for the withdrawal of the Artillery from the PURPLE to the RED LINE will be issued by the Divisions in the line. Brigades pass under the orders of the Division in Army Reserve on vacating their PURPLE LINE positions in order to take up their RED LINE Positions.

GROUPS.   3. The Artillery will be divided into two Groups:-

               Right Group - Serial letters L.S.T. (see below).
               Left   Group - Serial letters O.U.V.Q. with sub-
                             groups consisting of O.V. and U.Q.
The Senior Brigade Commander in each Group will be Group Commander.

ZONES.   4. The zones for which Groups will be responsible are as follows:-
             Right Group:- J.9.d.4.0. to D.28.c.8.0.
             Left   Group:- D.28.c.8.0. to Corps northern Boundary.
In arranging their S.O.S. Barrage Group Commanders will provide for overlap of 100 yards on each side of Group Sectors.
Dividing Line between Groups for purposes of harassing fire etc. will be the East and West Grid line between Squares E and J.

BRIGADE AREAS. 5. The areas shown below have been allotted by IV Corps to the Field Artillery covering the RED LINE. Under present arrangements they will be occupied by Brigades shown in last column, but these of course are liable to alteration as reliefs take place from time to time.

ROUTES OF WITHDRAWAL. The following emergency routes have been made in order that shelled areas may be avoided as far as possible:-

CHATEAU DE LA HAIE TRACK: J.6.b.0.4.- D.29.c.7.4.-
-D.28.c.0.3.- D.27.d.7.0.- D.27.b.2.1.- C.30.b.7.7.

WILLOW PATCH TRACK: E.13.c.9.8.- D.18.b.1.2.-
D.17.c.3.0.- D.16.c.9.1.- D.15.d.8.6.- D.15.c.6.3.

The following gaps exist in wire and trenches:-
(a). In HAIE SWITCH: (1) About J.6.d.8.8.;(2) About D.30.d.5.8.;(3) At SOUASTRE-FONQUEVILLERS road.

(b). In RED LINE: (1). At ROSSIGNOL FARM-BAYENCOURT Road; (2). About J.4.c.7.5.; (3). At track about D.28.d.2.2.; (4). At SOUASTRE - BAYENCOURT Road; (5). At SOUASTRE - SAILLY Road; (6). At SOUASTRE - Ch.DE LA HAIE Road; (7). At SOUASTRE - FONQUEVILLERS Road.

Areas allotted are as follows:-

Area.	Wagon Lines.	Allotted to
L. S.W. of PAS-COUIN Road in C.29.b.	C.16.b.	210 Bde 42nd D.A.
S. C.30.central.	C.17.a.	211 " " "
T. (N.E. of PAS-COUIN Road (in C.30.a. and C.24.c.; (C.23.b and c.	C.27.a.	26th A.F.A.Bde.
O. D.14.a.	C.16.a.	123 Bde.37th D.A.
U. D.9.a. and b.	C.15.c.	296 " 59th D.A.
V. D.8.d. and D.9.c.	C.15.d.	124 " 37th D.A.
Q. D.2.b. and c.	C.15.b.	295 " 59th D.A.

D.A.C's.	Areas allotted to D.A.C's are as follows:-	
	H.1.b. and H.2.a.	42nd D.A.C.
	H.2.b. and d.	37th D.A.C.
	C.27.a.	26th B.A.C.
	H.1.a. and c.	59th D.A.C.

BATTERY POSITIONS.

6. Brigades should reconnoitre their areas and routes of withdrawal in advance and should mark their Battery Positions with boards lettered and numbered as under.

Area	L	R.101 - R.104.
"	S	R.111 - R.114.
"	T	R.121 - R.124.
"	O	R.131 - R.134.
"	U	R.141 - R.144.
"	V	R.151 - R.154.
"	Q	R.161 - R.164.

Pinpoints of battery positions and of Brigade Headquarters should be reported to 41st D.A.H.Q. as early as possible.

COMMUNICATION.

7. Immediately a Brigade vacates its PURPLE Line positions it will send an Officer to report to D.A. Battle Headquarters for instructions and to give information bearing on fighting efficiency of Brigade, such as number of casualties, number of guns in action &c. As soon as the Brigade is in action in its RED Line Positions that fact is to be reported to D.A.H.Q.

A mounted or cyclist orderly per Brigade will be detailed, with rations for 24 hours, to remain at D.A.H.Q. This orderly will be relieved at 10 a.m. daily, and will be rationed, under Brigade arrangements.

D.T.M.Os will report at D.A.H.Q. immediately on receipt of orders to fall back from the PURPLE Line.

AMMUNITION.

8. Ammunition Dumps etc. are at the following places:-
   Divisional Dumps: D.26.d. D.15.d. D.20.b.
   Corps Dumps: I.14.d. I.12.a. C.23.b.
            H.3.a.(under construction)
   Ammunition Railheads: ST.LEGER I.12.
                        MONDICOURT C.2.

Ammunition will probably be delivered by rail at the following sidings:-

AUTHIE	I.15.a.
ORVILLE	H.10.a. and b.
AUTHIEULE	H.30.b.
AMPLIER	H.3.a.

In the event of withdrawal from PURPLE Line batteries will refill from Divisional Dumps until these are exhausted.

Dumps at battery positions will, in the absence of orders to the contrary, be brought up to 328 rounds per 18-pdr. and 204 rounds per 4.5" Howitzer immediately on occupation. D.A.Cs will assist to the extent of 76 rounds per 18-pdr. and 48 rounds per 4.5" Howitzer.

VISUAL SIGNALLING. 9. A D.A.H.Q. Central Visual Station has been established at D.19.d.7.0, and will be used in the initial stages of the occupation of the RED Line for communication between Advanced D.A.H.Q. and Groups.

Brigades should make themselves acquainted with this station with a view to establishment of communication with it when necessary.

O.P's. 10. The following suggestions are made for consideration by Brigades in the reconnaissance and establishment of their O.P's and communications from them to batteries.

RIGHT GROUP SECTOR.

<u>Right portion</u>   O.P. in Support Line S.E. of ROSSIGNOL FARM about J.9.b.0.8.
  Telephone line to Visual Station about 300 yards E of ROSSIGNOL FARM.
  Visual Station on Ridge in D.25.b. and d.

<u>Centre Portion.</u> O.P. in front line.
  Telephone Line to Visual Station about 300 yards E of ROSSIGNOL FARM.
  Visual Station either on Ridge in D.25.b. & d. or on Ridge S. of HENU-SOUASTRE Road.

<u>Left Portion.</u>   O.P. on Ridge S. of HENU-SOUASTRE Road.

LEFT GROUP SECTOR.

<u>Right Portion</u>   O.P. in front line near SOUASTRE-BAYENCOURT Road.
  Telephone Line to Visual Station in Support Line.
  Visual Station either on Ridge in D.25.b. & d. or on Ridge S. of HENU-SOUASTRE Rd.

<u>Right Centre Portion</u>) O.P's in front line.
<u>Left Centre Portion</u>) Telephone Lines to Visual Sta-
<u>Left Portion.</u>   )   tions in Support Line.
                     Visual Station on Ridge 3. and
                        F. of ST.AMAND.
                     Visual Stations on Ridge in D.4.

In case of area "O" visual signalling will probably present more difficulties than in the case of the other areas in this group. It may be preferable to establish an O.P. in front line near the SOUASTRE - SAILLY road with Visual Station in Support Line sending back to Visual Station near the Central Station referred to in para. 9.
Pin-points of O.P's and descriptions or diagrams of communications should be submitted to D.A.H.Q. as soon as determined by Brigades.

LIAISON WITH INFANTRY. 11. The RED Line will be held by the Division for the time being in Army Reserve, with two Infantry Brigades in the Line.
Right Brigade Battle Headquarters will be at I.11.b.60.05; Left Brigade at D.17.a.6.3.
Group Commanders will establish the usual Liaison with Brigades which they cover, and with Battalions when the necessary communications can be established.

12. ACKNOWLEDGE.

Issued at:- 7.30 p.m.

                                  Major, R.F.A.
                            Ag. Brigade Major,
                     41st Divisional Artillery.

Copy No.		
1 - 2		IV Corps.
3		IV Corps R.A.
4 - 5		57th Divn.
6 - 15		37th Divl. Arty.
16 - 20		42nd " "
21 - 22		59th " "
23 - 24		62nd " "
25		S.C.R.A. 41st Divn.
26		Sig. Offcr. 41st D.A.
27 - 31		War Diary and File.

SECRET.   COPY No. 31

42nd DIVISIONAL ARTILLERY DEFENCE SCHEME.

CENTRE DIVISION – IV CORPS.   Appendix "C"

Reference Map 1/20,000 Sheet 57.D. N.E.

1. **DIVISIONAL FRONT.**

    42nd Division holds the Centre Sector.IV Corps Front from K.10.d.4.0. to L.2.c.9.1.

    <u>Southern Boundary.</u> K.10.d.4.0. – K.4.c.0.0. – K.3.c.0.0. – Northern corner of SAILLY AU BOIS J.12.d.4.4. – J.11.c.0.4. – J.16.a.0.0.– thence due West.

    <u>Northern Boundary.</u> L.2.c.9.1.– S.W.edge of BIEZ WOOD to K.6.b.5.7.– E.30.a.0.3.– E.23.d.00.15.– E.27.d.0.3.– thence due West.

2. **GROUPING OF FIELD ARTILLERY.**

    The Artillery covering 42nd Division will be divided into 2 Groups as follows:-

    RIGHT GROUP. – 2 R.F.A.Bdes.

    Covering RIGHT Inf.Bde (H.Q.at E.27.c.8.7.)

    LEFT GROUP. – 3 R.F.A.Bdes.

    Covering LEFT Inf.Bde.(H.Q.at E.28.d.1.6.)

    The Inter-Brigade Boundary is at K.6.c.6.0.

    The composition of the Artillery Groups and location of Group H.Qrs., Batteries, &c., are shewn in the latest Disposition Report in which is also shewn the H.A.Bdes affiliated to the Division.

3. **ACTION OF ARTILLERY.**

    The action of the Artillery falls under 3 headings, viz:-

    (a) <u>COUNTER-PREPARATION.</u>
    i.e. Action to prevent a hostile attack from developing. This will be ordered when necessary by D.A.,H.Q.

para 3 cont/d.

(a) cont/d. ACTION.
Groups will engage tracks, hollows and likely assembly places within the limits of their Harassing Fire Zones with all 4.5" Hows. and one Section per battery of 18-pdrs. The remaining 18-pdrs stand by to fire on their S.O.S. Lines if required.

Group Commanders will select suitable objectives in consultation with Infantry Brigadiers and report to D.A., H.Q. the points selected.

RATE OF FIRE. - 18-pdrs. and 4.5" Hows.

½ round per gun per minute.

If Counter-Preparation is ordered for a period of not more than 15 minutes the above rates may be doubled

(b) COUNTER-BOMBARDMENT.
i.e. Action to be taken when the enemy opens an Artillery bombardment that appears to be the prelude of an attack.

ACTION.
All 18-pdrs and 4.5" Hows. will open fire on their S.O.S. lines for 15 minutes searching outwards for 300 yards.
It is impossible to say how long the enemy's Artillery preparation will last.
The above process, therefore, will be carried out at irregular intervals averaging 45 minutes apart.

RATE OF FIRE. - Half S.O.S. Rates.

Counter Bombardment will normally be ordered from D.A., H.Q., but in cases where communications are severed Group Commanders, or even Bde. or Battery Commanders, must act on their own initiative.

(c) S. O. S.
i.e. Action to deal with an Infantry attack that has actually developed.

ACTION.
On the S.O.S. Signal being received by Rocket, Telephone, Visual, Runner or Wireless from Aeroplane all batteries and T.Ms. will open fire on their S.O.S. lines for 10 minutes as follows:-

para 3,(c) cont/d.

First 3 minutes.

18-pdrs   - 4 rounds per gun per minute.
4.5" Hows. - 3 rounds per how per minute.
T.Ms.   - As fast as possible.

Next 7 minutes.

18-pdrs   - 2 rounds per gun per minute.
4.5" Hows. - 1 round per how per minute.
T.Ms.   - Normal rate.

AMMUNITION.

18-pdrs. - 50% Shrapnel - 50% H.E.(106 fuze if available)
4.5" Hows.- H.E. 106 fuze.

After 10 minutes batteries and T.Ms will STOP FIRING until further information is received or until the S.O.S. Signal is repeated.

4. ### GAS ATTACK.

A Gas attack, either in the form of a Gas Cloud or from Gas Projectors, will be met with the same procedure as laid down for "Counter Bombardment"

5. ### S.O.S.LINES.

S.O.S.Lines for 18-pdrs will be approximately 250 yards in front of the Infantry Front Line and will be arranged by Group Commanders in consultation with the Infantry Brigades they support.

Group Commanders will arrange for an over-lap of 50 yards at the junction of their S.O.S.Barrage.

On the flanks of the Division an over-lap of 100 yards with the S.O.S.Barrage of the Flank Divisions is arranged.

The 4.5" Hows will have their S.O.S.lines on selected trench junctions, hollows, likely places of assembly,&c, beyond the 18-pdr.Barrage.

If the 18-pdr Barrage becomes too thin it may be necessary to include some or all of the 4.5" Hows in the 18-pdr Barrage.

S.O.S.Points for T.Ms. will be selected in consultation with Infantry Brigadiers and finally approved by the C.R.A.

In addition to the above, 4 - 6" How.batteries, 1 - 8" How. battery and 1 - 9.2" How battery have S.O.S.lines on important road and trench junctions beyond the 18-pdr Barrage.

6. ADDITIONAL POINTS WITH REGARD TO S.O.S.

    (a) To ensure a quick response to all S.O.S. Calls detachments of 1 N.C.O. and 3 men per gun must always be in readiness near the battery position.
    One man per gun must always be close to each gun pit.

    (b) A dial with pointer will be established at all battery positions and Bde.O.Ps. to locate the portion of the front on which the S.O.S. Signal is sent up.

    (c) A look-out sentry will be maintained at all battery positions by day and night.
    This sentry must be familiar with the use of the dial mentioned in para 6 (b).

    (d) Groups will establish where necessary sufficient repeating stations for the S.O.S. rocket to ensure the signal being seen by all batteries.
    12 S.O.S. rockets will be kept at each such station.

7. ENFILADE FIRE.

    (a) The fullest use will be made of enfilade fire both in allotting S.O.S. lines and in carrying out Harassing Fire.

    (b) At S.O.S. the following enfilade fire will be given by 42nd D.A. to the N.Z. Division.

1 - 18-pdr battery of the RIGHT GROUP fires from -
    K.21.b.7.0. to K.27.b.7.8.

1 - 18-pdr battery of LEFT GROUP fires from -
    K.16.b.8.7. to K.17.c.1.6.

    These batteries will keep a special look-out for S.O.S. Signals on the RIGHT Division front.
    If there is an S.O.S. on the CENTRE Division front only, and not on the RIGHT Division front, these batteries may be superimposed on the CENTRE Division S.O.S. It must, however, be clearly understood that their normal/lines are on the RIGHT Division front.   S.O.S.

    The following enfilade fire is similarly given to the 42nd Division by flank Divisions.

1 - 18-pdr battery of the RIGHT Division fires from -
    K.11.c.8.3. to K.11.b.05.25.

1 - Section of 18-pdrs of the LEFT Division fire from -
    K.12.a.15.10 to K.11.d.90.60.

para 7.cont/d.

In addition 1 - 60-pdr battery 29th H.A.B. from a position N.W. of MAILLY-MAILLET enfilades the front in L.8.a.&.b.

8. **MUTUAL SUPPORT.**

GIVEN BY	GIVEN TO	CODE CALL	ACTION
Left Divn.	Centre Divn.	"HELP CENTRE DIVN"	Flank Bde R.F.A. of LEFT Divn. opens fire on their S.O.S. lines and search outwards 300 yards.
Centre Divn.	Left Divn.	"HELP LEFT DIVN".	Flank Bde R.F.A. of CENTRE Divn. opens fire on their S.O.S. lines and search outwards 300 yards.
Centre Divn.	Right Divn.	"HELP RIGHT DIVN".	18-pdrs of flank Bde R.F.A. fire on K.22.a. 4.6. to K.17.a.8.0.
Right Divn	Centre Divn	"HELP CENTRE DIVN"	18-pdrs of flank Bde R.F.A. fire on K.17. a.2.3. to K.11.d.5.6.

NOTE :- No Mutual Support will be given by Divisional Artilleries when there is an "S.O.S" on their own front.
This does not apply to the enfilade fire mentioned in para 7. (b) which will be brought to bear whenever there is an S.O.S. on the front of the Division concerned.

9. **HARASSING FIRE.**

The following zones are allotted to Groups in which to carry out Harassing Fire and in which to answer zone calls from the air.

RIGHT Group. Area between a line passing through K.10.d.4.0. and K.24.b.0.5. and a line passing through K.6.c.2.4. to Road Junction K.12.d.4.3. to L.14.c.0.0. up to limit of range.

LEFT Group. Area between a line through K.6.c.2.4. to Road Junction K.12.d.4.3. to L.14.c.0.0. and a line passing through L.2.c.9.1. and L.11.a.0.0. up to limit of range.

para 9 cont/d.

The Square L.13. will be common to both Groups for Harassing fire purposes.

The allotment of ammunition for daily Harassing Fire will be given to Groups from time to time and Groups will submit by 6 p.m. daily a programme of Harassing Fire for the 24 hours commencing 6 p.m. the following day.

10. O.Ps.

O.Ps. will be organised in depth as follows :-

    (a) Forward O.Ps.
    (b) Rear or Brigade O.Ps.
    (c) "HOME" O.Ps.

With reference to (c), each battery will select an O.P. near the battery position from which as much as possible of the ground between the Front Line and the Battery position can be seen and from which fire can be controlled by megaphone.

Two O.Ps. on the Divisional front will be manned by both H.A. and F.A. Officers.

For list of Artillery O.Ps. see APPENDIX 'A'.

One O.P. per Bde R.F.A. will be manned continuously day and night.

Of the remaining O.Ps. sufficient will be manned from DAWN to DARK to ensure the whole of the front being kept under observation.

11. LIAISON.

(a) Each Group will maintain a Senior Liaison Officer with the H.Q. of the Inf.Bde they support.
(b) An R.A. Liaison officer will be found with each Battalion in the line.
    By day this officer will usually man an O.P.

12 SILENT BATTERIES.

A certain proportion of the Batteries **will** be kept as "SILENT" batteries.

They will only fire on -

    (a) COUNTER-PREPARATION.
    (b) COUNTER BOMBARDMENT.
    (c) S.O.S.

They will be registered as unostentatiously as possible and every endeavour made to keep their positions undetected.

13. COMMUNICATIONS.

Arrangements must be made to supplement telephonic communication with visual and runner in all cases.

The Visual will be practiced daily.

Horses for mounted orderlies will be kept near all battery positions for use in case of an attack, when all lines are liable to be cut, these will be used daily for at least one message.

14. PRECAUTIONARY MEASURES.

In the event of it appearing probable, either by reason of Heavy Bombardment or on other grounds, that the enemy will attack the following precautionary measures will be taken on receipt of a wire or telephone order from D.A.H.Q.

"PRECAUTIONARY MEASURES"

1. Divisional Advanced Report Centre will be opened at J.5.d.45.00 and all telephone messages relating to operations will be addressed there.

2. Artillery Teams will be ready to move at short notice.

3. Each Artillery Brigade will detail 2 mounted men to be at the disposal of the Signal Officer near their H.Qrs.

15. CO-OPERATION WITH AIRCRAFT.

(a) N.F.Calls.
Fire on N.F, M.Q.N.F, and W.P.N.F. calls will be carried out by Groups within the zones given in para.9.

N.F. & WP.N.F.calls will be responded to by a synchronized concentration of all 4.5" How batteries 10 minutes after the first receipt of the call.

Each battery will fire 3 salvoes.

(b) G.F.Calls.
Three Field batteries will be used to reply to a G.F. call in the Inner zone.

Each battery will fire 20 rounds.

(c) L.L.Calls.
All pieces that can bear other than those in "SILENT" positions will respond - 6 rds per gun and How.

(d) L.L., G.F. and N.F.Calls.
"SILENT" batteries will not fire in response to L.L., N.F., or G.F.Calls.

para 15 cont/d.

Wireless Masts will be erected at the Howitzer Battery position of each Brigade.

16. LOW FLYING ENEMY AIRCRAFT.

Whenever possible, without danger to our Infantry, 18-pdrs will engage Low Flying E.A.

This is best done just before the machine crosses our lines by firing on S.O.S. lines and raising the angle of sight.

Lewis Guns at battery positions will also engage Low Flying E.A.

17. ANTI-TANK DEFENCE.

Batteries will at all times be prepared to engage enemy Tanks.

Those batteries that are situated some 400 yards behind a crest line are in an admirable position to do this.

In addition, a few 15-pdr guns will be available shortly for siting as Anti-Tank guns along the Corps front.

[margin note: ?Mobile Section]

18. TRENCH MORTARS.

T.Ms. will be distributed in depth, some to cover the present front line and others to cover the PURPLE LINE system.

They will be kept "SILENT" except for pre-arranged shoots.

75 rounds per Mortar will be maintained at each forward position and 100 rounds per Mortar at each PURPLE LINE position.

19. RETIRED POSITIONS.

(a) PURPLE LINE SYSTEM.

Positions to cover the PURPLE LINE are shown in APPENDIX 'B'.

Each battery will reconnoitre a route back to its Retired Position.

In the event of a retirement being ordered the Firing Battery Wagons and 1st Line Wagons of each battery concerned will at once proceed to the new position and dump ammunition there.

(b) RED LINE SYSTEM.

Areas for Bdes. R.F.A. to cover the RED LINE have not yet been allotted.

They will be selected from those areas not chosen by the French Artillery

20. AMMUNITION SUPPLY.   See APPENDIX 'C'.

2nd May. 1918.

APPENDIX 'C' — Issued with 42nd D.A. Defence Scheme.

INSTRUCTIONS REGARDING AMMUNITION SUPPLY

1. **NORMAL METHOD OF SUPPLY.**

   (a) By M.T. from Railhead or Corps Reserve Dump to Divisional A.R.P. at D.26.Central.

   (b) By wagons of D.A.Cs. from A.R.P. to Battery Wagon Lines.

   (c) Battery Wagons or pack horses from Wagon Lines to gun positions.

2. **ESTABLISHMENTS.**

	18-pdr.	4.5" How.	
(a) At gun positions.	450	350	per gun.
(b) In Bty Wagon Line.	176	108	" "
(c) In D.A.C.	100	114	" "
(d) At A.R.P.	100	100	" "
	826	672	

   All vehicles are kept full at all times.

   An establishment of 400 rounds of GAS Shell is kept at each 4.5" How. Battery in addition to the above.

   Gas, Smoke and Incendiary Ammunition is demanded as required as it is not desirable to keep large stocks in the forward area.

3. **MEDIUM TRENCH MORTAR AMMUNITION.** Is supplied by M.T. to A.R.P. and thence to gun positions by G.S. Wagon and carriers.

4. **PURPLE LINE.**

   In the event of a withdrawal to the PURPLE LINE being ordered D.A.Cs. of CENTRE Division will withdraw to positions in the AUTHIE Valley between AUTHIE and THIEVRES. Battery Wagon Lines will move to ST LEGER - COUIN AREA. Battery Wagon Lines will draw direct from D.26.Central until stocks are exhausted. Ammunition will then be drawn from ST LEGER Railhead I.12.b. where the A.R.P. will be established. In the event of this becoming untenable D.A.Cs. will draw from Corps Reserve Dump at X Roads I.14.d.

APPENDIX 'A'   → Issued with 42nd D.A. Defence Scheme.

LIST OF O.PS. of 42nd DIVISION (CENTRE DIVISION).

LOCATION.	BY WHOM MANNED.	REMARKS.
RIGHT GROUP.		
310th Bde R.F.A.		
@ K.3.d.0.7.	—	Bde Rocket O.P. manned day & night by Bties. of Bde. in turn. Direct communication by wire to 54th H.A. Bde. O.P. at K.3.d.15.10.
K.21.b.45.65	A/310 & D/310.Bties	Bty.O.P. Direct communication by wire to 56th H.A. Bde O.P. at K.21.b.15.90.
312th Bde R.F.A.		
@ K.3.c.85.40.	—	Bde Rocket O.P. manned day & night by Bties in turn.
K.5.a.0.2.	A/312 & D/312 Bties	Bty.O.P.
K.3.b.2.5.	B/312 & C/312 Bties	Bty.O.P.
LEFT GROUP.		
187th Bde R.F.A.		
@ L.1.b.5.7.	—	Forward Bde. Rocket O.P. manned day & night by Bties of Bde in turn
K.5.a.0.0.	—	Forward Bde.O.P. not regularly manned - used by Bties for shooting on ROSSIGNOL WOOD.
E.29.a.05.50	—	Bde Rear O.P.
K.6.c.3.5.	—	TANK, Manned by day by Liaison Officer with Left Bttn. telephone line to forward section of B/210 Bty. Manned occasionally.
E.29.a.5.5.	B/187 Bty.	
Trench in L.2.b. running N.&.S.	C/187 Bty.	Bty.O.P.
E.29.a.05.50.	D/187 Bty.	Bty.O.P. also Rear Bde O.P.

-2-

LOCATION.	BY WHOM MANNED.	REMARKS.
187th Bde R.F.A.		
E.30.c.4.0.	D/187.	Bty.O.P. used occasionally for shooting on FORK WOOD.
210th Bde R.F.A.		
@ E.29.a.45.80	-	Bde.O.P. manned day & night by Bties. of Bde in turn.
K.4.b.9.2.	C/210 Bty.	Bty.O.P.
F.25.c.8.9.	D/210 Bty.	Bty.O.P.
E.30.a.7.7.	B/210 Bty.	Bty.O.P.
211th Bde R.F.A.		
@ K.4.b.7.3.	-	Bde Rocket O.P. manned by day & night by Bties of Bdes in turn - Direct communication by wire to 54th H.A.Bde O.P. at K.3.d.15.10. A H.A. F.O.O. also mans this O.P. by day.
E.29.a.6.9.	-	Bde O.P.
K.10.d.4.3.	A/211 Bty. B/211 Bty. D/211 Bty.	Bty.O.P.

@ Bde.O.Ps manned day & night.

42nd D.A.No.B.M. 296.

Herewith Copy No...31... as below of 42nd Divisional
Artillery Defence Scheme with -

APPENDIX 'A' - LIST OF O.Ps. of 42nd DIVISION (CENTRE DIVISION)

& APPENDIX 'C' - INSTRUCTIONS REGARDING AMMUNITION SUPPLY.

Please Acknowledge.

APPENDIX 'B' - "POSITIONS TO COVER THE PURPLE LINE SYSTEM"
will be issued shortly.

P.R. Mitchell
Major., R.A.
2nd May.1918.   Brigade Major., R.A., 42nd Division.

Copy No. 1. - R.A. IV Corps.
         2. - 42nd Divn. 'G'
         3. - 42nd Divn. 'Q'
         4. - N.Z.,D.A.
         5. - 37th D.A.
      6 - 10 210th Bde R.F.A.
     11 - 15 211th Bde R.F.A.
     16 - 20 187th Bde R.F.A.
     21 - 25 310th Bde R.F.A.
     26 - 30 312th Bde R.F.A.
        31   41st D.A.   ✓
        32   IV Corps H.A.
        33   IV Corps C.B.S.O.
        34   125th Inf.Bde.
        35   126th Inf.Bde.
        36   127th Inf.Bde.
        37   54th H.A.Bde.
        38   56th H.A.Bde.
        39   S.C.,R.A. 42nd Divn.
        40   Officer i/c R.A.Sigs.
        41   H.A.Liaison Officer.
        42   O.C. 42nd M.G.Battn.
        43   R.C.,R.A., 42nd Division.

BM342

Reference 42nd Divisional Artillery Defence Scheme issued under this office No.B.M.296 dated 2nd May.1918.

Para 7. - ENFILADE FIRE.

1 - 18-pdr Battery of LEFT Group fires from

    K.16.b.8.7. to K.17.c.1.6.

should read

    K.17.a.5.0. to K.11.c.5.0.

and

1 - 18-pdr Battery of the RIGHT Divn. fires from

    K.11.c.8.3. to K.11.b.05.25

should read

    K.11.c.8.3. to K.11.b.25.05.

Please amend accordingly.

ACKNOWLEDGE.

P.R. Mitchell
Major, R.A.

5-5-18.   Brigade Major., R.A., 42nd Division.

To all recipients of 42nd D.A. Defence Scheme.

APPENDIX 'B' — Issued with 42nd D.A.Defence Scheme.

POSITIONS TO COVER PURPLE LINE SYSTEM.

	LOCATION.	POSITION BOARD No.	O.Ps.
RIGHT GROUP.	H.Q. CHATEAU DE LA HAIE. (Alternative J.10.c.7.9.)		
A/310.	J.5.c.3.2.	141	Bde O.Ps (Rear)
B/310.	J.5.c.5.0.	142	Chateau de la Haie Tower.
C/310.	J.12.d.5.5.	143	and K.1.c.6.8.
D/310.	J.11.a.5.7.	144 H	Forward O.Ps.
			(1) K.3.c.8.5.
			(2) K.3.c.8.6.
			(3) K.3.d.1.8.
A/312.	J.6.c.9.7.	149	Bde O.P.(Rear)
B/312.	K.7.a.3.8.	150	E.25.d.4.3.
C/312.	J.12.b.1.9.	151	Forward O.Ps.
D/312.	J.12.b.9.1.	152 H	(1) K.3.b.2.5.
			(2) K.3.d.0.7.
LEFT GROUP.	H.Q. SUNKEN ROAD in D.29.c.		
@ A/210	(a) E.15.c.6.5.	101	Bde O.P.(Rear)
	(b) D.24.c.8.2.		E.16.c.0.4.
@ B/210	(a) E.21.c.1.3.	102	Forward O.Ps.
	(b) D.30.a.4.3.		(1) E.28.d.5.4.
@ C/210	(a) E.20.d.2.2.	103	(2) E.29.a.4.8.
	(b) D.30.a.9.1.		
@ D/210	(a) E.21.c.5.3.	104 H	
	(b) D.30.c.3.3.		
A/211	D.29.d.4.1.	109	Bde O.P.(Rear)
B/211	D.29.d.5.5.	110	E.16.c.1.8.
C/211	D.29.d.9.5.	111	Forward O.Ps.
D/211	D.30.c.1.7.	112 H	(1) E.29.a.6.9.
			(2) K.4.b.7.5.

@ NOTE. Should it become necessary for 210th Bde to vacate their more forward positions they will retire to the positions marked (b) above.

R.O.   Appendix "D"   N° 43.

SECRET.

1st. AMENDMENT to 42nd D.A.DEFENCE SCHEME.

7th May 1918.

For para. 3 substitute the following:-

3. **ACTION OF ARTILLERY.**
    The action of the Artillery falls under three headings:-

(a). **COUNTER PREPARATION**
    i.e. Action to prevent a hostile attack from developing. This will be ordered when necessary by D.A.H.Q. and need not necessarily be put down in reply to hostile bombardment; the procedure will be similar to that adopted for (b).

(b). **COUNTER BOMBARDMENT.**
    i.e. Action to be taken when the enemy opens an Artillery bombardment that appears to be the prelude of an attack.
    Action.
    (i). All H.A. opens on a pre-arranged programme which is, roughly, that 6" Hows., and 60-pdrs. fire on approaches and strong points, while other natures carry out Counter Battery work.

    (ii). Should the hostile bombardment open at night, half an hour before dawn (which will be taken until further notice as 4 a.m.) 18-pdrs. will fire on the following programme which will be repeated at dawn and again half an hour after dawn.

    (iii). Bursts about 100 to 200 yards on enemy side of S.O.S. Lines, searching forward by bounds to a depth of 600 yards: each burst to be of 2 minutes duration, a pause of 1 minute between each burst: 3 or 4 bounds to be made according to the ground; the final burst to be on S.O.S.lines. When repeating this programme it will be varied by searching back from furthest burst to S.O.S. lines, or by searching from centre of area, forward and then back and so on; the final burst will however always be fired on S.O.S. lines.

    (iv). 4.5" Hows. will have their lines laid out on selected trench junctions, hollows, likely places of assembly &c. and linking up with 18-pdr. S.O.S. barrage and will search as above except when detailed to keep on a certain definite area.

    (v). T.M's on selected trench junctions and areas.

(vi) After 2 hours Counter Preparation certain 6", 8" and 9.2" Hows. are brought in closer on to their S.O.S. lines; information will, if possible, be sent to Groups as to the time at which Counter Preparation is ordered by B.G.C.H.A. and a burst in depth will be put down by Field Artillery 2 hours after H.A. open on the Counter Preparation programme and at the time the 6" and other Hows. move on to their S.O.S. Lines.
It is impossible to say how long the enemy's Artillery preparation will last.

(vii). Every effort is to be made to obtain observation, and send information as to the situation back to Groups, but no hard and fast rules can be laid down as to the precise action of the Field Artillery; should no information come in the procedure detailed above will be carried out at discretion of Group Commanders.

(viii). <u>Rate of fire.</u>
  18-pdrs. 3 rounds per gun per minute.
  4.5" Hows. 2 " " " " "
  T.M's. 3 " " " " "

Counter Bombardment will nominally be ordered from D.A.H.Q. but in cases where communications are severed Group Commanders or even Brigade Commanders must act on their own initiative, the principle being that all batteries on one area open fire simultaneously to ensure a heavy concentration.

(ix). Ammunition:- As for S.O.S.

(c). <u>S.O.S.</u>
i.e. action to deal with an Infantry Attack that has actually developed.
(i). <u>Action.</u> On the S.O.S. Signal being received by any means all batteries and T.M's will open fire on their S.O.S. lines for 10 minutes as follows:-
 First 3 minutes:-
  18-pdrs. 4 rounds per gun per minute.
  4.5" Hows. 3 " " " " "
  T.M's. As fast as possible.
 Next 7 minutes:-
  18-pdrs. 2 rounds per gun per minute.
  4.5" Hows. 1½ " " " " "
  T.M's. 3 " " " " "

Ammunition.
18-pdrs. 50% Shrapnel. 50% H.E. (106 fuze if available).

(ii). After 10 minutes batteries and T.M's will stop firing until further information is received or until S.O.S.Signal is repeated, except in the following circumstances:-
    (a). During hostile bombardment,
    (b). During a mist;
in both of which cases the procedure laid down of searching by bursts in depth as for Counter Bombardment will be followed with an interval of 20 minutes between the commencement of each series of bursts. Should however it be evident that a hostile attack is in progress this procedure will be repeated with an interval of one minute between series of bursts until the situation becomes clear.
F.O.O's and Infantry should be instructed to send up S.O.S. rockets at intervals until hostile attack is beaten off. This procedure will be continued for 2 hours or at the discretion of Group Commanders until the situation is cleared up.

For para.5 substitute the following:-

5. S.O.S.LINES.
(i). S.O.S.Lines of each 18-pdr. Brigade will be concentrated along likely lines of attack and be approximately 250 yards in front of Infantry Front Line. Under present arrangements they are as set out in Appendix D, issued herewith.

(ii). 4.5" Hows. will link up with 18-pdr. barrage except when detailed for some specific area.

(iii). T.M's will be on selected trench junctions and areas.

(iv). The principle adopted is to be strong at the most likely places of attack instead of weak all along the front.
Battalion M.G's have lines laid out on areas between 18-pdr. barrages.

(v). In addition to the above, 4 6" Hows., 1 8" How. and 1 9.2" How. Battery have S.O.S. lines on important road and trench junctions in rear of 18-pdr. S.O.S. lines, which in certain circumstances search in depth up to then.

Add to para. 14 new sub-para. 4 as follows:-

4. On opening of a heavy hostile bombardment 2 mounted orderlies per Group will be sent to D.A.H.Q. COUIN.

Add to para. 17 the following:-

Forward 18-pdr. Sections and flank guns of 18-pdr Batteries will prepare positions to which guns can be run out to deal with tanks.
One 18-pdr. gun will be placed by Right Group about K.3.a. with 100 rounds ammunition (50% A, 50% AX) and remain silent until needed. It will fire direct down valley and old NO MANS LAND between GOMMECOURT and HEBUTERNE.

A Mobile Section from the F.A. Brigade in Corps Reserve is detached under instructions from Corps and instructed to remain in neighbourhood of CH. DE LA HAIE to engage enemy Tanks on the first notice of their appearance. The Officer in charge of this section will have an orderly at Right Group Headquarters with the object of obtaining early information and orders if any; but he will watch the situation for himself, and failing the receipt of orders will move out to engage enemy tanks on receiving information of their approach.

Major, R.F.A.,
Ag. Brigade Major,
41st Divisional Artillery.

Issued to all recipients of 42nd D.A. Defence Scheme.

APPENDIX "D" to 42nd D.A. DEFENCE SCHEME.

7th May 1918.

1. S.O.S. Lines will be laid out as follows:-

   18-pdrs. A K.17.a.45.05 - K.11.c.50   C/211 A/310 C/310
            B K.11.d.25.65 - K.12.a.25.10.   A/312 B/312.
            C L.7.c.25.30 - L.7.d.6.2.   A/210 B/210 C/210.
            D L.8.c.8.9.   - L.8.b.45.60.   A/211 B/211.

   4.5" How. 1 Bty.(D/211) Along trench L.7.d.80 - L.8.c.85.60.
             1 Bty.(D/310) K.11.c.50 - K.11.d.25.70.
             1 Bty.(D/210) Search ROSSIGNOL WOOD.
             1 Section   Road K.12.a.04 - K.12.a.06.
             2 Sections   K.12.d.69. - L.7.c.25.45.

   6" T.M's 4 guns search ROSSIGNOL WOOD;
            remainder as detailed in 42nd D.A. Location
            Statement dated 5-5-18.

2. Searching during Counter Bombardment (see para.3 (b)(iii)
   1st Amendment to 42nd D.A. Defence Scheme) and when required during an attack will be from S.O.S. Lines as under:

   18-pdrs. A area from S.O.S. Lines (as above) to K.17.b.8.0-
                                                    K.17.b.8.9.
            B   -   K.12.c.55.00 - K.12.d.6.5.
            C   -   L.13.b.0.2. - L.14.a.25.05.
            D   -   L.8.d.7.2.   - L.9.c.35.90.

   4.5" Hows D/211: Area from S.O.S. lines to line of road
              L.14.a.35.05., L.14.a.60.08., L.8.d.25.25.
             D/310: Area from S.O.S. lines to line K.11.d.8.0.-
              K.12.c.05.25.
             Remaining 4.5" Howitzer and T.M. Batteries re-
                main on S.O.S. Lines.

   The searching by 18-pdrs will be in four bounds; including
   S.O.S. Line as one; that of 4.5" Hows in 3 bounds, one
   of which will be repeated; 4.5" Hows. and T.M's that do
   not search will fire 4 bursts to coincide with "bounds"
   of 18-pdrs.

SECRET.   Copy No. 43

Appendix "E"

2nd AMENDMENT to 42nd D.A. DEFENCE SCHEME.

10th May 1918.

In Para. 3(a), 1st Amendments to 42nd D.A. Defence Scheme:
Alter full stop after (b) to comma, and add "and is laid
down in Appendix E".

APPENDIX "E" to 42nd D.A. DEFENCE SCHEME.

1. Counter Preparation will be carried out as follows:-

18-pdrs.   Area E.   line K.17.d.75.77, K.17.b.95.65 to line
                           K.18.c.75.57, K.18.a.90.65.
               "   F.   line K.12.c.55.25, K.12.a.6.0. to line
                           K.12.d.65.10, K.12.d.65.85.
                         (Search ROSSIGNOL WOOD.
                         (Enfilade Trench K.12.d.70.95 to
               G.   {   L.7.c.25.50.
                         {   "   "   L.7.c.25.00. to
                         (L.13.c.75.65.
               "   D.   as in Appendix D (no change from Counter
                                            Bombardment area).

The batteries told off for Counter bombardment areas A and
B in Appendix D will search areas E and F shewn above in a
similar manner.
Batteries on area C will enfilade as shewn under G; area D,
no change.

4.5"Hows. Right Group. Sunken road E.18.a.15.90 to E.12.d.35.25.
                      Trench K.12.d.65.30 to K.18.b.70.45 and Trench
                      L.7.c.10.45 to L.7.c.15.00.

          Left Group. Trench L.7.c.50.15 to L.7.d.8.0.
                      Trench L.14.a.1.9. to L.8.d.1.7.

6" T.M's   4 guns search ROSSIGNOL WOOD; remainder,
                      Sunken roads and Trench system in K.17.b.,
                      K.11.d.

The searching by 18-pdrs. will be in four bounds, which will
be repeated after an interval of 10 minutes from conclusion
of last burst. Enfilade 18-pdrs., 4.5" Hows. and T.M's
will fire four bursts to coincide with "bounds" of 18-pdrs.

                                        E.R.Roper
                                            Major R.F.A.
                              for   Brigade Major, 41st Divl.Arty.
Issued to all recipients of 42nd D.A.Defence Scheme.

R.F.A.

<u>S E C R E T.</u>   <u>41st D.A.No.S628.</u>

                                                              <u>Copy No. 43</u>

<u>Reference Appendix E to 42nd D.A.Defence Scheme.</u>

     In consequence of change in front line the following alterations in Counter Preparation Tasks will be made at once:-

1.   Task G: Cancel lines 7 to 10 ("Enfilade Trench -------- L.13.c.75.65") and substitute the following:-

                "Enfilade road K.12.d.70.30 to L.7.c.10.00 and trench L.7.c.20.00 to L.13.a.75.65"

2.   4.5" Hows, line 20: For "L.7.c.10.45 to L.7.c.15.00" read "L.7.c.15.30 to Road L.13.a.30.85".

                                                         Major, R.F.A.
    11/5/18   for Brigade Major,
                                                   41st Divisional Artillery.

To all recipients of 42nd D.A.Defence Scheme.

S E C R E T.   Copy No. 40

CORRIGENDA to 1st AMENDMENTS 42nd D.A. DEFENCE SCHEME.
----

1. Last two lines of sub-para. 3(b)(vi) should be the beginning of sub-paragraph 3(b)(vii).

2. Add new para. 3(b)(x):-
   During "Counter Bombardment" should no hostile attack develop, the action of the Field Artillery will normally be limited to the action laid down in 3(b)(ii) and 3(b)(vi) but Group Commanders have complete liberty of action to order otherwise should the situation in their opinion call for it.

3. Cancel sub-para. 3(c)(ii) and substitute the following:-
   (ii). After 10 minutes reply to S.O.S. Call batteries and T.M's will stop firing until further information is received, except in the following circumstances:-

   (a). During hostile bombardment;
   (b). During a mist;
   (c). If it is evident, either from repetition of the S.O.S. signal or from other indications, that a hostile attack is in progress.

In cases (a) and (b) the procedure laid down for Counter Bombardment of searching by bursts in depth will be followed, with an interval of 20 minutes between the conclusion of each series of bursts and the next series.
This procedure will be continued for two hours or at the discretion of Group Commanders until the situation is clear.
In case (c) this procedure will be repeated with an interval of 4 minutes between the conclusion of each series of bursts and the next series, until it becomes clear that the attack has ceased.

F.O.O's and Infantry should be instructed to send up S.O.S. rockets at intervals until the hostile attack is beaten off.
It is to be clearly understood that after the first reply to an S.O.S. call, when all Field Artillery comes down on its S.O.S. lines, all fire intended to stop an attack will be put down by searching in depth, except where a battery or section is expressly detailed to remain on its S.O.S. lines. Batteries or sections so detailed will sweep to the extent necessary to cover their battery or section tasks. Enfilade batteries will search with the same object. T.M's will sweep 30 minutes unless a different amount of sweep is necessary for the execution of their S.O.S. tasks.

P.T.O.

4. In Appendix "D" para. 1 line 3, "18-pdrs "B", after B/312 insert B/310.

5. In Appendix "D" para. 1, line 9 should read "1 section D/312, Road K.12.a.45.00. - K.12.c.75.90; in line 10, insert "D/312" after "2 sections".

6. In Appendix "D" at end of para. 2 add "C/211 will fire alternately on its S.O.S. lines and on one "bound" beyond these lines, but will fire the same number of bursts on these lines as the other 18-pdrs. when searching. C/312 fires in enfilade on Right Division front from K.27.b.7.8. to K.21.d.70.95 and remains on that line and will fire bursts at times detailed for remaining 18-pdrs. of Right Group".

Major, R.F.A.
Ag. Brigade Major,
Issued at:- 5 p.m.   41st Divisional Artillery.

To all recipients of 1st Amendment to 42nd D.A. Defence Scheme.

Appendix "F"

41st. DIVISIONAL ARTILLERY INSTRUCTION No.1.

Copy No.

ENTRAINING.

(1) 41st.D.A. will entrain to-morrow in accordance with Table 'A' attached.

(2) Lieut. POPE and Lieut BLAND will be entraining Officers at the North and South Yard respectively. They will report to R.T.O.DOULLENS before 5.a.m. on 14th.inst. They will be present at the entraining of every train and travel on the last train from their respective stations.

(3) Transport must arrive at the Entraining Stations 3 hours before the advertised time of departure of the train. Officers Commanding Batteries or Sections and Officers or N.C.O's. i/c detached portions of D.A.C. will on arrival at the Station hand to the Entraining Officer for transmission to the R.T.O. an Entraining State on pro-forma attached. (Pro-forma 'B')

(4) Horses will be entrained unharnessed.

(5) The Senior Officer in each train will be O.C.Train. He will preserve strict discipline and ensure that once entraining is completed, no man leaves the train without the permission of an officer.

RATIONS.

(6) Units except as mentioned below will entrain with the unconsumed portion of the days rations, and one days rations (the meat portion of which will be an Iron Ration) carried on Supply Wagons. O.C. No.1 Coy, 41st.Divisional Train will send supply wagons loaded with supplies for consumption 15th, to join units to-night. Units entraining on Trains No's. 9 & 11 inclusive will entrain with rations for consumption 15th. only.

(7) O.C. D.A.C. will arrange that detached portions of D.A.C. carry their own rations with them.

(8) M.T.Coy. will move under orders of 4th.Corps to de-entraining station loaded with rations for consumption 16th.

BILLETING.

(9) Billeting parties consisting of 1 Officer per Brigade and D.A.C. Interpreter and 1 N.C.O. per Battery will travel in the first train of each Brigade and of the D.A.C. Detached portions of D.A.C. will wait at or near the Entraining Station for the arrival of their own Section.

LORRIES.

(10) Lorries have been detailed in accordance with Table 'C' attached.

CAMPS.

(11) All Camps and Billets must be left clean and in proper condition. All tents and shelters must be handed over to the Area Commandant of the Area concerned before departure, and receipts taken. Copies of receipts will be forwarded to this office, and numbers of tents and bivouacs handed over will be wired to this office before 10.a.m.14th. inst.

(12) ACKNOWLEDGE.

Churchill Captain,
Staff Captain, 41st. Divisional Artillery.,

Issued at _____

Copy No.1	187th B'de.	As are.	18.	4th.Corps 'Q'
6	190th. "		19.	4th.Corps R.A.
11.	41st.DAC	3 "	20.	Area Commdt. PAS. M Dwl. Sha
14.	D.T.M.O.	1 "	21.	" " COWIN.
16.	Lt.BLAND		22.	" " HTNU.
17.	Lt.POPE.			

TABLE 'A'.

14th instant.

No.	Entraining Station.	Time of departure.	UNIT.	Remarks.
1.	DOULLENS N.Yard.	8.42	A/190 1 G.S.Wagon & 5 limbered wagons of No.2 Sect.D.A.C. with teams.	
2.	DOULLENS S.Yard.	10.42	D/190. 1 G.S.Wagon & 5 limbered wagons and teams of No.2 Section D.A.C.	
3.	DOULLENS N.Yard.	12.42	H.Q.190th.B'de. No.2 Sect.D.A.C. less 4 G.S. Wagons and 15 limbered ammn. Wagons and teams.	
4.	DOULLENS S.Yard.	14.27	C/190. 1 G.S.Wagon and 5 limbered ext. Wagons and teams of No.2 Sect.	
5.	DOULLENS N.Yard.	16.27	D.A.C. 1 G.S.Wagon and team of D.A.C.	x It is probable that this train cannot accommodate the whole load.Any which cannot be entrained must be loaded on subsequent trains as opportunity offers.
6.	DOULLENS S.Yard.	18.27	H.Q.,D.A.C. No.1 Cav.41st.Div.Train. T.M. B's.	
7.	DOULLENS N.Yard.	20.42	H.Q.187th.B'de. No.1 Sect. D.A.C. less 4 G.S. Wagons and 16 limbered ammn. Wagons and teams.	
8.	DOULLENS S.Yard.	22.42	A/187. 1 G.S.Wagon and 4 limbered ammn. wagons and teams of No.1 Sect. D&C.	

15th.instant.

No.	Entraining Station.	Time of departure.	UNIT.	Remarks.
9.	DOULLENS N.Yard.	0.42	B/187. 1 G.S. Wagon & 4 limbered ammn. wagons and teams of No.1 Sect.D.A.C.	
10.	DOULLENS "	2.42	C/187. 1 G.S.Wagon & 4 limbered ammn. wagons & teams of No.1 Sect.DAC.	
11.	DOULLENS "	4.42	D/187. 1 G.S.Wagon & 4 limbered am. wagons of No.1 Section DAC with teams.	

PRO-FORMA 'B'

UNIT.

OFFICERS.	MEN.	HORSES		G.S.WAGONS.	AXLES.	BICYCLES.
		LD.	H.D.			

TABLE 'C'

Number.	Time & place to report.	How employed.	Remarks.
2.	HENU Church 6.0 a.m. 14th.inst.	Transport of T.M.B's to DOULLENS Station.	D.T.M.O. to send guide to HENU Church.
2.	COUIN Church 6.0 a.m. 14th.inst.	To assist 187th.B'de.in march to DOULLENS.	O.C.187th.B'de. to send guide to COUIN Chruch.
2.	PAS Church. 6.a.m. 14th.inst.	To assist 190th.B'de.in march to DOULLENS.	O.C.190th.B'de.to send guide to PAS Church.

Appendix "G"

SECRET. 41st D.A. No. S.646.

REAR LINES OF DEFENCE.

15th May 1918.

1. LINES OF DEFENCE. Five lines of defence have been constructed in rear of our present front line.

    A. RED   The "YPRES DEFENCES" Line.

    B. PURPLE   The "REAR ZONE" Line.

    C. GREEN   The "GREEN" or "VLAMERTINGHE" Line.

    D. YELLOW   The "YELLOW" or "BRANDHOEK" Line.

    E. BLUE   The "BLUE" or POPERINGHE EAST" Line.

2. Field Artillery positions for the defence of these lines have been reconnoitred and are enumerated below.

3. YPRES DEFENCES.

Right Artillery Brigade
  Brigade Headquarters - GOLDFISH CHATEAU (H.11.a.85.25).
  6 - 18-pdrs.   -   H.11.b.0.6.
  6 - 18-pdrs.   -   H.11.b.05.30.
  6 - 18-pdrs.   -   H.5.d.25.05.
  6 - 4.5" Howitzers - H.11.b.4.8.
      Main O.P. - RAMPARTS at I.14.b.15.95.

Left Artillery Brigade.
  Brigade Headquarters - MACHINE GUN FARM (H.5.c.9.9.)
  6 - 18-pdrs.   -   H.4.d.90.15.
  6 - 18-pdrs.   -   H.5.c.8.1.
  6 - 18-pdrs.   -   H.5.b.2.0. ∅
  6 - 4.5" Howitzers - H.4.c.80.86.
      Main O.P. - RAMPARTS at I.8.b.05.75.

Notes.
(1). All above positions have been occupied except that marked ∅.
(2). Buried cables run from D.A. Advanced Exchange at VLAMERTINGHE CHATEAU to both MACHINE GUN FARM and GOLDFISH CHATEAU.
(3). Buried cables run from GOLDFISH CHATEAU to the RAMPARTS close to the O.P. at I.1.b.7.2..
    Buried cables run from MACHINE GUN FARM to DEAD END at I.2.c.05.55.

4. REAR ZONE LINE. Positions have been chosen to defend the REAR ZONE LINE as an outpost line only, the main line of resistance being the GREEN LINE.
The positions chosen are :-

Right Artillery Brigade
  6 - 18-pdrs.   -   H.1.c.9.9.
  2 - 4.5" Howitzers - H.1.a.90.45.
      Main O.P. - GOLDFISH CHATEAU.

Left Artillery Brigade.
  6 - 18-pdrs.   -   A.25.c.1.8.
  2 - 4.5" Howitzers - A.30.d.45.50.
      Main O.P. - Buildings at H.5.b.0.0.

All other units would be disposed as for defence of GREEN LINE.

Note. Buried cables run from D.A. Advanced exchange at VLAMERTINGHE CHATEAU to both GOLDFISH CHATEAU and MACHINE GUN FARM.

5. GREEN and YELLOW LINES.

Battery positions and Brigade Headquarters chosen for the defence of GREEN Line are also suitable for the defence of the YELLOW Line.

<u>Right Artillery Brigade.</u>
Brigade Headquarters — Farm at A.28.b.7.1.
6 - 18-pdrs. — A.28.d.5.2.
6 - 18-pdrs. — G.5.a.6.5.
6 - 18-pdrs. — G.5.a.15.55.
6 - 4.5" Howitzers — G.4.b.7.0.
Main O.Ps (For GREEN Line - VLAMERTINGHE CHATEAU.
(For YELLOW Line - Houses at G.5.b.7.8.

<u>Left Artillery Brigade.</u>
Brigade Headquarters — Farm at A.28.b.7.1.
6 - 18-pdrs. — A.29.c.6.3.
6 - 18-pdrs. — A.28.d.8.5.
2 - 18-pdrs. — A.29.c.90.45.
4 - 18-pdrs. — A.29.c.95.20.
6 - 4.5" Howitzers — A.29.c.15.80.

Main O.Ps. { For GREEN Line { B.26.d.9.6. or
{ { B.26.d.7.3.
{ For YELLOW Line { Building at
{ { A.30.d.9.5.

<u>Notes.</u>
(1). Sand-bagged elephants have been erected at farm at A.28.b.7.1. There will be accommodation in the cellar of the farm and sand-bagged elephants could be erected in the barns of the farm as soon as it is vacated by the inhabitants.
(2). Work has been commenced at both YELLOW Line O.Ps.
(3). One telephone line in the emergency buried route from LOVIE CHATEAU to PESELHOEK has been allotted to D.A.
From PESELHOEK two lines run overland to farm at A.28.b.7.1.
(4). Armoured cables have been laid from farm at A.28.b.7.1. to Battery positions.
(5). One armoured cable has been laid from farm at A.28.b.7.1. to VLAMERTINGHE CHATEAU for GREEN Line O.P. Work of Right Artillery Brigade, and to cable head at B.25.a.1.3. for GREEN Line O.P. work of Left Artillery Brigade.
A buried cable runs through the GREEN Line at about B.26.d.6.9. If time permits the bury may be opened up at this point for use of Left Artillery Brigade O.Ps.
(6). The armoured cables mentioned in Note (5) above have been laid via their respective Brigade YELLOW Line O.Ps.

6. BLUE LINE.

<u>Right Artillery Brigade.</u>
Brigade Headquarters — Farm at L.5.b.05.95.
6 - 18-pdrs. — L.5.b.40.05.
6 - 18-pdrs. — L.5.b.40.65.
2 - 18-pdrs. — F.30.c.15.20.
4 - 18-pdrs. — F.29.d.70.15.
6 - 4.5" Howitzers — L.5.b.15.90.

Left Artillery Brigade
    Brigade Headquarters — House at F.29.d.5.9.
    6 - 18-pdrs. -   - F.29.d.6.4.
    6 - 13-pdrs. -   - F.29.a.70.85.
    2 - 13-pdrs. -   - F.30.c.5.7.
    4 - 18-pdrs. -   - F.29.d.7.9.
    2 - 4.5" Howitzers - F.29.b.45.90.
    4 - 4.5" Howitzers - F.29.b.50.25.

Notes.
    (1). Divisional Boundaries West of BLUE Line have not yet been notified.
    (2). O.Ps have not yet been reconnoitred.
    (3). No cables have yet been laid and no work has been done on positions or Headquarters.

F.N. MacFarlane

                              Brigade Major,
                        41st Divisional Artillery.

Copy No. 1 to 5   187th Brigade R.F.A.
  " " 6 " 10   190th   "   "
  " " 11   S.C.R.A. 41st Divn.
  " " 12   Signal Officer, 41st D.A.
  " " 13 to 15 War Diary and File
  " " 16 " 18   Spare.

Appendix "H"

41" O.A. No. S.654.

SECRET.

Copy No. 26

17th May 1918.

Reference 29th D.A. Instructions No.52 dated 15th May 1918. The following alterations will be made.:-

Para 4 S.O.S. Lines.

Right Brigade
    18-pdr. S.O.S.Line:-
    The barrage will be thinned out opposite MOATED GRANGE to thicken up the two flanks.

4.5" Howitzer Tasks.

    Delete I.16.d.5.8. and substitute I.16.d.65.15.
      "   I.16.c.85.30 and substitute I.22.b.35.85.
      "   I.10.d.50.15 and substitute I.10.d.75.10.

Left Brigade
    18-pdr. S.O.S.Line:-

The superimposed battery will cover the line I.16.b.25.60 to I.10.d.30.60.
One section 18-pdrs will be withdrawn from the portion from I.10.b.central - JAMES FARM/ and will fire on the Railway cutting about I.11.c.1.8.

4.5" Howitzer Tasks.

    Delete I.10.d.7.7. and substitute Railway cutting about I.11.c.3.9.
    Delete CRUMP FARM and substitute Railway cutting about I.11.c.3.9.

for Brigade Major,
41st Divisional Artillery.

Issued to all recipients of 29th D.A. Instructions No.52.

Appendix "I"

S E C R E T.   Copy No. 18

41st. DIVISIONAL ARTILLERY INSTRUCTIONS No.2.

18th May 1918.

1. To increase the lack of depth in the present dispositions of the 41st Divisional Artillery the following moves will take place:-

2. Two 18-pdr. Batteries of 187th Brigade (one of which will be A/187) will move to positions in H.5.d. and H.6.d. already selected.

   One 18-pdr. Battery of 190th Brigade will move to a position about B.29.d.9.1.

3. Moves will take place by sections as soon as possible. Brigades will report when ready to commence move and will await sanction from C.R.A. before moving.

4. The Batteries in H.5.d. and B.29.d. will be "silent" Batteries. One gun only per Battery will be registered. Batteries will fire S.O.S. and Counter Preparation only. The greatest care is to be taken as regards camouflage.

5. Brigades will report the amount of ammunition left at positions on vacation when orders as to its disposal will be issued.

F.H. MacFarlane
Captain R.F.A.
Brigade Major,
41st Divisional Artillery.

Issued at:- 10 p.m.

Copy No.	1	187th Bde. R.F.A.	Copy No.	10	122 Infy. Bde.
" "	2	190th Brigade R.F.A.	" "	11	123 Infy. Bde.
" "	3	41st Division G.	" "	12	124 Infy. Bde.
" "	4	41st Division Q.	" "	13	C.R.E. 41st Divn.
" "	5	II Corps R.A.	" "	14	A.D.M.S. 41st Divn
" "	6	II Corps H.A.	" "	15	S.C.R.A. 41st Divn.
" "	7	C.B.S.O.	" "	16	Sigs. 41st D.A.
" "	8	41st D.A.C.	" "	17-20	War Diary & File
" "	9	41st M.G.Battn.			

S E C R E T.

AMENDMENT No. 1 to 41st D.A. INSTRUCTIONS No.2.

19-5-18.

Cancel para. 5 and substitute "One Section from each of the above batteries will remain in action in its present position for normal harassing fire purposes".

F.H. MacFarlan
Captain R.F.A.
Brigade Major,
41st Divisional Artillery.

Issued to all recipients of 41st D.A. Instructions No.2.

Appendix "J"

S E C R E T.   Copy No. 18

41st DIVISIONAL ARTILLERY INSTRUCTIONS No.3.

Harassing Fire.   19th May 1918.

In future harassing fire will be carried out by Brigades within their own Boundaries between a line approximately 1000 yards E of our Front Line Trench and the extreme limits of their range.

No Harassing fire will take place further W than this line except on localities known to be occupied.

The minimum expenditure will be reduced to 75 rounds per gun 18-pdr. and 40 rounds per gun 4.5" Howitzer.

Captain R.F.A.
Brigade Major,
Issued at:- 4 p.m.   41st Divisional Artillery.

To all recipients of 41st D.A. Instructions No. .2

Appendix "K"

S E C R E T. 41st D.A. No. S.672.

Reference 41st D.A. Instructions No.4 of date.

Zero hour will be 12 midnight 21st/22nd May.

187th and 190th Brigades acknowledge BY WIRE.

                                    for Captain R. F. A.
                                    Brigade Major,
21-5-19.   41st Divisional Artillery.

Issued to all recipients of 41st D.A. Instructions No.4.

SECRET.   Copy No. 6

41st DIVISIONAL ARTILLERY INSTRUCTIONS No.4.

24th May 1918.

1. 6th Division are carrying out a raid tonight in I.27.b, c and d.

2. 41st Divisional Artillery will co-operate as follows:-

   (a). 187th Brigade will assist Left Group 6th D.A. under orders of O.C. Left Group, 6th D.A.

   (b). 190th Brigade will open fire on the following tasks at zero.
       1 section 18-pdrs. will search N edge of BILLEBEKE lake from a point 400 yards in front of our front line as far as HALLEBLAST Corner.
       2 sections 18-pdrs. will search and sweep the area N.E. of this line as far as the TUTURIEN.
       1 battery 18-pdrs. will search and sweep the area I.22.b.4.6. I.16.d.4.6. I.17.c.0.5. I.23.a.0.5.
   One 4.5" Howitzer will be detailed to engage each of the following:-
      (a). T.M. at I.22.b.6.4.
      (b). M.G. at I.22.b.3.7.
      (c). Road junction at I.22.b.75.40.
      (d). Road Junction at I.16.d.68.12.
      (e). " " " I.16.c.4.5.
      (f). HALLEBLAST Corner.

3. **Rates of fire**
   Zero to Zero plus 5'   18-pdrs. 2 rounds per gun per minute.
                             4.5"How. 2 " " " " "
   Zero plus 5' to Zero plus 45' 18-pdrs. 1 rd. " " " "
                             4.5"How.1 " " " " "

4. Zero hour will be notified later.
   Watches will be synchronised from this office.

5. 187th and 190th Brigades to ACKNOWLEDGE.

                                          Captain, R.F.A.
                                          Brigade Major,
                                         41st Divisional Artillery.

Issued at:- 11 p.m.

Copy No. 1 to 187th Bde.
   " " 2 " 190th "
   " " 3 " 41st Division G.
   " " 4 " 6th D.A.
   " " 5-6 War Diary and File.

War Diary. Appendix "Z"

S E C R E T.　　　　　　　　　　　　　　　　Copy No. 27

41st. DIVISIONAL ARTILLERY DEFENCE SCHEME No.1.

Reference Maps:-　　　　　　　　　　　　　　19th May 1918.
Sheets 27 N.E.& 28 N.W. 1/20,000.

1. (a). The Field Artillery covering the 41st Divisional front is
DISPOSITIONS. disposed as follows:-

    Covering Right Infantry Brigade front,　　　　A)
        187th Brigade R.F.A.
        H.Q. I.1.d.15.50.　　　　　　　　　　　　　B) 187 Batteries
        Lt. Col.C.D.G.LYON,D.S.O.,R.F.A.　　　　　C)　R.F.A.
        　　　　　　　　　　　　　　　　　　　　　D)

    Covering Left Infantry Brigade front,　　　　A)
        190th Brigade R.F.A.　　　　　　　　　　　B) 190 Batteries
        H.Q. H.6.b.25.55.　　　　　　　　　　　　　C)　R.F.A.
        Lt.Col.G.A.CARDEW,C.M.G.,D.S.O.,　　　　　D)
                      R.F.A.

(b). Locations of units of 41st Divisional Artillery are given
    in Appendix "A" and 41st D.A.Instructions No.2 attached.

(c). Y/41 T.M.Battery has 6 - 6" Newton Trench Mortars in ac-
    tion as shewn in Appendix "A" for the defence of the YPRES
    defences.
    X/41 T.M.Battery is in reserve at C.4.a.2.3.

(d). The Heavy Artillery covering the Divisional front consist
    of the following R.G.A.Brigades of II Corps H.A.:-

Covering from Northern Divisional) 8th Bde.R.G.A.　14 - 6" Hows
   Boundary to I.16.a.6.8.　　　　) H.Q. A.18.a.1.8　 2 - 9.2"
                                                      Hows.

Covering from I.16.a.6.8. to) 53rd Bde.R.G.A.　　6 - 6" Hows
Southern Divisional Boundary.) H.Q. A.30 a 7.7.　　6 - 60 Prs.
                                                     6 - 9.2"
                                                     Hows.

2.　　List of O.Ps manned day and night by 41st Divisional
O.Ps.　Artillery and affiliated Heavy Artillery is attached in
     Appendix "B".

3.
LIAISON.
A senior Officer from each Artillery Brigade stays with the Headquarters of its affiliated Infantry Brigade in the line at MACHINE GUN FARM.

An Officer from each Artillery Brigade will stay with headquarters of each of the two Battalions of its affiliated Infantry Brigade in the line.
In the case of the Right Artillery Brigade, liaison with the Infantry Battalion Headquarters in the ECOLE will be maintained by the F.O.O. at ECOLE O.P.
41st Divisional Artillery Instructions No.5 as to Liaison duties are attached in Appendix "C".

4.(a). Southern boundaries of Right Artillery Brigade.
ARTILLERY For S.O.S. Northern edge of ZILLEBEKE LAKE.
BOUNDARIES, For all other purposes:-
I.21.b.00.65 - I.28.a.2.9. along road through
I.28.a. b. & d and I.35.a. & c. inclusive.

(b). Inter-Brigade Boundary:-
I.10.c.40.55 - I.10.d.40.55 - I.10.d.7.1. thence along MENIN Road inclusive to Left Brigade.

(c). Northern Boundary of Left Artillery Brigade:-
East and West grid line through I.4.b.5.5.

5.
S.O.S.
S.O.S. instructions and tasks are attached in Appendix "D".

6.
MUTUAL SUPPORT.
Mutual support with Field Artillery on the flanks will be as detailed in Appendix "E" attached.

7.
AMMUNITION
The following dumps of ammunition will be maintained at gun positions:-
18-pdr. 300 rounds per gun. (50% A and AX.)
4.5"How. 250 " " " including 50 chemical.
Ammunition to cover the normal daily expenditure should be kept at gun positions in addition to the above amounts which should always be available.
18-pdr. ammunition should be fired in the percentage of 75% A and 25% AX.

8. (a). The dividing line between Field and Heavy Artillery for
HARASSING harassing fire is,
FIRE. I.28.b.0.0. - I.22.d.0.0. - I.23.d.0.0.
- I.11.d.0.0. - I.12.a.0.0. - C.30.c.0.0.

(b). Harassing fire will be carried out on selected objectives within Brigade areas by day and night.
Expenditure of ammunition 18-pdr. 100 rounds per gun in action.
4.5" How. 50 " " " "

(c). Gas shoots will be carried out according to the weather and tactical situation under orders of D.A.H.Q.

9. CALLS FROM THE AIR.
"S.O.S." calls from the air will be taken up in the same manner as if the call had been sent by Light Signal etc.

"LL" Calls
1 section per battery will be turned on if it can reach the target, firing 3 rounds gun fire, irrespective of whether it is in the Brigade Area or not. The "LL" Call will be repeated if a further concentration is required. If not engaged on other tasks at the time, batteries will take up "LL" Calls with all their guns, firing 3 rounds gun fire

"N.F." Calls will be answered by all batteries which can reach, firing 10 to 15 rounds a call.

"G.F." Calls, will not be answered by Field Artillery.

10. COUNTER-BATTERY WORK.
Both 4.5" Howitzer Batteries have been placed at the disposal of C.B.S.O. II Corps for Counter-Battery work which will take precedence over all other work except S.O.S. for these batteries.
When Counter-Battery concentrations are ordered all 18-pdrs that can reach and are not otherwise employed will take part.
Active hostile batteries engaged by Brigades by order of C.B.S.O. will be included in the harassing fire tasks by day and night.

11. WIRELESS MASTS.
Wireless masts of Brigades will be in action with their Howitzer batteries.
Wireless mast of D.A.H.Q. will be at VLAMERTINGHE Chateau exchange.

12. COUNTER PREPARATION.
Counter Preparation will be ordered by D.A.H.Q. when necessary and will take the form of heavy bursts of fire with intervals on known occupied localities and likely assembly positions within harassing fire boundaries. Time tables will be issued by D.A.H.Q. in each case and careful synchronization must be ensured.

13. REAR POSITIONS. The Field Artillery dispositions for the rear lines of defence are attached under 41st D.A. No.S.646, attached as Appendix "F".

14. COMMUNICATION. A tracing of existing communications is attached. Visual signalling between O.Ps and Batteries, Batteries and Brigades and Brigades and affiliated Infantry Brigades will be tested twice a week. C.W. wireless sets will be allotted stations on receipt.

15. REDISPOSITION OF T.Ms. The 12 6" Newton Stokes will shortly be redistributed as under:-
```
for defence of line of resistance   4.
   "      "    "  YPRES defences.   4.
   "      "    "  Rear Zone defences 4.
```

16. ADMINISTRATION. Administration and salvage arrangements are attached as Appendix "G".

17. ACKNOWLEDGE.

F.H. MacFarlan
Captain, R.F.A.
Brigade Major,
41st Divisional Artillery.

Issued at:- 5 p.m.

```
Copy No. 1 - 5    187th Bde.R.F.A.
         6 - 10   190th Bde.R.F.A.
         11       41st Division G.
         12       41st Division Q.
         13       II Corps R.A.
         14       II Corps H.A.
         15       C.B.S.O.
         16       41st D.A.C.
         17       41st M.G.Battn.
         18       122nd Infy. Bde.
         19       123rd    "    "
         20       124th    "    "
         21       C.R.E. 41st Divn.
         22       A.D.M.S. 41st Divn.
         23       S.C.R.A. 41st Divn.
         24       Sigs. 41st D.A.
         25       No.7 Squadron R.A.F.
         26 - 30  War Diary and File.
```

S E C R E T.   APPENDIX "A".   17th May 1918.
Issued with 41st D.A. Defence Scheme No.1.

Ref. Map - Sheets 27 & 28.

	Position in action.	Main Wagon Lines.	Adv. Wagon Lines Gun Limbers.
Headquarters 41st Divl. Arty.	LOVIE CHATEAU. 27/F.16.d.4.5.	A.25.b.0.8.	
190th Brigade R.F.A.H.Q.	(REIGERSBURG. (H.6.b.25.55	A.23.c.2.8.	
A/Bty.R.F.A. 6-18-pdrs.	I.7.a.5.8.	A.28.a.9.3.)	
B/Bty.R.F.A. 6-18-pdrs.	H.6.b.99.50.	A.22.b.5.4.)	H.3.d.9.4.
C/Bty.R.F.A. 6-18-pdrs.	H.6.b.6.4.	A.22.b.5.4.)	
D/Bty.R.F.A. 6-4.5" Hows.	I.7.a.6.9.	A.23.c.3.7.	H.4.a.7.3.
187th Brigade R.F.A.H.Q.	(RED HOUSE (I.1.d.15.50.	A.28.c.7.8.	
A/Bty.R.F.A. 6-18-pdrs.	I.1.b.65.90.	A.26.b.1.9.)	
B/Bty.R.F.A. 6-18-pdrs.	I.1.d.10.15.	A.27.d.4.1.)	
C/Bty.R.F.A. 6-18-pdrs.	I.1.c.5.9.	A.28.d.8.7.)	H.2.b.6.0.
D/Bty.R.F.A. 6-4.5" Hows.	I.1.b.5.3.	A.28.d.2.7.)	

6" Newton Trench Mortars.

1. at I.8.d.10.55.
1. at I.8.d.05.47.
1. at I.14.a.52.54.
1. at I.14.a.46.49.
1. at I.14.a.42.48.
1. at I.14.a.38.60.

41st Divisional Ammunition Column.

Headquarters.	A.25.b.0.8.	A.25.b.0.8.
No.1 Section	-	27/F.24.a.9.4.
No.2 Section.	-	27/F.24.c.9.7.
No.3 (S.A.A.)Section.	-	A.29.d.central.

S E C R E T.   O.P's.   20th May 1918.
                     APPENDIX "B".
            Issued with 41st W.A. Defence Scheme No.1.

Brigade.	Name	Co-ordinate.	When manned.
8th Bde.R.G.A.	CONCRETE.	I.9.c.20.90.	Day and night.
53rd.Bde.R.G.A.	DUCK.	H.18.d.60.40.	" " "
	DAVE.	H.2.b.95.20.	" " "
	DRAKE.	I.14.b.30.25.	" " "
187th Bde.R.F.A.	ECOLE.	I.9.c.65.50.	" " "
190th Bde.R.F.A.	SAPPER.	I.3.c.95.00.	" " "

SECRET.   "C".   Copy No.

41st. DIVISIONAL ARTILLERY INSTRUCTIONS No. 5.

Liaison between Artillery and Infantry.

The following procedure will be adopted regarding Liaison with and visiting of Infantry in the line.

1. A specially selected senior Liaison Officer, who may be one of the Lieutenant Colonels other than the Group Commander, will be detailed for duty with each Infantry Brigade in the line when any active operations either defensive or offensive are in prospect; this Officer will remain with the Infantry Brigadier for the whole period of these operations. In normal circumstances a senior Liaison Officer will be told off for a tour of duty with Infantry Brigade and this Officer should be changed as seldom as possible having due regard to the efficiency of his unit; if possible he should remain during the whole tour of the Infantry Brigade.

Should Group Headquarters and Infantry Brigade Headquarters be adjacent, which is the ideal arrangement, the above does not apply.

2. Liaison Officers will be detailed with Battalions on either of the following principles:-

(a). For a period of 3 or 4 days: which duty does not necessitate his sitting at Battalion Headquarters for the whole period. This Officer should be responsible for all R.A. Signalling communications with Battalion Headquarters and should work with the Battalion Signal Officer; he should know all O.P's in his area, his way about all trenches, the whereabouts of Company and Platoon Headquarters and be personally acquainted with the Commanders themselves; he should be prepared to accompany the Battalion Commander on his rounds if required and able to furnish information as to what batteries cover the front, and their respective zones, and generally to advise the Battalion Commander on any Artillery points which may arise.

(b). For a night only, in which case an Officer who has done a tour by day at an O.P. will proceed at dusk to Battalion Headquarters and stay there the night, returning to his Battery next morning; his duty being to advise the Battalion Commander on Artillery matters and acquaint the Group Commander with the situation.

Method (a) will be adopted as soon as possible; arrangements are being made for accommodation for the Liaison Officer to be provided where this does not already exist. This Officer should not be relieved at the same time as the Infantry Battalion.

P.T.O.

It is obvious that the value of a Battalion Liaison Officer is much reduced without direct communication with the Artillery covering the Sector, but this cannot always be provided at present owing to shortage of wire.

3. Each Group Commander will arrange that not only Infantry Brigade Headquarters is visited by him or his representative daily but that each Battalion Headquarters is similarly visited by the O.C.Brigade covering it and if possible Company Commanders also.

Each Battalion will be visited daily by at least one of the Battery Commanders covering it and whenever possible Company and Platoon Commanders also will be visited by this Officer. A roster of Battery Commanders will be kept for this purpose, but this does not mean that no Battery Commander is to go near his Battalion except when detailed.

4. Battalion Commanders should be provided with a sketch shewing Artillery dispositions of all guns covering their front.

5. All Artillery Officers should know their sectors intimately; complaints have been made that Liaison Officers with Battalions are not fully acquainted with the Sectors they cover: this is perhaps unavoidable with the large number of young Officers who have recently joined the Artillery but it should be a matter of personal pride that all Artillery Officers know at least as much of the Sectors as the Infantry holding them. This can be arranged by Officers not actually required for duty with the guns visiting the trenches and becoming acquainted as much as possible with all O.P's, Battalion, Company and Platoon Headquarters &c. &c.

6. The object aimed at in the foregoing instructions is the closest possible touch with the Infantry; the moral support afforded to the latter by the constant and daily presence of Artillery Officers amongst them is very great. This is particularly so in times of stress when all Artillery Officers are needed with their batteries and the Infantry then realize that it is not want of will that prevents the daily visits of their comrades in the Artillery, which will be resumed at the earliest possible moment.

It is fully understood that the procedure outlined above is carried out already to a very great extent and attention is only drawn to these points on a fresh Division coming into the line with Artillery from various other Divisions covering it.

J.H.MacFarlane
Captain, R.F.A.
Brigade Major,
41st Divisional Artillery.

30-4-18.

SECRET.
APPENDIX "D".
Issued with 41st D.A. Defence Scheme No.1

20th May 1918.

S.O.S. Instructions.

TASKS. 1. The following tasks will be engaged by the 41st D.A. on receipt of an S.O.S. Call on the divisional front:-

Right Brigade

4.5" How. Bty.
(1 How.   I.22.a.30.65.
(2 Hows. I.16.d.05.50 - 05.65.
(3 Hows. sweeping from I.22.a.30.65 -
(I.16.c.65.00.

1 18-pdr. Bty.   I.16.c.78.10 - I.16.d.00.45.
1 18-pdr. Bty.   I.16.b.10.37 - I.16.b.20.95.
1 18-pdr. Bty.   I.16.b.20.95 - I.10.d.25.65.

Left Brigade

4.5" How. Bty.
(2 Hows. I.10.b.40.30 - I.10.b.45.45.
(2 Hows. I.4.d.70.10 - I.4.d.75.28.
(2 Hows. I.4.b.90.15 - I.4.b.95.40.

1 18-pdr. Bty.   I.10.d.25.60 - I.10.b.40.20.
1 18-pdr. Bty.   I.16.b.30.95 - I.10.d.25.65.
1 18-pdr. Bty.   I.4.d.80.40 - I.4.b.90.00.

6" Newton T.M's when in action will be given S.O.S. lines to help the 3" Stokes and Machine Gun Barrage to fill the gaps in I.16.b.& d. and I.10.b. in the field artillery barrage, and will be laid out on the following points:-
I.16.b.05.95., I.16.b.05.20., I.10.b.50.60., I.4.d.60.00.

SIGNAL. 2. The S.O.S. signal in present use is a Rifle grenade bursting into 3 red parachute lights one above the other.

PROCEDURE AND RATES OF FIRE. 3. An S.O.S. Call in any shape or form on the divisional front will be immediately answered in preference to any other task by all batteries. If any doubt exists fire will be opened at once till the situation is cleared up, at the following rates:-
18-pdrs. 4 rounds per gun per minute)
4.5" Hows. 3   "   "   "   "   "   ) for 10 minutes.

Subsequent action will be governed by the situation at the time except that in the following circumstances:-

P.T.O.

(a) during hostile bombardment.
(b) during a mist.
(c) If it is evident either from repetition of the S.O.S. Signal or from other indications that the hostile attack has not been beaten off.

the procedure laid down for S.O.S. will be repeated at the following rates:-

  18-pdrs. 3 rounds per gun per minute.
  4.5" Hows. 2 " " " " " "

with intervals between the 10 minute bursts of 20 minutes in the case of (a) and (b) and 4 minutes in the case of (c). This procedure will be carried on for 2 hours or at the discretion of Group Commanders in the case of (a) and (b) and until it becomes clear that the attack has been beaten off in case (c).

F.O.O's and Infantry should be instructed to send up S.O.S. rockets at intervals till the hostile attack fails.

4. AMMUNITION.   18-pdrs. 50% each Shrapnel and H.E.106 fuze. By day
       H.E. 106 fuze   By night.
   4.5"Hows. H.E. 106 Fuze.

5.   Any Battery receiving an S.O.S.Call will immediately inform its Brigade Headquarters and neighbouring Batteries.
Brigade Headquarters will inform D.A.H.Q. and their affiliated Infantry Brigades.

6.   A tracing shewing the S.O.S.barrage lines of M.G's, field and heavy artillery is attached.

SECRET.   20th May 1918.

APPENDIX "E".

Issued with 41st D.A.Defence Scheme No.1.

Serial No.	Situation.	Code Call.	Brigade to take action	Action to be taken.
1.	Attack on the Division on our right and no attack on our Division.	"HELP FRENCH FARM."	Left Artillery Brigade Supporting 41st Division.	1-18-pdr Bty.to barrage the line I.27.c.central - I.27.b.central - I.21.b.8.1.
2.	Attack on the Division on our left and no attack on our Division.	"HELP POTTER."	(Right Arty. Bde.Supporting (41st Division (Left Artillery Bde.Supporting (41st Division.	(1-18pdr.Bty.to barrage (the line,CRUMP FARK I.5. (a.90.45 to EITEL FRITZ (FARM I.5.b.65.60 (1 How. to engage OUTPOST (BUILDINGS. (1 How.to engage MILL (COTTS I.5.a.00.65.
3.	Attack on 41st Division.	"HELP HORTE."	24th Bde. R.F.A.	Barrages Line I.22.b.3.6 -I.16.b.2.0 - I.10.d.cen.
		"HELP BURKE"	Left Artillery Bde. of Division on our Left.	1-18-pdr.Baty. to barrage Valley from the STABLES I.5.b.3.5. to OSCAR FARM I.6.c.00.96. 1 How. to engage EITEL FRITZ FARM I.5.b.65.60. 1 How. to engage OSKAR FARM I.6.c.00.95.

SECRET.   41st D.A. No.S.646.

APPENDIX "F".
Issued with 41st D.A.Defence Scheme No.1

REAR LINES OF DEFENCE.   20th May 1918.

1. LINES OF DEFENCE.

Five lines of defence have been constructed in rear of our present front line.

   A. **RED.**   The "YPRES DEFENCES" Line.

   B. **PURPLE.**   The "REAR ZONE" Line.

   C. **GREEN.**   The "GREEN" or "VLAMERTINGHE" Line.

   D. **YELLOW.**   The "YELLOW" or "BRANDHOEK" Line.

   E. **BLUE.**   The "BLUE" or "POPERINGHE EAST" Line.

2. Field Artillery positions for the defence of these lines have been reconnoitred and are enumerated below.

3. YPRES DEFENCES.

Right Artillery Brigade
Brigade Headquarters - GOLDFISH CHATEAU (H.11.a.85.25).
    6 - 18-pdrs. - - H.11.b.0.6.
    6 - 18-pdrs. - - H.11.b.05.30.
    6 - 18-pdrs. - - H.5.d.25.05.
    6 - 4.5" Hows.- - H.11.b.4.8.
       Main O.P. - RAMPARTS at I.14.b.15.95.

Left Artillery Brigade.
Brigade Headquarters - MACHINE GUN FARM (H.5.c.9.9.).
    6 - 18-pdrs. - - H.4.d.90.15.
    6 - 18-pdrs. - - H.5.c.8.1.
    6 - 18-pdrs. - - H.5.b.2.0.   ⌀
    6 - 4.5" Hows.- - H.4.c.30.86.
       Main O.P. - RAMPARTS at I.8.b.05.75.

Notes.
   (1). All above positions have been occupied except that marked ⌀.
   (2). Buried cables run from D.A.Advanced Exchange at VLAMERTINGHE CHATEAU to both MACHINE GUN FARM and GOLDFISH CHATEAU.
   (3). Buried cables run from GOLDFISH CHATEAU to the RAMPARTS close to the O.P. at I.1.b.7.2.
      Buried cables run from MACHINE GUN FARM to DEAD END at I.2.c.05.55.

4. REAR ZONE LINE.

Positions have been chosen to defend the REAR ZONE LINE as an outpost line only, the main line of resistance being the GREEN LINE.
The positions chosen are:-

Right Artillery Brigade.
    6 - 18-pdrs.   -   - H.1.c.9.9.
    2 - 4.5" Hows. - - H.1.a.90.45.
                   Main O.P. - GOLDFISH CHATEAU.

Left Artillery Brigade.
    6 - 18-pdrs.   -   - A.25.c.1.8.
    2 - 4.5" Hows. - - A.30.d.45.50.
                   Main O.P. - Buildings at H.5.b.0.0.

All other units would be disposed as for defence of GREEN LINE.

Note. Buried cables run from D.A.Advanced exchange at VLAMERTINGHE CHATEAU to both GOLDFISH CHATEAU and MACHINE GUN FARM.

5. GREEN and YELLOW LINES.

Battery positions and Brigade Headquarters chosen for the defence of GREEN LINE are also suitable for the defence of the YELLOW LINE.

Right Artillery Brigade.
Brigade Headquarters - Farm at A.28.b.7.1.
    6 - 18-pdrs. - - A.28.d.5.2.
    6 - 18-pdrs. - - G.5.a.6.5.
    6 - 18-pdrs. - - G.5.a.15.55.
    6 - 4.5" Hows. - - G.4.b.7.0.
       Main O.Ps.(For GREEN LINE - VLAMERTINGHE CHATEAU.
                (For YELLOW LINE - Houses at G.5.b.7.8.

Left Artillery Brigade.
Brigade Headquarters - Farm at A.28.b.7.1.
    6 - 18-pdrs. - - A.29.c.6.3.
    6 - 18-pdrs. - - A.28.d.8.5.
    2 - 18-pdrs. - - A.29.c.90.45.
    4 - 18-pdrs. - - A.29.c.95.20.
    6 - 4.5" Hows. - - A.29.c.15.80.

                (For GREEN LINE (B.26.d.9.6. or
                ((B.26.d.7.3.
   Main O.Ps.(
                (For YELLOW LINE (Building at
                ((A.30.d.9.5.

Notes.
(1). Sand-bagged elephants have been erected at farm at A.28.b.7.1. There will be accommodation in the cellar of the farm and sand-bagged elephants could be erected in the barns of the farm as soon as it is vacated by the inhabitants.

(2). Work has been commenced at both YELLOW Line O.Ps.

(3). One telephone line in the emergency buried route from LOVIE CHATEAU to PESOLHOEK has been allotted to D.A. From PESOLHOEK two lines run overland to farm at A.28.b.7.1.

(4). Armoured cables have been laid from farm at A.28.b.7.1. to Battery positions.

(5). One armoured cable has been laid from farm at A.28.b.7.1. to VLAMERTINGHE CHATEAU for GREEN LINE O.P. Work of Right Artillery Brigade, and to cable head at B.25.a.1.3. for GREEN LINE O.P. work of Left Artillery Brigade.

A buried cable runs through the GREEN LINE at about B.26.d.6.9. If time permits the bury may be opened up at this point for use of Left Artillery Brigade O.Ps.

(6). The armoured cables mentioned in Note (5) above have been laid via their respective Brigade YELLOW LINE O.Ps.

6. BLUE LINE.

Right Artillery Brigade.

Brigade Headquarters	– Farm at L.5.b.05.95.
6 – 18-pdrs.	– L.5.b.40.05.
6 – 18-pdrs.	– L.5.b.40.65.
2 – 18-pdrs.	– F.30.c.15.20.
4 – 18-pdrs.	– F.29.d.70.15.
6 – 4.5" Hows.	– L.5.b.15.90.

Left Artillery Brigade

Brigade Headquarters	– House at F.29.d.5.9.
6 – 18-pdrs.	– F.29.d.6.4.
6 – 18-pdrs.	– F.29.a.70.85.
2 – 18-pdrs.	– F.30.c.5.7.
4 – 18-pdrs.	– F.29.d.7.9.
2 – 4.5" Hows.	– F.29.b.45.90.
4 – 4.5" Hows.	– F.29.b.50.25.

Notes.(1). Divisional Boundaries West of BLUE Line have not yet been notified.

(2). O.Ps have not yet been reconnoitred.

(3). No cables have yet been laid and no work has been done on positions or Headquarters.

APPENDIX "G" 21st. May 1918.

Issued with 41st.D.A.Defence Scheme No.1.

ADMINISTRATIVE ARRANGEMENTS.

(1) **AMMUNITION.**

(a) Normal supply to all batteries (other than C/190 and D/187) is by light railway direct to battery positions. Demands for ammunition to be delivered by light railway to batteries reach this office by 12 noon the preceding day. If this is not done the ammunition cannot be supplied.

(b) Ammunition is carried to MACHINE GUN SIDING. An Officer detailed by O.C., 41st.D.A.C. is responsible for distribution in front of that point. He is located at 190th.Brigade R.F.A. H.Q. Wagon Lines at A.23.c.2.8 which is on the telephone.

(c) Ammunition supply to C/190 and D/187 and to other batteries in case of breakdown of railway supply is by 41st.D.A.C. from Corps Dump at E.22.b.4.6 Sheet 27, to rear wagon lines, thence by battery wagons under Brigade arrangements. Ammunition at Corps Dump is issued on demand.

(2) **ORDNANCE.**

Ordnance Mobile Workshops No.10 & 15 (Light) are at Sheet 27, E.28.a.7.2.

(3) **BATHS.**

Baths are situate at :-
FOSTER CAMP   H.1.c.5.5
DIRTY BUCKET   A.30.Central.
P Camp   A.18.d.Central.

O.C.Baths has his H.Q. at P Camp.
Application for Baths are made to him direct stating :-
(a) Number to be bathed.
(b) Most convenient time.
(c) "   "   bath.

(4) **SALVAGE.**

(1) O.C.,41st.D.A.C. details an Officer to be O.C.Salvage. His duties are :-
(a) To reconnoitre the area and locate ammunition to be salved.
(b) To arrange for collection of ammunition by wagon or pack as may be most convenient.
(ii) Salvaged ammunition is dealt with as follows:-
(a) If in the opinion of the Officer i/c Salvage it is unsafe to move, it is buried in situ.

(b) If it is damaged but safe, it is collected to BARRIE Salvage Dump, H.1.b.2.8.
(c) If it is serviceable, it is collected to the most convenient Siding on the railway.

O.C. D.A.C. provides necessary wagons and personnel. He calls on D.T.M.O. for assistance up to 8 men per day.

(iii) Officer i/c Salvage reports to this office daily by 12 noon :-
(a) Amount of serviceable ammunition collected in preceding 24 hours, and exact description of siding where dumped.
(b) Amount of unserviceable ammunition dumped at BARRIE DUMP.
(iv) Arrangements are made for trains for the removal of serviceable ammunition and for the examination of unserviceable ammunition.
(v) Empty boxes and cartridge cases are sent by returning empty ammunition trains to XG3 (SWISS COTTAGE)
(vi) Officers Commanding batteries are responsible for loading on to returning trains and for labelling each truck clearly "XG3".

Signal Communications.

Issued with 1st. D.A. Defence Scheme No. 1.

Appendix "M"

41st D.A. No. S.871.

Headquarters,
   187th Bde. R.F.A.
   190th   "   "
   41st Division G.
   122nd Inf. Bde.
   123rd   "   "
   124th   "   "
   R.A. II Corps.
   H.A. XI Corps.

     The new S.O.S. Lines as laid down in 41st D.A. Defence Scheme No.1 will come into operation at 12 noon 22nd May.

21-5-18.

                              Captain, R.F.A.
                              Brigade Major,
                41st Divisional Artillery.

SECRET.   War Diary Appendix "N"   Copy No. 23

41st. DIVISIONAL ARTILLERY INSTRUCTIONS No.6.

24th May 1918.

The undermentioned harassing fire programmes in conjunction with 41st M.G.Battn. and heavy artillery when practicable will be used when ordered by D.A.H.Q. Ammunition expended on these programmes will come out of the normal harassing fire allotment.

Code word of programme for the night if any will be wired to all concerned by 7 p.m. at which hour Field Artillery Brigade watches will be synchronized.

D.A.H.Q. and H.Q. M.G.Battalion will synchronize at the same hour.

Each target will be engaged at the hour named by one section 4.5" Hows. and 1 battery 18-pdrs, of the Field Artillery Brigade in whose zone it lies.

Rates of fire:- 18-pdrs. 3 rounds per gun per minute.
              4.5" Hows. 2   "   "   "   "

for 3 minutes, commencing with a salvo as a signal to the Machine Guns.

Programme No.	Code name.	Time.	Target.
I	COW	(a). 10.15 p.m. (b). 11.30 p.m. (c). 1 a.m. (d). 2.30 a.m. (e). 3 a.m.	RIFLE FARM. THATCH BARN - BOUNDARY FARM. HALFWAY HOUSE. TUILERIES. I.5.c.85.38.
II.	CAT	(a). 10.30 p.m. (b). 12 midnight (c). 12.45 a.m. (d). 2.45 a.m.	I.22.b.55.35. I.10.d.90.70. I.16.d.60.00. DILLY FARM.
III.	DOG	(a). 10 p.m. (b). 11.15 p.m. (c). 12.30 a.m. (d). 2.15 a.m.	WEST FARM. I.5.a.90.50 - 90.80. I.16.d.6.4. I.11.b.25.50.
IV.	RAT	(a). 10.45 p.m. (b). 11 p.m. (c). 1 a.m. (d). 1.15 a.m. (e). 2.45 a.m.	I.10.d.90.70. RIFLE FARM. HALFWAY HOUSE. HALLEBLAST CORNER. I.16.d.60.00.

187th and 190th Brigades to ACKNOWLEDGE.

F.H. Macfarlane
Captain R.F.A.
Brigade Major,
41st Divisional Artillery.

Issued at:- 6.30 p.m.

Copy No. 1 - 6 187th Bde.(1 for Liaison Officer).
       7 -12 190th " ("   "   "   "   ).
      13   41st M.G.Battn.   Copy No. 19 8th Bde. R.G.A.
      14   41st Divn. G.   20 53rd "   "
      15   II Corps R.A.   21 H.A.II Corps.
      16   122nd Infy. Bde.   22- 24 War Diary & File.
      17   123rd "   "
      18   124th "   "

Appendix "O"

S E C R E T.   25th May 1918.

AMENDMENT No.1 to 41st. D.A.DEFENCE SCHEME No.1.

Reference para.15.
Positions to cover the present line of resistance have been selected for 4 6" Newtons at:-

       I.3.d.30.40.
       I.3.d.40.42.
       I.9.c.67.32.
       I.9.c.69.38.

Work has been commenced on the above and they will be occupied very shortly.

   4 6" Newtons will remain in action in the following positions:-
       I.8.d.10.55.
       I.8.d.05.47.
       I.14.a.38.60.
       I.14.a.46.49.

to cover the YPRES Defences Line.

   Positions in the Purple Line have been selected for two sections as under:-

   1 section   H.12.a.23.52.
   1 section   H.11.b.85.43.

Work has been commenced on these.

                                       Captain R.F.A.
                                       Brigade Major,
                                 41st Divisional Artillery.

Issued to all recipients of 41st D.A.Defence Scheme No.1.

Appendix "P"

PROGRAMME
for
Visit of G.O.C. to Wagon Lines, 25-5-18.

    Leave H.Q.   9. 0 a.m.
    D.A.C.   9.15 a.m.
    A/187   10 a.m.
    B/187   10.30 a.m.
    C/187   10.45 a.m.
    D/187   11. 0 a.m.
    A/190   11.15 a.m.
    D/190   11.30 a.m.
B & C/190   11.45 a.m.
    S.A.A.   12.15 p.m.

Appendix "Q"

S E C R E T.   25th May 1918.

1st. AMENDMENT to APPENDIX "F" 41st. D.A.
DEFENCE SCHEME No.1

Rear Lines of Defence.

Para.3. - Delete, with the exception of notes (2) and (3) and substitute the following:-

3. YPRES DEFENCES.

Positions have now been selected and work is in progress as follows:-

Right Artillery Brigade

Brigade Headquarters.	MACHINE GUN FARM dugouts.
A Battery	H.5.b.1.6. (3 guns already in action here).
B Battery 3 guns.	H.10.b.72.62.
3 guns.	H.10.b.35.90.
C Battery	H.11.a.2.6.
D Battery	H.11.b.4.8.
Main O.P. RAMPARTS I.14.b.15.95.	

Left Artillery Brigade.

Brigade Headquarters.	H.5.a.05.85.
A Battery.	H.5.b.2.0.
B Battery.	H.4.d.90.15.
C Battery.	B.29.d.25.10.
D Battery.	H.4.c.80.86.
Main O.P. RAMPARTS I.8.b.05.75.	

Captain R.F.A.
Brigade Major,
41st Divisional Artillery.

Issued to all recipients of 41st D.A. Defence Scheme No.1.

"Appendix R"

S E C R E T.   27th May 1918.

AMENDMENT No.2 to 41st.D.A.DEFENCE SCHEME No.1.

Reference para. 12, during heavy hostile bombardment, should all communication be cut, Group Commanders will order "Counter-Preparation" on their own initiative on the following general principle.

(a). Fire to come down on S.O.S. Lines and search about 600 yards East; 4.5" Hows. and 18-pdrs. will be utilized for this searching fire, 4.5" How. 106 fuze.

(b). Rates of fire:- 18-pdrs. 3 rounds per gun per minute.
                    4.5 Hows. 2   "   "   "   "   "

(c). Bursts to be fired as under, and to be of 5 minutes duration each.
     Half an hour before dawn, at dawn and half an hour after dawn.

(d). In ordering further bursts of fire Group Commanders will be guided by the situation at the time and the necessity of having sufficient ammunition in hand to deal with a hostile attack.

                                    M.W. Green.
                                    for Major
                                    Captain R.F.A.
                                    Brigade Major,
                                    41st Divisional Artillery.

Issued to all recipients of 41st D.A.Defence Scheme No.1.

SECRET. Appendix "S" Copy No. 4

41st. DIVISIONAL ARTILLERY INSTRUCTIONS No. 7.

29th May 1918.

1. An Alternative position for every battery in action which has not already got one is to be reconnoitred and prepared forthwith: this does not apply to "silent" batteries.

    These Positions should be fairly close to present occupied positions and 50 rounds per gun will be dumped at them.

    In the case of Battery positions occupied at present and in all future positions, guns should be dotted about irregularly and spread out to avoid organised Counter Battery work and gas shelling putting entire units out of action.

    One section should always be some way apart from the remainder.

2. As far as circumstances permit the training of scouts and patrols is to be carried out by all Batteries as thoroughly as possible.

    At present this cannot very well go beyond training a certain number of men in each unit to find their way accurately to any given point on a map.

3. Once a week all telephone communication will be stopped from 9 a.m. to 5 p.m. During this period telephones will not be used except in case of urgent tactical necessity.

    All communication routes should be tested and a message sent by two different methods along each route.

    A report on the results of each of these periods will be forwarded to this office on the following day.

                                    Captain R.F.A.
                                    Brigade Major,
                                    41st Divisional Artillery.

Copy No. 1   187th Brigade R.F.A.
 "   "   2   190th   "   "
 "   "   3-6 War Diary & File.

Army Form C. 2118.

WAR DIARY
or
INTELLIGENCE SUMMARY.

Headquarters, 41st. Divisional Artillery

(Erase heading not required.)

Instructions regarding War Diaries and Intelligence Summaries are contained in F.S. Regs., Part II. and the Staff Manual respectively. Title pages will be prepared in manuscript.

Place	Date	Hour	Summary of Events and Information	Remarks and references to Appendices
LA LOVIE (BELGIUM)	1918 June 1st.		Warning Order was received that the 49th. Division (less Artillery) would relieve the 41st. Division (less Artillery) as shewn in Appendix "A".	App "A"
-do-	June 2nd.		Warning Order was issued that 49th. Divisional Artillery would relieve 41st. Divisional Artillery on night 4th/5th and 5th/6th. June. (Appendix "B").	App "B"
-do-	June 3rd.		Detailed orders as to relief of 41st. Divisional Artillery issued (Appendix "C"). 190th. Brigade Headquarters moved from REIGERSBURG to area of MACHINE GUN FARM.	App "C"
-do-	June 4th.		Relief of 190th. & 187th. Brigades by Brigades of the 49th. Divisional Artillery commenced on night 4th/5th. June (Appendix "C")	App "C"
-do-	June 5th.		Relief of 41st. Divisional Artillery by 49th. Divisional Artillery completed on night 5th/6th.	App "C"
BAMBECQUE (FRANCE)	June 6th.		41st. Divisional Artillery marched to DROGLANDT and BAMBECQUE area (Appendices "C" & "D")	Apps: "C" & "D"
ZEGGERS-CAPPEL	June 7th.		41st. Divisional Artillery marched to ZEGGERS-CAPPEL area (Appendix "E")	App: "E"
POLINCOVE	June 8th.		41st. Divisional Artillery marched to POLINCOVE area (Appendix "E") Accommodation was available as shown in Appendix "F"	App: "E" App: "F"
- do-	June 9th. to 15th.		41st. Divisional Artillery in rest. Training carried out.	
- do-	June 16th.		Field Firing operations carried out with the 30th. American Division to illustrate the Artillery support afforded to an Infantry Brigade in the attack on a long straggling village with strong points. The exercise was carried out successfully. (Appendices "G" & "H")	App: "G" App: "H"
- do-	June 17th. to 23rd.		Training and Route marching carried out.	
-do-	June 24th.		Units of 41st. Divisional Artillery inspected by General PLUMER, Commanding Second Army, accompanied by General BUCKLE, M.G., R.A., Second Army.	

Army Form C. 2118.

WAR DIARY
or
INTELLIGENCE-SUMMARY.

(Erase heading not required.)

Instructions regarding War Diaries and Intelligence Summaries are contained in F. S. Regs., Part II. and the Staff Manual respectively. Title pages will be prepared in manuscript.

Headquarters, 41st. Divisional Artillery.

Place	Date 1918	Hour	Summary of Events and Information	Remarks and references to Appendices
ZEGGERS-CAPPEL	June 25th.		41st.Divisional Artillery, No.1 Company, 41st.Divisional Train, and No.52 Mobile Veterinary Section marched to ZEGGERS-CAPPEL area (Appendix "I")	App: "I"
ABEELE area. (BELGIUM)	June 26th.		41st.Divisional Artillery moved to ABEELE area and relieved units of 27th.French Divisional Artillery in Reserve positions on night 26th/27th June. (Appendix "J") Captain F.N.Mason-Macfarlane, M.C., Brigade Major, 41st.D.A., admitted to Hospital (Sick).	App: "J"
--do--	June 27th.		Orders regarding forthcoming relief of 7th.French Divisional Artillery in the SCHERPENBERG front by 41st.Divisional Artillery issued (Appendix "K")	App: "K"
--do--	June 28th.		Owing to the greater range of the French Field Artillery the positions occupied by them were in many cases unsuitable for our Field Artillery. Positions were accordingly reconnoitred for positions further forward. Positions for a forward section for each battery were chosen with a view to using them for harassing fire, the remaining four guns in each case being silent. Reconnaissance of the positions was carried out by C.R.A., Brigade Majors and Battery Commanders. D.T.M.O. carried out reconnaissance of forward area with a view to selecting positions for 6" T.Ms.	
--do--	June 29th.		Further reconnaissance of positions and O.Ps carried out.1 Section per Battery occupied positions prepared during the day of the 29th, on night 29th/30th.June.	
--do--	June 30th.		On night 30th June/1st.July, one further section per battery occupied positions prepared and camouflaged. Orders regarding Liaison with Infantry Brigades in the line were issued. 187th. Brigade found a Liaison Officer with Right Infantry Brigade, 190th.Brigade with Left Infantry Brigade, the Liaison Officer for the Centre Infantry Brigade being found alternately by 190th. Brigade, R.F.A., and 187th.Brigade, R.F.A.	App: "L"

2nd.July 1918.

Brigadier General,
Commanding 41st.Divisional Artillery.

Appendix 'A'

S E C R E T.   41st D.A. No. S.737.

41st Division less Artillery will be relieved by 49th Division as follows:-

Night 2nd/3rd June   123 Brigade will be relieved by 148 Bde.

       3rd June   124   "   "   "   "   "   146 "

Night 3rd/4th June   122   "   "   "   "   "   147 "

Forward and YPRES defences Machine Guns will be relieved as follows:-

   Right Brigade Sector on night 2nd/3rd June.

   Left   "   "   "   "   3rd/4th June.

Remaining Machine Gun Companies, Field Companies etc. will be relieved on the 3rd June.

F. MacFarlane

Captain R.F.A.,
Brigade Major,
41st Divisional Artillery.

31st May 1918.

187th Brigade R.F.A. (5 copies).
190th   "   "   (5 copies).
D.T.M.O. 41st Division (3 copies).
41st D.A.C. (2 copies).
S.C.R.A. 41st Divn.
R.A.Sigs. 41st Divn.
War Diary.
File.

Appendix "B"

SECRET.

41st D.A. No. S.746.

Headquarters,
    187th Brigade R.F.A.
    190th   "   "
    41st D.T.M.O.
    41st D.A.C.

WARNING ORDER.

41st Divisional Artillery will be relieved by 49th Divisional Artillery on the nights 4th/5th and 5th/6th instant.

Details will be issued later.

On relief, the 41st Divisional Artillery will move to the DROGLANDT, BAMBECQUE area.

Captain R.F.A.,
Brigade Major,
41st Divisional Artillery.

2-6-18.

Appendix "C"

S E C R E T.   Copy No. 26

41st. DIVISIONAL ARTILLERY ORDER No. 4.

3rd June 1918.

1. 41st Divisional Artillery will be relieved by 49th Divisional Artillery on the nights 4th/5th and 5th/6th June.

2. Guns will not be exchanged.

3. One section per Battery will be relieved on the night 4th/5th.
Two sections on the night 5th/6th.
Relief in each case to be completed by 12 midnight.

Command of each group and battery will pass on completion of relief on second night.

The limbers and teams which take in the ingoing guns to the positions will bring away the outgoing guns.

All S.O.S. rockets, Trench Stores, maps, defence Schemes, aeroplane photographs and documents relating to the front will be handed over.

Completion of relief will be wired to this office each night using code word "BOGRAT".

4. Details of relief will be arranged direct between Brigade Commanders concerned.

5. On completion of relief, Batteries of 41st Divisional Artillery will withdraw to their Wagon lines.

6. 41st Divisional Artillery will march to the DROGLANDT BAMBECKE area on the morning of the 6th June. Detailed orders will be issued later.

Rear of the column will be clear of the cross roads in L.6.a. by 10 a.m.

7. 41st Divisional Artillery will hand over present Wagon lines to 49th Divisional Artillery who will arrange to send advance parties to take them over on 6th June before 41st Divisional Artillery move out.

8. Supply of ammunition will be taken over by 49th D.A.C. at 9 a.m. on June 6th.

9. 49th Divisional Artillery will please arrange that no movement of wagon lines or D.A.C. to new Wagon lines will take place before 10 a.m. June 6th.

10. Time at which C.R.A. 41st Division will hand over command of the Artillery covering the 49th Division front to C.R.A. 49th Division will be notified later.

11/- over.

11. The 12 6" Newton Trench Mortars complete now in action on the 41st Division front will be handed over to 49th Divisional Artillery.

Personnel of 41st Trench Mortar Batteries will be relieved by personnel of 49th Trench Mortar Batteries by 4 p.m. on 5th June.

Details to be arranged direct between D.T.M.O's.

12. ACKNOWLEDGE.

F. MacFarlan
Captain R.F.A.
Brigade Major,
Issued at:- 5 p.m.   41st Divisional Artillery.

```
Copy No. 1 - 5    187th Brigade R.F.A.
         6 - 10   190th Brigade R.F.A.
         11       41st Division G.
         12       41st Division Q.
         13       II Corps R.A.
         14       II Corps H.A.
         15       C.B.S.O.
         16       41st D.A.C.
         17       41st M.G.Battn.
         18       122nd Infy. Bde.
         19       123rd Infy. Bde.
         20       124th Infy. Bde.
         21       C.R.E. 41st Division.
         22       A.D.M.S. 41st Division.
         23       S.C.R.A. 41st Division.
         24       Sigs. 41st D.A.
         25       No.7 Squadron R.A.F.
         26       War Diary.
         27       File.
         28       53rd Brigade R.G.A.
         29       6th Divl. Arty.
         30       56th Divl. Arty.
         31       D.T.M.O. 41st Division.
         32       8th Brigade R.G.A.
         33       29th Divl. Arty.
         34       No.1 Coy. 41st Divl. Train.
         35       49 Divl Arty
```

War Diary   Appendix "D"

COPY NO. 20

SECRET.
41st. DIVISIONAL ARTILLERY ADMINISTRATIVE INSTRUCTION No.4,
      issued in connection with 41st.D.A. Order No.5.

(1) **CAMPS.**
    All camps must be left in a clean and proper condition. Wherever possible a certificate will be obtained from the incoming unit or Area Commandant concerned that this has been done.

(2) **TENTS.**
    12 Tents issued to B/187, 4 Tents issued to 187th.Brigade H.Q. and any other tents issued to units in this area will be handed over to incoming unit, if required by them, and if not handed in to Camp Commandant HAMHOEK before marching. In either case a receipt will be taken, and a copy forwarded to this office.

(3) **RATIONS.**
    Units will draw rations in this area for last time on 5th. for consumption 6th.
    Supply wagons of 187th.Brigade loaded with rations for consumption 7th. will join units of that Brigade on evening of 5th. and march with them on 6th. On arrival at DROGLANDT these wagons will un-load and re-join No.1 Coy.41st.Divnl.Train in BAMBECQUE area. On 6th.inst., 190th.Brigade, D.A.C., and T.M.B's will send guides to D.A.H.Q. BAMBECQUE at 3.p.m. to guide supply wagons to their camps. On the 7th.inst. all units will send guides to D.A.H.Q. ZEGGERS-CAPPEL to guide supply wagons to their camps.

(4) **ACCOMMODATION.**
    Accommodation for night 6/7th. is contained in Schedule 'A' attached, and for night 7/8th. in Schedule 'B' attached. Advance parties will be sent forward by all units each day to locate and take over billets.

(5) **BILLETS.**
    Before billets are vacated, they must be inspected by an Officer who will satisfy himself that they clean, and if possible got a certificate to that effect.

(6) **LEAVE.**
    Personnel proceeding on leave on 6th. and 7th. insts. will report at MENDINGHEM on 6th.inst. Personnel proceeding on 8th. and subsequent days will report to R.T.O. WATTEN. Personnel Train leaves WATTEN 14.50 hrs. daily.

(7) **AMMUNITION.**
    Brigades and D.A.C. will wire to this office by 6.p.m. tomorrow night amounts of ammunition with which they will march out.

                                              _____ Captain,
4th.June 1918.   Staff Captain,41st.Divisional Artillery.
Issued at 10.0 p.m.
DISTRIBUTION

Copy No.1 - 5   187th.B'de.RFA.
        6 -10   190th. "   "
       11 -14   41st.D.A.C.
       15 -16   41st.D.T.M.O.
       16 -17   41st.Divnl.Train.
                (No 1 Coy)
           18. War Diary.
           19. File.
       20 -25. Spare.

SCHEDULE 'A'.

ACCOMMODATION Night 6/7th. June 1918.

UNIT.	LOCATION.	BILLET No.	PROPRIETOR.	Remarks.
H.Q.D.A.	BAMBECQUE.	76.		
187th.Bde. H.Q.	DROGLANDT. (K.1.a.8.4)			Detail of billeting attached. (187th.B'de. only)

NOTE. If tents are required, application should be made to Camp Commandant, DROGLANDT.

UNIT.	LOCATION.	BILLET No.	PROPRIETOR.	Remarks.
190th.Bde. H.Q.	BAMBECQUE.	36.	LELIEUR.	Mess and Office.
		5.	BEGUE.	1 Officer.
		6.	PAUWELS.	----do----
		30.	WAELS.	----do----
		38.	YVOZ.	----do----
		39.	VANDENAMEELE.	----do----
		41.b.		Horse Lines.
1 Battery.	----"---- (27/E.2.d.9.5) (27/E.3.c.5.1)	52. 53.	MERCHIER. PATTYN.	
1 Battery.	(27/E.2.b.8.3)	51.	VANDENABEELE.	
1 Battery.	(27/E.2.c.6.7)	48.	OUTTERS.	
1 Battery.	(19/W.27.a.9.2) (19/W.26.b.5.3)	4. 3.	LASCURE.) LELIEUR.)	Balance of Officers and men at ROUSBRUGGE Camp. (19/W.20.c)
D.A.C. H.Q.	BAMBECQUE.	70.	VANNEE	Mess. 1 Officer.
		4.	DUESEIGNE.	1 Officer.
		7.	OUTTERS.	2 Officers.
		Farm.	MOENECLAY.	Horse Lines.
No's 1 & 2 Sections and T.M.B's.	(19/W.20.c) (19/W.20.a.7.2)	7.	ROUSBRUGGE Camp. DEVAELE.	
No.1 Coy, 41st. Dvnl.Train.	(27/E.2.a.7.3) (27/E.2.a.9.0)	49. 50.	MARTEYN. VERHAEGE.	

NOTES. (a) Camp Wardens are at Billet 51 (E.2.b.9.2) and ROUSBRUGGE Camp.
(b) Water Points for drinking water at YSER BRIDGE, S. of BAMBECQUE.

SCHEDULE 'B'.

ACCOMMODATION Night 7/8th. June 1918.

UNIT.	LOCATION.	Billet No.	REMARKS.
D.A.H.Q.	ZEGGERS-CAPPEL.	72.	
187th.Bde. H.Q.	------"------	1.	Details of billeting attached (187th.Brigade only)
190th.Bde. H.Q.	ERINGHEM.	E.27.V.	Details of billeting attached (190th.Brigade only)
D.A.C. H.Q.	(B.14.d.1.7)	E.122.	Details of billeting attached (D.A.C. only)
T.M.B's.	Will billet with D.A.C. If more accommodation is required, apply to Camp Commandant ZEGGERS-CAPPEL.		
No.1.Coy. 41st.Div.Train.	(B.13.a.2.5)	E.114.	Details of billeting attached. (No.1 Coy.only)

War Diary Appendix "E"

SECRET.   Copy No. 17

41st DIVISIONAL ARTILLERY ORDER No. 6.

5th June 1918.

1. 41st Divisional Artillery will march to ZEGGERS CAPELLE area on 7th instant and to POLINCOVE area on the 8th inst. in accordance with the following march table:-

Unit.	Date and Time.	Starting Point.	Route	Remarks
No.1 Coy, 41 Divl. Train.	6 a.m. 7th.	Road Junction 27/E.1.d.0.7.	HERZEELE WORMHOUDT ESQUELBECQUE ZEGGERS CAPELLE.	
190th Bde. R.F.A.	7 a.m. 7th.	ditto.	ditto.	
41st D.A.C. (less S.A.A. Sect.) & 41st T.M.Bs.	8 a.m. 7th.	Road Junction 19/W.25.d.1.7.	ditto.	
187th Bde. R.F.A.	9 a.m. 7th.	Cross Roads 27/E.13.c.5.7.	ditto.	HOUTKERQUE will be avoided.
No.1 Coy, 41 Div. Train.	6 a.m. 8th.	Cross Roads 27/B.19.d.6.7.	HERKEGHEM WATTEN POLINCOVE area.	
41st D.A.C. (less S.A.A. Sect) & 41st T.M.Bs.	7 a.m. 8th.	ditto.	ditto.	
187th Bde. R.F.A.	7.45 a.m. 8th	ditto.	ditto.	
190th Bde. R.F.A.	8.30 a.m. 8th.	ditto.	ditto.	Battery at 27/A.3.d.3.4 will join its Bde at 27/A.23.b.1.1.

2. Billeting and administrative arrangements for the POLINCOVE area will be notified later by S.C.R.A.

3. Usual road distances and strict march discipline will be maintain.

4. H.Q.R.A. 41st Division will be located as follows:-
   10 a.m. 6th - 9 a.m. 7th BAMBECQUE Billet No.76.
   10 a.m. 7th - 9 a.m. 8th ZEGGERS CAPELLE Billet No.72.
   from 10 a.m. 8th POLINCOVE.

5. 187, 190, D.A.C. and D.T.M.O. to acknowledge.

F.H. MacFarlane
Captain R.F.A.
Issued at:- 6.30 p.m.   Brigade Major 41st Divisional Arty.

To all recipients of 41st D.A. Order No. 5.

War Diary   Appendix F

S E C R E T.   Copy No. 18

41st. DIVISIONAL ARTILLERY ADMINISTRATIVE
INSTRUCTIONS No.5

                                              6th June 1918.

1. Accommodation in the POLINCOVE Area is contained in Appendix "A" hereto.

2. Billeting parties will go forward to POLINCOVE Area on 7th instant to locate and take over Billets.

3. Area Orders are contained in Schedule "B" hereto. Units will render direct list referred to in order No.2

4. The Area Commandant in RECQUES. Billet Wardens will be at the MAIRIE, RUMINGHEM, No. 6 billet MUNCQ NIEURLET and the Area Commandant's Office POLINCOVE at 11 a.m. on the 8th instant.

5. Particulars of water supply are contained in Schedule "C".

6. Baths are at MUNCQ NIEURLET and will be got into working order as soon as possible.

7. Commanding Officers will ensure that all orders received from the Area Commandant are strictly complied with, and that a high standard of cleanliness and general discipline is maintained.

8. ACKNOWLEDGE.

                                    C W Anderson Lt.
                                         Captain,
                                      Staff Captain,
Issued at 7.30 p.m.   41st Divisional Artillery.

Issued to all recipients of 41st D.A. Administrative Instructions No.4.

APPENDIX "A"

Unit.	Location.	Billet No.	Remarks.
D.A.H.Q.	POLINCOVE	1.	
187th Bde.	ditto.	18.	Particulars of billeting, plans etc attached (187 Bde. only).
190th "	MUNCQ NIEURLET	6.	ditto. (190th Bde only)
41st D.A.C.	RUMINGHEM	32.	ditto. (D.A.C. only).
D.T.M.O.	ditto.	12,17,18,16b.	Officers.
		12,15,17,18)	Other ranks.
		11.)	
		16b.	Mess.
No.1 Coy. Div.Train.	ditto.	4,6,7,8,	Officers.
		2,3,4,10.	Other ranks.
		8a.	Mess.
			Horses, Field near 2 - Field B.

NOTES:- (a). Tents for Officers where required in Billets at MUNCQ NIEURLET can be drawn from Area Commandant RECQUES. They must be returned to his Office before leaving the area.
(b). Canvas water troughs where required can be obtained in the same way.

SCHEDULE "B".

AREA ORDERS.

1. Marching in state to be rendered at once.

2. Distribution list as per Billet list handed to units, to be rendered within 48 hours, or before departure if occupation is of less duration. It must show actual numbers occupying each Billet.

3. No new ground is to be taken for horse lines.

4. The latrines are not to be taken away, and not to be moved from one billet to another without notice to the Brigade Area Commandant.

5. There must be no lights nor any smoking in billets where straw, hay, or other fodder is stored.

6. Lights must be extinguished or properly screened from 1 hour after sunset. All lights out by 9.30 .

7. Estaminets are only open to British troops from 10.30 a.m. to 1.30 p.m. and from 5.30 p.m. to 9 p.m.

SCHEDULE "C".

POLINCOVE

Billot No.	Scoops.
12	1
13	1
18	2
23	1
28	1
30	1
31a	1
33	1 (spring).

MUNCQ NIEURLET

1a)	
4)	
16)	1
17)	
22)	

Note:- Horses at Billet 20 water at the river at RECQUES.

RUMINGHEM

| 40 | 1 |
| 48 | 1 |

Note:- 41st Div. Train should go to Watton for water. The key can be obtained from Office of Area Commandant WATTON.

Appendix C. War Diary

ADDENDUM to 41st DIVISIONAL ARTILLERY
INSTRUCTION No. 9.

14th June 1918.

1. Location of units in action will be as follows:-

41st D.A.H.Q. advanced	P.12.a.3.5.	
rear	J.28.a.1.5.	
187th Bde. H.Q.	P.9.c.5.6.	
	Battery.	O.P.
A/187 Battery	P.15.d.25.60.	P.17.b.80.15.
B/187 "	P.9.d.30.40.	P.11.c.70.10.
C/187 "	P.9.d.10.90.	P.11.d.20.70.
D/187 "	P.15.b.50.50.	P.17.b.50.20.
190th Bde. H.Q.	P.4.c.6.9.	
	Battery.	O.P.
A/190 Bty.	P.9.b.15.90.)	
B/190 "	P.3.d.6.4.)	area about
C/190 "	P.4.c.1.7.)	P.11.d.35.90.
D/190 "	P.4.c.95.45.)	
41st D.A.C.H.Q.)		
No.1 Section D.A.C.)	J.26.d.9.7.	
No.2 Section D.A.C.)		
No.1 Coy.Div. Train.	RECQUES.	

2. Guides as detailed in para. 8 will be at the rendezvous named therein at 10.30 a.m.

Captain R.F.A.
Brigade Major,
41st Divisional Artillery.

SECRET.   Copy No. 31

41st. DIVISIONAL ARTILLERY INSTRUCTIONS No.9.

                                                14th June 1918.

1. 41st Divisional Artillery will carry out Field firing with the 30th American Division by arrangement with 39th Division on 16-6-18 S.E. of NORTLEULINGHEM.

2. A general outline of the operations is attached. The Scheme and detailed orders will be issued later to all concerned.

3. The following units of the 41st Divisional Artillery will take part:-
   - D.A.H.Q.
   - 187th Bde.   Firing batteries only.
   - 190th Bde.   Firing batteries only.
   - D.A.C.   Ammunition Wagons of Nos. 1 & 2 sections only.
   - No.1 Coy. 41 Divl. Train. Skeleton only.

   Dress - F.S. marching order.

4. The following proportions of ammunition will be carried:-
   - 4.5" Hows.   All BX (delay fuze).
   - 18-pdrs.   All A, except one Battery 190 Brigade which will carry All AX (101 fuze).

   One 18-pdr. Battery, which will be detailed later from 187th Brigade, will carry 24 rounds per gun smoke shell.

5. The march to the range will take place in accordance with the following March Table:-

Unit.	Starting Point.	Time.	Route.	Destination.
187 Bde.	J.15.b.6.0.	7.30a.m.	) NORDAUSQUES	(Positions in
190 Bde.	ditto.	8.0 a.m.	) J.36.c.0.3.	(action already
D.A.C.	ditto.	8.30a.m.	) NORTLEULIN-	(reconnoitred by
D.A.H.Q.	ditto.	8.45a.m.	) GHEM.	(O.C. Units.

   NORDAUSQUES must be cleared by 9 a.m.

6. Batteries must be in action and prepared to commence registration by 11 a.m. Zero hour will be 1.20 p.m. All ammunition will be dumped at the guns.

7. Once units reach their positions in action all roads will be kept clear till 11 a.m.
   Teams should be watered during the operations between 11 a.m. and 1 p.m. between NORDAUSQUES and TOURNEHEM.

8. Each battery will have a guide at P.11.c. (hill 90) to take a party of American Officers to its O.P. to watch registration

                                                        P.T.O.

Each Battery 187th Brigade will have a guide at Cross Roads at LA RONVILLE in P.9.c. and each Battery 190th Brigade at the mill in P.4.a. to take a party of American Officers to the Battery Position to watch the work at the guns during registration.

9. Operations will cease at 1.30 p.m.
At this hour all units will limber up and return to their billets in the reverse order to which they marched out and by the same route.
It is very important that the area should be cleared of Artillery early to enable the Infantry to get back as soon as possible to their billets.

10. Brigades, D.A.C. and No.1 Coy. 41st Divl. Train to ACKNOWLEDGE.

Issued at:- 1 p.m.

[signature]
Captain, R.F.A.
Brigade Major,
41st Divisional Artillery.

Distribution.

Copy No.		
1 - 5	187th Brigade R.F.A.	
6 - 10	190th " "	
11 - 14	41st D.A.C.	
15.	41st D.T.M.O.	
16.	41st Division G.	
17.	41st Division Q.	
18.	39th Division G.	
19.	A.P.M. 41st Divn.	
20.	A.P.M. 39th Divn.	
21.	A.P.M. VII Corps.	
22.	VII Corps R.A.	
23.	Second Army R.A.	
24.	122nd Infantry Bde.	
25.	123rd " "	
26.	124th " "	
27.	41st M.G.Batth.	
28.	C.R.E. 41st Divn.	
29.	A.D.M.S. 41st Division.	
30.	No. 1 Coy, 41st Divl. Train.	
31.	War Diary.	
32.	File.	

Outline of Field Firing operations to be carried out by 41st Divisional Artillery in conjunction with 39th Division (Training Division with American Army), on 16-6-18.

General Idea.   To illustrate the Artillery support afforded to an Infantry Brigade in the attack on a long straggling village with strong points.

The Artillery available consists of the 41st Divisional Artillery comprising 187th and 190th Brigades R.F.A. each 3 18-pdr. Batteries and 1 4.5" How. Battery - Total 36 18-pdrs., 12 4.5" Hows.

During the Infantry Advance all batteries will open fire on the objective at a slow rate, 18-pdrs. on edge of village 4.5" Hows. on strong points: as the Infantry approach the village the Artillery fire will be quickened up until the Infantry reach within assaulting distance when they will take cover or lie down - as soon as the Infantry are ready to assault, the Artillery will fire at the rate of 4 rounds
x per gun per minute (4.5" Hows. 3 rounds per gun per minute) for 5 minutes and lift off the objective simultaneously to form a protective barrage beyond it: the intense fire of the Artillery is a signal to the Infantry to be ready to assault and the lift off the objective is the signal for the actual assault.

It is proposed to illustrate the screening of the attack from a hostile O.P. by means of a smoke barrage.

Rates of fire of the Artillery:-

ø (Zero - 20' to Zero - 15'   Very Slow.
  (Zero - 15' to Zero - 5'   Slow.
  (Zero - 5' to Zero   Normal.

Zero to Zero plus 5'   Intense (to prepare the
                                                    assault.)

Zero plus 5' to Zero plus 10'   Slow(protective barrage
                                                    which would in practice be continued as required, usually in bursts of fire at uncertain intervals).

Zero plus 10'   Stop.

ø From Zero - 20 to Zero - 5' one 18-pdr. Battery will form the Smoke Screen outlined above at a rate of fire which will depend on weather conditions.
   At Zero - 5' this Battery will switch on to its bombardment task.

The objective is represented by detached screens; strong points will be spit locked in the chalk.

x This will take place either:-
    (a). When the Artillery F.O.O's see them formed up,
    (b). A light signal is sent up from the attacking Infy,
    (c). At some given Zero hour.

War Diary

41st D.A. ADMINISTRATIVE INSTRUCTION
issued in connection with 41st D.A. Instructions, No. 10.

(1) A rear Echelon of 41st D.A., H.Q. will be established at Cross Roads NORDAUSQUES, K.27.b.8.9. at 9.30 a.m. on 16th inst.

(2) As soon as wagon lines are established each Brigade will send 2 mounted orderlies to rear H.Q. One will be employed for inter-communication, and one to establish touch with supplies. These orderlies will report the exact location of wagon lines and the time of their arrival will be recorded.

(3) As soon as the 41st D.A.C. reach their wagon lines in action, they will send a mounted orderly to report arrival and location to rear H.Q. They will also send mounted orderlies to establish touch with each Brigade wagon lines. Ammunition will not be supplied to wagon lines in action by 41st D. A. C.

(4) As soon as 41st Divl. Train has selected a camp in the RECQUES Area, they will send a mounted orderly to rear H.Q. to report arrival and location. This mounted orderly will join there the guides from Bde. wagon lines. The time when touch is established between the Train orderly and orderlies from Brigade wagon lines will be recorded and they will all then return to their own units.

(5) As soon as the operations are completed and units have returned to their own camps, 41st D.A.C. will immediately refill Brigade wagon lines under arrangements to be made direct between units concerned. Brigades will report to 41st D.A., H.Q. by 6 p.m. 16th inst. amount of ammunition expended.
Arrangements for refilling the D.A.C. will be notified later.

(6) All empty cartridge cases must be collected by batteries, brought back to camp, and handed in to Salvage.

(7) Proper latrines will be dug at all battery positions and wagon lines and filled in before leaving.

(8) An ambulance will be in NORDAUSQUES Village during the operations, if required by Medical Officers.

15-6-18.

Captain,
Staff Captain, 41st Divisional Artillery.

Copy No. 31

Appendix H... heavy

41st. DIVISIONAL ARTILLERY INSTRUCTIONS No.10.

15th June 1918.

1. The 41st Divisional Artillery will co-operate with the 117th American Infantry Regiment in an attack on the village of X in P.18.b. in accordance with Scheme already issued by 39th Division.

2. All units of 41st Divisional Artillery will take up positions in action according to 41st D.A.Instructions No.9 of 14th instant.

3. All 18-pdr. Batteries will fire time shrapnel and both 4.5" How. batteries H.E. with delay fuze with the exception of C/190 which will fire H.E. with delay fuze and A/187 which for the first 15 minutes will fire smoke.

4. Zero hour will be 1.20 p.m.

5. Table of tasks and barrage time table is attached.

6. Registration will be carried out simultaneously by both Brigades between 11 a.m. and 1 p.m.
Fire will not be opened till ordered by D.A.H.Q.

7. An Officer from D.A.H.Q. will visit Brigade Headquarters with a watch between 10.30 a.m. and 11 a.m. for synchronization purposes.

8. 187th, 190th Brigades and D.A.C. to acknowledge.

J.P. MacFarlane
Captain R.F.A.,
Brigade Major,
41st Divisional Artillery.

Issued at:- 8 a.m.

To all recipients of 41st D.A.Instructions No.9.

18-pdr. Task and Time Table.

Time.	Guns.	Target.	Rate of fire.
Zero - 30' to Zero - 15'	18-pdrs. 187th Bde. (less A Bty.)	Front edge of village of X from P.18.b.1.1.- P.18.b.5.5. Road exclusive	Very slow.
	18-pdrs. 190th Bde.	Front edge of village of X from P.18.b.8.9.- P.18.b.5.5. Road inclusive	
Zero - 15' to Zero - 5'	ditto.	ditto.	slow.
Zero - 5' to Zero.	ditto.	ditto.	Normal.
Zero to Zero plus 5'	ditto & A/187.	ditto.	intense.
Zero plus 5' to Zero plus 10'	18-pdrs. 187 Bde.	Protective barrage line from P.18.c.8.8. to P.13.a.20.15.	slow.
	18-pdrs. 190 Bde.	Protective barrage line from P.13.a.20.15. to P.13.a.5.6.	
Zero - 20' to Zero - 5'	A/187 Bde.	P.18.c.95.10 to P.18.d.20.10.	will be notified later.

4.5" How. Table over.

4.5" How. Task and Time Table.

Time.	Hows.	Target.	Rate of fire.
Zero - 20' to Zero - 15'	D/187.	Southern strong point in rear of village of X.	Very slow.
	D/190.	Northern strong point in rear of village of X.	
Zero - 15' to Zero - 5'	ditto.	ditto.	slow.
Zero - 5' to Zero.	ditto.	ditto.	normal.
Zero to Zero plus 5'	ditto.	ditto.	intense.
Zero plus 5' to Zero plus 10'	D/187.	Protective Barrage from P.13.a.0.0. to P.13.a.20.15.	slow.
	D/190.	Protective barrage from P.13.a.20.15. to P.13.a.3.3.	

18-pdr. Table over.

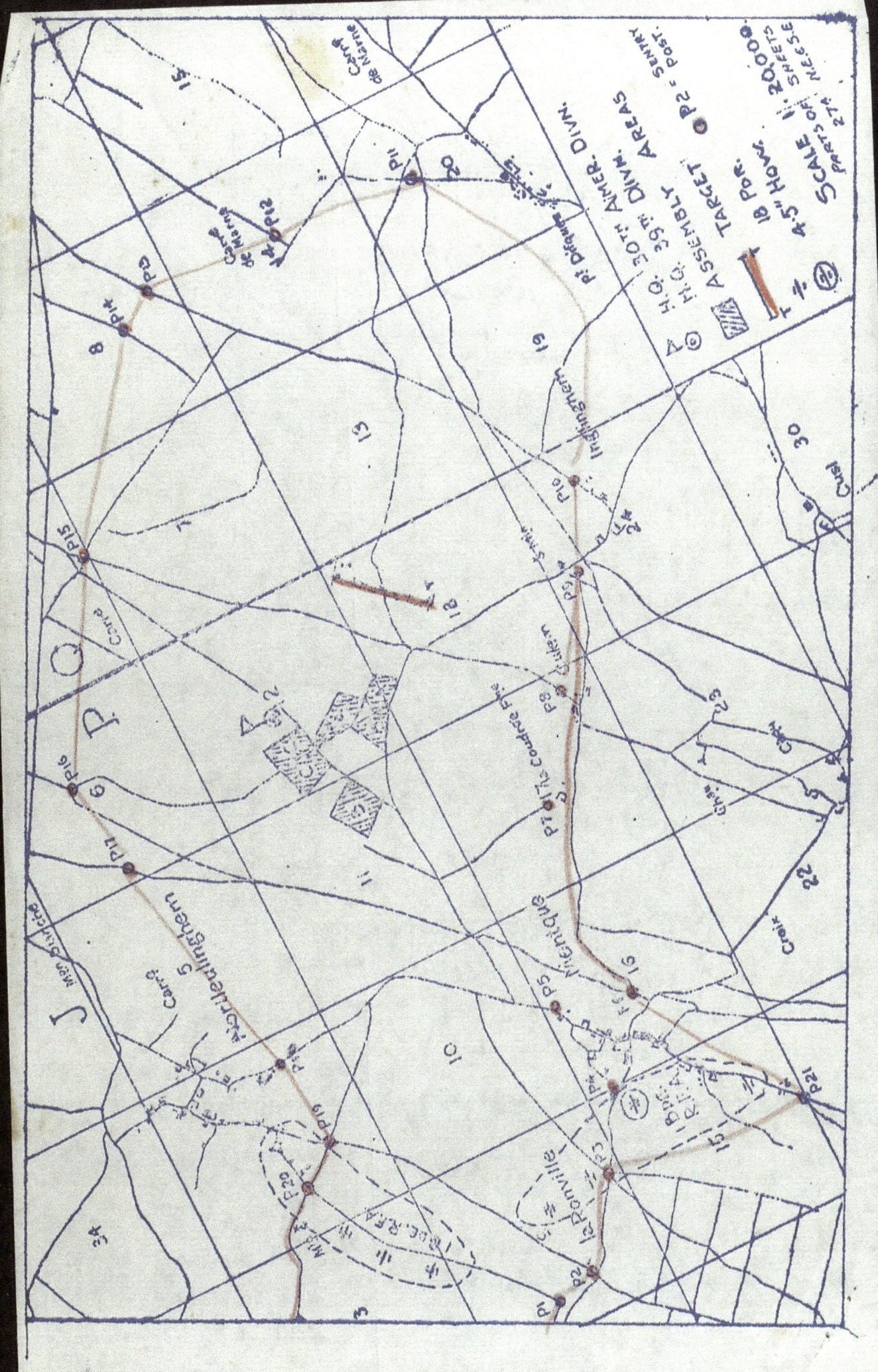

War Diary   Appendix "1"

S E C R E T.   Copy No. 25

41st DIVISIONAL ARTILLERY ORDER No. 7.

Reference:-   24th June 1918.
  HAZEBROUCK 5A 1/100,000.
  Sheet 27A N.E.1/20,000.

1. 41st Divisional Artillery will move to ZEGGERS CAPPEL area tomorrow 25th instant in accordance with the following march table:-

Unit.	Starting Point.	Time.	Route.
No.1 Coy. 41 Div. Train.	L.1.c.9.3.	6.30 a.m.	HALTE LIB LES CLITRES. MILLAIN MERCKEGHEM
41st D.A.C.	E.28.c.6.2.	6.45 a.m.	ditto.
190th Bde. R.F.A.	E.26.d.2.5.	7.30 a.m.	RUMINGHEM thence as above.
187th Bde. R.F.A.	D.30.c.3.5.	8.0 a.m.	ditto.

2. Destination in each case will be the Billets in the ZEGGERS CAPPEL area occupied on the recent march to present area. Units will make their own arrangements about sending on advanced parties.

3. The usual march distances and halts will be strictly observed.

4. 41st T.M.Batteries will remain at LEULINGHEM and will move on the 26th or 27th inst. under arrangements which will be notified later.
The 4 G.S.Wagons for T.M.Batteries will march empty with the D.A.C.
No.1 Coy, 41st Divl. Train will be prepared to ration 41st T.M.B's who will then be with D.A.C. for consumption on 27th instant.

5. No. 1 Coy. 41st Divl. Train and all units 41st Divisional Artillery will send guides for supply wagons to H.Q.D.A. opposite ZEGGERS CAPPEL Church at 1 p.m. 25th instant.

6. 187th and 190th Brigades will each send a guide to D.A.H.Q. POLINCOVE at 7 a.m. 25th instant for a lorry each which will be attached to them during the march.

7. All latrines must be filled in and all billets left clean and in proper condition before units leave the area. An Officer must be left behind to see that this has been done. A certificate from the proprietor will be obtained wherever practicable stating that he is satisfied and has no outstanding claim.

                                                       P.T.O.

8. Baggage wagons will be sent to rejoin units forthwith.

9. All tents, troughs and other area stores which have been drawn in this area must be returned to Area Commandant's Office RECQUES before moving and a receipt obtained.

10. D.A.H.Q. will close at POLINCOVE at 9 a.m. 25th instant and re-open at ZEGGERS CAPPEL at 10 a.m. on same date.

11. Brigades, D.A.C., No.1 Coy. Divl. Train and D.T.M.O. to ACKNOWLEDGE.

F. H. MacFarlane
Captain R.F.A.
Brigade Major,
41st Divisional Artillery.

Issued at 7 p.m.

```
Copy No. 1 - 5    187th Bde.
         6 - 10   190th    "
        11 - 14   41st D.A.C.
        15        No.1 Coy. Divl. Train.
        16        D.T.M.O. 41st Div.
        17        41st Divn. G.
        18        41st Divn. Q.
        19        A.P.M. 41st Divn.
        20        VII Corps R.A.
        21        A.P.M. VII Corps.
        22        A.D.M.S. 41st Divn.
        23        D.A.D.O.S. 41st Divn.
        24        Area Commdt. RECQUES.
        25        War Diary.
        26        File.
        27)
        28) Spare.
        29)
```

War Diary

S E C R E T.   Copy No. 8

41st Divisional Artillery Order No. 6.

24th June 1918.

1. 52nd Mobile Veterinary Section will be attached to 41st D.A.C. during the march commencing tomorrow 25th inst.

2. 52nd M.V.S. will march to EECCERS CAPPEL area on the 25th instant by the following route:-

    GANSPETTE
    WATTEN
    MERCKEGHEM

    It will be clear of WATTEN by 8 a.m.

3. A representative of 52nd M.V.S. will be met at Area Commandants Office EECCERS CAPPEL at 8 a.m. 25th instant by a member of 41st D.A.C's billeting party to arrange accommodation.

4. 52nd M.V.S. will send a guide for supply wagon to D.A.H.Q. opposite church in EECCERS CAPPEL at 1 p.m. 25th inst.

                                            Captain R.F.A.
                                            Brigade Major,
Issued at:- 7.15 p.m.   41st Divisional Artillery

Copy No. 1   52nd Mobile Vety. Sect.
       2.   41st D.A.C.
       3.   41st Divn. G.
       4.   41st Divn. Q.
       5.   A.P.M. 41st Divn.
       6.   No.1 Coy Divl. Train.
       7.   File.
       8.   War Diary.

War Diary

Officer Commanding,
   187th. Brigade, R.F.A.,
   190th. Brigade, R.F.A.,
   41st. D.A.C.
----

1.   Reference 41st.D.A. Order No.7, para.7.
    A certificate will be rendered to Sub-Area Commandants concerned that all billets have been left clean and in a sanitary condition. On arrival in ZEGGERS CAPPEL area copies of these certificates will be forwarded to D.A., Headquarters.

2.   Four lorries will report at 187th. Brigade Headquarters at 8 a.m., on 25th. instant, and not at D.A., Headquarters as previously stated. They are allotted as follows:-

        D.A., H.Q.   1 Lorry
        187th. Brigade   1 "
        190th. Brigade   1 "
        187th. Bde.)
        190th. Bde.) shared 1 "

Lorries may do two journeys if required for carriage of sick. Lorries will remain with units till night of 26th. instant, when they will rejoin the M.T. Company.

3.   Sick who are being treated regimentally and who are unfit to march will be evacuated to the affiliated Field Ambulance forthwith.
    Artillery sick to 138th. Field Ambulance.

                                                Captain,
24.6.18.   Staff Captain, 41st. Divisional Artillery.

Appendix "J"

SECRET.   Copy No. 27

41st. DIVISIONAL ARTILLERY ORDER No.9.

25th June 1918.

Reference
    HAZEBROUCK. 5A 1/100,000.

1. 41st D.A. will move to ABEELE area tomorrow the 26th inst in accordance with March Table attached.

2. All latrines must be filled in and all billets left clean and in proper condition before units leave the area. An Officer must be left behind to see that this has been done. A certificate from the Proprietor will be obtained wherever practicable stating that he is satisfied and has no outstanding claim.

3. Usual march distances and halts will be strictly observed. All transport will be brigaded and march in rear of Brigades under an Officer.

4. 187th Brigade and 190th Brigade will not pass cross roads 1¼ miles S.S.E. of WATOU before 9.30 p.m. Brigades will select suitable places to pull off the road for water and feed as necessary.
    D.A.C. will march direct in to wagon lines and will arrive during the hours of darkness.

5. 187th Brigade will relieve Group in area I.3.40.95. with 4 hows. and 2 18-pdr. batteries (4 guns each only). 1 18-pdr. battery 187th Brigade (6 guns) and 1 18-pdr battery 190th Brigade (6 guns) will relieve the Group in area I.3.45.85. and come under the orders of O.C. 187th Bde.

    190th Brigade will relieve Group in the area I.2.70.10. with 1 4.5" How. battery (4 Hows. only) and 2 18-pdr.batteries (4 guns each only).

    The remaining guns and hows. will be kept in wagon lines, and be brought into action in the event of hostile attack.

6. Ammunition dumped at positions will be made up to 100 rounds per gun and 60 rounds per How. by night of 27th/28th inst. The D.A.C. will refill the Brigades on 29th inst. Instructions as to refilling D.A.C. will be issued later.

7. All Maps, Defence Schemes, telephone wires etc. will be taken over.

8. R.A.H.Q. will close at ZEGGERS CAPPEL at 10 a.m. and re-open at the same hour at H.2.70.15. (¼ mile E. of K in MOENAARTBEEK).

9. A lorry will start from D.A.H.Q. ZEGGERS CAPPEL at 8 a.m. tomorrow, calling at 190th H.Q. at 8.15 a.m. Adjutants of Brigades and 2 Officers per Battery will travel in this lorry to new R.A.H.Q. given above.

10. Units of 41st Divisional Artillery will send guides for supply wagons to No. 1 Coy. 41st Divl. Train (see location in march table) at 4 a.m. on 27th instant. These wagons will be loaded with rations for consumption 27th instant.

11. On completion of March lorries with Brigades will rejoin M.T. Company.

12. Brigades, D.A.C. and No. 1 Coy. Train to ACKNOWLEDGE.

T.Mitchell Capt
Brigade Major,
41st Divisional Artillery.

Issued at:- 1·0 p.m.

```
Copy No.  1 -  6   187th Bde.
          7 - 12   190th    "
         13 - 16   41st D.A.C.
              17   No. 1 Coy. Divl Train.
              18   D.T.M.O. 41st Divn.
              19   41st Divn G.
              20   41st Divn. Q.
              21   A.P.M. 41st Divn.
              22   VII Corps R.A.
              23   A.P.M. VII Corps.
              24   A.D.M.S. 41st Divn.
              25   D.A.D.O.S. 41st Divn.
              26   Area Commandant ZEGGERS CAPPEL.
              27   War Diary.
              28   File.
              29   Signal Officer.
              30   Staff Capt. 41st D.A.
              31   French 14th Corps Artillery.
              32   D.A.N.
              33   2nd Regt. of Artillery (French).
              34   52nd M.V. Section.
```

S E C R E T.

M A R C H   T A B L E

Issued with 41st Divisional Artillery Order No.9   25th June 1918.

Unit.	Starting Point.	Time.	Route.	Destination	Remarks.
187th Bde. R.F.A.	Cross Road E.2.85.70. (on ZEGGERS CAPPEL - ESQUELBECQUE Rd.)	2 p.m.	WORMHOUDT - HOUT-KERQUE, WATOU.	French Wagon lines in area about H.2.95.05.	Reconnoitred to-day.
190th Bde. R.F.A.	ditto.	3 p.m.	ditto.	ditto in area about I.2.10.10.	ditto.
D.A.C. and 52nd M.V.S.	ditto.	8 p.m.	ditto.	ditto in area about I.2.30.12.	ditto.
No.1 Coy. 41st.Div.Train.	ditto.	Can move under own arrangements provided it clears above units.		ditto. in area H.3.35.95.(WATOU FRANCE) about 1¾ miles N.E. of STEENVOORDE.	

War Diary   Appendix "K"

SECRET.   Copy No. 25

41st DIVISIONAL ARTILLERY INSTRUCTIONS No.12.

Reference Sheet 27 & 28 1/40,000
                                              27th June 1918.

1.   The Artillery covering 41st Division will shortly consist of:-

   187th Brigade R.F.A.
   190th Brigade R.F.A.
   One Brigade R.F.A. to be detailed later "X" Brigade,

in three Brigade Groups, each covering one Infantry Brigade in the Line.

   All arrangements are made on the assumption that "X" Brigade will arrive shortly and will cover the Left Brigade in the line; until this takes place the line will be covered by 41st Divisional Artillery only, 187th Brigade on Right half, 190th Brigade on Left: the line of demarcation within Divisional Sector being approximately N.20.central - N.14.c.0.0.

2.   Owing to the greater range of the French Field Artillery the positions now occupied by them are in many cases unsuitable for British Artillery: as explained at conference to-day, where they are suitable they will be occupied.
   No positions exist suitable for 187th Brigade; these will be reconnoitred on the 28th instant.
   Brigades will select positions wherever possible within the following areas:-

187th Brigade.   Southern boundary; Divisional Boundary
                    N. of WESTOUTRE - Road M.17.a.4.0.
                 Northern boundary; M.3.central, M.4.d.0.1.,
                    M.11.central.

190th Brigade.   Southern boundary; M.3.central, M.4.d.0.1.,
                    M.11.central.
                 Northern boundary; Track G.34.c.0.6.,
                    G.34.d.0.6., road junction G.34.d.8.2.,
                    Track junction M.6.c.00.75.

"X" Brigade.   Southern boundary; Track G.34.c.0.6.,
                    G.34.d.0.6., road junction G.34.d.8.2.,
                    Track junction M.6.c.00.75.
                 Northern boundary; Northern Divisional
                    Boundary.

3.   Brigades should be distributed in depth between ranges of 3,000 and 5,000 yards from the Front Line with sections or single guns in advance; the line of the SCHARPENBERG-BEEK appears to offer facilities for the latter.

4.   Group Headquarters will be those occupied by the French i.e.:-

   187th Brigade approximately M.3.a.2.4.
   190th Brigade   "   G.33.c.8.8.
   "X" Brigade.   "   G.29.c.1.1.

5.   French Right Group, being at too great a range for 18-pdrs. will not be relieved and will remain covering the line. (See appendix attached paras. 3 & 4).
       French Centre Group will be relieved by 190th Brigade as detailed in Appendix attached paras. 3 & 4.
       French Left Group, unless "X" Brigade arrives, will not be relieved and will remain covering the Line. (See Appendix paras. 3 & 4). Should "X" Brigade arrive before the relief is complete, the arrangements for relief will be similar to those of 190th Brigade.

6.   It is of the utmost importance that the relief should not be noticed.
       As little movement as possible is to take place by day; when reconnoitring front areas Officers and Other Ranks will borrow French Helmets.
       Registration will be reduced to an absolute minimum, very little should be necessary now that all guns are calibrated.
       Any firing that takes place for purposes of registration will be with H.E.
       Movement in view of MONT KEMMEL or hostile balloons should be restricted as much as possible; this is particularly the case near Headquarters.

7.   Wagon Lines will be reconnoitred in the following areas:-

       187th Brigade R.F.A.   S. of an EAST & WEST Line through track crossing railway at L.32.c.6.4. to within Divisional Southern Boundary.

       "X" Brigade R.F.A.   N. of an EAST & WEST Line through Ch L.26.c.6.3. to within Divisional Northern Boundary.

       190th Brigade R.F.A.   Between the above limits.

       D.A.C. less S.A.A.Sect. In or about BOIS de BEAUVOORDE, in agreement with French A.C.D. already there.

       Until instructions are issued to shift Wagon Lines they will remain in present position.

8.   Result of reconnaissance of gun positions and Wagon Lines to be sent to this Office with Map references as soon as possible.

9.   Relief is to be completed by 3 a.m. 2nd July at which time command passes.
       On completion of relief French A.C.D.7 will take over present reserve line gun positions of 41st Divisional Artillery with all maps, Defence Schemes, wires, aeroplane photographs and documents relating to the Front.

10.   Attached appendix shews details of relief.

11. Completion of reliefs nightly to be reported to this Headquarters by code word "DUNNIT".

12. Arrangements will be made with French Group Commanders for an Officer per Battery to be attached to French Batteries for a period of two days before completion of relief.

13. On completion of relief H.Q.R.A. 41st Division will be established at approximately L.26.a.8.7.

14. Brigades and D.A.C. to ACKNOWLEDGE.

                                                         (signature) Capt.
                                                           Brigade Major,

Issued at:- 10 p.m.   41st Divisional Artillery.

```
Copy No.  1 -  6   187th Brigade R.F.A.
          7 - 12   190th Brigade R.F.A.
         13 - 16   41st D.A.C.
              17   D.T.M.O. 41st Divn.
              18   41st Division G.
              19   41st Division Q.
              20   14th French Corps Artillery.
              21   7th French Divl. Arty.
              22   A.P.M. 41st Division.
              23   S.C.R.A. 41st Divn.
              24   Signal Officer 41st D.A.
              25   War Diary.
              26   File.
         27 - 36   Spare.
```

S E C R E T.

A P P E N D I X
issued with 41st Divisional Arty. Instructions No. 12.

27th June 1918.

Relief of 7th (French) D.A. (A.C.D.7) by 41st British)
D.A.

1. **28th June.**

    Brigade Commanders.
    Battery Commanders and one Officer per Battery.

    Reconnoitre positions to be occupied and select fresh ones.

    Meet C.R.A. at 9.30 a.m. in hollow G.32.a.9.5.

    During night 28th/29th two wagon loads of ammunition per gun and How. (i.e. 12 Wagon loads per Battery) will be dumped at gun positions and camouflaged. Where necessary a party will prepare and camouflage positions in each battery for a section which will be occupied on night 29th/30th.

    D.T.M.O. to reconnoitre front area with a view to selecting positions for 6" T.M.

    Captains of batteries to reconnoitre area for Wagon Lines. (See Instructions No. 12 para. 7.).

2. **29th June.**

    Further reconnaissance of positions and O.P's.

    During the night one Wagon load of ammunition per Gun and How. will be dumped at gun positions and camouflaged - further positions for a section per battery will be prepared and camouflaged ready for occupation on night 30th/1st July.

    The positions prepared on night 28th/29th will be occupied by a section per battery and ammunition in gun limbers dumped in addition.

3. **30th June.**

    During the night one wagon load of ammunition per Gun and How. will be dumped at gun positions; further positions for a section per battery will be prepared and camouflaged ready for occupation on night 1st/2nd July and the positions prepared on night 29th/30th will be occupied and ammunition in gun limbers dumped.
    Where these coincide with French battery positions, a section per battery of French A.C.D. will be relieved under arrangements by Group Commanders.
    Where French A.C.D. is not being relieved one section per French Battery will be withdrawn to positions vacated by 41st Divisional Artillery covering the Reserve line.

P.T.O.

4. **1st July** During the night one Wagon load of ammunition per Gun and How. will be dumped at Gun positions and the final positions already prepared will be occupied and ammunition in gun limbers dumped.

The relief to be completed by 3 a.m.

Remaining sections of French A.C.D. will be withdrawn, either on being relieved or under instructions of French Group Commanders, all maps, Defence Schemes, wires, aeroplane photographs and documents referring to the Reserve Line will be handed over by 41st D.A. to Groups and Batteries of French A.C.D. taking over defence of Reserve Line.

5. Unless orders are received to the contrary 41st D.A. will retain their present Wagon Lines and French A.C.D. their lines in BOIS de BEAUVOORDE.

6. During relief the following roads will be used:-

187th Brigade R.F.A.

WIPPENHOEK, ABEELE - RENINGHELST Road as far as road junction G.32.c.1.2. Track to M.2.a.7.3. - Cross roads M.2.a.9.6. thence via HEKSKEN CABT. to positions - return same route.

190th Brigade R.F.A.

Road Junction L.17.b.1.1. - Cross roads G.32.d.80.35 -Road junction G.33.c.8.4. thence to positions. Return same route.

French relief.

2 Groups   RENINGHELST - ABEELE Road to reserve gun positions.

1 Group   RENINGHELST - ABEELE Road, road through K of LIJSSENTHOEK to reserve gun positions (Ref. French Map ELVERDINGHE 1/20,000).

SECRET.   41st D.A. No. S. 344.

1st AMENDMENT TO 41st DIVISIONAL ARTILLERY
                INSTRUCTIONS No. 12.

                                              29th June 1918.

Page 1, 3rd line from Bottom,

        For "N.3.a.2.4."

        Read " O.32.b.5.2."

                                        Brigade Major,
                                    41st Divisional Artillery.

Copy to:-
        187th Bde. R.F.A.
        190th   "   "
        41st D.A.C.
        D.T.M.O. 41st Divn.
        41st Division G.
        41st Division Q.
        War Diary.
        File.

SECRET   Copy No..........

         41st. DIVISIONAL ARTILLERY ADMINISTRATIVE
         INSTRUCTIONS No.12 issued in connection
         with 41st.D.A., Instructions No.12, dated
         28th.June 1918.

                                                29th.June 1918

1. ACCOMMODATION

         From and after 12 noon, to-morrow, 30th.June 1918, the
Divisional Artillery will be accommodated as shewn in Table
"A" attached.
         On completion of relief the Division (less Artillery)
will be accommodated as shewn in Table "B" attached.

2. AMMUNITION

         Ammunition at guns will be made up to 400 rounds per
gun and How. as soon as possible after completion of relief.

3. SUPPLIES

         Railhead. - STEENVOORDE from 29th. instant.
         No.1 Company, 41st.Divisional Train will deliver to
Battery Wagon Lines by horse transport in the usual way.
         Batteries will communicate any changes in Wagon Lines
direct to No.1 Company, Divisional Train, and will arrange
guides for supply wagons if required.

4. WATER.

         The Water supply in the Forward area is poor, and is
reported as being badly contaminated, the greatest care must
therefore be taken as regards chlorination.
         There are Water cart filling points at:-
                  REMY SIDING
                  S.W. of HOOGRAAF CABT.
                  ABEELE STATION
         Barrel reservoirs have been made by the French at:-
                  Right Brigade   - M.11.b.6.2.
                  Centre Brigade - M.5.a.6.6.
                  Left Brigade   - M.6.a.0.9.

5. RE.STORES

         Divisional Dump - STEENAKER - L.32.d.4.0.
         Lieut.STRATTON, M.C., R.E., is accommodated at D.A.,H.Q.,
and will advise on all constructional work. All indents for
material will be forwarded direct to him.
         There is a great quantity of material to be salvaged in
the forward area, and until this is used up, indents for new
material should be restricted to an absolute minimum.

6. MEDICAL ARRANGEMENTS

   (A) Headquarters Forward Field Ambulance   WIPPENHOEK,L.28.d.5.6.
        (139th.Field Ambulance)   (Sheet 27)
    i. Headquarters Forward Bearers and   G.21.c.5.9)RENINGHELST
        Collecting Post, also Car Post.   (Sheet 28)-POP, Road
   ii. Collecting Post, also Car Post.   G.34.d.5.5.(Sheet 28)
                                                  (Cellars of old 41st.D.H.Q)

6. **MEDICAL ARRANGEMENTS (Contd)**

    iii. Collecting Post, also Car Post.   ZEVECOTEN, G.35.d.5.6.
                                                   To be moved later when post is finally constructed to ZEVECOTEN SIDING YARD at G.36.c.2.2. (Sheet 28)

    iv. Collecting Post.   M.5.b.6.1. (Sheet 28)
         Relay Post.   M.11.central (Sheet 28)
    v. Collecting Post   M.18.a.1.8. (Sheet 28)

  (B) Main Dressing Station, Gas Centre   REMY SIDING.
       & Sorting Station for Sick.   Old site No 2 Canadian C.C.S.
       140th. Field Ambulance.   L.23.a.1.1.

  (C) D.R.S. for sick and lightly   RWELD, J.27.b.3.2.
       wounded.
       (138th. Field Ambulance)
       (not open at present)

    i. At present no Advanced Dressing Stations - cases will be sent from R.A.Ps direct to Bearer Collecting Post and from thence direct in wheeled stretchers and Divisional Cars to M.D.S. at REMY SIDING.

    ii. All sick will be sent to M.D.S. REMY SIDING until the D.R.S. at RWELD can be organised and opened.
        Cars kept at No.1, 2, and 3, Collecting Posts REMY SIDING, WIPPENHOEK, and RWELD.

  (D) R.A.P. will be notified later.

7. **TRAFFIC**

  (i) Lorries may not proceed further East than BOESCHEPE - WIPPENHOEK Road in daylight.
       Horse Transport may not proceed further East than the N.& S. Grid Line between squares G.31 and 32. in daylight.

  (ii) Steel helmets and Box Respirators in the alert position, will be worn by all ranks East of the N.& S. Grid Line between squares G.31 and 32.

8.   ACKNOWLEDGE.

                                                    T H Bischoff
                                                        Captain,

Issued at:-   Staff Captain, 41st. Divisional Artillery.
   4 pm

Distribution:-

     Copy No.1 - 6   187th. Brigade, R.F.A.,
          No.7 -12   190th. Brigade, R.F.A.,
          No.13-16   41st. D.A.C.
          No.17-18   41st. D.T.M.O.
          No.19   No.1 Company, 41st. Divl: Train,
          No.20   41st. Division, "Q".
          No.21   File

TABLE "A"

ACCOMMODATION of 41st. DIVISIONAL ARTILLERY

Reference Sheets 27 & 28 - 1/40,000

Unit	Co-ordinate
41st. D.A. Headquarters	K.18.a.85.90.
187th. Brigade, R.F.A.	
Brigade Headquarters)	
"A" Battery)	R.1.a.80.80.
"B" Battery	R.3.a.80.30.
"C" Battery	R.1.a.80.80.
"D" Battery	R.2.a.90.90.
190th. Brigade, R.F.A.	
Brigade Headquarters	L.31.a.10.50.
"A" Battery	L.32.a.20.20.
"B" Battery	L.31.a.10.50.
"C" Battery	L.31.a.10.50.
"D" Battery	L.31.b.10.30.
41st. Divl: Ammn: Column	
Headquarters	L.16.c.40.50.
No.1 Section)	
No.2 Section)	L.15.b.90.20.
No.3 (S.A.A.) Section	K.21.d.95.80.
41st. D.T.&.O.	
Headquarters	K.21.d.95.80.
No.1 Company, 41st. Divl: Train	K.21.d.70.40.

TABLE "B"

Reference Sheet 27 - 1/40,000

Unit	Personnel Line	Transport "A" Echelon	"B" Echelon
122nd. I. Brigade	Line (Left)	LAPPE)	BEAUVOORDE WOOD
123rd. I. Brigade	Line (Centre)	LOYE)	
124th. I. Brigade	Line (Right)	K.36.central	L.26.a.1.4.
Machine G.Bn.	Line	L.33.central	(K.31.b.1.8.
			(K.25.c.8.6.
-do- (Res.Coy)	L.23.c.1.2.		
Royal Engineers	Line		STEEN AKKER
-do- 1 Company	ABEELE AERODROME		
19th. Middlesex	L.28.d.1.9.		STEEN AKKER
138th. Field Amb.			R ELD.
139th. Field Amb.	IPPENHOEK		R ELD
140th. Field Amb.			REMY SIDING
Divl: Train:-			
No.1 Company			
No.2 Company)			ATON, FRANCE
No.3 Company)			
No.4 Company)			ST. ELOY
Mobile Vet. Section			ST. ELOY

Appendix "I"

S E C R E T.   Copy No. 8

41st. DIVISIONAL ARTILLERY INSTRUCTIONS No.13.

30th June 1918.

1. Provisional orders for Liaison with Infantry Brigades in the line.

   Until the arrival of "X" Brigade R.F.A. the Divisional front is covered by 41st Divisional Artillery, 107th Brigade R.F.A. on right, 190th Brigade R.F.A. on the left:

   All three Infantry Brigades of 41st Division are in the line.

   O.C. 107th Brigade R.F.A. will find a Liaison Officer with Right Infantry Brigade (124th Infantry Brigade) Headquarters at R.17.b.0.5. approximately, under arrangements to be made direct with O.C. Right Infantry Brigade.

   O.C. 190th Brigade R.F.A. will similarly find a Liaison Officer with Left Infantry Brigade (122nd Infantry Brigade) Headquarters at C.30.c.1.1. approximately.

   The Liaison Officer with Centre Infantry Brigade (123rd Infantry Brigade) Headquarters at M.6.c.5.4. approximately will be found alternately by 107th Brigade R.F.A. and 190th Brigade R.F.A. for a tour of 4 days, commencing with 107th Brigade R.F.A. at 5 p.m. 1st July; this Liaison Officer will be relieved by 190th Brigade R.F.A. at 5 p.m. 5th July and so on until the arrival of "X" Brigade R.F.A. when further instructions on the subject will be issued.

2. Under instructions from C.C.R.A. XXXth Corps a proportion of guns of the 41st Divisional Artillery have been pushed forward and away from the main battery positions; these guns will do the shooting and the main battery positions will be "silent" except in the case of "S.O.S." or "Counter preparation".

3. S.O.S. Signal 5 white stars, now used by 7th (French) Division will remain in force until 8 a.m. 2nd July after which hour the 2nd Army S.O.S. Signal RED will be used.

4. O.P's. Each R.F.A. Brigade will man one O.P. permanently, i.e. both by day and night. Arrangements will be made by O.C. Brigades direct with O.C. Groups (French) for relief of the latter so that the lookout is continuous during the passing of command.

5. Instructions regarding "S.O.S." and "Counter preparation" will be issued shortly; in the meantime the principles laid down in previous 41st Divisional Artillery Defence Scheme for YPRES sector will be adhered to under Brigade arrangements.

6. New Wagon Lines will be occupied during the night of 1st/2nd July if this has not been previously carried out. French A.C.D.7 will occupy vacated wagon lines in Woods L.80. area on same night. Wagon Lines to be vacated by 12 midnight.

7. ACKNOWLEDGE.

                                        [signature] Capt.
                                        Brigade Major,
                                        41st Divisional Artillery.

Issued at:-

Copy No. 1 107th Bde.R.F.A.   Copy No. 5 124th Infy.Bde.
         2 190th   "   6 41st Divn. G.
         3 122nd Infy. Bde.   7 XXXth Corps R.A.
         4 123rd   8-9 War Diary & File.

NORAH D
Sept 27

Bedford
Major RE

On His Majesty's Service.

A.P. Office
Base

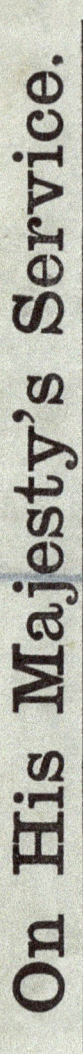

R | A.P.O. S.21
No. 281

Army Form C. 2118.

WAR DIARY
or
INTELLIGENCE-SUMMARY.
(Erase heading not required.) Headquarters, 41st.Divisional Artillery

Instructions regarding War Diaries and Intelligence Summaries are contained in F. S. Regs., Part II. and the Staff Manual respectively. Title pages will be prepared in manuscript.

Place	Date	Hour	Summary of Events and Information	Remarks and references to Appendices
BELGIUM ABEELE Area.	1918 July 1st. July 2nd.		During the night 1st/2nd, remaining sections of batteries of 41st.Divisional Artillery /MM occupied positions prepared, relief being completed by 3 a.m.; (Appendix "A") C.R.A. took over command of the Artillery covering the 41st.Division at 3 a.m. on the 2nd. MM	App:"A"
"	"	3rd.	Temporary Defence Scheme issued (Appendix "B") MM	App:"B"
"	"	6th.	Captain F.N.Mason-Macfarlane, M.C.,Brigade Major, returned from Hospital. MM	
"	"	7th.	41st.D.A., Headquarters moved to new Headquarters about 1½ miles N.W. of ABEELE. MM	
"	"	9th.	G.O.C., 41st.Division proceeded on leave to England; Brigadier-General A.S.COTTON, D.S.O., C.R.A.,41st.Division, assumed command of 41st.Division; Lieut.Col. G.A., CARDEW, C.M.G., D.S.O., 190th.Brigade, R.F.A., assumed command of 41st.Divisional Artillery. 41st.D.A.,Defence Scheme issued.(Appendix "C") MM	App:"C"
"	"	11th.	Addendum issued to 41st.D.A.,Defence Scheme regarding O.Ps.for Main line of resistance. (Appendix "C") MM	App:"C"
"	"	13th.	Orders were issued regarding co-operation of 41st.Divisional Artillery in an attack to be carried out by the 6th. and 33rd.Divisions. (Appendix "D") MM	App:"D"
"	"	14th	41st.D.A.,co-operated in the attack by the 6th. and 33rd.Divisions by prolonging the 6th.Divisional Artillery's Creeping barrage, and blinding enemy O.Ps on the Northern face of MONT KEMMEL with smoke and Gas. The attack was completely successful; 6 Officers & 356 Other ranks being taken prisoners. MM	
"	"	16th.	Names of the various lines of Defence issued (Appendix "E") MM	App:"E"
"	"	17th.	Counter preparation carried out at 11.30 p.m., as an attack was expected, and at 2.45 a.m. the following morning (18th). MM	
"	"	18th.	Concentrations of Gas fired in conjunction with XIXth.Corps Heavy Artillery on various targets in the vicinity of MONT KEMMEL from 11.55 p.m. to 2.19 a.m. 19th.(Appendix "F") G.O.C.,41st.Division returned from leave; G.R.A.,resumed Command of 41st.Divisional Artillery. G.A.CARDEW, C.M.G., D.S.O.,resumed Command of 190th.Brigade, R.F.A. MM	App:"F"

A6945 Wt.W14422/M160 350,000 12/16 D. D. & L. Forms/C./2118/14

.1.

WAR DIARY
or
INTELLIGENCE-SUMMARY.

(Erase heading not required.) Headquarters, 41st.Divisional Artillery

Army Form C. 2118.

Instructions regarding War Diaries and Intelligence Summaries are contained in F.S. Regs., Part II. and the Staff Manual respectively. Title pages will be prepared in manuscript.

Place	Date	Hour	Summary of Events and Information	Remarks and references to Appendices
Area of ABEELE, BELGIUM	July 19th.1918		Raid carried out by 11th.R.W.Surrey Regiment ("Queens") at 1.30 a.m. Raid was successful 3 prisoners being captured and an identification established (Appendix "G") MWm	App: "G"
"	21st.		**Two** bombardments carried out by batteries of 41st.D.A., in conjunction with XIXth.Corps Heavy Artillery on Hostile Trench Mortars and Trench Mortar Dumps (Appendix "H")	App: "H"
"	"		Captain F.N.Mason Macfarlane, M.C., Brigade Major, 41st.D.A., proceeded on leave to England; Major R.L.CREASY, M.C., O.C., "D" Battery, 190th.Brigade, R.F.A., came to 41st.D.A., Headquarters as acting Brigade Major. MWm	
"	22nd.		Work commenced on forward positions for three Brigades in the vicinity of LA CLYTTE & SCHERPENBERG. These positions were to be occupied to support a Counter stroke in the event of a hostile attack being made. It was intended by a counter stroke to push the enemy from MONT KEMMEL. The battery positions had accordingly to be chosen close up to our forward area. Arrangements were made for the dumping of ammunition at all these positions. MWm	
"	23rd.		Small raid carried out on night 23rd/24th. Assistance was given by the Artillery. All objectives were reached but there was no trace of the enemy. MWm (Appendix "I".)	App: "I"
"	26th.		41st.D.A., co-operated with XIXth.Corps H.A., on night 26th/27th. in a gas shell bombardment MWm	App "J"
"	27th.		41st.D.A., supported a raid carried out by the 26th.Royal Fusiliers (41st.Division) on night 27th/28th. The raid was successful; 2 prisoners being taken. The prisoners belonged to the 58th.Saxon Division (Appendix "K") MWm	App "K"
"	30th.		150th.(Army) Brigade, R.F.A. withdrawn from action. One 18pdr. Battery, and one 4.5"Howitzer Battery of the 11th (Army) Brigade, R.F.A. replaced the Two 18pdr. and One 4.5" Howitzer Batteries of the 150th (Army) Brigade, R.F.A. The two batteries of the 11th.Brigade remained in their present positions in the 6th.Divisional Area (Appendix "L") MWm	App "L"

1st.Aug.1918.

Brigadier General,
Commanding 41st.Divisional Artillery.

Appendix "A"

SECRET.   Copy No. 27

41st DIVISIONAL ARTILLERY INSTRUCTIONS No.12.

Reference Sheet 27 & 28 1/40,000
27th June 1918.

1. The Artillery covering 41st Division will shortly consist of:-

    187th Brigade R.F.A.
    190th Brigade R.F.A.
    One Brigade R.F.A. to be detailed later "X" Brigade,

    in three Brigade Groups, each covering one Infantry Brigade in the Line.

    All arrangements are made on the assumption that "X" Brigade will arrive shortly and will cover the Left Brigade in the line; until this takes place the line will be covered by 41st Divisional Artillery only, 187th Brigade on Right half, 190th Brigade on Left: the line of demarcation within Divisional Sector being approximately N.20.central - N.14.c.0.0.

2. Owing to the greater range of the French Field Artillery the positions now occupied by them are in many cases unsuitable for British Artillery: as explained at conference to-day, where they are suitable they will be occupied.

    No positions exist suitable for 187th Brigade; these will be reconnoitred on the 28th instant.

    Brigades will select positions wherever possible within the following areas:-

    187th Brigade.   Southern boundary; Divisional Boundary
                        N. of WESTOUTRE - Road M.17.a.4.0.
                     Northern boundary; M.3.central, M.4.d.0.1.,
                        M.11.central.

    190th Brigade.   Southern boundary; M.3.central, M.4.d.0.1.,
                        M.11.central.
                     Northern boundary; Track G.34.c.0.6.,
                        G.34.d.0.6., road junction G.34.d.8.2.,
                        Track junction M.6.c.00.75.

    "X" Brigade.   Southern boundary; Track G.34.c.0.6.,
                        G.34.d.0.6., road junction G.34.d.8.2.,
                        Track junction M.6.c.00.75.
                     Northern boundary; Northern Divisional
                        Boundary.

3. Brigades should be distributed in depth between ranges of 3,000 and 5,000 yards from the Front Line with sections or single guns in advance; the line of the SCHARPENBERG-BEEK appears to offer facilities for the latter.

4. Group Headquarters will be those occupied by the French i.e. :-

    187th Brigade approximately ~~M.3.a.2.4.~~ G.32.b.5.2.
    190th Brigade   "   G.33.c.8.8.
    "X" Brigade.   "   G.29.c.1.1.

1.

5.   French Right Group, being at too great a range for 18-pdrs, will not be relieved and will remain covering the line. (See appendix attached paras. 3 & 4).
       French Centre Group will be relieved by 190th Brigade as detailed in Appendix attached paras. 3 & 4.
       French Left Group, unless "X" Brigade arrives, will not be relieved and will remain covering the Line. (See Appendix paras. 3 & 4). Should "X" Brigade arrive before the relief is complete, the arrangements for relief will be similar to those of 190th Brigade.

6.   It is of the utmost importance that the relief should not be noticed.
       As little movement as possible is to take place by day: when reconnoitring front areas Officers and Other Ranks will borrow French Helmets.
       Registration will be reduced to an absolute minimum, very little should be necessary now that all guns are calibrated.
       Any firing that takes place for purposes of registration will be with H.E.
       Movement in view of MONT KEMMEL or hostile balloons should be restricted as much as possible; this is particularly the case near Headquarters.

7.   Wagon Lines will be reconnoitred in the following areas:-

       187th Brigade R.F.A.   S. of an EAST & WEST Line through track crossing railway at L.32.c.6.4. to within Divisional Southern Boundary.

       "X" Brigade R.F.A.   N. of an EAST & WEST Line through Ch L.26.c.6.3. to within Divisional Northern Boundary.

       190th Brigade R.F.A.   Between the above limits.

       D.A.C. less S.A.A.Sect. In or about BOIS de BEAUVOORDE, in agreement with French A.C.D. already there.

       Until instructions are issued to shift Wagon Lines they will remain in present position.

8.   Result of reconnaissance of gun positions and Wagon Lines to be sent to this Office with Map references as soon as possible.

9.   Relief is to be completed by 3 a.m. 2nd July at which time command passes.
       On completion of relief French A.C.D.7 will take over present reserve line gun positions of 41st Divisional Artillery with all maps, Defence Schemes, wires, aeroplane photographs and documents relating to the Front.

10.   Attached appendix shews details of relief.

11. Completion of reliefs nightly to be reported to this Headquarters by code word "DUNNIT".

12. Arrangements will be made with French Group Commanders for an Officer per Battery to be attached to French Batteries for a period of two days before completion of relief.

13. On completion of relief H.Q.R.A. 41st Division will be established at approximately L.26.a.8.7.

14. Brigades and D.A.C. to ACKNOWLEDGE.

Issued at:- 10 p.m.

Brigade Major,
41st Divisional Artillery.

Copy No. 1 - 6   187th Brigade R.F.A.
         7 - 12   190th Brigade R.F.A.
        13 - 16   41st D.A.C.
             17   D.T.M.O. 41st Divn.
             18   41st Division G.
             19   41st Division Q.
             20   14th French Corps Artillery.
             21   7th French Divl. Arty.
             22   A.P.M. 41st Division.
             23   S.C.R.A. 41st Divn.
             24   Signal Officer 41st D.A.
             25   War Diary.
             26   File.
        27 - 36   Spare.

SECRET.

APPENDIX
issued with 41st Divisional Arty. Instructions No.12.

27th June 1918.

Relief of 7th (French) D.A. (A.C.D.7) by 41st British) D.A.

1. **28th June.**

   Brigade Commanders.
   Battery Commanders and one Officer per Battery.

   Reconnoitre positions to be occupied and select fresh ones.

   Meet C.R.A. at 9.30 a.m. in hollow G.32.a.9.5.

   During night 28th/29th, two wagon loads of ammunition per gun and How. (i.e. 12 Wagon loads per Battery) will be dumped at gun positions and camouflaged. Where necessary a party will prepare and camouflage positions in each battery for a section which will be occupied on night 29th/30th.

   D.T.M.O. to reconnoitre front area with a view to selecting positions for 6" T.M.

   Captains of batteries to reconnoitre area for Wagon Lines. (See Instructions No.12 para. 7.).

2. **29th June.**

   Further reconnaissance of positions and O.P's.

   During the night one Wagon load of ammunition per Gun and How. will be dumped at gun positions and camouflaged - further positions for a section per battery will be prepared and camouflaged ready for occupation on night 30th/1st July.

   The positions prepared on night 28th/29th will be occupied by a section per battery and ammunition in gun limbers dumped in addition.

3. **30th June.**

   During the night one wagon load of ammunition per Gun and How. will be dumped at gun positions; further positions for a section per battery will be prepared and camouflaged ready for occupation on night 1st/2nd July and the positions prepared on night 29th/30th will be occupied and ammunition in gun limbers dumped.

   Where these coincide with French battery positions, a section per battery of French A.C.D. will be relieved under arrangements by Group Commanders.

   Where French A.C.D. is not being relieved one section per French Battery will be withdrawn to positions vacated by 41st Divisional Artillery covering the Reserve line.

P.T.O.

4. 1st July   During the night one wagon load of ammunition per Gun and How. will be dumped at Gun positions and the final positions already prepared will be occupied and ammunition in gun limbers dumped.

The relief to be completed by 3 a.m.

Remaining sections of French A.C.D. will be withdrawn, either on being relieved or under instructions of French Group Commanders, all maps, Defence Schemes, wires, aeroplane photographs and documents referring to the Reserve Line will be handed over by 41st D.A. to Groups and Batteries of French A.C.D. taking over defence of Reserve Line.

5.   Unless orders are received to the contrary 41st D.A. will retain their present Wagon Lines and French A.C.D. their lines in BOIS de BEAUVOORDE.

6.   During relief the following roads will be used:-

187th Brigade R.F.A.

WIPPENHOEK. ABEELE - RENINGHELST Road as far as road junction G.32.c.1.2. Track to M.2.a.7.3. - Cross roads M.2.a.9.6. thence via HEKSKEN CABT. to positions - return same route.

190th Brigade R.F.A.

Road Junction L.17.b.1.1. - Cross roads G.32.d.8.0.35 - Road junction G.33.c.8.4. thence to positions. Return same route.

French relief.

2 Groups   RENINGHELST - ABEELE Road to reserve gun positions.

1 Group   RENINGHELST - ABEELE Road, road through K of LIJSSENTHOEK to reserve gun positions (Ref. French Map ELVERDINGHE 1/20,000).

War Diary Appendix "B"

S E C R E T.   Copy No. 19

41st. DIVISIONAL ARTILLERY DEFENCE SCHEME (TEMPORARY).

Reference Maps:- 27 N.E. 28 N.W.) 1/20,000
                 27 S.E. 28 S.W.)

3rd July 1918.

1. Until more detailed information is available regarding the sector held by 41st Division the following will be the arrangements for S.O.S. and Counter Preparation.

    In subsequent Defence Scheme the fire of Heavy Artillery and Machine Guns will be co-ordinated with that of 41st Divisional Artillery.

2. Artillery Boundaries:-

    Southern Boundary   M.24.d.00.60. - Cross
                                roads N.31.a.85.80.

    Inter-Brigade Boundary. N.20.central - N.14.c.0.0.

    Northern Boundary   N.16.d.0.2. - N.9.d.15.00.

3. The dividing line between Field and Heavy Artillery for Harassing Fire will be a line drawn through Cross Roads N.31.a.85.80. and N.16.d.0.2.

4. (a). Until further instructions are issued the S.O.S. Tasks will be those laid down by French A.C.D.7.

    i.e. Right Brigade:-
        M.24.d.5.0. - N.19.a.8.2. - N.20.a.20.95.
        Hows. on selected points either in rear of this line or in the barrage.

    Left Brigade:-
        N.20.a.00.85. - N.14.c.95.55. - N.14.b.68.35. -
        N.14.b.8.8. - N.15.b.15.40.
        Hows. on selected points either in rear of this line or in the barrage.

    (b). An S.O.S. Call in any shape or form on the Divisional Front will be immediately answered in preference to any other task by all batteries. If any doubt exists fire will be opened at once at the following rates:-

        18-pdrs.   4 rounds per gun per minute)
        4.5" Hows. 3   "   "   "   "   "   ) for 10 minutes.

    when fire will cease unless again called for.

    (c). Under the following circumstances:-
        (a). during hostile bombardment,
        (b). during a mist,
        (c). if it is evident, either from repetition of S.O.S. Signals or from other indications that the hostile attack has not been beaten off
    the procedure laid down for S.O.S. will be repeated at the following rates:-

18-pdrs.   3 rounds per gun per minute.
4.5" Hows. 2   "   "   "   "   "

with intervals between the 10 minute bursts of 20 minutes in the case of (a) and (b) and 4 minutes in the case of (c). This procedure will be carried on for 2 hours or at the discretion of Group Commanders in case of (a) and (b) and until it becomes clear that the attack has been beaten off in case (c).

(d). F.O.O's and Infantry should be instructed to send up S.O.S. rockets at intervals until the hostile attack fails.

(e). Ammunition.   if available
18-pdrs. 50% Shrapnel, 50% H.E.(106 Fuze)by day.
          H.E. 106   by night.
4.5" Hows. H.E. 106 Fuze.

(f). Any battery receiving an S.O.S. Call will immediately inform its Brigade Headquarters and neighbouring batteries. Brigade Headquarters will inform D.A.H.Q. and their affiliated Infantry Brigades.

(g). A tracing shewing S.O.S. barrage lines of Machine Guns, field and heavy artillery will be prepared when the lines are finally fixed.

5. (a). "Counter preparation A" will be ordered by D.A.H.Q. when necessary and will take the form of heavy bursts of fire, with intervals, on known occupied localities and likely places of assembly within Field Artillery boundaries.
Time tables will as a rule be issued by D.A.H.Q. and in all cases careful synchronization must be ensured.

(b). A Counter preparation map is being prepared and will shortly be issued to all concerned.

(c). During heavy hostile bombardment, should all communications be cut, Group Commanders will order "Counter Preparation A" on their own initiative on the following general principle:-

(i). Fire to come down on S.O.S. Lines and search 600 yards S.E. from S.O.S.line, repeating same after an interval of 3 minutes.
4.5" Hows. (106 Fuze) as well as 18-pdrs. will be utilized for this searching fire.

(ii). Rates of fire:-
18-pdrs.   3 rounds per gun per minute.
4.5" Hows. 2   "   "   "   "   "

(iii). The two bursts referred to in para.(c) to be fired as under and to be of 6 minutes duration each:-
Half an hour before dawn, at dawn, and half an hour after dawn.
Dawn to be taken at present as 3.30 a.m.

(iv). In ordering further bursts of fire Group Commanders will be guided by the situation at the time and the necessity of having sufficient ammunition in hand to deal with a hostile attack.

6. Harassing fire will be carried out by day and night at uncertain intervals after receipt of orders from D.A.H.Q. that it is to be initiated; it will be arranged by Group Commanders in consultation with Infantry Brigades so that all roads, approaches and tracks are dealt with. This fire will be distributed in depth and so arranged that when possible approaches are enfiladed.

Programme as made out by Group Commanders will be submitted to D.A.H.Q. daily.

The daily allotment of ammunition for harassing fire will be notified later. At present all firing is to be reduced as much as possible consistent with the defence of the line; when this is threatened ammunition is limited only by the amount that can be brought up. The Divisional artillery will not remain "silent" but a minimum of 100 rounds per Brigade will be fired per 24 hours.

Group concentrations will be ordered by Group Commanders as may be necessary, and the normal procedure for engaging movement, located M.G's, T.M's &c will be carried out in addition.

7. Mutual Support.

See Appendix "A" attached.

8. Complete and detailed Defence Scheme will be issued later.

9. ACKNOWLEDGE.

Brigade Major,
41st Divisional Artillery.

Issued at:- 12 noon.

```
Copy No. 1 - 5     187th Bde. R.F.A.
         6 - 10    190th Bde. R.F.A.
         11        41st Divn. G.
         12        XIX Corps R.A.
         13        6th Divl. Arty.
         14        71st French Divl. Arty.
         15        D.T.M.O. 41st Divn.
         16        122nd Infantry Bde.
         17        123rd      "       "
         18        124th      "       "
         19        War Diary.
         20        File.
```

SECRET.

APPENDIX "A".

Issued with 41st Divisional Artillery Defence Scheme (Temporary)

3rd. July 1918.

Serial No.	Situation.	Code Call.	To whom sent.	Brigade to take action.	Action taken.
1.	Attack on Division on our right, and no attack on 41st Division.	Artillerie NORT-HOMME demande appui Artillerie LINGE.	41st Divl. Arty.	Left Artillery Brigade 41st D.A. (190 Bde. R.F.A.)	1 Bty. 4.5" Hows. area N.30.a.4.0.—M.30.b.0.5. 1 Bty. 18-pdrs. road M.30.b.2.0.—M.30.b.2.6. 1 Bty. 18-pdrs. valley M.30.b.55.00.—M.30.b. 55.65.
2.	Attack on Division on our Left, and no attack on 41st Division.	HELP LA POLKA.	41st Divl. Arty.	Right Artillery Brigade 41st D.A. (187 Bde. R.F.A.)	1 Bty. 18-pdrs. search and sweep area N.14.d.7.3.—M.14.b.7.1.—M.15.a.7.1.—N.15.c.7.3. to limit of range. 1 Bty. 18-pdrs. search and sweep area N.15.d.0.2.—N.15.d.0.9.—N.15.d.9.9.—N.15.d.9.2. to limit of range. 1 Bty. 4.5" Hows. Road Junctions in KEMMEL village, N.21.d.0.2. and N.of cross roads N.21.d.4.4.

P. T. O.

Serial No.	Situation.	Code Call.	To whom sent.	Brigade to take action.	Action taken.
3.	Attack on 41st Division.	Artillerie LINGE demande appui Artillerie HEET HOMME.	A.D. 71 French.	71st.French Divl. Artillery.	1 Bty. 75 m.m. valley N.30.b. 55.30. N.30.b.55.65. 1 Bty. 75 m.m. roads N.25.b.15.85.- N.19.c.7.1. 2 Btys. 75 m.m. Trench N.19.d.3.1.- N.19.c.6.6. 1 Bty. 150 Courte Road N.30.d.2.8. 1 Bty. 150 Courte Cross Roads N.25.b.2.2. 1 Bty. 150 Courte Valley N.30.b. 75.30.
		HELP ROSSIGNOL.	6th D.A.	6th Divl. Arty.	2 Btys. 18-pdrs. Barrage road N.20.b.9.5. - N.15.a.7.1. and trenches parallel to this road. 2 4.5" Hows. on Northern exits of KENG EL village. 2 4.5" Hows. on road & trenches N. of ROSSIGNOL WOOD.

SECRET.

ADDENDUM No.1 to 41st D.A. DEFENCE SCHEME
(Temporary) dated 3rd July 1918.

6th July 1918.

10. Calls from the air.

"S.O.S." calls from the air will be taken up in the same manner as if the call had been sent by light signal etc.

"L.L." Calls. One section per battery will engage the target if it is within range, firing 3 rounds gun fire, and irrespective of whether target is in Brigade area or not. The "L.L." Call will be repeated if a further concentration is required. If not engaged on other tasks at the time, batteries will answer "L.L." Calls with all guns, firing 3 rounds gun fire.

"N.F." Calls will be answered by all batteries that are able to reach the target, firing 10 to 15 rounds a call.

"G.F." Calls will not be answered by Field Artillery.

E H Poe Capt RFA
Brigade Major
41st Divisional Artillery.

To all recipients of 41st D.A. Defence Scheme (Temporary).

Appendix "C" 37

41st. DIVISIONAL ARTILLERY DEFENCE SCHEME No. 2.

APPENDICES.

"A". LOCATION STATEMENT.

"B". T.M. ARRANGEMENTS.

"C". LIST OF O.P's.

"D". LIAISON INSTRUCTIONS No. 5.

"E". S.O.S. ORDERS AND TRACING.

"F". MUTUAL SUPPORT BARRAGES.

"G". COUNTER PREPARATION MAP "A".

"H". REAR DEFENCES.

"I". COMMUNICATIONS.

"J". ADMINISTRATIVE INSTRUCTIONS.

Distribution over.

41st D.A. DEFENCE SCHEME No. 2.

DISTRIBUTION.

Copy No.	1 - 7	187th Brigade R.F.A.
	8 - 13	190th Brigade R.F.A.
	14	41st Division G.
	15	41st Division Q.
	16	XIX Corps R.A.
	17	XIX Corps H.A.
	18	XIX Corps C.B.S.O.
	19	41st D.A.C.
	20	41st M.G. Battalion.
	21	122nd Infantry Brigade.
	22	123rd Infantry Brigade.
	23	124th Infantry Brigade.
	24	C.R.E. 41st Division.
	25	A.D.M.S. 41st Division.
	26	No. 10 Squadron R.A.F.
	27	No. 39 K.B.S.
	28	65th Brigade R.G.A.
	29	6th Brigade R.G.A.
	30	25th H.A.G.
	31	6th Divl. Arty.
	32	35th Divl. Arty.
	33	D.T.M.O. 41st Division.
	34	S.O.R.A. 41st Division.
	35	41st Divl. Arty. Signal Officer.
	36	R.A.R.A. 41st Divn.
	37 - 40	War Diary and File.

SECRET.   Copy No. 37

41st. DIVISIONAL ARTILLERY DEFENCE
SCHEME No.2.

9th July 1918.

Reference Maps:-
27 & 28 1/20,000.

1. DISPOSITIONS. (a). The Field Artillery covering the 41st Divisional front on the LA CLYTTE - SHERPENBERG Sector is disposed as follows:-

Right Group   Batteries.

H.Q. G.32.b.50.20.   A, B, C & D/187th Brigade.
Lt. Col. C.D.G.LYON,D.S.O.,   C & D/150th Brigade.
R.F.A.

Left Group.

H.Q. G.33.a.85.05.   A, B, C & D/190th Brigade.
Lt. Col. G.A.CARDEW,C.M.G.,   B/ 150th Brigade.
D.S.O.,R.F.A.

(b). Locations of units of 41st Divisional Artillery are given in Appendix "A" attached.

(c). Distribution of 41st Trench Mortar Batteries is given in Appendix "B" attached.

(d). The following units of XIX Corps R.A. cover the Divisional Front:-

65th Bde. R.G.A.   6   9.2" Hows.
                         12   6"   Hows.

6th Bde. R.G.A.   4   9.2" Hows.
(part of)   2   6"   Hows.
                         12   60 - pdrs.

25th H.A.G.   2   15"   Hows.
(part of)   2   12"   Hows.

The 65th Brigade R.G.A. is affiliated to 41st D.A.

2. O.P's. A list of O.P's manned day and night by 41st D.A. and affiliated Heavy Artillery is attached in Appendix "C".

3. LIAISON. Until the re-distribution of the Divisional Front as a two Brigade front the following will be the Liaison arrangements:-

Right Group will find a Liaison Officer with each of the following:-
Right Infantry Brigade H.Q.
Centre Infantry Brigade H.Q.
H.Q. Right Battalion in the Line.

1.

Left Group will find a Liaison Officer with each of the following:-
  Left Infantry Brigade H.Q.
  Hd.Qrs.Centre Battalion in the Line.
  Hd.Qrs.Left Battalion in the Line.

41st D.A. Instructions No.5 re liaison duties are attached in Appendix "D".

4. ARTILLERY BOUNDARIES.

Southern Boundary   M.24.d.00.60. - N.31.a.85.80.

Inter-Group   "   N.20, central - N.14.c.0.0.

x Northern Boundary   N.9.c.0.0. - N.22.central.

x Point of junction between S.O.S. lines of 6th and 41st Divisional Artilleries will be N.15.a.0.7. each D.A. arranging an overlap of about 100 yards.

5. S.O.S.

S.O.S. instructions and tasks are attached in Appendix "E".

6. MUTUAL SUPPORT.

Field Artillery Mutual support arrangements are attached in Appendix "F".

7. AMMUNITION.

The following dumps of ammunition will be maintained at gun positions:-

  18-pdrs.   500 rounds per gun. (50% A & AX).
  4.5" Hows. 400   "   "   " (including 50 chemical).

Ammunition to cover normal daily expenditure should be kept at gun positions in addition to the above amounts which should always be available.

8. HARASSING FIRE.

(a). The dividing line between Field and Heavy Artillery for harassing fire purposes (Inner and Outer Zones) is a line drawn through
  N.25.c.45.45.
  N.15.d.70.30.
i.e. 1,200 yards from our outpost line.

(b). Harassing fire will be carried out by day and night at uncertain intervals and will be arranged by Group Commanders in consultation with Infantry Brigades so that all roads, approaches and tracks are dealt with. This fire will be distributed in depth and will be so arranged that when possible approaches are enfiladed.

Ammunition allotment for harassing fire is as follows per 24 hours.

  18-pdr.   450 rounds per Group.
  4.5" How. 150 rounds per Battery.

(c). Gas shoots will be carried out according to the weather and the tactical situation under orders of 41st D.A.H.Q.

9. CALLS FROM THE AIR.

S.O.S. calls from the air will be taken up in the same manner as if the call had been sent by light signal etc:-

"L.L." calls one section per battery will engage the target if it is within range firing 3 rounds gun fire and irrespective of whether the target is in the Brigade area or not.
The "L.L." call will be repeated if a further concentration is required. If not engaged on other tasks at the time, batteries will answer "L.L." calls with all guns firing 3 rounds gun fire.

"N.F." Calls will be answered by all Batteries that are able to reach the target firing 10 - 15 rounds per call.

"G.F." Calls will be answered by Field Artillery in the same way as LL Calls but under no circumstances will more than one section per Battery be used.

10. COUNTER BATTERY WORK.

Counter Battery work will take precedence with the 4.5" How. Batteries over all other tasks except S.O.S. C.B.S.O. XIX Corps will notify tasks to Batteries through D.A.H.Q.

In those Counter Battery concentrations in which the C.B.S.O. asks for Field Artillery co-operation all 18. pdrs. that can reach the objective and are not otherwise employed will take part.

Active hostile Batteries engaged by Brigades by order of the C.B.S.O. will be included in their harassing fire tasks by day and night.

11. WIRELESS MASTS.

Wireless Masts of Brigades will be in action with their respective howitzer batteries.

Wireless mast of D.A.H.Q. will be at D.A.H.Q.

12. (a). COUNTER PREPARATION.

Counter Preparation "A" will be ordered by D.A.H.Q. when necessary. It will take the form of heavy bursts of fire with pauses on suspected assembly places and occupied localities within the inner zone beyond a line 600 yards in front of our outpost line.

Time tables with rates of fire and tasks will be issued as necessary and careful synchronization will be ensured.

A map shewing detailed tasks for Counter-preparation "A" is attached as Appendix "G".

(b). Counter preparation "B" will be ordered by D.A.H.Q. or by Group Commanders on their own initiative, if communications are cut, during heavy hostile bombardment on the following general principles:-

    (1). Two bursts of fire each of 6 minutes duration with a pause of 2 minutes between bursts will be put down on S.O.S. lines searching 600 yards S.E. from them.

        18-pdrs. 3 rounds per gun per minute 50% A 50% AX 106 fuze
        4.5" Hows. 2 " " " " " BX 106 fuze.

    (2). If the situation is obscure and a hostile attack apparently imminent Counter preparation "B" as above will be fired at the following times:-
        half an hour before dawn
        dawn
        half an hour after dawn.
dawn will be taken at present as 3.40 a.m.

    (3). In ordering further bursts of Counter preparation "B" Group Commanders will be guided by the situation at the time and the necessity of having sufficient ammunition in hand to deal with a hostile attack.

13. REAR POSITIONS. The Field Artillery dispositions for the rear lines of defence in the divisional area are attached in Appendix "H".

14. COMMUNICATIONS. A tracing of existing communications is attached as Appendix "I".

Visual signalling between O.P's and Batteries, Batteries and Groups and Groups and affiliated infantry Brigades will be tested twice a week.

Each Group O.P. is equipped with a message rocket apparatus and the right group O.P. is in communication with C/187 Battery by trench wireless.

15. ADMINISTRATION. Administrative and salvage arrangements are attached as Appendix "J".

16. ACKNOWLEDGE.

                                          F.N. MacFarlane
                                          Captain R.F.A.
                                          Brigade Major,

Issued at:- 7 p.m.   41st Divisional Artillery.

SECRET.   41st D.A. No. S.890.

ADDENDUM to 41st D.A. DEFENCE SCHEME No.2.
───────────────
                                          11th July 1918.
                                          ─────────────

1.   The inter group Artillery boundary will run as follows in rear of the present front line

           N.14.c.0.0.
           N.7.c.32.56.
           M.4.a.70.56.

II.   Groups will arrange for O.P's to be selected and constructed as far as wire permits on the following lines:-

   (a).   One O.P. per Battery for the main line of resistance.

   (b).   One O.P. per forward section to cover the ground between it and the SCHERPENBERG - LA CLYTTE crest. These O.P's should, if possible, be within voice control distance of and form command posts for these sections and be in communication with the main battery positions.

   (c).   Command post O.P's for close defence of main Battery positions.

                                          Captain R.F.A,
                                          Brigade Major,
                                     41st Divisional Artillery.

Issued to all recipients of 41st D.A. Defence Scheme No.2.

(Appendix "F")

ADDENDUM to 41st D.A. Defence Scheme No. 2.

15th July 1918.

Lewis Guns and Small Arms.

1. In normal circumstances each Battery will keep one of its Lewis guns with its forward section and one with its main Battery position.

2. These guns will be permanently mounted for A.A. defence and fitted for this purpose with A.A. sights and efficient A.A. mountings.

3. The siting of these guns for the close defence of sections and main positions is to be carefully done in conjunction with the wiring in of positions. Where necessary alternative emplacements will be constructed.

4. 2,000 rounds S.A.A. per gun will be maintained at each gun.

    A small proportion of this should be tracer ammunition.

    16 drums will be maintained with each gun.

5. The D.A.C. Lewis guns will be permanently mounted for the A.A. defence of D.A.C. camp and the Divisional A.R.P.

    The Guns and teams of the D.A.C. must be prepared at short notice to replace casualties in Batteries.

6. 6 Rifles will be kept in each Gun pit and 50 rounds S.A.A. per man in bandoliers.

Captain R.F.A.
Brigade Major,
41st Divisional Artillery.

APPENDIX "A"
Issued with 41st D.A. Defence Scheme No. 2.

Reference Sheets 27 & 28 – 1/40,000.   9th July 1918.

Headquarters, 41st Divisional Artillery.   –   K.24.c.15.15.

			Position in action.	Wagon Lines
RIGHT GROUP.				
	Brigade Headquarters		G.32.b.50.20.	Q.12.b.20.80.
187th Brigade.	("A" Battery	(4 guns)	M. 3.d.80.90.)	R. 1.a.80.80.
	(	(2 guns)	M.10.b.65.55.)	
	("B" Battery	(2 guns)	M. 9.c. 65.95.)	
	(	(2 guns)	M. 9.a.85.30.)	R.3.d.80.30.
	(	(2 guns)	M.10.c.75.55.)	
	("C" Battery	(4 guns)	M. 9.a.80.95.)	R. 1.a.80.80.
	(	(2 guns)	M.10.a.00.60.)	
	("D" Battery	(4 hows)	M. 9.b.20.35.)	R. 2.a.90.90.
	(	(2 hows)	M.10.b.15.70.)	
	C/150 Battery	(4 guns)	G.35.a.60.50.	L.25.a.30.30.
	D/150 Battery	(4 hows)	G.35.b.20.80.	
		(2 hows)	M. 4.d.90.40.	L.19.d.10.40.
LEFT GROUP.				
	Brigade Headquarters		G.33.a.85.05.	L.33.a.90.00.
190th Bde.	("A" Battery	(4 guns)	M. 4.d.40.80.)	
	(	(2 guns)	M.11.a.70.40.)	L.32.a.20.90.
	("B" Battery	(4 guns)	M. 4.d.20.60.)	
	(	(2 guns)	M.11.b.20.35.)	L.25.c.30.25.
	("C" Battery	(4 guns)	M. 3.b.40.95.)	
	(	(2 guns)	M. 5.d.80.40.)	L.25.c.20.45.
	("D" Battery	(4 hows)	M. 4.a. 40.20.)	
	(	(2 hows)	M. 6.c.30.10.)	L.33.d.50.50.
	B/150 Battery	(4 guns)	G.33.d.80.20.)	
		(2 guns)	N. 1.a.10.10.	L.15.c.40.90.

41st DIVISIONAL AMMUNITION COLUMN.

	Position in action.	Wagon Lines
Headquarters	K.21.c.60.30.	K.21.c.60.30.
No. 1 Section.	–	K.34.b.90.90.
No. 2 Section.	–	K.35.a.70.40.
No. 3 (S.A.A.) Section.	–	K.21.d.95.80.
41st D.A.Ammunition Dump.	R. 2.b.50.80.	–

41st D. T. M. O.

Headquarters.	G.31.b.80.50.	–

Appendix "C"

AMENDMENT to APPENDIX "B"
41st D.A. Defence Scheme No. 2.

Para. (1).

    Line 6   for M.13.a.10.15.
                   read N.18.b.80.40.

                                    Captain R.F.A.
                                    Brigade Major,
12-7-16.   41st Divisional Artillery

Issued to all recipients of 41st D.A. Defence Scheme No.2.

SECRET.   41st D.A. No. S.973.

ADDENDUM to APPENDIX "B" 41st D.A. DEFENCE SCHEME No.2.

Para. (1) b.

    add

        2 T.M's at M.17.a.5.8.

                              Captain R.F.A.
                              Brigade Major,
19-7-18.   41st Divisional Artillery.

To all recipients of 41st D.A. Defence Scheme No.2.

APPENDIX "B"
issued with 41st D.A.Defence Scheme No.2.

(1.) Positions for the Trench Mortars of "X" and "Y"/41 Trench Mortar Batteries have been reconnoitred as follows:-

(a). To cover the outpost line.
 x 2 T.M's at   M.18.c.60.90.
    2 T.M's at   ~~M.18.a.10.15.~~ N.18.b.80.40.

x work has already been commenced on these emplacements.

(b). To cover the line of resistance.
 1 T.M. at   M.12.c.42.57.
 1 T.M. at   M.12.c.53.61.
 2 T.M's at   N.7.a.32.20.

(2.) The remaining 4 T.M's will be sited in positions which will shortly be reconnoitred to cover the WESTOUTRE line.

(3.) Work on (1) (a) and (b) will be proceeded with as rapidly as possible.

Work on (2) will not be commenced till the Trench Mortar personnel now engaged on burying cable complete their task.

(4). 75 rounds per mortar will be maintained at each emplacement.

APPENDIX "C".
Issued with 41st D.A. Defence Scheme No.2.

9th July 1918.

O. P's.

41st DIVISIONAL ARTILLERY.

PIN-POINT.	CODE NAME	BY WHOM MANNED.
M.17.d.75.85.	LANCASTER.	Right Group.
N.7.c.40.02.	DOVER.	Left Group.

41st. DIVISION OBSERVATION SECTION.

M.17.d.75.85.	-	)
N.7.c.40.02.	-	) Divisional Observers.

XIX CORPS HEAVY ARTILLERY.

| M.18.b.90.90. | EATON. | 6th Brigade R.G.A. |
| M.12.d.80.00. | - | 65th Brigade R.G.A. |

SECRET.   "D"   Copy No.

41st. DIVISIONAL ARTILLERY INSTRUCTIONS No. 5.

Liaison between Artillery and Infantry.

The following procedure will be adopted regarding Liaison with and visiting of Infantry in the line.

1. A specially selected senior Liaison Officer, who may be one of the Lieutenant Colonels other than the Group Commander, will be detailed for duty with each Infantry Brigade in the line when any active operations either defensive or offensive are in prospect; this Officer will remain with the Infantry Brigadier for the whole period of these operations. In normal circumstances a senior Liaison Officer will be told off for a tour of duty with Infantry Brigade and this Officer should be changed as seldom as possible having due regard to the efficiency of his unit; if possible he should remain during the whole tour of the Infantry Brigade.

Should Group Headquarters and Infantry Brigade Headquarters be adjacent, which is the ideal arrangement, the above does not apply.

2. Liaison Officers will be detailed with Battalions on either of the following principles:-
   (a). For a period of 3 or 4 days: which duty does not necessitate his sitting at Battalion Headquarters for the whole period. This Officer should be responsible for all R.A. Signalling communications with Battalion Headquarters and should work with the Battalion Signal Officer; he should know all O.P's in his area, his way about all trenches, the whereabouts of Company and Platoon Headquarters and be personally acquainted with the Commanders themselves; he should be prepared to accompany the Battalion Commander on his rounds if required and able to furnish information as to what batteries cover the front, and their respective zones, and generally to advise the Battalion Commander on any Artillery points which may arise.

   (b). For a night only, in which case an Officer who has done a tour by day at an O.P. will proceed at dusk to Battalion Headquarters and stay there the night, returning to his Battery next morning; his duty being to advise the Battalion Commander on Artillery matters and acquaint the Group Commander with the situation.

Method (a) will be adopted as soon as possible; arrangements are being made for accommodation for the Liaison Officer to be provided where this does not already exist. This Officer should not be relieved at the same time as the Infantry Battalion.

P.T.O.

It is obvious that the value of a Battalion Liaison Officer is much reduced without direct communication with the Artillery covering the Sector, but this cannot always be provided at present owing to shortage of wire.

3. Each Group Commander will arrange that not only Infantry Brigade Headquarters is visited by him or his representative daily but that each Battalion Headquarters is similarly visited by the O.C. Brigade covering it and if possible Company Commanders also.

Each Battalion will be visited daily by at least one of the Battery Commanders covering it and whenever possible Company and Platoon Commanders also will be visited by this Officer. A roster of Battery Commanders will be kept for this purpose, but this does not mean that no Battery Commander is to go near his Battalion except when detailed.

4. Battalion Commanders should be provided with a sketch showing Artillery dispositions of all guns covering their front.

5. All Artillery Officers should know their sectors intimately; complaints have been made that Liaison Officers with Battalions are not fully acquainted with the Sectors they cover: this is perhaps unavoidable with the large number of young Officers who have recently joined the Artillery but it should be a matter of personal pride that all Artillery Officers know at least as much of the Sectors as the Infantry holding them. This can be arranged by Officers not actually required for duty with the guns visiting the trenches and becoming acquainted as much as possible with all O.P's, Battalion, Company and Platoon Headquarters &c. &c.

6. The object aimed at in the foregoing instructions is the closest possible touch with the Infantry; the moral support afforded to the latter by the constant and daily presence of Artillery Officers amongst them is very great. This is particularly so in times of stress when all Artillery Officers are needed with their batteries and the Infantry then realize that it is not want of will that prevents the daily visits of their comrades in the Artillery, which will be resumed at the earliest possible moment.

It is fully understood that the procedure outlined above is carried out already to a very great extent and attention is only drawn to these points on a fresh Division coming into the line with Artillery from various other Divisions covering it.

F. MacFarlane
Captain, R.F.A.
Brigade Major,
41st Divisional Artillery.

30-4-18.

SECRET.   41st D.A. No. S.979.

2nd AMENDMENT to APPENDIX "E" 41st D.A. DEFENCE SCHEME No.2.

1. The Rifle Grenade Signal mentioned in Amendment to Appendix "E" of 41st D.A. Defence Scheme No.2 dated 17-7-18 to show that the enemy is attacking or preparing to attack the SCHERPENBERG - DICKEBUSCH LAKE line will be changed to a Rifle Grenade bursting into RED over RED over RED from 12 noon 20th July.

2. After S.O.S. Barrage II has commenced the ordinary S.O.S. Signal in force on the front will be used in the event of any further attack.

3. The 6 6" Newton T.M's covering the SCHERPENBERG - DICKEBUSCH LAKE line will open fire on their S.O.S. lines in S.O.S. Barrage II as soon as the signal denoting an attack on that line is sent up without waiting for orders from D.A.H.Q. as previously ordered.

F.H. MacFarlan
Captain R.F.A.
Brigade Major,
41st Divisional Artillery.

20th July 1918.

Issued to all recipients of 41st D.A. Defence Scheme No.2.

SECRET.   41st D.A. No. S.949.

AMENDMENT to 41st D.A. Defence Scheme No.2, Appendix "E".

Cancel para. 4 and substitute the following:-

S.O.S. barrage II will only come into force by order from D.A.H.Q.

In the event of all other means of communication having failed the signal that the enemy is attacking or preparing to attack the SCHERPENBERG - DICKEBUSCH LAKE Line will be a rifle grenade signal - White turning to Green - sent up from the SCHERPENBERG by an Officer who will be detailed for this duty by Right Infantry Brigade.

The signal will be repeated from the other infantry Bde. H.Q's and will be reported, immediately it is seen, by Artillery Group Commanders to D.A.H.Q.

F.M. MacFarlane
Captain R.F.A.
Brigade Major,
41st Divisional Artillery.

17-7-18.

Issued to all recipients of 41st D.A. Defence Scheme No.2.

APPENDIX "E".

Issued with 41st D.A.Defence Scheme No.2.

9th July 1918.

S. O. S. INSTRUCTIONS.

1. The defence of the forward system of the divisional sector falls into the following phases.

    (a). The defence of the forward zone.

    (b). The defence of the SHERPENBERG - LA CLYTTE main line of resistance.

2. The S.O.S. barrage for (a) will be known as:-
    S.O.S. Barrage I.
    The S.O.S. barrage for (b) will be known as:-
    S.O.S. Barrage II.

3. The four forward T.M's will fire on S.O.S.Barrage I as laid down; during phase (a); if and when requested by Infantry holding defended localities (SCHERPENBERG spur, FERMOY FARM) they will bring in their fire to the following points to assist by close fire in the defence of these posts M.18.c.85.05; M.18.d.7.3.; N.13.c.1.4.; N.13.d.4.8. Should the infantry holding the posts be compelled to withdraw the T.M.personnel will accompany the rear guard, using rifles as opportunity offers - it is of the utmost importance that the T.M. fire be kept up to the last as a premature withdrawal might emperil the defenders of the posts.
    The closest liaison is to be maintained between T.M's and Infantry holding these posts.

    Beyond the four T.M's mentioned above, no guns will be withdrawn from S.O.S.Barrage I.

4. S.O.S.Barrage II will only come into force by order from Divl. H.Q. or, should all communications fail, on a signal which will be notified later from the SCHERPENBERG; this signal will be repeated from Infantry Brigade H.Q. The Officer Commanding on the SCHERPENBERG is responsible for this signal being sent up. Immediately it is seen all batteries (and T.M's covering main line of resistance) will come down on S.O.S.Barrage II.

5. Tasks for S.O.S. Barrages I and II are attached.

6. The S.O.S. signal at present in use is a rifle grenade bursting into 3 red parachute lights one above the other or the "ALARM" sounded on bugles.

7. An S.O.S. Call in any shape or form on the divisional front will be immediately answered in preference to any other task by all Batteries. If any doubt exists fire will be opened at once till the situation is cleared up.

P.T.O.

The following will be the rates of fire:-

18-pdrs. 4 rounds per gun per minute)
4.5" Hows. 3   "   "   "   "   ") for 10 minutes.
6" Newtons.4   "   "   "   "   ")

18-pdrs. 50% A and AX (106 fuze)
4.5" Hows. BX 106 fuze.

Fire will cease after 10 minutes unless called for again or under the following circumstances:-

(a). during a hostile bombardment
(b). during a mist
(c). if it is evident that a hostile attack has not been beaten off

in which case the procedure laid down for S.O.S. will be repeated at the following rates:-

18-pdrs. 3 rounds per gun per minute.
4.5" Hows. 2   "   "   "   "   "

with intervals between the 10 minute bursts of 20 minutes in the case of (a) and (b) and 4 minutes in the case of (c)

This procedure will be carried out for 2 hours or at the discretion of Group Commanders in case of (a) and (b) and until it becomes clear that the attack has been beaten off in case (c).

8. F.O.O's and Infantry should be instructed to send up S.O.S. rockets at intervals until the hostile attack fails

9. Any Battery receiving an S.O.S. call will immediately inform its Brigade Headquarters and neighbouring Batteries

Brigade Headquarters will inform D.A.H.Q. and their affiliated infantry Brigades.

10. Tracings shewing S.O.S. Barrage lines I and II of M.G's, T.M's, field and heavy Artillery are attached.

SECRET. 41st D.A. No. S.1068.

To all recipients of 41st D.A. Defence Scheme No. 2.

1. Present tasks for S.O.S. Barrages I and II are as set out in annexed sheet.

2. Boundary between Right and Centre Groups as set out in 41st D.A. No. S.1023 of 25th instant ("Para. 4 Artillery Boundaries") should read "N.19.a.8.8. - N.26.a.6.6."

                                              Major, R.F.A.
                                              A/Brigade Major,
31-7-18.   41st Divisional Artillery.

S.O.S. TASKS. BARRAGE I (covering Front Line).

Right Group

18-pdrs. 1 bty.	M.30.b.40.95. — M.24.d.80.25.	
1 "	N.19.a.9.3. — N.19.b.60.65.	
1 "	ditto.	(superimposed).
4.5"Hows 6 hows.	M.24.d.85.35. — N.19.c.30.80.	

Centre Group.

18-pdrs. 1 bty.	N.19.b.98.85. — N.14.c.30.05.
1 "	N.14.c.63.25. — N.14.d.25.75.
4.5"Hows 1 Section	N.19.a.70.15. — N.19.a.85.25.
1 "	N.19.b.7.7. — N.19.b.85.75.
1 "	N.14.c.37.07. — N.14.c.53.20.

Left Group.

18-pdrs. 1 bty.	N.14.c.63.25. — N.14.d.25.75.
2 sections	N.14.b.40.00. — N.14.b.60.30.
1 section	N.14.b.85.75. — N.15.a.3.6.
4.5"Hows.1 "	N.14.d.30.80. — N.14.d.35.92.
2 sections	N.14.b.65.35. — N.14.b.85.65.

Trench Mortars. 3 T.M's. N.19.a.45.00, N.19.c.35.85,, N.19.a.66.10.

1 T.M. N.14.c.40.15.

P. T. O.

31-7-18.

S.O.S. TASKS. BARRAGE II (covering SCHERPENBERG - LA CLYTTE LINE).

Right Group

18-pdrs.	2 btys.	M.24.a.1.9. - M.18.c.5.4.
	1 " 4 guns.	M.18.b.3.3. - M.18.b.52.48.
	2 guns.	M.18.b.8.4. - M.18.b.95.40.

4.5" Hows. 6 hows.   M.18.c.5.4. - M.18.b.3.3.

Centre Group.

| 18-pdrs. | 1 bty. | N.13.a.64.50. - N.13.a.95.73. |
| | 1 " | N.13.b.30.90. - N.13.b.70.92. - N.7.d.98.26. |

4.5" Hows. 6 hows.   M.18.b.45.60.
M.18.b.66.44.
N.13.a.22.38.
N.13.a.32.40.
N.13.a.46.42.
N.13.a.56.47.

Left Group.

18-pdrs.	1 bty.	N.13.b.30.90. - N.13.b.70.92. - N.7.d.98.26.
	1 " 2 guns	N.8.c.45.70. - N.8.c.68.75.
	4 "	N.8.d.13.86. - N.8.d.76.88.

4.5" Hows. 6 Hows.   N.8.c.10.27.
N.8.c.23.41.
N.8.c.32.53.
N.8.c.37.63.
N.8.c.87.83.
N.8.c.98.87.

Trench Mortars.   M.23.b.78.60.
M.23.b.97.86.
M.24.a.18.82.
N.13.a.04.26.
N.13.a.13.31.
N.13.b.78.88.

31-7-18.   ----------

S E C R E T.   APPENDIX "F".   Issued with 41st D.A. Defence Scheme No.2.   10th July 1918.

Serial No.	Situation.	Code Call.	To whom sent.	Brigade to take action.	Action taken.
1.	Attack on Division on our Right, and no attack on 41st Division.	HELP LOCRE.	41st Divl. Arty.	Left Group 41st D.A.	1 Bty. 4.5"Hows.area M.30.a.4.0.-M.30.b.0.3. 1 Bty. 18-prs. road M.30.b.2.0.-M.30.b.2.6. 1 Bty. 18-prs. valley M.30.b.55.00-M.30.b.55.65.
2.	Attack on Divn.on our Left, and no attack on 41 Division.	HELP LA POLKA	41st Divl. Arty.	Right Group 41st D.A.	1 Bty. 18-prs. search & sweep area N.14.d.7.5.-N.14.b.7.1. N.15.a.7.1. N.15.c.7.3. to limit of range. 1 Bty. 18-prs. search & sweep N.15.d.0.2.-N.15.d.0.9. N.15.d.9.3. N.15.d.9.2. to limit of range. 1 Bty. 4.5"Hows. Road Junctions in KEMMEL village, N.21.d.0.2. and N.of cross roads N.21.d.4.4.
3.	Attack on 41st Divn.	HELP SCHERPENBERG.	35th D.A.	detailed by 35th D.A.	1 Bty.18-prs. M.30.d.80.30.to M.30.b.50.00. 1 Bty.18-prs. Cross Roads N.19.c.30.00. 1 Bty.18-prs. M.19.c.90.50.- N.19.d.50.10. 2 4.5"Hows. M.30.d.10.20.- N.30.d.20.60. 2 4.5"Hows. N.25.a.00.00.- N.25.a.10.20. 2 4.5"Hows. N.25.b.40.10.- N.25.b.10.50.
		HELP ROSSIGNOL.	6th D.A.	detailed by 6th Divl.Arty.	2 Btys.18-prs.Barrage road N.20.b.9.5.- N.15.a.7.1.& trenches parallel to this road. 2 4.5"Hows.on Northern exits of KEMMEL Village 2 4.5"Hows.on road & trenches N.of ROSSIGNOL WOOD.

RFA

SECRET. 　　　　　　　　　　　　　41st D.A. No. S.1030.

AMENDMENT No. 2 to Appendix "H" 41st D.A. Defence Scheme No. 2.

Positions for E.POP Line in accordance with Add. No. 2 of the above Defence Scheme are re-allotted as under:-

	4 guns.	2 guns
187th Brigade,	R.1.d.60.20.	R.5.c.90.40.
H.Q., R.2.d.70.70.	R.2.c.60.50.	R.5.c.90.60.
	R.3.d.40.80.	R.5.c.65.90.
Hows.	R.2.d.85.30.	R.5.b.30.15.
190th Brigade.	R.2.a.20.65.	R.3.b.80.90.
	R.3.b.70.40.	L.36.c.40.80.
	R.4.c.20.65.	G.31.d.00.80.
Hows.	L.32.b.00.20.	G.31.d.20.50.
150th Army Brigade.	L.32.c.75.80.	L.35.a.70.40.
	L.33.b.30.25.	L.35.a.75.25.
	L.33.d.90.80.	L.36.a.50.00.
Hows.	L.27.c.25.65.	L.35.a.65.50.

　　　　　　　　　　　　　　　　R L Creasy
　　　　　　　　　　　　　　　　Major, R.F.A.
　　　　　　　　　　　　　　　　A/ Brigade Major,
26-7-18.　　　　　　　　　　　　41st Divisional Artillery.

APPENDIX "H" to 41st D.A.
Defence Scheme No.2.

17-7-18.

1. In the event of an enemy attack penetrating our defences and our troops falling back to the REDOUBT LINE, Group Commanders will exercise their discretion as to ordering Batteries to withdraw.

2. In the event of such a withdrawal Group Commanders will each detail one Battery to retire gradually fighting its way back while the remainder of the Batteries in the group retire to positions covering the EAST POPERINGHE Line (a trace of which is attached).

3. Positions are allotted as follows:-

	4 guns.	2 guns.	
187th Bde.	R.1.d.60.20.	R.5.c.90.40.	)
H.Q.,R.2.d.70.70.	R.2.c.60.50.	R.5.c.90.60.	)
	R.3.d.40.80.	R.5.c.65.90.	) Right
	Hows.R.2.d.85.30.	R.5.b.30.15.	) Group.
			)
150th Bde.	ˣR.2.a.20.65.	R.3.b.80.90.	)
H.Q.R.3.a.30.40.	ˣR.3.b.70.40.	L.36.c.40.80.	)
(if functioning)	R.4.c.20.65.	G.31.d.00.60.	)
	How. L.32.b.00.20.	G.31.d.20.50.	)
			) Left
190th Bde.	L.32.c.75.80.	L.35.a.70.40.	) Group.
H.Q.L.33.c.90.90.	L.33.b.30.25.	L.35.a.75.25.	)
	L.33.d.90.80.	L.36.a.50.00.	)
	How. L.27.c.25.65.	L.35.a.65.50.	)

ˣ one of these positions to be left vacant for A/150.

4. The following positions will be left vacant for a reinforcing Brigade:-

	L.28.a.60.50.	G.31.b.20.20.
H.Q.L.34.b.40.25.	L.35.c.55.15.	L.35.d.45.20.
	R.5.b.20.60.	R.5.b.50.80.
	How.L.33.b.85.40.	L.36.a.10.35.

5. No work has been done on above positions but all are easy of access.

6. Group Commanders will sub-allot positions to batteries as soon as possible.
Batteries retiring first will occupy those positions closest up to the line.

7. The inter-group Artillery boundary will be continued from M.4.a.7.6. to G.32.d.8.3.

8. The Divisional Sector of the E. POP Line extends from G.26.d.5.5. to M.1.d.9.4.

9. The E. POP. Line will be held by the 27th American Division.

10. Anything in the nature of a premature withdrawal will be avoided and all ground fought for to the last possible moment as the re-establishment of our line on the SCHERPENBERG if lost will be attempted at all costs.

SECRET.   41st D.A. No.S.977.   20th July 1918.

ADDENDUM to APPENDIX "H" 41st D.A.
DEFENCE SCHEME No.2.

1. O.P's.

The following two O.P's for the E. POP. Line have been selected and work is being commenced forthwith.

Left Group. Pillbox at G.32.b.94.40.

Right Group. Pillbox at M.2.b.67.92.

2. COMMUNICATIONS.

Air lines are being laid to all Brigade Headquarters for the E.POP line from D.A.H.Q.

The two O.P's mentioned above are being connected to the bury running throught G.32. and 26.

F.N. MacFarlane
Captain R.F.A.
Brigade Major,
41st Divisional Artillery.

To all recipients of 41st D.A.Defence Scheme No.2.

SECRET.

AMENDMENT to APPENDIX "H" of 41st D.A. DEFENCE SCHEME No. 2.

Cancel para. 2 and substitute the following:-

2.   In the event of such a withdrawal Right Group batteries will retire to their forward section positions for the E.POP Line from which they will cover their sector of the WESTOUTRE - GOED MOET MILL Line.

    They will occupy these forward section positions with all available guns so long as this line holds and will withdraw all guns except one section per battery to their main battery positions for the defence of the E. POP Line when an attack on that line appears imminent.

    Left Group Batteries will send one section per Battery to their forward section positions for the E. POP Line.

    The remainder of the Left Group guns will come into action in positions which will be notified later in the valley in G.32. to cover the WESTOUTRE GOED MOET MILL Line.

    These guns will retire to their main battery positions for covering the E.POP Line when an attack on the latter develops.

    All retirements will be carried out as far as the exigencies of the situation permit so as to ensure not more than half the guns of a Group being out of action at the same time.

                                              Captain R.F.A.
                                             Brigade Major,
18-7-18.   41st Divisional Artillery.

SECRET.

ADDENDUM No.2 to APPENDIX "H" 41st D.A. Defence Scheme No.2.

1. In the event of a withdrawal to the E.POP Line, 41st British D.A. will come under the orders of the C.R.A. 27th American Division (C.R.A. 66th British Division), and will be disposed as follows:-

    (a). 187 and 190th Bdes.- Subgroups covering CONDIMENT CROSS Subsector (RIGHT Subsector) in positions already reconnoitred (vide 41st D.A. Defence Scheme No.2 App.H.)

    Regimental Headquarters.- COMMANDANTS HOUSE L.34.a.7.8.

    Battalion H.Q.   FRENCH HOUSE G.31.b.6.0.

    C.R.A. 41st British Division will establish his H.Q. with RIGHT AMERICAN INFANTRY Bde. at ABEELE AERODROME L.31.a.

    (b). 150th Army Bde. R.F.A. will form a group with 11th Army Bde. R.F.A. under O.C. 150th Brigade covering HOOGRAAF Subsector (Centre Subsector).

    Regimental Headquarters.- BODO FARM L.28.b.1.3.

    Battalion H.Q.   EBDEN HOUSE - G.25.d.45.50.

    This group will come under the orders of either C.R.A. 6th or C.R.A. 41st British Divisions according to the situation.

2. Officer i/c 41st D.A. Signals will make the necessary arrangements for communication for both (a) and (b) as above.

3. Groups of 66th British D.A. at present covering E POP Line will remain directly under C.R.A. 66th British Divn. until such time as a re-adjustment can be made. They will then come as Subgroups under the orders of the respective Group Commanders.

4. ACKNOWLEDGE.

                                R.A. Creasy
                                Major R.F.A.
                                A/Brigade Major,
25th July 1918.   41st Divisional Artillery.

Issued to all recipients of 41st D.A. Defence Scheme No.2.

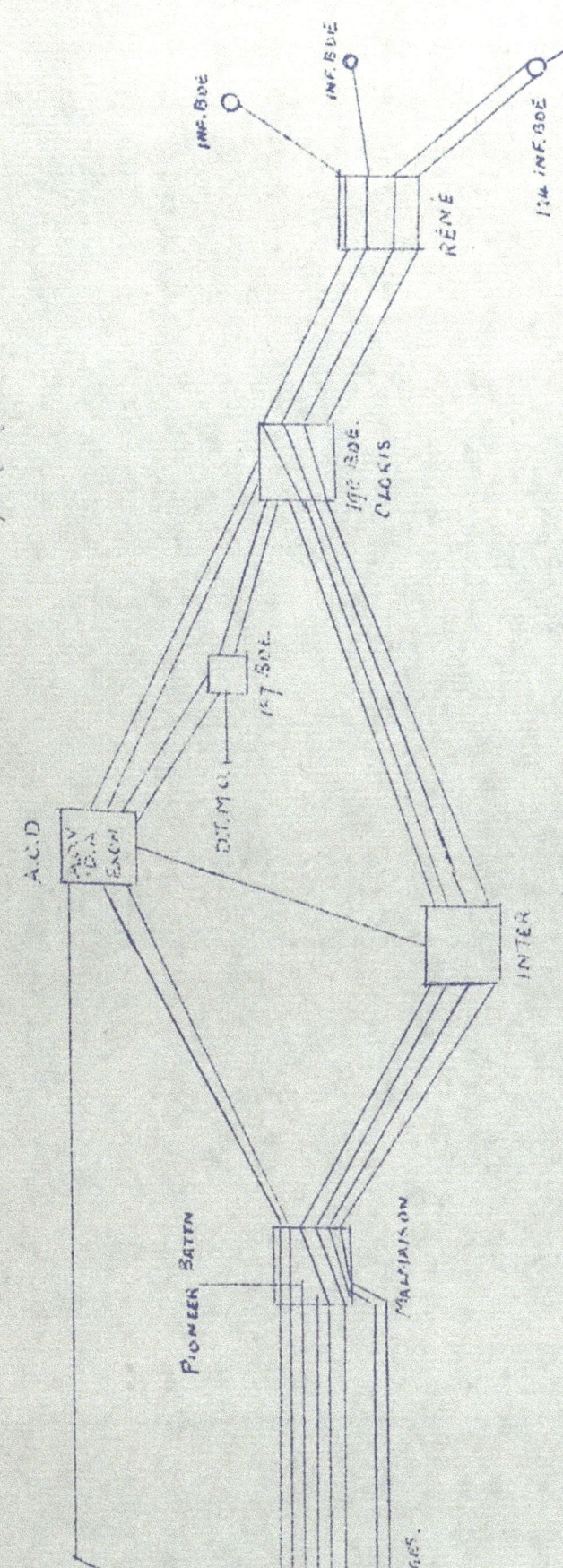

SECRET.   APPENDIX "J"

ADMINISTRATIVE ARRANGEMENTS.

(1) ACCOMMODATION.

The D.A. is accommodated as shown in Schedule of Accommodation attached (
Sub-area Commandants in the Divisional Area are located as follows:-

    LAPPE Sub-area - 2/Lieut. D.E. CARLEY   27/L.34.a.8.8.
    ABEELE   do   Lt.Col. B. FLETCHER   27/L.31.d.0.5.
    ST. ELOY "   2/Lieut. SKINNER.   27/K.35.d.5.5.

(2) AMMUNITION.

Army and Corps Railheads are as follows:-

	XK	ESQUELBECQ		27/C.7.b.8.8.
%	XGD	HEIDEBEEK		19/X.19.b & d.
%	XGA	STRAFFEHEM		27/F.2.c.
%	XGF	WATOU		27/E.18.c.8.9.
	XD	BLENDECQUES STN.		
	XDA	CAMPAGNE		
% x	XG	SWISS COTTAGE	11 Corps	20/S.28.a.
x	XOB	PESELHOEK	11 Corps	28/A.14.c.
% x	XOA	WESTONHOEK		28/G.4.a.
x	XC	PACIFIC		28/G.10.a.
	ODA	EBBLINGHEM	No.1 Dump	27/U.21.cent.
x	ODB	HONDEGHEM	" 2 "	27/T.6.b.
% x	OKB	ABEELE SIDING		27/L.27.b.
	XKA	BAVINCHOVE	Heavy	27/O.21.a.8.5.
			Light	27/I.23.b.4.4.

    % Empties may be sent.
    x Advanced Corps Railheads.

XIXth Corps Reserve Dumps are as follows:-

    LE NOUVEAU MONDE for Field Ammunition S.A.A. Grenades etc.) not yet
    WINNEZEELE SOUTH for Heavy and Siege Ammunition   ) in oper-
)   ation.

The Divisional Dump is located at STEEN AKKER, R.2.b.5.8. to which ammunition is delivered by Light Railway. Issues will not be made from this Dump until existing dumps at K.35.b.1.7 and K.27.a.9.3. are exhausted.

At present D.A.C. draws by horse transport and delivers to battery wagon lines, whence ammunition is taken by battery wagons to gun positions.

(3) SUPPLY.

Railhead is at STEENVOORDE.
No. 1 Coy. 41st Divl. Train draws from STEENVOORDE and delivers to wagon lines in the usual way.
Artillery units notify O.C. No. 1 Coy direct of any change in location and arrange guides, if required.

(4) PERSONNEL.

Railhead for personnel MENDINGHEM.

P.T.O.

(5) ORDNANCE.

D.A.D.O.S., 41st Division is located at ABEELE AERODROME.

Nos. 11 and 12 Light Mobile Workshops are located at Sheet 27, K.17.b.2.2.

(6) R.E. STORES.

Divisional Dump is at STEEN AKKER, L.32.d.4.0, but is in process of being moved to LOYE, R.5.b.0.9.

Lieut. STRATTON, M.C., R.E. is accommodated at 41st D.A.H.Q. and advises on constructional work. All indents for R.E. material are forwarded direct to him.

Lieut. MACWHINNEY, R.F.A. Corps Camouflage Officer is accommodated by 6th D.A. Indents for camouflage are forwarded direct to him.

(7) WATER SUPPLY.

Water cart refilling points are at,

REMY SIDING.
S.W. of HOOGRAAF CABT.
ABEELE STATION.

Barrel reservoirs are at,

Right Brigade. M.11.b.6.2.
Centre Brigade M.5.a.6.6.
Left Brigade   M.6.a.0.9.

(8) BATHS

Baths are situate at K.29.b.central and L.29.c.7.2.

(9) TRAFFIC.

Lorries do not proceed further east than BOESCHEPE - WIPPENHOEK road in daylight.

Horse transport does not proceed further east than the N & S grid line between squares G.31 and G.32 in daylight.

(10) MISCELLANEOUS.

Steel helmets and box respirators in the alert position are worn by all ranks east of the N & S grid line between squares G.31 and G.32.

SECRET.   41st D.A. No. S.1023.

1.   In consequence of the division of the Field Artillery covering 41st Division front into 3 groups, the following amendments will be made in 41st D.A. Defence Scheme No.2 dated 9th instant.

Para.1 **Dispositions.**   Cancel sub para. (a) and substitute -

Right Group   **Batteries**

H.Q. M.2.a.9.9.   A, B, C, D 187.
Lt. Col. C.D.G. LYON, D.S.O. R.F.A.

Centre Group

H.Q. G.33.d.7.5.   A, B, C, D 190.
Lt. Col. G.A. CARDEW, C.M.G., D.S.O., R.F.A.

Left Group

H.Q. G.29.c.15.15.   B, C, D 150.
Lt. Col. F.A. DIXON, D.S.O., R.F.A.

Each Group will cover an Infantry Brigade in the line.

Para. 3 **Liaison**   cancel and substitute -

Each group will find a Liaison Officer with the Headquarters of its Infantry Brigade and Battalion in the line if required.

Para. 4 **Artillery Boundaries**   Cancel and substitute -

Southern Boundary - M.24.d.00.60 - N.31.a.85.80.
Boundary between Right & Centre Groups N.19.a.6.0.-N.26.a.6.8.
   "   "   Centre & Left   "   LA CLYTTE-KEMMEL road
                                        (inclusive to Centre Group)

Northern Boundary - N.9.c.0.0. - N.22.central.

Para.8 HARASSING FIRE; Sub para (b) - Cancel lines 7 - 10 - substitute -

Ammunition allotment for harassing fire is as follows per 24 hours:-

     18-pdr.   230 rounds per battery.
     4.5" How. 200   "   "   "

2. ACKNOWLEDGE.

                                  R.J. Cecil
                                         Major R.F.A.
                                         A/Brigade Major,
25th July 1918.   41st Divisional Artillery.

Issued to all recipients of 41st D.A. Defence Scheme No.2.

AMENDMENTS to APPENDICES 41st D.A. Defence Scheme No. 2.

1. APPENDIX "A"   To be amended in accordance with foregoing.

    ADD following location:-
        LEFT GROUP (150 Bde. R.F.A.)
        H.Q. G.29.c.25.45   Wagon lines K.23.a.25.20.

2. APPENDIX "C"   O.P's

    In column 3 "By whom manned" for Left Group read "Left Group and Centre Group".

    N.B. The necessary communications will be arranged forthwith.

3. APPENDIX "E". S.O.S. Tasks. Barrage I and II.

    Cancel and Substitute tables attached.

4. APPENDIX "F". Mutual support.

    Serial No.1   Brigade to take action
        For "Left Group 41st D.A."
        Read Centre Group 41st D.A.   1 Bty 4.5" Hows.
              Left Group 41st D.A.   1 Bty 18-pdrs.
                                        1 Bty 18-pdrs.

    Serial No.2   For "Right Group 41st D.A."
        Read Right Group 41st D.A.   1 Bty. 18-pdrs.
                                        1 Bty. 18-pdrs.
             Centre Group 41st D.A.   1 Bty. 4.5" Hows.

    Pinpoints of targets to be engaged as before.

5. APPENDIX "G"

    Boundaries of C.P. areas should be altered in tracing to correspond with new group boundaries.

6. APPENDIX "H"   Para. 3.

    187 Bde. remains Right Group as before.
    190 Bde. becomes Centre Group.
    150th Bde.   "   Left Group.
    but see ADD. 2 to App. H. issued herewith.
    Para.7   Cancel and substitute :-

    The inter group artillery boundaries will be continued as follows:-

    Between Right & Centre - M.2.b.1.4. - M.12.c.4.4 - N.19.a.8.3.
    Between Centre & Left - G.33.c.2.7. - M.6.c.5.5. -
                             M.12.b.5.7. - M.7.central -
                             N.14.a.1.5.

7. APPENDIX "K"   Forward Wagon Lines:-
    The necessary re-grouping into Right, Centre & Left Group instead of Right and Left Group.

8. ADDENDUM No.S.898 dated 11th July.
    Para.1. Cancel lines 3, 4 & 5 & substitute "boundaries as shewn in amended App. "H" para.7.

S.O.S. TASKS. BARRAGE I (covering outpost line).

Right Group

18-pdrs. 1 Bty.   M.30.b.40.95. - M.24.d.80.25.

1 Bty.   N.19.a.9.3. - N.19.b.60.05.

1 Bty.   Ditto   (superimposed.)

4.5" Hows. 6 Hows.   M.24.d.85.35. - N.19.c.30.80.

Centre Group

18-pdrs. 1 Bty.   N.19.b.98.85. - N.14.c.30.05.

1 Bty.   N.14.c.63.25. - N.14.d.25.75.

1 Bty.   Ditto   (superimposed)

4.5"Hows. 1Section   N.19.a.70.15. - N.19.a.85.25.

1Section   N.19.b.7.7   - N.19.b.85.75.

1Section   N.14.c.37.07. - N.14.c.53.20.

Left Group

18-pdrs. 1 Bty.   N.14.b.40.00. - N.14.b.60.30.

1 Bty.   N.14.b.85.75. - N.15.a.3.6.

4.5"Hows. 1Section   N.14.d.30.80. - N.14.d.35.92.

2Sections N.14.b.65.35. - N.14.b.85.65

Outpost line T.M's. 3 T.M's   N.19.a.45.00, N.19.c.35.85,
                               N.19.a.66.10.

1 T.M.   N.14.c.40.15.

P. T. O.

S.O.S. TASKS. BARRAGE II. (Covering SCHERPENBERG - LA CLYTTE LINE).

Right Group.

18-pdrs. 1 Bty.	M.24.a.1.9.	- M.18.c.5.4.
1 Bty. 4 guns.	M.18.a.85.15.	- M.18.b.52.48.
2 guns.	M.18.b.8.4.	- M.18.b.95.40.
1 Bty.	M.18.a.85.15.	- M.18.b.52.48. (superimposed).

4.5" Hows. 6 Hows.   M.18.c.65.45.
M.18.c.80.55.53
M.18.c.93.62.
M.18.c.98.82.
M.18.c.95.95.
M.18.d.92.08.

Centre Group.

18-pdrs. 1 Bty.	N.13.a.64.50.	- N.13.a.95.73.
1 Bty.	N.13.b.30.90.	- N.13.b.70.92. - N.7.d.98.26.
1 Bty.	ditto.	(superimposed).

4.5" Hows. 6 Hows.   M.18.b.45.60.
M.18.b.66.44.
N.13.a.22.38.
N.13.a.32.40.
N.13.a.46.42.
N.13.a.56.47.

Left Group.

18-pdrs. 1 Bty. 2 guns.	N.8.c.40.70.	- N.8.c.51.72.
4 guns.	N.8.d.13.86.	- N.8.d.76.88.
1 Bty. 4 guns.	N.8.d.13.86.	- N.8.d.76.88. (superimpose
2 guns.	N.8.c.63.73.	- N.8.c.74.77.

4.5" Hows. 6 Hows.   N.8.c.10.27.
N.8.c.23.41.
N.8.c.32.53.
N.8.c.37.63.
N.8.c.87.83.
N.8.c.98.87.

Trench Mortars.   M.23.b.78.60.
M.23.b.97.96.
M.24.a.18.82.
N.13.a.04.26.
N.13.a.13.31.
N.13.b.78.88.

(Appendix "D")

SECRET.   Copy No. 24

41st DIVISIONAL ARTILLERY INSTRUCTIONS No. 14.

1. The 6th and 33rd Divisions are attacking on 14-7-18 with the object of regaining our old front line.

    Objective

    Trench running from

    N.5.c.7.9. - N.5.b.12.08 - N.5.b.80.77 - H.36.b.45.30.

2. Zero hour will be about 6 a.m.

3. 41st Divisional Artillery will co-operate as follows:-

    (i). All 18-pdrs. of both groups will prolong the 6th Divisional Artillery creeping barrage as far as the KEMMEL - LA CLYTTE Road.

    (ii). All 4.5" Hows. of both groups will blind the enemy O.P's on the northern face of MOUNT KEMMEL with smoke and gas.

4. 18-pdr. tasks are shewn on the attached map "A".

    Rates of fire:- Zero to zero plus 11'   intense.
                     Zero plus 11' to Zero plus 40'   normal.

    Ammunition:-   Zero to zero plus 11'   A.
                    Zero plus 11' to zero plus 40'   50% A
                                                      50% AX.

    If weather conditions are favourable 18-pdrs will fire 10% smoke shell.
    This will be notified later by wire as follows:-

    Smoke to be used   "Rations will be delivered".

    Smoke not to be used   "Rations will not be delivered".

5. 4.5" How. tasks are shewn on attached map "B".

    Rates of fire and Ammunition.

        Zero to zero plus 10'   3 r.p.g.p.m. smoke.
    Zero plus 10' to zero plus 40'   ½ r.p.g.p.m. smoke
                                        2 r.p.g.p.m. gas B.C.B.R.)

6. A special weather forecast in connection with this operation will be issued at 12 midnight 13/14th and another at 3 a.m. 14th.
    On receipt of the latter, orders will be issued by D.A. as to which of the alternative Barrages shewn on map "B" will be employed.

7. For a period of 24 hours after Zero a special S.O.S. Signal will be employed on the front of attack. This will be a rifle grenade bursting into 3 stars RED over GREEN over YELLOW.

                                                    P.T.O.

8. As this operation is to be a surprise attack no registration beyond the normal will be carried out prior to Zero.

9. Zero hour and synchronization arrangements will be issued later.

10. ACKNOWLEDGE.

F.M. MacFarlane
Captain R.F.A.
Brigade Major,
Issued at:- 12 noon.   41st Divisional Artillery.

Copy No. 1 - 7   Right Group.
        8 - 13   Left Group.
         14   6th Divl. Arty.   )
         15   41st Divn. G.   )
         16   122nd Infy. Bde.   )
         17   123rd "   "   ) for information
         18   124th "   "   )
         19   D.T.M.O. 41st Divn.   ) without maps.
         20   35th Divl. Arty.   )
         21   XIX Corps R.A.   )
         22   XIX Corps H.A.   )
        23 - 28 War Diary & File   )

S E C R E T.   41st D.A. No. S.915.

ADDENDUM to 41st D.A. INSTRUCTIONS No.14.

1. It is possible that the 4.5" How. gas shell demanded for this operation will not arrive in time.

2. This will be notified to all concerned at 6 p.m.

3. In this eventuality the following changes in Barrage tasks will take place:-

   (a). O.C. Right Group will form the creeping Barrage with two 18-pdr. Batteries only.
      The remaining two 18-pdr. Batteries of the Right group will fire on the following tasks on Map "E"

        1 section task "A".
        2 sections " "B".
        2   "   " "C".
        2   "   " "D".

Rates of fire:-

    0 to 0 plus 10'   3 r.p.g.p.m. *smoke*
    0 plus 10' to 0 plus 40'   2 r.p.g.p.m. *smoke*

   (b). Rates of fire for 4.5" Hows. will be changed as follows:-

    0 to 0 plus 10'   2 r.p.g.p.m. *Smoke*
    0 plus 10' to 0 plus 35'   1 r.p.g.p.m. *Smoke*

                          Jh. MacFarlan
                          Captain R.F.A.
                          Brigade Major,
13-7-18.   41st Divisional Artillery.

Issued to all recipients of 41st D.A. Instructions No.14.

SECRET.

ADDENDUM to 41st D.A. INSTRUCTIONS No. 14.

1. In those portions of the 18-pdr. creeping barrage which are beyond shrapnel range for the batteries concerned, H.E. will be used.

2. From O plus 11' to O plus 40' those Batteries which can reach will search and sweep up to 500 yards beyond the line of the barrage.

13-7-18.

Captain R.F.A.
Brigade Major,
41st Divisional Artillery.

Issued to all recipients of 41st D.A. Instructions No. 14.

WD Appendix "E"

SECRET.　　　　　　　　　　　　　41st Div,
　　　　　　　　　　　　　　　　　G.17C.
　　　　　　　　　　　　　　　　　(3922).

41st. DIVISION INSTRUCTION No.5.

1. In future the various systems of defence in the XIX Corps area will be described as follows:-

   (a). The most advanced line occupied and its support and reserve trenches or posts will be called:-

   "THE FRONT SYSTEM".

   (b). The SCHERPENBERG - LA CLYTTE - N.8.b.4.5. - N.3.c.4.0.- N.3.d.5.8. - N.4.a.1.5. - H.34.c.3.2. line will be called:-

   "THE SCHERPENBERG - DICKEBUSCH LAKE LINE".

   (c). The line of supporting posts about M.10.b., M.11.b., M.6.d., N.1.central, H.32.d., H.26.d., H.27.a. will be called :-

   "THE REDOUBT LINE".

   (d). The line WESTOUTRE - East of ZEVECOTEN (G.35.d) - GOED MOET MILL (G.30.b) - junction of VLAMERTINGHE and BRANDHOEK lines in G.24.d. will be called:-

   "THE WESTOUTRE - GOED MOET MILL LINE".

   (e). The East POPERINGHE Line will be called :-

   "THE EAST POP. LINE".

2. No line will be designated "THE OUTPOST LINE" or "LINE OF RESISTANCE".

3. The necessary alterations will be made to all previous references in 41st Division Instructions Nos. 2 and 3 &c.

　　　　　　　　　　　　　　　(sd) E.A.Beck,
　　　　　　　　　　　　　　　Lieut-Colonel,
16th July 1918.　　　　　　　　General Staff.

　　　　　　　　　　　　　　　41st D.A. No. S.943.

The necessary alterations will be made to all previous references in 41st D.A.Defence Scheme No.2, etc.

　　　　　　　　　　　　　　　F.M.MacFarlane
　　　　　　　　　　　　　　　Captain R.F.A,
　　　　　　　　　　　　　　　Brigade Major,
16th July 1918.　　　　　　　　41st Divisional Artillery.

Left Group (6 copies)
Right Group (7 copies)
D.T.M.O.
D.A.C.　　(4 copies)
S.C.R.A.
R.C.R.A.

Appendix "F"
17/7/18

SECRET.   Right Group. (6 cos.)   41st D.A. No. S.953.
           Left   "   (2 ")

1. A Gas shell bombardment in conjunction with XIXth Corps H.A. will take place on night 18/19 or the first suitable night afterwards in accordance with bombardment table over.   July

2. The area to be shelled is divided into the following Sectors.

   Targets to be engaged in each sector are as follows:-

Sector A.	Sector B.	Sector C.
1. N.26.b.40.25.	1. N.26.b.10.10.	1. N.26.c.60.60.
2. N.26.b.30.60.	2. N.26.a.90.10.	2. N.26.c.40.60.
3. N.26.b.10.60.	3. N.26.c.70.90.	3. N.26.c.30.00.
4. N.26.a.90.60.	4. N.26.c.20.90.	4. N.26.c.10.40.
5. N.26.a.70.50.	5. N.25.b.85.05.	5. N.26.c.00.00.
6. N.26.a.00.45.	6. N.25.d.80.90.	6. N.25.d.90.20.
7. N.26.a.00.25.	7. N.25.d.80.60.	7. N.25.d.70.20.
8. N.25.b.80.30.	8. N.25.d.50.60.	8. N.25.d.30.10.

3. Targets in Sectors will be engaged by the following:-

   Sector A.   D/150 Battery, Right Group.
   Sector B.   D/187th Battery, "   "
   Sector C.   D/187th Battery, Left Group.

4. 18-pdrs. will co-operate as follows firing 50% A and 50% AX.

   Sector A.   1 forward Section Right Group.
   Sector B.   1   "   "   "   "
   Sector C.   1   "   "   "   "

5. From 1.30 a.m. to 1.55 p.m. D/190 will be required to support a raid on Centre Brigade front, details of which will be issued later.

   Targets Nos. A6, B6 and C6 will therefore be engaged by the following:-

   A6.   5 hows.   D/150.
   B6.   3 hows.   D/187.
   C6.   3 hows.   D/187.

6. Orders as to whether the bombardment will take place or not will be sent out by 10.30 p.m. from this office by the following code:-
   Bombardment will take place   CAT
   Bombardment will NOT take place   DOG.

7. Synchronization details will be issued later.

8. ACKNOWLEDGE.

                                    F. MacFarlan
                                    Captain R.F.A.
   Issued at:- 9.35 p.m.   Brigade Major, 41st Divl. Arty.

Copy for information to:-
   41st Divn. G.   122nd Infy. Bde.   D.A.C.   P.T.O.
   XIX Corps R.A.   123rd   "   "   D.T.M.O.
   XIX Corps H.A.   124th   "   "   41st M.G.Battn.

BOMBARDMENT TABLE.

Target.	TIME		No. & NATURE OF ROUNDS 41st D.A.		
	From.	To.			
A.1.	11.55 p.m.	11.57 p.m.	30 B.C.G.	8 A	8 AX.
	11.57 p.m.	12. 3 a.m.	60 B.N.C.	18 A	18 AX.
B.1.	11.55 p.m.	11.57 p.m.	30 B.C.G.	8 A	8 AX.
	11.57 p.m.	12. 3 a.m.	60 B.N.C.	18 A	18 AX.
C.1.	11.55 p.m.	11.57 p.m.	30 B.C.G.	8 A	8 A.X.
	11.57 p.m.	12. 3 a.m.	60 B.N.C.	18 A	18 AX.
A.2.	12. 8 a.m.	12.10 a.m.	"	"	"
	12.10 a.m.	12.16 a.m.	"	"	"
B.2.	"	"	"	"	"
C.2.	"	"	"	"	"
A.3.	12.21 a.m.	12.23 a.m.	"	"	"
	12.23 a.m.	12.29 a.m.			
B.3.	"	"	"	"	"
C.3.	"	"	"	"	"
A.4.	1. 0 a.m.	1. 2 a.m.	"	"	"
	1. 2 a.m.	1. 8 a.m.			
B.4.	"	"	"	"	"
C.4.	"	"	"	"	"
A.5.	1.13 a.m.	1.15 a.m.	"	"	"
	1.15 a.m.	1.21 a.m.			
B.5.	"	"	"	"	"
C.5.	"	"	"	"	"
A.6.	1.26 a.m.	1.28 a.m.	"	"	"
	1.28 a.m.	1.34 a.m.			
B.6.	"	"	"	"	"
C.6.	"	"	"	"	"
A.7.	2. 4 a.m.	2. 6 a.m.	"	"	"
	2. 6 a.m.	2.12 a.m.			
B.7.	"	"	"	"	"
C.7.	"	"	"	"	"
A.8.	2.17 a.m.	2.19 a.m.	"	"	"
	2.19 a.m.	2.25 a.m.			
B.8.	"	"	"	"	"
C.8.	"	"	"	"	"

Appendix "G"

SECRET. Copy No. 12

41st D.A. INSTRUCTION No.15.

18th July 1918.

1. On the night 18th/19th July the 11th Queens will carry out a small raid, with the object of obtaining identification, on the enemy's positions in the area bounded by the lines running from

   N.13.d.96.40. - N.20.a.27.90. and from
   N.14.c.72.15. - N.14.c.43.67.

2. 41st Divisional Artillery will co-operate in accordance with the attached programme "A".

3. 41st M.G. Battalion and 123 T.M.B are also co-operating.

4. 6th D.A. and 35th D.A. will co-operate as follows:-

   Each will put down a small box barrage on that portion of their divisional front closest to this divisional sector from Zero plus 5' to Zero plus 25'.
   The number of guns and the rate of fire to be employed is left to the discretion of C.R.As concerned but a box barrage is requested in each case sufficiently realistic to make the enemy suspect a raid at each point.

5. XIX Corps H.A. will ~~also co-operate~~ with Counter Battery work.

6. The following code will be used in connection with the operation:-

   TROUT - operation postponed 60 minutes.
   SALMON - operation cancelled.
   SHRIMPS - cease fire.
   MUSSELS - Resistance.
   PIKE   - party returning.
   COD   - all in.

7. Zero hour will be 1.30 a.m.

8. Time will be given over the telephone at 7.30 p.m. to Flank D.As. and 123rd Infantry Brigade. + C B 50
   An Officer to be detailed by O.C. 190th Brigade R.F.A. will be at H.Q. 123rd Infantry Brigade at that hour with a watch.

9. No mention of this operation is to be made on the telephone.

10. ACKNOWLEDGE.

F. MacFarlan
Captain R.F.A.
Brigade Major,
41st Divisional Artillery.

Issued at :- 10.30 a.m.

Copy No. 1 Left Group.   6. 122 Infy. Bde.
       2 6th Divl. Arty.   7. 123rd   "   "   12 War Diary.
       3. 35th Divl. Arty.   8. 124th   "   "   13)
       4. XIX Corps H.A.   9. Right Group.   14) File.
       5. 41st Divn. G.   10. L.T.M.O.   15)
                             11. XIX Corps R.A.   16 11th Queens.

TABLE "A" Issued with 41st D.A.
Instructions No.15.

18th July 1918.

x one of these with only 4 guns.

Left Group.

18-pdrs.	x 5 guns	Zero to Zero plus 25'	N.13.d.88.04.-N.20.a.22.55.
	x 5 guns	Zero to Zero plus 25'	N.14.c.70.65.-N.14.c.96.12
	6 guns	Zero to Zero plus 3'	N.19.b.94.96.-N.14.c.82.42.
	6 guns	Zero to Zero plus 3'	N.20.a.03.78.-N.14.c.84.38
	12 guns	Zero plus 3' to Zero plus 5')	N.20.a.03.78.-N.14.c.84.38
	"	Zero plus 5' to Zero plus 25')	N.20.a.22.55.-N.14.c.96.12
4.5"Hows.	2 hows.	Zero to Zero plus 25'	N.20.a.9.7. - N.20.b.0.5.
	1 how.		N.20.d.25.60.
	1 how.		N.19.b.8.9.
	1 how.		N.14.c.95.85.
	1 how.		N.14.c.94.50.
	All guns & hows.)	Zero plus 25'	Stop.

Rates of fire.

Zero to Zero plus 5'	Intense.
Zero plus 5' to Zero plus 15'	Rapid.
Zero plus 15' to Zero plus 25'	Normal.

If the Barrage is required for a longer period than laid down above, Officer Commanding Raid will fire a light signal bursting into 4 white stars.

On receipt of this all guns and hows. will go on shooting at normal rates for a further 15 minutes on the tasks they are firing on at Zero plus 25'.

O.C. Left Group will make the necessary arrangements for ensuring that this signal is transmitted without delay to Batteries.

W.D. Appendix "H".

SECRET. Copy No. 24

41st DIVISIONAL ARTILLERY ORDER No.10.

21st July 1918.

1. (i). Two bombardments by Heavy and Field Artillery of Hostile Trench Mortars and Trench Mortar Ammunition dumps will take place on the night July 21st/22nd.

   (ii). Each bombardment will be of 10 minutes duration and will take place at the following time:-

   1st Bombardment - 10.55 p.m. to 11.5 p.m.

   2nd Bombardment - 1.50 a.m. to 2.0 a.m.

2. (i). List of targets to be engaged by Field Artillery is as follows:-

   RIGHT GROUP.

   Target 1. T.M. N.14.c.20.05. to 30.05
   2. Dump N.20 a.45.85.
   3. T.M. N.20 a.83.62.
   5. Dump N.21.a.45.95.

   LEFT GROUP.

   Target 6. Dump N.21.b.25.84.
   7. T.M. N.15.a.10.35.
   8. Dump N.15.a.50.20.

   These will be engaged by all available howitzers during each bombardment. Delay action fuzes will be used.

   (ii). During both bombardments harassing fire with 18-pdr shrapnel will be carried out on all of the above targets within range, each target being engaged, if possible, by one full 18-pdr. battery.

3. Rates of fire all natures for both bombardments:-

   1st five minutes - INTENSE.
   2nd five minutes - RAPID.

4. Infantry will be withdrawn after dark from any portion of the front trenches where necessary on account of proximity of targets, such places being re-occupied before daylight.

5. Time will be synchronized to Brigades at 2.30 p.m. and 6.30 p.m. on 21st July by telephone.

6. ACKNOWLEDGE.

Captain R.F.A.
Issued at:- 9 a.m. Brigade Major, 41st Divl. Arty.

Copies Nos.1 - 7 Right Group.   Copy No.18 41st Divn G.
   8 -13 Left Group   19 XIX Corps H.A.
   14 D.T.M.O.   20 122nd Infy. Bde.
   15 D.A.C.   21 123rd   "   "
   16 S.C.R.A.41 D.A.   22 124th   "   "
   17 R.A.XIX Corps.   23- 28 War Diary & File.

Appendix "T"

SECRET.   Copy No. 14

41st DIVISIONAL ARTILLERY INSTRUCTIONS No.16.

21st July 1918.

1. A small raid will be carried out on night of 23rd/24th July, under arrangements made by Brigade Commander 122nd Infantry Brigade, to obtain identifications and to do as much damage as possible to the enemy in personnel and material.

2. OBJECTIVE.

   Light Railway Line from N.14.c.90.70 to N.14.b.35.35, which is believed to be the enemy outpost line.

3. STRENGTH OF RAIDING PARTY   2 Platoons.

4. Zero hour will be notified as soon as it is received from 122nd Infantry Brigade.

5. The raid will be carried out without actual Artillery covering fire. The following assistance will however be given:-

   (a). Officer Commanding Right Group 41st D.A. will arrange to put down a feint Box barrage from Zero to Zero plus 20' in the neighbourhood of N.19.c. in consultation with G.O.C. 124th Infantry Brigade.

   (b). In consultation with G.O.C. 122nd Infantry Brigade Officer Commanding Left Group will arrange to neutralise the following T.M. emplacements during the operation with 4.5" Hows.:-

   N.15.c.1.5.
   N.14.c.94.16.
   N.20.a.5.3.
   N.20.a.85.73.
   N.14.d.83.42.
   N.20.b.68.85.
   N.20.a.43.85.

   Fire will be maintained from Zero plus 3 until Zero plus 25 or until notification is sent by 122nd Infantry Brigade that it is no longer required.

   O.C. Left Group will also arrange for artillery support to be ready if required to cover the withdrawal.

   (c). The Heavy Artillery are arranging to neutralise enemy batteries known to be active on the sector between Zero minus 5 and Zero plus 25

6. The whole operation is not expected to take more than 10 to 15 minutes; the signal for recall of raiding troops will be a GREEN VEREY Light.

7. No mention of this operation is to be made over the telephone.

                1.   P.T.O.

8. Synchronization

(a) With H.A. – By telephone 9.15 p.m. on 23rd inst.

(b) F.A. Groups – O.C. Left Group will arrange for an Officer to synchronize at 122nd Infantry Brigade H.Q. at 9 p.m. 23rd instant. O.C. Right Group will arrange to synchronize with Left Group.

9. ACKNOWLEDGE.

R.A. Creasy
Major R.F.A.
A/ Brigade Major,
Issued at 6.30 p.m.   41st Divisional Artillery.

Copy No. 1   Right Group. 41st D.A.
        2   Left Group.   "   "
        3   41st Divn. G.
        4   35th Divl. Arty.
        5   6th Divl. Arty.
        6   R.A. XIX Corps.
        7   H.A. XIX Corps.
        8   122nd Infantry Bde.
        9   123rd   "   "
       10   124th   "   "
       11   S.O.R.A. 41st Divn.
       12   D.T.M.O.
       13   D.A.C.
       14   War Diary.
       15)
       16) File.
       17)

SECRET. 22nd July 1918.

ADDENDUM No.1 to 41st D.A. INSTRUCTIONS No.16.

The operation foreshadowed in 41st D.A. Instructions No.16 dated 21st instant may have to be cancelled owing to bright moonlight.
If, however, weather permits, the programme will hold good.

In the event of the affair being cancelled, the Code "NOTHING DOING" will be sent by telephone to all concerned about 11.30 p.m. on 23rd instant.

R L Creasy
Major R.F.A,
A/Brigade Major,
41st Divisional Artillery.

Issued to all recipients of 41st D.A. Instructions No.16, in addition copy to H.A. Xth Corps.

(Appendix "J")

SECRET.   41st D.A. No. S.1017.

   Right Group. (7 copies).
   Left Group (5 copies).
   ----

1.   A gas shell bombardment in conjunction with XIXth Corps
   H.A. will take place on night July 26th/27th or the first
   suitable night afterwards in accordance with table below.

2.   Two forward sections 18-pdrs. per Group will co-operate
   firing 50% A 50% AX.

3.(a). Targets and times are as under:-

        F1 - N.22.c.15.72. - 12.15 a.m. - 12.17 a.m.
                              12.17 a.m. - 12.24 a.m.

        F2 - N.21.d.9.3.   - 12.34 a.m. - 12.36 a.m.
                              12.36 a.m. - 12.43 a.m.

        F3 - N.21.d.4.4.   - 12.53 a.m. - 12.55 a.m.
                              12.55 a.m. - 1. 2 a.m.

        F4 - N.21.d.3.3.   -   1.12 a.m. - 1.14 a.m.
                               1.14 a.m. - 1.21 a.m.

   (b). Each Group will expend the following ammunition on each
        target -

        30 BCG.   30 BNC   36 A   36 AX

4.(a). Targets are arranged in series to allow of the down wind
       target being dealt with first.

  (b). Safety limits for wind will be between S.W. by S. and
       E.N.E.

  (c). If there is any W. in the wind, targets will be engaged
       in the order as above viz:- F1, F2, F3, F4.

       Code word for this will be "DOWN".

  (d). If there is any E. in the wind targets will be engaged
       in reverse order, viz:- F4, F3, F2, F1.

       Code for this will be "UP".

5.   Orders as to whether the bombardment will take place
      or not will be sent from this office by 10.30 p.m. by the
      following code:-
           Bombardment will take place   RAT.
           Bombardment will NOT take place   MOUSE.
      If RAT is sent it will be followed by the code words men-
      tioned in para. 4.(c) and (d).   one of

6.   Watches will be synchronized by telephone prior to the
      shoot.

7.   Groups to ACKNOWLEDGE.

                                          R L Creasy.
          25-7-18.   Major R.F.A.
                                          A/Brigade Major, 41st Divl. Arty.
Copies to:-   S.C.R.A. 41st Divn.
41st Divn. G.   122nd Infy. Bde.   41st D.A.C.
XIX Corps R.A.   123rd   "   "   41st D.T.M.O.
XIX Corps H.A.   124th   "   "

Appendix K

SECRET. COPY No. 24

41st D.A INSTRUCTIONS No. 17.

1. 26th Royal Fusiliers (124th Infantry Brigade) are carrying out a raid tonight 27th/28th July on an enemy post at N.19.a.80.16.

    The Raiders will be formed up by Zero at or about N.19.a.73.42 and will rush the post on lift of barrage at Zero plus 4'.

2. 41st Divisional Artillery will support this operation as per attached table.

3. Zero hour will be notified later.

4. At the same hour a destructive shoot will be carried out on the enemy's front from N.14.c.90.70. to N.14.b.36.35. Infantry Patrols from 122nd Infantry Brigade will investigate the area after this bombardment with a view to obtaining identifications.

    O.C. 190th Brigade R.F.A. will issue necessary orders for this destructive shoot and will have at his disposal for the purpose the following batteries:-

    B/150, D/150, B/190, C/190, D/190
    2 guns A/190.

5. Heavy Artillery have been asked to neutralize certain hostile batteries active on 41st Divisional Front.

6. No mention of the above operations are to be made over the telephone forward of Divisional H.Q.

7. SYNCHRONIZATION   Watches will be synchronized over the telephone from this Headquarters at 6 p.m. and 9 p.m. 27th instant.

8. ACKNOWLEDGE.

R L Creagy
Major, R.F.A.
A/Brigade Major,
41st Divisional Artillery.

27-6-18.
Issued at:- 7 a.m.

```
Copy No.  1 -  5  187th Bde. R.F.A.
          6 - 10  190th   "      "
         11 - 14  150th   "      "
         15       41st Divn. G.
         16       122nd Infy. Bde.
         17       123rd   "     "
         18       124th   "     "
         19       XIX Corps H.A.
         20       XIX Corps R.A.
         21       35th D.A.
         22       6th D.A.
         23       S.C.R.A. 41st Divn
         24       R.O.R.A.
         25 - 30  War Diary & File.
```

P.T.O

SECRET.   TABLE issued with 41st D.A. Instructions No.17.   27th July 1918.

Battery.		Time.	Task.	Ammunition.
C/150	6 guns	Zero to Zero plus 25'	N.19.a.35.25.-N.19.c.3.6.	A throughout.
B/187	6 guns	Zero to Zero plus 25'	N.19.c.3.6. - N.19.a.1.8.	AX "
C/187	6 guns	Zero to Zero plus 25'	N.19.d.128. - N.19.b.37.05.	AX "
A/190	4 guns	Zero to Zero plus 25'	N.19.b.37.05.-N.19.a.96.58.	A "
A/187	6 guns	Zero to Zero plus 4'	N.19.a.70.05.-N.19.a.9.2.	
A/187	3 guns	Zero plus 4' to Zero plus 25'	N.19.a.5.0. - N.19.c.3.9.	AX "
A/187	3 guns	Zero plus 4' to Zero plus 25'	N.19.b.1.4. - N.19.b.3.6.	
D/187	1 how.	Zero to Zero plus 25'	M.G.Post N.19.d.0.5.	
D/187	1 how.	Zero to Zero plus 25'	Strong point N.19.d.42.42.	
D/187	1 how.	Zero to Zero plus 25'	M.G. at N.19.c.15.75.	BX 106.
D/187	3 hows.	Zero to Zero plus 25'	T.M's at N.14.c.55.00. N.20.a.90.65. N.13.c.15.55.	

Rates of fire:—
Zero to Zero plus 5'   -   Intense.
Zero plus 5' to Zero plus 10'   -   Rapid.
Zero plus 10' to Zero plus 20'   -   Normal.
Zero plus 20' to Zero plus 25'   -   Slow.
Zero plus 25'   -   Cease fire.

Appendix "L."

SECRET.   Copy No. 17

41st DIVISIONAL ARTILLERY INSTRUCTIONS No.19.

30th July 1918.

1. The 150th Army F.A.Brigade will withdraw from action to its wagon lines on the night July 30th/31st, and will be prepared to proceed by rail out of Second Army Area on August 1st.

2. On withdrawal of 150th Army Bde. R.F.A. the Left Group 41st D.A. will be composed as follows:-

   H.Q. 11th Army Bde. R.F.A.
   A/190th Bde. R.F.A.
   85th Battery R.F.A.
   D/11 Bde. R.F.A.

   These Headquarters and Batteries will remain in their present positions. A/190 will remain under Centre Group until telephonic communication has been established between it and Left Group Headquarters, but not later than 8 p.m. on the 31st July.

3. O.C. 11th Army Brigade R.F.A. will assume responsibility for Artillery support of Left Infantry Brigade at 9 p.m. on the 30th July.

4. S.O.S. lines of Left Group will be as follows:-

   One 18-pdr. Battery : N.14.c.63.25 - N.14.d.25.75. (A/190).

   One 18-pdr. Battery { 2 Section. N.14.b.4.0.-N.14.b.6.3.
                       { 1 Section N.14.b.85.75.-N.15.a.3.6.

   One 4.5"How. Battery.{ 1 Section. N.14.d.3.8.-N.14.d.35.92.
                        { 2 Sections.N.14.b.65.35-N.14.b.85.65.

5. Centre Group will consist of 190th Brigade R.F.A. less A Battery.

   S.O.S. lines of this Group will be as follows:-

   One 18-pdr.Battery. N.19.b.98.85. - N.14.c.30.05.

   One 18-pdr. Battery. N.14.c.63.25. - N.14.d.25.75.

   One 4.5" How. Battery. As at present.

6. ACKNOWLEDGE.

                                        Major, R.F.A.
                                        A/Brigade Major,
Issued at:- 6.45 p.m.   41st Divisional Artillery.

Copy No. 1 150th Army Bde.   Copy No. 9 66th Divl. Arty.
        2   187th Bde.R.F.A.   10 32nd D.A.
        3   190th   "   "   11 11th Army Bde.R.F.A.
        4   D.T.M.O.   12 XIX Corps H.A.
        5   41st D.A.C.   13 S.C.R.A. 41st Divn.
        6   41st Divn. G.   14 Sigs. 41st D.A.
        7   XIX Corps R.A.   15 R.O.R.A. 41st Divn.
        8   6th Divl. Arty.   16-20 War Diary & Files.
                                           21 122nd Infy. Bde.

Army Form W.3091.

Appendix "J"

HQ RA 4th /8/28

Cover for Documents.

Nature of Enclosures.

OPERATION ORDERS

Minor operation
8/9 Aug '18

~~Finished~~ (War Diary)
with map.

Notes, or Letters written.

Army Form C. 2118.

WAR DIARY
— or —
INTELLIGENCE-SUMMARY.
(Erase heading not required.) Headquarters, 41st.Divisional Artillery

Instructions regarding War Diaries and Intelligence Summaries are contained in F. S. Regs., Part II. and the Staff Manual respectively. Title pages will be prepared in manuscript.

Place	Date	Hour	Summary of Events and Information	Remarks and references to Appendices
(BELGIUM) ABEELE Area	1918 1st Aug.		Orders issued regarding co-operation of Right Group, 41st.Divisional Artillery, with 35th. Divisional Artillery on the Right, in an attack to capture DRANOUTRE RIDGE (App:"A")	App: "A"
—do—	2nd Aug.		The operation in which the Right Group, 41st.D.A., was to co-operate, was postponed owing to bad weather (App:"B")	App: "B"
—do—	5th Aug.		Orders issued regarding co-operation by 41st.D.A., in an attack to be carried out by 15th. Hants.Regiment, 122nd.Infantry Brigade, (Left Infantry Brigade) to straighten the present front line. The 41st.D.A. was aided by units of the 6th.& 66th. Divisional Artilleries (Appendix "D") It was arranged that during this attack 124th.Infantry Brigade (Right Infantry Brigade) would carry out a raid in the BRULOOZE Area, the necessary artillery support being given by Right Group, 41st.D.A. (Appendix "D") Captain T.H.BISCHOFF, M.C., Staff Captain, 41st.D.A., proceeded on leave to England, Captain E.H.COE, Adjutant, 187th.Brigade, R.F.A., acting as Staff Captain in his absence.	App: "C" App: "D"
—do—	7th Aug.		The operation to be carried out by 35th.Division on the Right to capture DRANOUTRE RIDGE was cancelled (Appendix "C") Captain F.N.MASON MACFARLANE, M.C., Brigade Major, 41st.Divisional Artillery, returned from 14 days leave in England.	App: "C"
—do—	8th Aug.		Attack carried out by 15th.Hants.Regt., supported by artillery, at midnight 8th/9th. was successful, 30 prisoners being taken. The raid carried out by the 124th.Infantry Brigade was also successful, 1 prisoner & 1 M.G. being taken.	
—do—	10th Aug.		Brigadier-General A.S.COTTON, D.S.O., C.R.A., 41st.Division, proceeded on 14 days leave of absence to England, Lieut.Col.G.A.CARDEW, C.M.G., D.S.O., O.C., 190th.Brigade, R.F.A., acting as C.R.A., in his absence. On night 9th/10th.batteries of 330th.Brigade, R.F.A., which had been specially brought up for attack by 15th.Hants.Regt. withdrew 1 section per battery from action (Appendix "D")	App: "D"
—do—	11th Aug.		Counterpreparation On night 10th/11th.batteries of 330th.Brigade withdrew remaining section (Appendix "D")	App: "D"

Army Form C. 2118.

WAR DIARY
INTELLIGENCE-SUMMARY.
Headquarters, 41st.Divl:Artillery

(Erase heading not required.)

Instructions regarding War Diaries and Intelligence Summaries are contained in F. S. Regs., Part II. and the Staff Manual respectively. Title pages will be prepared in manuscript.

Place	Date	Hour	Summary of Events and Information	Remarks and references to Appendices
BELGIUM ABEELE Area	1918 11th Aug (contd)		As the enemy had attempted to retake the ground gained by us on the night 8th/9th., two batteries of the 66th.D.A., were brought into action on night 11th/12th. (Appendix "E") Counter preparation fired during night 11th/12th. (Appendix "F")	App: "E" & "F"
-do-	13th Aug		Counter preparation fired from 3 a.m., to 3.55 a.m. (Appendix "F")	App: "F"
-do-	14th Aug		Counter preparation again fired between 3 a.m., to 4 a.m. 41st.Divisional Artillery co-operated with XIXth.Corps H.A., in a Road blocking shoot on Roads S. and W. of MONT KEMMEL (Appendix "G")	App: "G"
-do-	15th Aug		Between 3 a.m., and 4 a.m., batteries stood to on their Counter preparation lines ready to open fire in the event of any heavy enemy bombardment. The night was quiet (Appendix "H") The S.O.S.Lines of Right batteries of Right Group altered (Appendix "I") A/330th.Battery, & C/350th.Battery, 66th.D.A., withdrawn from action (Appendix "J")	App: "H" App: "I" & "J"
-do-	16th Aug		Gas shell bombardment carried out by 4.5"How Batteries of Right and Centre Groups in conjunction with XIXth.Corps H.A. (Appendix "K")	App: "K"
-do-	17th Aug		Relief of 41st.D.A., by 66th.D.A., commenced on night 17th/18th (Appendix "L")	App; "L"
-do-	18th Aug		Relief completed on night 18th/19th. (Appendix "L"). Gemmand	App: "L"
FRANCE ST.LAURENT	19th.Aug.		Command of Artillery covering 41st.Divisional front passed from C.R.A.,41st.Division to C.R.A., 41st.D.A.,Headquarters moved to ST.LAURENT	App: "L",
-do-	20th Aug.		Capt.T.H.BISCHOFF,M.C.,Staff Captain, 41st.D.A., returned from leave	
-do-	22nd Aug.		Lieut.Colonel G.A.CARDEW, C.M.G.,D.S.O.,190th.Brigade,R.F.A., acting C.R.A.,41st.Division,proceeded on 14 days leave to England;Lieut.Col.C.D.G.LYON,D.S.O.,O.C.,187th.Brigade,acting as C.R.A.,41st.Division in his absence.	
-do-	24th Aug.		Brigadier-General A.T.COTTON D.S.O., C.R.A.,41st.Division returned from 14 days leave and assumed command of the 41st.Division, in the absence of the G.O.C.,41st.Division, on leave.	
-do-	26th Aug		Relief of 66th.D.A., by 41st.D.A., commenced on night 26th/27th (Appendix "M")	App: "M"
-do-	27th Aug		Relief of 66th.D.A., completed on night 27/28th.(Appendix "M")	
BELGIUM ABEELE Area	28th Aug		Lieut.Col.C.D.G.LYON,D.S.O.,a/G.R.A.,41st.Division assumed Command of the artillery covering 41st.Division at 9 a.m., moved to ABEELE Area (Appendix "M")	App: "M"

Army Form C. 2118.

WAR DIARY
or
INTELLIGENCE SUMMARY.

(Erase heading not required.) Headquarters, 41st.Divl: Artillery

Instructions regarding War Diaries and Intelligence Summaries are contained in F. S. Regs., Part II. and the Staff Manual respectively. Title pages will be prepared in manuscript.

Place	Date	Hour	Summary of Events and Information	Remarks and references to Appendices
BELGIUM. ABEELE Area.	1918 29th. Aug.		34th.Division (less Artillery) relieved 41st.Division (less Artillery)	
-do-	30th. Aug.		Information was received that the enemy had evacuated BAILLEUL and was retiring East of it. In the evening the Division on our right had patrols in the vicinity of DRANOUTRE and were moving on. Harassing fire on night 30th/31st. was fired at as long range as possible in order to interfere with the enemy retirement. Our infantry carried out active patrolling.	
SCHERPENBERG Area.	31st. Aug.		During the early morning patrols of our Right Infantry Brigade pushed forward to MONT KEMMEL in touch with Division on our Right, with very little opposition. Machine gun nests interfered with the movement of our Left Infantry Brigade, but by about mid-day our troops had crossed MONT KEMMEL. Batteries were moved up into their forward section positions during the day. At 7 p.m., 41st.D.A., Headquarters moved with advanced Divisional Headquarters, 34th.Division, to the Headquarters vacated by Right Infantry Brigade in the vicinity of SCHERPENBERG.	

5th.Sept.1918.

(signature)
Brigadier General,
Commanding 41st.Divisional Artillery.

Appendix A

SECRET.   Copy No. 11

41st. DIVISIONAL ARTILLERY INSTRUCTIONS No.20.

1st August 1918.

1. The Division on our Right will attack DRANOUTRE RIDGE on the morning of the 3rd instant.

2. Right Group of this Divisional Artillery will co-operate by putting down a barrage during the attack, for which orders have already been issued.

3. After the capture of the Ridge this Divisional Artillery will cover the consolidation of the ground taken by putting up two smoke screens on KEMMEL HILL from 4.45 to 5.15 a.m. with the object of blinding enemy observation posts thereon.

4. The screens will if weather conditions are normal, be put up as follows:-

   Screen No.1: N.25.c.80.47. - N.25.a.70.05: Right Group.

   Screen No.2: N.26.a.48.25. - N.26.a.30.70: Centre Group and A/190.

5. The object of screen No.1 is to blind suspected O.P. at N.25.d.1.7. and high ground in that area.

   The object of Screen No.2 is to blind the high ground about BELLE VUE CABARET.

6. The exact line on which this smoke shell is dropped will of course depend upon the direction of the wind. If, for instance, a 10 f.s. wind is blowing from East to West the rounds will require to be placed 100 yards further East, and vice versa; if a 10 f.s. wind is blowing from North to South rounds will require to be dropped 100 yards further North and vice versa (vide "Notes on the Use of Smoke" par.7)

7. Ammunition expenditure will be:-

   360 rounds per 18-pdr. battery.
   166   "   " 4.5" How. battery
   fired at an even rate through the half hour.

8. Watches will be synchronized at 35th D.A. H.Qrs. (R.15.a.1.5.) at 12.30 p.m. on the 2nd instant.

9. Zero hour will be about 2 a.m. on the 3rd August. The exact hour will be notified by telegram; e.g. if zero hour is fixed for 2.10 a.m. the telegram will read:-

   "Instructions No. 20. Add ten minutes."

10. ACKNOWLEDGE.

                                                    Major R.F.A.
   Issued at 7 p.m.   A/Brigade Major, 41st Divl. Arty.

1. 11th A Bde.   5. D.A.C.   9. S.C.R.A. 41st Divn.
2. 187th Bde.   6. 41 Div G.   10. Bigs. 41st D.A.
3. 190th "   7. XIX Corps R.A.   11. R.O.R.A. 41st Divn.
4. D.T.M.O.   8. XIX Corps H.A.   12 - 16 War Diary & File.

Appendix "B"

SECRET.

41st D.A. No. S.1089.

To all recipients of 41st D.A. Instructions No.20.

The operation referred to in these instructions has been postponed.

ACKNOWLEDGE.

2-8-18.

Captain R.F.A.
for Brigade Major,
41st Divisional Artillery.

Appendix C

SECRET.   41st D.A. No. S.1119.

To all recipients of 41st D.A. Instructions No.20.

1.   The operation referred to in the above Instructions will probably take place on the night 6th/7th August with Zero Hour about 2.5 a.m. Wednesday 7th August.

2.   If the weather is not favourable the operation will be cancelled. The decision will be made by 3 p.m. 5th August.

3.   The following Code Words will be employed to notify the decision.

   Operation will be carried out } ADEN.
       on night 6th/7th August   }

   Operation is cancelled.   ICELAND.

4.   A C K N O W L E D G E.

                                   E.R. Roper
                                   Major, R.F.A.
                                   A/Brigade Major,
5th August 1918.   41st Divisional Artillery.

S E C R E T   41st D.A. No. S.1148.

SECOND AMENDMENT to 41st D.A. Operation Order No.11.

Cancel para. 16 and substitute the following:-

"Synchronization will be carried out by telephone at about 11 a.m. and 9 p.m. on 8th instant from this Office with
           Right Group.
           Left Group
           Centre Group.
           6th Divl. Arty.
           XIXth Corps H.A.

                                       Captain R.F.A.
                                       Brigade Major,
7-8-18.   41st Divisional Artillery.

Right Group.
Left Group.
Centre Group.
6th Divl. Arty.
XIX Corps H.A.

SECRET.　　　　　　　　　　　　　　　41st D.A. No. S.1149.

6th Divl. Arty.

Your Operation Order No. 146.

C.R.A. 41st Division would be glad if you could arrange to continue to fire in support of ~~xx~~ the operation mentioned in para. 5 till Zero plus 45' so that the cease fire in all the operations would be simultaneous.

[signature]

Captain R.F.A.
Brigade Major,
41st Divisional Artillery.

7-8-18.

SECRET.   41st D.A. No. S.1150.

Headquarters,
    187th Bde. R.F.A.

Your Order No.43.

C.R.A. would like you to continue firing till zero plus 45' at the rates you leave off at so that your cease fire will coincide with the end of the major operation.

[signature]

Captain R.F.A.
Brigade Major,
41st Divisional Artillery.

7-8-18.

SECRET.　　　　　　　　　　　　　　41st D.A. No. S.1140.

FIRST AMENDMENT to 41st D.A. Operation Order No.11.

Para.5, L : Cancel first two lines (lines 20 and 21, p.2) and substitute the following:-

"Lane L opens on the line 'd' (N.15.a.63.58 - N.15.a.81.75) at zero and moves forward with lane K at zero plus 8 to line 'g'."

E R Roper
Major, R.F.A.
for Brigade Major,
41st Divisional Artillery.

7th August 1918.
Issued at 2 p.m.

Issued to all recipients of 41st D.A. Operation Order No.11.

SECRET.   41st D.A. No. S.1156.

Right Group.
Left   "
Centre "   6th Divl. Arty.

    With reference to 41st D.A. Operation Order No. 11 dated 5th August 1918.

    ZERO Hour will be 12 midnight 8th/9th August.

    Acknowledge by wire.

                                          Captain R.F.A.
                                          Brigade Major,
8th August 1918.   41st Divisional Artillery.

SECRET.   41st D.A. No. S.1155.

Right Group.
Left   "
Centre "
6th Divl. Arty.
XIX Corps H.A.

My No. S.1148.

Synchronization this evening will take place at 8 p.m. at 122nd Infantry Brigade Headquarters C.36.c.1.2. and not by phone as therein stated.

A representative of each group will be there at the hour named and 6th Divl. Arty. and XIX Corps H.A. will also please arrange to send representatives.

Acknowledge by wire.

8-8-18.

Captain R.F.A.
Brigade Major,
41st Divisional Artillery.

SECRET.   41st D.A. No. S.1142.

              FIRST ADDENDUM to 41st D.A. Operation Order No.11.

       The following should be added to Appendix "D" of 41st
D.A. Operation Order No.11:-

HEAVY ARTILLERY TASKS.

    15.   BEAVER CORNER   N.15.c.25,35.

                                          [signature]
                                          Captain R.F.A.
                                          Brigade Major,
    7th August. 1918.   41st Divisional Artillery.

       Issued to all recipients of 41st D.A. Operation Order No.11.

SECRET.   Copy No. 45

41st. DIVISIONAL ARTILLERY INSTRUCTIONS No.21.

8th August 1918.

1. Units of 41st Divisional Artillery and attached batteries will return to their normal locations in accordance with attached March Table.

2. 41st Divisional Artillery will issue orders by wire using the code given below according to the tactical situation.

   Move will take place .... COD.

   Move will not take place .... TAG.

3. S.O.S. lines from 8 p.m. 9th inst for those guns and hows. of 330 and 331 Brigades not moving till night 10th/11th will be as follows:-

   A 330   2 guns)
) N.14.d.40.75. - N.14.d.98.92.
   B 330   4 guns)

   B 331   2 guns)
) N.14.d.98.92. - N.15.a.43.08.
   D 330   2 hows)

   C 330   4 guns   N.15.a.43.08. - N.15.a.78.18.

4. Completion of moves in all cases where guns are moving into action again will be notified by wire to this office by Groups concerned on each night using Code Word FISH.

5. ACKNOWLEDGE.

                                        F. MacFarlane
                                        Captain R.F.A.
                                        Brigade Major,
   Issued at:- 11.30 p.m.   41st Divisional Artillery.

Copy No. 1 - 7   Right Group.
         8 - 13 Centre Group.
        14 - 19 Left Group.
        20 - 28 66th D.A.
             29 35th D.A.
             30 6th D.A.
             31 122nd Infy. Bde.
             32 123rd Infy. Bde.
             33 124th Infy. Bde.
             34 41st Divn. G.
             35 41st Divn. Q.
             36 XIX Corps R.A.
             37 XIX Corps H.A.
             38 XIX Corps C.B.S.O.
             39 41st M.G.Battn.
             40 D.T.M.O. 41st Divn.
             41 S.C.R.A. 41st Divn.
             42 Sig. Officer 41st D.A.
             43 RORA 41st D.A.
        44 - 48 War Diary & File.

SECRET.

MOVEMENT TABLE
issued with 41st D.A. Instructions No.21.

8th August 1918.

Battery.	No. of guns.	From.	To.	Night of
A/330	2	M.12.a.75.45	W.L.	9/10 Aug.
"	2	M. 6.d.05.30	"	9/10 "
"	2	M.12.a.75.45.	"	10/11 "
B/330	2	M.12.b.00.65.	"	9/10 "
"	2	M.12.b.00.65.	"	10/11 "
"	2	M.11.a. 7. 4.	"	10/11 "
C/330	2	M. 6.d.15.72.	"	9/10 "
"	2	M. 6.d.15.72	"	10/11 "
"	2	M. 6.d.05.30.	"	10/11 "
D/330	4	G.35.b. 2. 8.	"	9/10 "
"	2	G.35.b. 2. 8.	"	10/11 "
B/190	2	M.11.b.20.85.	M.4.d. 2.6.	9/10 "
C/190	2	M. 5.d.80.40.	M.3.b. 20.60.	9/10 "
85th Bty.	2	M.10.b. 4. 2.	G.35.b. 9.8.	9/10 "
"	2	H.31.a. 2. 6.	G.35.b. 9.8.	9/10 "
B/331	2	M.10.b. 7. 7.	W.L.	10/11 "

S E C R E T. Copy No. 55

Appendix "D"

41st. DIVISIONAL ARTILLERY OPERATION ORDER No.11.

5th August 1918.

Reference Maps 28 S.W.1.) 1/10,000.
                  28 N.W.3.)

ATTACK. 1. In order to straighten the present front line on the left of the Divisional Front the 122nd Infantry Brigade will attack with a view to gaining the following objective:-

From Farm at N.14.c.82.96 to Pond at N.15.a.87.65. On the Right touch will be established with the present Front line at N.14.a.55.05. On the left the 6th Division will co-operate by advancing their present line of posts, pivoting on N.9.d.4.0., to join up with the Left of our objective at N.15.a.87.65.

ZERO. 2. Zero hour will be notified later, and will probably be on night 8th/9th August 1918.

ARTILLERY ACTION. 3. The 41st Divisional Artillery aided by units of the 6th and 68th Divisional Artilleries will co-operate by firing a barrage under which the attacking troops will advance and consolidate the objective when gained, and by bombarding machine gun posts etc. in the neighbourhood of the attack.

Corps R.A. will also co-operate (see para.9).

BARRAGE. 4. The Barrage will be as shewn in the tracing annexed marked "A".

The Barrage is arranged in lanes, four 18-pdrs being allotted to each lane; the lanes are lettered A, B, C, etc, from the right.

The successive lifts of the Barrage are marked a, b, c, etc. commencing from the opening line, and are of 100 yards each.

Owing to configuration of the Front Line it is impossible to place the opening line of the Barrage parallel with the line of attacking troops. The attackers will therefore approach the Barrage at an angle; it has in consequence been so arranged that the Lane which is first approached is the first to lift, the remaining lanes lifting in succession as the Infantry approach, commencing with Lane K.

LIFTS. 5. Lifts are at intervals of two minutes.
Lanes A to K open on the line a.

K. At Zero plus 2 Lane K will move forward by 2 minute lifts to line 'f' which it reaches at Zero plus 10. It then pivots on its right and reaches final barrage line at Zero plus 12 where it remains.

Lane

J. At Zero plus 4/J will similarly move forward to line 'e', which it reaches at Zero plus 10 and leaves at Zero plus 12 to form its portion of the protective barrage.

I. At Zero plus 6 Lane I moves forward in similar manner to line 'e', pivoting on its right at Zero plus 14 to form its portion of protective barrage.

G. H. At Zero plus 8 Lanes G and H move forward in similar manner to line 'd', pivoting on right flank of G at Zero plus 14 to reach their portion of protective barrage line.

E. F. At Zero plus 10 Lanes E and F move forward in similar manner to line 'c', pivoting on right flank of E at Zero plus 14 to reach their portion of protective barrage line.

A. B. C. D. At Zero plus 10 lanes A, B, C, and D move forward and A and B stand on line 'b'; C and D at Zero plus 14 pivot on right flank of C in order to reach their portion of protective barrage line.

L. Lane L opens on the line d at zero and moves forward with lane K at Zero plus 10 to line 'g', which it reaches at Zero plus 14 and on which it stands to form its portion of the protective barrage.

M. N. Lanes M and N open on line 'g' at zero forming the left flank of the protective barrage, and remain there throughout.

The line 'gg' is the final protective barrage and S.O.S. line.

4.5" HOW.
BATTERIES. 6. 4.5" How. batteries of Centre and Left Groups will engage the following points:-

1 Battery. (N.14.c.91.19.
(N.14.c.90.08.
(N.20.a.88.90.
Task W. (N.20.a.90.72.
(N.20.a.99.58.
(N.20.b.05.50.

1 Battery: (N.20.a.97.28.
(N.20.b.18.32.
(N.20.b.35.72.
Task X. (N.20.b.48.69.
(N.20.b.60.48.
(N.20.b.70.49.

1 Battery: (N.14.b.98.15.
(N.15.a.10.25.
(N.15.a.05.06.
Task Y. (N.15.c.20.98.
(N.15.a.28.15.
(N.15.a.39.04.

lifting at Zero plus 6 to
(N.14.d.80.18.
(N.14.d.85.05.
Task Z. (N.15.c.63.62.
(N.15.c.70.70.
(N.15.c.95.88.
(N.15.d.05.84.

PROTECTIVE BARRAGE. 7. The protective barrage will remain on the line 'gg' until Zero plus 45. This will be S.O.S. Line if called for.

8. Allotment of guns for the various tasks and lanes are given in Appendix "B".

HEAVY ARTILLERY. 9. XIXth Corps H.A. will co-operate by bombarding selected targets in back areas during the attack; these are shewn on Appendix "D". Counter batteries will neutralize known active hostile batteries from Zero to Zero plus 45.

DIVERSIONS. 10. During the attack 124th Infantry Brigade will create a diversion by carrying out a raid, with Artillery support, in the BRULOOZE area.

The O.C. Right Group will provide the necessary support. Allotment of guns for this task is given in Appendix "B".
Detailed orders on this subject will be issued by O.C. Right Group.

A similar diversion will be carried out by 6th Division on our Left.

AMMUNITION. 11. Rates of fire and Allotment of Ammunition are as follows:-

<u>18-pdrs:</u>
  Zero to Zero plus 15: 3 rounds per gun per minute.
  Zero plus 15 to Zero plus 45: 2 rounds per gun per minute.

<u>4.5" Hows:</u>
  Zero to Zero plus 15: 2 rounds per how. per minute.
  Zero plus 15 to Zero plus 45: 1½ rounds per how. per minute.

<u>Ammunition:</u>

<u>18-pdrs.</u> Lanes A,B,C,D. AX direct action fuze throughout.
  " E,F,G,H,I,J,K,L,M,N, Zero to Zero plus 15. A.
  Zero plus 15 to Zero plus 45 AX direct action fuze.

<u>4.5" Hows.</u> BX 106 fuze.

Ammunition for incoming batteries for this operation will, where necessary, be dumped by Brigades now in the Line, up to an amount of 300 rounds per 18-pdr. and 250 rounds per 4.5" Howitzer.

GROUPING. 12. Reinforcing Artillery will be grouped as follows:-

330th Bde. R.F.A.: 1 Section of B Battery will reinforce Forward Section of A/190 in Left Group.
Howitzer battery will join Left Group.
Remainder will form a sub-group under Centre Group.

<u>331st Bde. R.F.A.</u>: 1 Section will reinforce forward section A/187 under Right Group.

<u>11th Army Bde. RFA.</u>: 1 Section of 85th Battery will reinforce Forward section of B/187 and will be temporarily in Right Group.

Reinforcing batteries of 6th Divisional Artillery are grouped under and act under the orders of Right Group of that Divisional Artillery.

OCCUPATION OF POSITIONS.	13.	Positions to be occupied are shewn in Appendix "B". Guns which require to be moved into new positions for this operation will do so in accordance with the Movement Table given in Appendix "C".

All movement east of N. and S. Grid Line through G.31.central will take place during the hours of darkness.

WITHDRAWAL FROM POSITIONS.	14.	After conclusion of the operation guns which have been moved into new positions for the operation, will remain there until the night of the 9th/10th or 10th/11th August, being withdrawn after dark on these nights under instructions which will be issued at the time.
EMPTIES.	15.	All empties are to be removed by the batteries or sections which have fired them.
SYNCHRONIZATION.	16.	Watches will be synchronized at 122nd Infantry Brigade Headquarters (G.36.c.1.2.) at 9 p.m. on the evening of the attack.
PASS WORD.	17.	Pass word on night of the attack will be "MURDOCH".
S.O.S. SIGNAL.	18.	S.O.S. Signal will be that now in force, namely:- RED / GREEN / YELLOW.
BOUNDARIES AND S.O.S. LINES.	19.	On the night following the operation the 6th Division will take over East of the line N.15.a.35.60 - MILKY WAY JUNCTION and present Divisional Boundary. S.O.S. lines of Left Group will be re-arranged from 8 p.m. on that night as follows; these will be their normal S.O.S. lines in future:

One 18-pdr. Bty.: N.14.c.63.25 - N.14.d.25.75.
"   "   "   : N.14.d.98.92 - N.15.a.43.08.
4.5" How. Bty.: 2 Sections N.14.d.45.78 -
                            N.14.d.90.90.
               1 Section   N.15.a.52.10. -
                            N.15.a.75.18.

20. A C K N O W L E D G E.   N.15.a.20.00
                              N.15.c.10.98.
N.14.d.98.92.   N.15.c.00.95
N.14.d.82.88.
N.14.d.56.82.   *E.R. Roper*
Issued at 2 p.m.   Major, R.F.A.
                              A/Brigade Major,
                              41st Divisional Artillery.

Distribution over/

Distribution:-

Copy No. 1	- 7	Right Group.
8	- 13	Centre Group.
14	- 19	Left Group.
20	- 28	66th D.A.
29	- 31	35th D.A.
32	- 37	6th D.A.
38	- 39	122nd Infantry Bde.
	40	123rd　　"　　"
	41	124th　　"　　"
	42	41st Divn. G.
	43	41st Divn. Q. (without map)
	44	XIX Corps R.A.
	45	XIX Corps H.A. (without map).
	46	XIX Corps C.B.S.O.　"　　"
	47	41st M.G. Battalion.
	48	65th Bde. R.G.A. (without map.)
	49	6th　"　　"　　"　　"　　"
	50	25th A.Bde R.G.A.　"　　"
	51	D.T.M.O.
	52	S.C.R.A. 41st Divn. (without map).
	53	Sig. Officer 41st D.A.　"　　"
	54	R.O.R.A. 41st Divn.　"　　"
55	- 60.	War Diary & File.

LEGEND

18 Pdr Barrage

4.5 How. "

— ditto —

Reference Letter for Map Squares N.

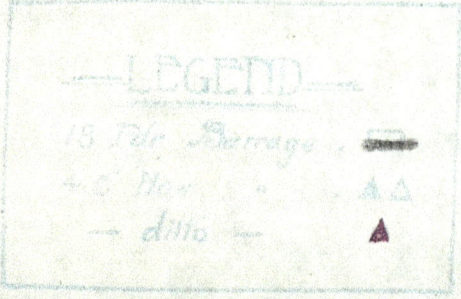

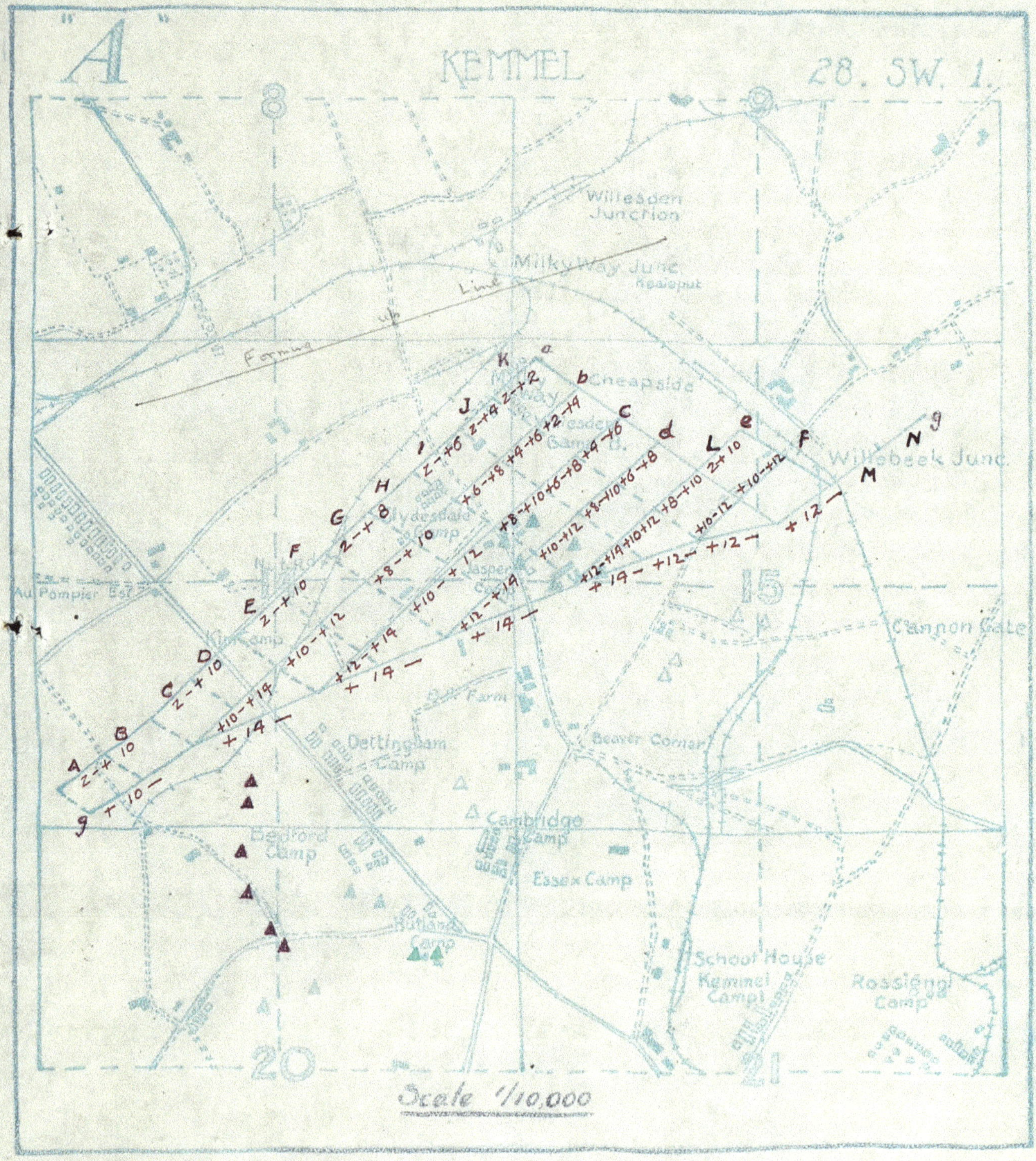

Scale 1/10,000

SECRET.   A P P E N D I X "B"
             Issued with 41st D.A. Operation Order No.11.
                                                           5-8-18.
                   A L L O T M E N T of G U N S.

	Battery.	No. of Guns.	Position.	Task.
I. BARRAGE.	B/187. 85th Bty.	2) 2)	M.10.b.4.2.	Lane A.
	A/187. B/331.	2) 2)	M.10.b.7.7.	" B.
	B/190.	4	M.11.b.2.8.	" C.
	C/190.	4	M.5.d.8.4.	" D.
	B/330.	4	M.12.b.00.65.	" E.
	A/330.	4	M.12.a.75.45.	" F.
	A/330. C/330.	2) 2)	M.6.d.05.30.	" G.
	C/330.	4	M.6.d.15.72.	" H.
	A/190. B/330.	2) 2)	M.11.a.7.4.	" I.
	85th Bty.	4	H.31.a.2.6.	" J.
	6th D.A.	4		" K.
	6th D.A.	4		" L.
	6th D.A.	4		" M.
	6th D.A.	4		" N.
II. 4.5" HOW. TASKS.	D/190.	4 2	M.4.a.40.20. M.12.a.50.80.	W.
	D/330.	6	G.35.b.2.8.	X.
	D/11.	4	G.30.a.57.55.	Y and
	D/11.	2	G.36.d.75.30.	Z
III. RAID BY 124th INFY.BDE.	A/187.	4	M.3.d.8.9.	
	B/187.	4	M.9.c.65.95. and M.9.a.85.30.	
	C/187.	6	Present.	
	D/187.	6	Present.	
	A/190.	4	M.4.d.40.80.	
	B/190.	2	M.4.d.20.60.	
	C/190.	2	M.3.b.20.60.	
	35th D.A.	6 18-pdrs.		

SECRET.

APPENDIX "C"
Issued with 41st D.A. Operation Order No.11.

5-8-18.

MOVEMENT TABLE.

Battery.	No. of guns.	From	To.	Night of
A/330.	2	W.L.	M.12.a.75.45.	6/7th Aug.
"	2	"	M. 6.d.05.30.	6/7th "
"	2	"	M.12.a.75.45.	7/8th "
B/330.	2	"	M.12.b.00.65.	6/7th "
"	2	"	M.12.b.00.65.	7/8th "
"	2	"	M.11.a 7. 4.	7/8th "
C/330	2	"	M. 6.d.15.72.	6/7th "
"	2	"	M. 6.d.15.72.	7/8th "
"	2	"	M. 6.d.05.30.	7/8th "
D/330.	4	"	G.35.b. 2. 8.	6/7th "
"	2	"	G.35.b. 2. 8.	7/8th "
B/190.	2	M.4.d.2.6.	M.11.b.20.85.	6/7th "
C/190.	2	M.3.b.20.60.	M. 5.d.80.40.	7/8th "
85th Bty.	2	G.35.b.9.8.	M.10.b. 4. 2.	6/7th "
"	2	G.35.b.9.8.	H.31.a. 2. 6.	7/8th "
B/331.	2	W.L.	M.10.b. 7. 7.	6/7th "

SECRET.

APPENDIX "D"
Issued with 41st D.A. Operation Order No.11.

5-8-18.

HEAVY ARTILLERY TASKS.

1. Area N.25.a.15.85. - suspected M.G's.
2. " N.25.d.00.70. - " "
3. " N.26.a.6.7. - N.26.b.20.75. (M.KEMMEL).
4. " N.20.d.1.6. - N.20.d.5.7. (O.P's and M.G's.)
5. " N.20.a.50.25. (Coy. or Battalion H.Qrs. & tracks).
6. Cross roads at N.20.b.90.55.
7. Area N.21.b.35.82. (Centre of activity and Dumps).
8. " N.15.d.28.50. (Centre of activity).
9. N.16.c.20.88. (Suspected M.G.).
10. Area N.22.a.85.85. (Suspected M.G's).
11. N.21.c.90.65. (Track junction).
12. N.15.c.6.9. (Track junction - to be bombarded from Zero to Zero plus 10').
13. N.15.c.05.55. (R.E.FARM) (Zero to Zero plus 10').
14. N.15.a.05.15. (Farm) (Zero to Zero plus 4').

Appendix E

SECRET.   Copy No. 31

41st. DIVISIONAL ARTILLERY INSTRUCTIONS No. 22.

11th August 1918.

A. 1. Two 18-pdr. Batteries 66th Divisional Artillery will go into action in positions "Y" and "W" in M.6.d. and "T" in M.12.a. and must be in action at the earliest possible moment after dark tonight 11th instant.

 2. 66th Divisional Artillery will please issue the necessary orders.

 3. These Batteries will form a sub-group under Left Group R.F.A. 41st Divisional Artillery.
    R.A.Signals 41st Divisional Artillery are arranging the necessary communications.

 4. S.O.S. lines for Batteries of 66th D.A. will be as follows:-

    1 battery N.14.d.40.76 - N.14.d.98.92.
    1 battery N.14.a.43.08 - N.15.a.78.18.

B. 1. Counter preparation will be fired tonight between 3.15 and 3.45 a.m. in accordance with the attached table "K".

 2. XIX Corps H.A. will co-operate by searching a belt in the Left Group Zone between 500 yards and 800 yards from our front line at the same times as the Field Artillery are firing.

 3. 6th Divisional Artillery will also co-operate.

 4. In the event of a heavy hostile bombardment of the Left Group front, Groups will open fire on their Counter-preparation tasks except Left Group which will open on its S.O.S. lines at once without waiting for orders, and will continue firing at S.O.S. rates until the situation becomes quiet at the discretion of Group Commanders.

    XIX Corps H.A. will immediately commence intense Counter Battery work.

 5. Watches will be synchronized by telephone from this Office at 10 p.m.

 6. A C K N O W L E D G E.

                                          F. MacFaran
                                          Captain R.F.A.
    Issued at:- 3 p.m.   Brigade Major, 41st Divisional Arty.

Copy No.1 – 5 Right Group.	21 XIX Corps R.A.	29 S.C.R.A.
6 – 10 Centre "	22 XIX Corps H.A.	30 Sigs 41 D.A.
11 – 15 Left "	23 C.B.S.O. XIX Corps.	31 R.O.R.A.41.
16 122 I.Bde.	24 41st Divn. G.	32 War Diary.
17 123 I.Bde.	25 D.T.M.O.	33-37 File.
18 124 I.Bde.	26 35th D.A.	
19 6th D.A.	27 41st D.A.C.	
20 66th D.A.	28 41st M.G.Battn.	

P T O

TABLE K.
COUNTER PREPARATION TABLE
issued with 41st D.A. Instructions No.22.

11th August 1918.

A. TASKS.

W.	All guns and hows Left Group.	Search 400 yards on S.O.S.lines.	
V.	2 18-pdr.batteries Centre Group.	Search area N.15.a.78.18 – N.15.d.3.5. – N.15.c.35.15. – N.14.d.70.75.	
X.	1 18-pdr Battery Right Group.	Search area N.14.d.70.75. – N.15.c.35.15. – N.20.b.6.8. – N.14.d.00.48.	
Y.	4 Howitzers Centre Group.	R.E.Farm. N.14.c.25.40. N.14.c.90.20. N.20.b.05.55.	
Z.	4 Howitzers Right Group.	N.20.b.10.40. N.20.d.18.90. N.20.d.25.70. N.20.a.85.70.	

B. RATES OF FIRE.

3.15 – 3.23 a.m.   W.V.X.Y.Z.   Rapid

3.23 – 3.30 a.m.   pause

3.30 – 3.35 a.m.   W.V.X. normal Y.Z. Rapid.

3.35 – 3.38 a.m.   pause

3.38 – 3.45 a.m.   W.V.X. rapid Y.Z. Rapid.

Appendix "F"

SECRET.   Copy No 32

41st. DIVISIONAL ARTILLERY INSTRUCTIONS No.24.

                                                12th. August 1916.

1. Counter preparation will be fired to-night 12th/13th.inst.
    on the same tasks as last night in accordance with the
    following table :-

Time.	Rate of fire.
3. a.m. - 3.5 a.m.	All tasks normal.
3.5 " - 3.13 "	Pause.
3.13 " - 3.20 "	All tasks rapid.
3.20 " - 3.28 "	Pause.
3.28 " - 3.35 "	W V X Normal, Y Z rapid.
3.35 " - 3.48 "	Pause.
3.48 " - 3.55 "	W V X Intense, Y Z rapid.

2. XIXth. Corps H.A. and 6th. D.A. are co-operating.

3. Watches will be synchronized from this office at 10.p.m.

4. ACKNOWLEDGE.

                                            F. MacFarlane
                                            Captain R.F.A.
                                            Brigade Major,
Issued at 4.p.m.   41st. Divisional Artillery.

Issued to all recipients of 41st. D.A. Instructions No.22.

Appendix E

SECRET.   ADDENDUM to 41st D.A. Instructions No.22.

11th August 1918.

In the event of an S.O.S. on the Right or Centre Group fronts Right and Centre Group batteries will at once revert to normal S.O.S. lines and procedure.

F. MacFarlane
Captain R.F.A.
Brigade Major,
41st Divisional Artillery.

Issued at:- 3.30 p.m.

To all recipients of 41st D.A. Instrons. No.22.

Appendix G.

SECRET.   Copy No. 12

41st DIVISIONAL ARTILLERY INSTRUCTIONS No.23.

12th August 1918.

1. 41st Divisional Artillery will co-operate with XIX Corps H.A. in a road blocking shoot on the 14th inst. as under:-

2. TASKS

   18-pdrs.
   - (a). N.27.c.9.8. - N.27.a.85.15.
   - (b). N.27.a.85.15. - N.27.b.00.50.
   - (c). N.27.b.00.50. - N.27.b.18.80.
   - (d). N.27.b.18.80. - N.21.d.30.08.
   - (e). N.21.d.30.08. - N.21.d.45.38.

   4.5" How.
   - (f). N.27.c.9.8. - N.27.c.49.90.
   - (g). N.27.c.49.90. - N.27.a.0.0.
   - (h). N.27.a.0.0. - N.26.b.60.15.

3. Each task will be engaged by searching and sweeping with 2 guns or hows. by groups as follows:-

   Left Group (a), (b) and (f).

   Centre Group (c), (d) and (g).

   Right Group (e).

4. Zero hour will be 10.10 p.m.

5. Rate of fire:-

   Zero to Zero plus 5'   Intense.
   Zero plus 5'   Stop.

6. Ammunition:-

   18-pdrs.   A.
   4.5" Hows. BX. 106 fuze.

7. Watches will be synchronized from this office at 8 p.m.

8. ACKNOWLEDGE.

F.M. MacFarlane
Captain R.F.A.
Brigade Major,
Issued at 9 a.m.   41st Divisional Artillery.

Copy No.	
1	Right Group.
2	Centre "
3	Left "
4	41st Divn. G.
5	122nd Infy. Bde.
6	123rd " "
7	124th " "
8	XIX Corps R.A.
9	XIX Corps H.A.
10	S.C.R.A. 41st D.A.
11	Sigs. 41st D.A.
12	R.O.R.A. 41st D.A.
13	War Diary.
14 - 18	File.

Appendix H.

SECRET. Copy No. 30

41st DIVISIONAL ARTILLERY INSTRUCTIONS No. 26

14th August 1918.

1. Between 3 and 4 a.m. tonight 14th/15th inst. all batteries detailed for Counter preparation in 41st Divisional Artillery Instructions No.22 of 11th inst. will stand to on the C.P. lines therein ordered.

2. In the event of any heavy enemy bombardment on the front effected, all batteries will at once open fire on these C.P. tasks except Left Group Batteries which will fire on their S.O.S. lines without searching.

3. Fire will be intense for 5 minutes after which Group Commanders will use their own discretion as regards rate and duration of fire according to the situation.

4. Three Groups and Infantry Brigades ACKNOWLEDGE.

Captain R.F.A,
Brigade Major,
Issued at 4.30p.m. 41st Divisional Artillery.

```
Copy No. 1 - 6 Right Group.
         7 -11 Centre Group.
        12 -16 Left Group.
           17 122nd Infy. Bde.   )
           18 123rd    "    "    )
           19 124th    "    "    )
           20 41st Divn. G.      )
           21 XIX Corps R.A.     )
           22 XIX Corps H.A.     )
           23 6th Divl. Arty.    )  For information.
           24 30th Divl. Arty.   )
           25 D.T.M.O. 41st Divn.)
           26 S.C.R.A. 41st Divn.)
           27 Sigs. 41st D.A.    )
           28 R.O.R.A. 41st D.A. )
        29- 32 War Diary & File.
```

Appendix I

SECRET.   41st D.A. No. S.1198.

1.   S.O.S. lines of the two Right Batteries of the
   Right Group 41st Divisional Artillery will be changed
   forthwith to the following tasks:-

        18-pdr.Bty. on right of Group to

            M.24.d.38.00. to M.24.d.08.45.
                                      (80)

        How. Battery
            Along Road from

            N.19.a.15.00. to M.24.d.80.45.

2.   Right Group and 124th Infantry Bde. to ACKNOWLEDGE.

                                    F.M. MacFarlan
                                    Captain R.F.A.
                                    Brigade Major,
14th August 1918.   41st Divisional Artillery.

To all recipients of 41st D.A. Defence Scheme No.2.

Appendix J

SECRET.   Copy No. 9

41st DIVISIONAL ARTILLERY ORDER No.12.

15th August 1918.

1. A/330 and C/330 Batteries will withdraw from action after dark tonight 15th inst. and will rejoin 66th D.A. in accordance with 66th D.A. Order No.42 of 14th inst.

2. Positions will be left carefully camouflaged and all ammunition remaining in the positions will be left clean and weatherproof.

3. Left Group will report when these Batteries are clear of their positions using code word "PINK".

4. Left Group ACKNOWLEDGE.

                                              Captain R.F.A.
                                              Brigade Major,
Issued at:- 10 a.m.   41st Divisional Artillery.

Copy No. 1   Left Group.
         2   Centre Group.
         3   8th Divl. Arty   )
         4   66th Divl. Arty.   )
         5   122nd Infy. Bde.   ) for information
         6   41st Divn. G.   )
         7   XIX Corps R.A.   )
         8   S.O.R.A. 41st Divn.   )
         9   War Diary.
        10   File.

SECRET.   Copy No. 14

41st DIVISIONAL ARTILLERY INSTRUCTIONS No.27.

                                            15th August 1918.

1.   4.5" Howitzer Batteries of Right and Centre Groups
will co-operate with XIXth Corps H.A. in a gas shell
bombardment on night 16th/17th inst. or the first suitable night afterwards in accordance with enclosed
instructions No. XIX Corps R.A. 42/180 of 14th instant.
                                    ―
                                    G

2.   All howitzers at forward sections and main positions
will be employed.

        Rate of fire "Intense" throughout.

3.   O.Cs. Right Group and Centre Group will arrange to
harass each target on the bombardment table within range
during each 2 minute burst with one section 18-pdrs.

        Rate of fire "Intense".

4.   Watches will be synchronized from this Office at an
hour to be notified later.

5.   ACKNOWLEDGE.

                                    [signature]
                                        Captain R.F.A.
                                        Brigade Major,
        Issued at:-10.30 a.m.   41st Divisional Artillery.

Copy No. 1 Right Group.
        2   Centre   "
        3   41st Divn G.   ) For information without
        4   122nd Infy.Bde.   ) detailed bombardment orders.
        5   123rd   "   "   )
        6   124th   "   "   ) Bombardment will consist of
        7   XIX Corps R.A.   ) short intense bursts between
        8   XIX Corps H.A.   ) 9.45 p.m. and 1.17 a.m.
        9   S.C.R.A.41st D.A.   )
       10   S.O. 41st D.A.   ) Code words:-
       11   D.T.M.O.   )
       12   41st D.A.C.   ) HOT = Bombardment on.
       13   Left Group.   ) COLD = Bombardment off.
       14   War Diary.
    15 - 18 File.

Appendix I.

SECRET   Copy No. 95

41st DIVISIONAL ARTILLERY ORDER No. 13.

Ref. sheets 27-28.

1.   41st D.A. will be relieved by 66th D.A. on nights 17/18th and 18/19th August.

2.   H.Q. 11th Army Brigade R.F.A., 85th Battery R.F.A., D/11th Battery R.F.A., and T.M's of 41st Division will remain in action under 66th D.A.

3.   41st D.A. will take over responsibility for defence of 2nd POSITION on relief.

4.   Commands will pass as follows:-

       D.A.H.Q. at 9 a.m. 19-8-18.
       Groups   ) on completion of relief.
       Batteries)

5.   187th Brigade R.F.A. will be relieved by 330th Bde. R.F.A.
       190th   "   "   "   "   "   "   331st   "   "

       41st D.A.C. will not move.

       No. 1 Coy. 41st Divisional Train will not move.

       11th B.A.C. will not move.

6.   Guns will be exchanged in situ (see G.R.O.3202)
       Guns of 66th D.A. in Wagon Lines will be handed over to representatives of Batteries of 41st D.A. on afternoon of 18th inst.
       Units of 41st D.A. will obtain receipts for all material handed over to 66th D.A.

7.   Details of relief will be arranged direct between Brigade Commanders concerned subject to the following:-

     (a). All forward sections of 41st D.A. will be relieved on evening of the 17th inst.

     (b). All sections of 66th D.A. in observation in 2nd POSITION will be relieved on 18th inst. Also the 2 Anti-Tank guns.

     (c). Brigade Headquarters and remainder of 41st D.A. Batteries in action will be relieved on evening of 18th inst.

     (d). Wagon lines will be exchanged on 19th inst. Moves to be completed by 2 p.m.

8.   One officer per Battery of 41st D.A. will remain with relieving Battery of 66th D.A. for 24 hours after relief if required.
       All defence schemes, map boards, tactical instructions, orders and documents relating to the sector, air photos, maps etc:- will be handed over and receipts taken.

9.   41st D.A. Batteries will hand over and obtain receipts for all ammunition on their charge, less echelons, and will take over all ammunition at 2nd POSITION positions reporting amounts to this office.

                                   P.T.O.

10. Sections of 41st D.A. on going into action in 2nd POSITION positions will come under orders of 66th D.A. till 9 a.m. 19th inst.

11. Completion of each gun line relief will be reported to this office by groups by wire using code word "LILAC".

12. 41st D.A.C. will hand over ammunition supply of the D.A. in the line to 66th D.A.C. at 9 a.m. 19th inst.

13. One lorry per battery on first night and one per Battery and Brigade Headquarters on second night of relief will bring 66th D.A. personnel to G.32.c.9.3. at 5 p.m. Units of 41st D.A. will send guides to this point to meet them and conduct the relieving parties to gun positions. They will also send a man to remain with their opposite numbers lorry who will remain with the lorry till the outgoing personnel get down from the guns, when the lorry will take them to their Wagon Lines.

14. H.Q. 41st D.A. will close at K.24.c.1.1. and reopen at ST LAURENT J.18.d. at 9 a.m. 19th inst.

15. ACKNOWLEDGE.

F.N. MacFarlane
Captain R.F.A.
Brigade Major,
41st Divisional Artillery.

17th August 1918.
Issued at:- 2 a.m.

Copy No. 1 187th Bde. R.F.A.) with copy 66th D.A. Order No.43 & 66th
2 190th " ") D.A. location statement.
3 11th Army Bde. R.F.A.
4 D.T.M.O. 41st Divn.
5 41st D.A.C.
6 66th Divl. Arty. (4 copies).
7 41st Divn. G.
8 41st Divn. Q.
9 No. 1 Coy. 41st Divl. Train.
10 30th Divl. Arty.
11 6th Divl. Arty.
12 XIX Corps R.A.
13 XIX Corps H.A.
14 XIX Corps C.B.S.O.
15 41st M.G.Battn.
16 C.R.E. 41st Divn.
17 122nd Infy. Bde.
18 123rd " "
19 124th " "
20 No.10 Squadron R.A.F.
21 39th K.B.S.
22 D.A.D.O.S. 41st Divn.
23 A.P.M. 41st Divn.
24 S.C.R.A. 41st Divn.
25 Signal Officer 41st D.A.
26 R.O.R.A. 41st Divn.
27 War Diary.
28)
29) File.
30)

App "L"

SECRET.   COPY No. 23

ADMINISTRATIVE INSTRUCTION ISSUED WITH
41st. D.A. Order No. 13, dated 17th.Aug:'18.

1. Wagon Lines (less D.A.C. and No.1 Coy.Divnl.Train) will be exchanged on 19th.inst. as directed by abovementioned Order. Locations of new Wagon Lines are attached.

2. 41st.D.A.C. and No.1 Coy.Divisional Train will not move.

3. Area Stores will be handed over and receipts given and taken.

4. Wagon Lines will be left clean and sanitary.

5. Units will move with echelons full.

6. D.A.C. will detail one G.S.Wagon and team to report at each battery and B'de. H.Q.wagon line at 9.a.m. 19th.inst. to assist in removal. Where a Battery or H.Q. wagon line already has a D.A.C. wagon, less team, in its possession, a team only will be sent.

7. D.A.C. will detail one Officer and 5 O.R. to take over 66th.D.Arty. A.R.P. at K.22.a.5.2 at 7.p.m. 17th.inst. This will be A.R.P. for 41st. D.A. after completion of relief.

8. The A.R.P. at STEENAKKER will remain on charge of 41st. D.A.C. who will retain 1 Officer and 15 O.R. there for work in the improvement of the Dump, which will not issue.

9. A return will be rendered to this office by 12 noon 19th.inst., showing separately amount and nature of all ammunition :-

   (a) Handed over by batteries to 66th.D.A. at Btty.positions.
   (b)   "   "   "   "   "   "   "unoccupied"
   (c) Taken over by batteries from 66th.D.A.at Bty. positions.
   (d) In Echelons.

10. D.A.C. return will show amount and natures:-

    (a) Taken over at 66th.D.Arty. A.R.P.
    (b) Remaining on charge at STEENAKKER.
    (c) In Echelons.

11. RATIONS. The working party of 23 men at present rationed by A/190th.Bde. will be so rationed for the last time for consumption 18th. For consumption 19th. and following days the 11 men of the party from 187th.Bde. will be rationed by 187th.Bde. and the remaining 12 men from 331 Bde. by 66th.D.A. Except as above ration supply will remain as at present, the first delivery being made to new wagon lines on 20th.inst.

12. Arrangements regarding Baths, Railhead etc. will be notified later.

                                              Captain,
17-8-1918.   a/Staff Captain,41st.Divisional Arty.
Issued at 2.a.m.

LOCATIONS OF WAGON LINES TO BE OCCUPIED
by 41st.Div: ARTY. on & from 19th.Aug.1918.

UNIT.	LOCATION OF WAGON LINE.	TAKEN OVER FROM.
41st.D.A.H.Q.	ST.LAURENT (J.18.d.9.2)	---
H.Q.187th.Bde.	K.28.a.90.65	H.Q.330th.Bde.
"A" Bty. "	K.27.a.3.8	"A" Bty. "
"B" " "	K.27.a.3.8	"B" " "
"C" " "	K.22.c.7.6	"C" " "
"D" " "	K.15.d.5.6	"D" " "
H.Q.190th.Bde.	K.22.a.9.7	H.Q.331st.Bde.
"A" Bty. "	K.16.d.75.75	"A" Bty. "
"B" " "	K.23.c.2.0	"B" " "
"C" " "	K.22.a.9.7	"C" " "
"D" " "	K.22.a.9.7	"D" " "
H.Q.41st.D.A.C.	K.21.c.60.30	
No.1 Section.	K.34.b.90.90	---
" 2 "	K.35.a.70.40	---
" 3 (SAA)"	K.21.d.95.80	---
No.1 Coy.Divnl.Train.	K.21.d.70.40	

Copy No.1 - 5 187th.Brigade R.F.A.
     6 - 10 190th. " "
    11 - 14 41st.D.A.C.
    15. 11th.(Army) Bde.R.F.A.
    16. D.T.M.O. 41.
    17. B.M. 41st.D.A.
    18. 41st.Divnl.Train.
    19. 41st. Divn. 'Q'.
    20. 66th. D.A.
    21. A. R. P.
    22. War Diary.
   23.- 26. File.

Appendix M

SECRET   Copy No. 43

41st DIVISIONAL ARTILLERY ORDER No.14.

25-8-18.

1. 41st Divisional Artillery will relieve 66th Divisional Artillery in the line on night ~~29th/30th~~ 26/27 and ~~30th/31st~~ 27/28 inst.

2. Trench Mortars 41st Division, H.Q. 11th Army Bde.R.F.A., 85th Battery R.F.A., D/11th Battery R.F.A. and 11th B.A.C. will come under the orders of 41st Divisional Artillery on relief.

3. Commands will pass as under.

   Brigades & Batteries   on completion of relief.
   D.A.H.Qs   at 9 a.m. ~~31st instant.~~ 28th

4. 41st Divisional Artillery will hand over responsibility for defence of 2nd position to 66th Divisional Artillery on relief.
   All R.F.A. units detailed for the defence of the 2nd Position will be under the orders of 41st D.A. till 9 a.m. 31st inst. when they come under the orders of 66th D.A.

5. All units 41st D.A. will relieve the same units of 66th D.A. as relieved them during last relief.
   41st D.A.C., 41 T.M.Bs and No.1 Coy. 41st Divisional Train will not move.

6. All details of relief will be arranged direct between Brigade Commanders concerned subject to the following:-

   Forward sections will be relieved on first night.
   2nd Position sections   "   "   " ~~30th inst.~~ 27th
   Brigade H.Q. and re-)   "   "   " ~~2nd night~~ 28th
   mainder of batteries)
   Wagon lines will be exchanged on ~~31st inst.~~ 29th before 2 p.m.

   No movement of vehicles except M.T., E of a N & S line through G.31.central before dark.

7. M.T. arrangements and all details regarding handing over will be the same as for last relief.

8. Guns and sights will be exchanged in situ. Brigade Commanders will arrange that on completion of relief every unit is in possession of its own guns and sights.

9. 41st D.A.C. will take over ammunition supply, including relief of A.R.P. personnel, from 66th D.A.C. at 9 a.m. 31st inst.

10. H.Q. 41st D.A. will close at K.19.a.9.9. and re-open at K.24.c.2.3. at 9 a.m. ~~31st inst.~~ 28th

11. ACKNOWLEDGE.

                                    F.H. MacFarlane
                                    Captain R.F.A.
                                    Brigade Major,
Issued at:- 12 noon.   41st Divisional Artillery.

                                    Distribution over.

```
Copy No.  1 -  5   187th Bde. R.F.A.
          6 - 10   190th  "    "
         11 - 14   41st D.A.C.
              15   D.T.M.O. 41st Divn.
              16   41st Divn. G.
              17   41st Divn. Q.
              18   No. 1 Coy. 41st Divl. Train.
              19   XIX Corps R.A.
              20   XIX Corps H.A.
              21   XIX Corps C.B.S.O.
         22 - 25   66th Divl. Arty.
              26)  122nd)
              27)  123rd) Infy. Bdes.
              28)  124th)
              29   C.R.E. 41st Divn.
              30   A.D.M.S. 41st Divn.
              31   D.A.D.O.S. 41st Divn.
              32   30th Divl. Arty.
              33   6th Divl. Arty.
              34   27th American Division.
              35   65th Bde. R.G.A.
              36   6th Bde. R.G.A.
              37   10th Squadron R.A.F.
              38   39th K.B.S.
              39   41st Signal Coy.
              40   S.C.R.A. 41st Divn.
              41   Sigs R.A. 41st Divn.
              42   R.O.R.A. 41st Divn.
              43   War Diary.
         44 - 48   File.
```

Army Form C. 2118.

WAR-DIARY
or
INTELLIGENCE SUMMARY
Headquarters, 41st. Divisional Artillery

(Erase heading not required.)

Instructions regarding War Diaries and Intelligence Summaries are contained in F. S. Regs., Part II. and the Staff Manual respectively. Title pages will be prepared in manuscript.

Place	Date	Hour	Summary of Events and Information	Remarks and references to Appendices
	1918			
BELGIUM SCHERPENBERG Area.	1st.Sept.		An attack, with the final objective the old enemy front line of 1916, was carried out by 101st. and 102nd. Infantry Brigades supported by 41st.Divisional Artillery. The attack was only partially successful. Our infantry reached approximately the old British front line of 1915.	
--do--	2nd.Sept.		102nd.Infantry Brigade relieved 101st. and 103rd.Infantry Brigades; the changes in the artillery arrangements being as shown in Appendix "A".	App:"A"
--do--	5th.Sept.		Relief of 41st.Divisional Artillery by 34th.Divisional Artillery carried out as in Appendix "B" Programme for Harassing fire issued; special attention was to be paid to the CRATERS, PETIT BOIS, and WYTSCHAETE WOOD (Appendix "C").	App:"B" App:"C"
--do--	6th.Sept.		Relief continued (Appendix "B")	App:"B"
--do--	7th.Sept.		Relief continued (Appendix "B") In consequence of the re-adjustment of the Divisional boundaries the S.O.S. lines of Groups were altered. (Appendix "D")	App:"B" App:"D"
ABEELE Area.	8th.Sept.		34th.Divisional Artillery took over from 41st.Divisional Artillery at 10 a.m. 41st.D.A.,H.Q., on relief, rejoined Headquarters, 41st.Division, near ABEELE. Batteries of 11th.(Army) Brigade, R.F.A., withdrawn from action. Groups make the necessary alteration in S.O.S. lines. (Appendix "E").	App:"E"
--do--	9th.Sept.		Capt. F.N.MASON MACFARLANE, M.C.,R.F.A., Brigade Major, 41st.Divisional Artillery, selected for Staff Appointment in INDIA, proceeded to England. Temp.Major E.R.ROPER, D.S.O., M.C., R.F.A., O.C. "A" Battery, 187th.Brigade,R.F.A., appointed Brigade Major R.A., 41st.Division, assuming duties on 10th.Sept.1918.	
--do--	10th.Sept.		Captain T.H.BISCHOFF, M.C., Staff Captain, R.A.,41st.Division, admitted to Hospital (Sick). Captain W.A.MACKENZIE,M.C.,R.F.A., Adjutant,190th.Brigade, R.F.A., assumed duties of Staff Captain, 41st.D.A.	
--do--	13th.Sept.		Provisional Defence Scheme issued (Appendix "F")	App:"F"

-1-

Army Form C. 2118.

WAR DIARY
— or —
INTELLIGENCE SUMMARY

Headquarters, 41st. Divisional Artillery

(Erase heading not required.)

Instructions regarding War Diaries and Intelligence Summaries are contained in F. S. Regs., Part II. and the Staff Manual respectively. Title Pages will be prepared in manuscript.

Place	Date	Hour	Summary of Events and Information	Remarks and references to Appendices
BELGIUM				
ABEELE Area.	14th. Sept.		Work commenced on forward positions by 190th. and 187th. Brigades, R.F.A. These positions were situated about 2,000 to 3,000 yards from our Front line, and were intended for use in future operations.	
—do—	16th. Sept.		Dumping of Ammunition for forward positions commenced. D.A.C. assisted Brigades with pack animals; the ammunition being taken up by light railway as far as possible.	
—do—	18th. Sept.		During the pending offensive it was arranged that 190th. Brigade should support the attack by the 14th. Division on ST. ELOI CRATERS and the BLUFF, from its present positions, whilst 187th. Brigade supported attack, by 35th. Division north of the YPRES – COMINES CANAL, from positions prepared in the vicinity of BELGIAN CHATEAU, S.W. of YPRES. As soon as these two Divisions had gained their final objectives, 187th. and 190th. Brigades were to revert to C.R.A., 41st. Division in support of attack by 41st. Division.	
—do—	21st Sept.		187th. Brigade, R.F.A., relieved by a Brigade of 34th. Divisional Artillery, and withdrew to its Wagon lines, pending occupation of the offensive positions near BELGIAN CHATEAU. They came under orders of C.R.A., 35th. Division.	
—do—	23rd. Sept.		190th. Brigade, R.F.A., came under 14th. Divisional Artillery, but remained in their present positions.	
—do—	26th. Sept.		Instructions as to attack by XIXth. Corps issued. (Appendix "H")	App: "H"
BUSSEBOOM Area.	27th. Sept.		41st. Divl: H.Q., R.A. moved to MERSEY CAMP (BUSSEBOOM Area). Captain S. COKE, R.G.A., XIXth. Corps H.A., was attached to 41st. D.A., H.Q., as Liaison Officer for pending operations.	
—do—	28th. Sept.		Attack commenced at 5.30 a.m. Enemy resistance was slight, and there was little M.G. or rifle fire. At 7.45 a.m., news was received that 35th. Division had taken CANADA TUNNELS and HILL 60, and that 14th. Division's attack was progressing well, the BLUFF and ST. ELOI CRATERS being taken. Lieut. Col. G.A. GARDEW, C.M.G., D.S.O., Commanding 190th. Brigade, R.F.A., slightly wounded whilst reconnoitring forward positions. During the day 190th. Brigade moved to the vicinity of LA CHAPELLE FARM, where they came into action in support of an attack by 124th. Infantry Brigade East of the YPRES–COMINES CANAL. Artillery arrangements as shown in Appendix "H". The attack was successful. Positions in the vicinity of HOLLEBEKE CHATEAU to be occupied	App: "H"

Army Form C. 2118.

WAR DIARY
—or—
INTELLIGENCE SUMMARY.
(Erase heading not required.)

Headquarters, 41st. Divisional Artillery

Instructions regarding War Diaries and Intelligence Summaries are contained in F.S. Regs., Part II. and the Staff Manual respectively. Title pages will be prepared in manuscript.

Place	Date	Hour	Summary of Events and Information	Remarks and references to Appendices
BELGIUM MERSEY CAMP (BUSSEBOOM Area.)	1918 28th.Sept (contd)		by the 187th.Brigade the following day were reconnoitred. Orders were issued for the advance to be continued by the 123rd. and 124th.Infantry Brigades. (Appendix "I")	App:"I"
--do-- & LANKHOF FM., nr. YPRES - COMINES Canal.	29th.Sept		The advance was continued. 123rd.Infantry Brigade passed through 124th.Infantry Brigade (as shown in Appendix "I"). 187th.Brigade, R.F.A., pushed forward sections to vicinity of HOLLEBEKE CHATEAU. Owing to the state of the roads great difficulty was experienced in moving forward. During the day both Brigades succeeded in pushing forward to positions in the vicinity of HOLLEBEKE CHATEAU. 41st.D.A.,H.Q., moved to LANKHOF FARM in the vicinity of YPRES - COMINES CANAL.	App:"I"
--do--	30th Sept		Orders issued for an approach march on MENIN to be carried out by 41st.Division; 190th.Brigade R.F.A., being grouped with 122nd.Infantry Brigade, and 187th.Brigade, R.F.A., with 123rd. Infantry Brigade.	

15.10.18.

Brigadier General,
Commanding 41st. Divisional Artillery.

War Diary

Appendix A.

SECRET   Copy No. 25

41st DIVISIONAL ARTILLERY ORDER No. 15.

2nd September 1918.

1.   102nd Infantry Brigade will take over the 34th Divisional front tonight, with two Battalions in line, and one in support.

2.   In consequence of the above the Artillery covering the front will be formed into one Group under O.C. 187th Brigade R.F.A.

Present Right Group will be known as Right Sub-Group and will cover the Right Battalion. Headquarters with 102 Infantry Brigade.

Present Left Group will be known as Left Sub-Group and will cover the Left Battalion. Headquarters as under.

O.C. 187th Brigade R.F.A. will accompany G.O.C. 102 Infantry Brigade.

Left Sub-Group Headquarters will be established at N.7.d.2.1.

3.   A Liaison Officer with each Battalion in the line will be found by each Sub-Group.

4.   The above will come into force on completion of relief or at 6 a.m. 3rd. September, whichever occurs first.

5.   ACKNOWLEDGE

F. MacFarlane
Captain R.F.A.
Brigade Major,
41st Divisional Artillery.

Issued at:- 5.30 p.m.

Copy No. 1 - 6   Right Group.
         7 - 12 Left   "
         13   41st Divn. G.
         14   34th   "   G.
         15   101 Infantry Bde.
         16   102   "   "
         17   103   "   "
         18   6th Divl. Arty.
         19   30th Divl. Arty.
         20   XIX Corps R.A.
         21   XIX Corps H.A.
         22   C.B.S.O. XIX Corps.
         23   S.C.R.A. 41st Divn.
         24   R.A. Sigs.
         25   War Diary.
         26 - 30 File.

WD   Appendix B

SECRET   Copy No. 48

41st DIVISIONAL ARTILLERY ORDER No. 16.

5th September 1918.

1. 41st Divisional Artillery will relieve 34th Divisional Artillery covering 41st Division in the DICKEBUSCH Sector as follows.

2. All Headquarters, gun positions, wagon lines and dumps will be exchanged.

3. Moves will take place as follows:-

5th September.   A/187 exchange Wagon Lines with A/160.
                  D/187   "   "   "   "   D/160.
                  A/190   "   "   "   "   A/152.

Night 5th/6th September   Above Batteries exchange gun positions.

6th September   B/187 exchange Wagon lines with B/160.
                 B/190   "   "   "   " B/152.

Night 6th/7th September.   Above Batteries exchange gun positions.

7th September   C/187 exchange Wagon lines with C/160.
                 C/190   "   "   "   " C/152.
                 D/190   "   "   "   " D/152.

Night 7th/8th September.   Above batteries exchange gun positions.

8th September.   187th Brigade Headquarters and Wagon Lines will be exchanged with those of 152 Brigade.
   190th Brigade Headquarters and Wagon Lines will be exchanged with those of 160 Brigade.
   41st D.A.C. exchange Wagon Lines with 34th D.A.C., and personnel at A.R.P.
   41st T.M.Bs. exchange Wagon lines with 34th T.M.Bs.
   No.1 Coy, 41st Divl. Train will exchange Wagon lines with No.1 Coy. 34th Divl. Train.

4. Batteries of 11th Army Brigade R.F.A., and 41st D.A.C. S.A.A.Section will not move. 11th Army Brigade Batteries will come under the orders of the incoming group commanders when commands pass.

5. Commands will pass as under:-
       D.A.H.Qs.   10 a.m. on 8th September.
       Groups.   10 a.m. on 8th September.
       Batteries   on completion of relief.

6. Location statement of 34th D.A. is issued herewith as Appendix "A" to all concerned.

7. All ammunition and camouflage at gun positions, and maps and documents relating to the front will be handed over and receipts taken.
   The above will also be taken over from 34th D.A. units at the new positions, and amounts of ammunition so taken over reported at once to S.C.R.A.

1.

8. All details of relief subject to the above will be arranged direct between units concerned.

Group Commanders and Battery Commanders will endeavour to make themselves as much acquainted as possible with the new sector before moving.

9. Completion of relief in the case of each unit will be wired to 41st D.A. and 34th D.A. using code word "BOB"

10. Headquarters 41st Divisional Artillery will close at M.10.d.6.6. and re-open at L.14.a.2.0. at 10 a.m. on 8th September.

11. A C K N O W L E D G E.

F. MacFarlan
Captain R.F.A.
Brigade Major,
41st Divisional Artillery.

Issued at 2 p.m.

Distribution:-

Copy No. 1 - 6 Right Group.
        7 - 12 Left "
       13 - 18 34th Divl. Arty.
       19 - 22 41st D.A.C.
           23 41st D.T.M.O.
           24 No. 1 Coy. 41st Divl. Train.
           25 41st Divn. G.
           26 34th Divn. G.
           27 41st Divn. Q.
           28 34th Divn. Q.
           29 XIX Corps R.A.
           30 XIX Corps H.A.
           31 XIX Corps C.B.S.O.
           32 30th Divl. Arty.
           33 66th " "
           34 122nd Infy. Bde.
           35 123rd " "
           36 124th " "
           37 101st " "
           38 102nd " "
           39 103rd " "
           40 A.D.M.S. 41st Divn.
           41 A.D.V.S. 41st Divn.
           42 D.A.D.O.S. 41st Divn.
           43 A.P.M. 41st Divn.
           44 A.P.M. 34th Divn.
           45 S.C.R.A. 41st Divn.
           46 R.A.Sigs. 41st Divn.
           47 R.O.R.A. 41st Divn.
           48 War Diary.
      49 - 53 File.

SECRET

APPENDIX "A" to 41st D.A. ORDER No. 16.

LOCATIONS of 34th DIVISIONAL ARTILLERY.

Ref: Sheets 27 & 28 1/40,000.

Unit.	Location.	Wagon Lines.
R.A.H.Q. 34th Div.	DOUGLAS CAMP (L.14.a.2.0.)	L.13.d.9.9.
Right Group (160) H.Q.	H.32.a.5.0.	G.22.b.7.7.
A/160 6 guns.	N. 3.c.1.7.	G.22.a.5.4.
B/160 6 "	N. 3.a.4.2.	G.22.
C/160 6 "	H.32.d.1.0.	G.22.a.2.4.
D/160 6 Hows.	N. 3.b.2.7.	G.22.c.8.7.
83rd. Battery.	N. 3.b.6.1.	G.25.b.5.3.
Left Group (152) H.Q.	H.27.b.6.7.	H.8.c.65.10.
Rear Bde. H.Q.	H. 8.c.65.10.	
A/152. 6 guns.	H.33.b.8.9.	G.16.b.4.9.
B/152. 6 "	H.29.c.45.15.	G.10.c.7.2.
C/152. 4 "	H.28.d.30.65.	G.16.d.45.80.
2 "	H.28.a.4.6.	(ELGIN FARM)
D/152. 6 Hows.	H.28.c.50.15.	G.11.a.2.2.
84th Battery.	H.29.a.0.7.	(QUERY FARM)
34th D.A.C., H.Q.		L.16.d.5.5.
No. 1 Section.		L.14.c.4.4.
No. 2 Section.		L.16.d.5.8.
34th T.M.Bs.		L. 2.d.6.6.
34th A.R.P.		CORDOVA (G.24.d.4.4.)
No. 1 Coy. Train.		L.17.c.2.8.

5th September 1918.

S E C R E T   41st D.A. No. S.1314.

Right Group.   XIX Corps R.A.
Left   "   S.C.R.A. 41st Divn.
34th Divn. G.

     Bombardments of craters and PETIT BOIS and WYTSCHAETE WOOD will not take place on the 7th instant.
     4.5" Hows. will fire up to 50 rounds per Battery during night 7/8th on likely routes of approach in group zones.
     This is in addition to 18-pdr harassing fire as already laid down.

                                                                Captain R.N.A.
                                                                Brigade Major,
6-9-18.   41st Divisional Artillery

SECRET Copy No. 14

41st DIVISIONAL ARTILLERY INSTRUCTION No. 30.

5th September 1918.

1. 101 Brigade is relieving 102 Brigade in the southern half of the Division front between WORMWOOD - PECKHAM road just N of PECKHAM craters (incl. to 101 Brigade) and the southern Divisional Boundary on night 5th/6th inst.

2. 41st Divisional Artillery will be grouped as follows:-

With 101 Brigade :-
   Right Group   H.Q. 187 Brigade   SCHERPENBERG
   A, B, C and D/187 and D/190.

With 102 Brigade :-
   Left Group   H.Q. 190 Brigade   N.20.d.1.4.
   A, B & C/190. 85th and D/11.

3. The above re-grouping will come into force at 8 p.m. 5th instant.

4. Groups will maintain Liaison Officers with each Battalion in the line in their sector.

5. 41st D.A. Group and Sub-Groups to ACKNOWLEDGE.

                                   Captain R.F.A.
                                   Brigade Major,
Issued at 7 a.m.   41st Divisional Artillery.

Copy No. 1   41st D.A. Group.
         2 - 7   Right Sub-Group.
         8 -13   Left Sub-Group.
         14   34th Divn. G.
         15   30th Divl. Arty.
         16   34th Divl. Arty.
         17   101 Infy. Bde.
         18   102 "   "
         19   103 "   "
         20   XIX Corps R.A.
         21   XIX Corps H.A.
         22   XIX Corps C.B.S.O.
         23   C.R.E. 34th Divn.
         24   A.D.M.S. 34th Divn.
         25   Sigs. 41st D.A.
         26   S.C.R.A. 41st Divn.
         27   War Diary.
         28 -30 File.

Appendix C

SECRET.   Copy No. 22

41st DIVISIONAL ARTILLERY INSTRUCTION No.31.

5th September 1918.

Harassing & Bombardment Programme

A. (1). 4.5" Hows. 2 shoots daily (one in the morning and one in the afternoon):-

   (a). Left Group   -   PETIT BOIS.
   (b). Right Group -   WYSCHAETE WOOD.

   100 rounds each.

   Two 18-pdr. batteries will fire shrapnel on these areas during those shoots.

(2). One shoot of 40 rounds on each crater (there are two in each area) with one 18-pdr. battery firing shrapnel at the same time.

   The time and duration of all the above shoots will be fixed by Group Commanders and communicated to this Office.

B.   18-pdrs. Harassing fire up to a maximum of 150 rounds per battery will be carried out by night on likely routes of approach in Group Areas.

   Groups ACKNOWLEDGE.

F.W. MacFarlan
Captain R.F.A.
Brigade Major,
41st Divisional Artillery.

Issued at:- 11 p.m.

Copy No. 1 - 6 Right Group.
          7 - 12 Left   "
             13 34th Divn. G.
             14 101 Infy. Bde.
             15 102 "   "
             16 103 "   "
             17 XIX Corps R.A.
             18 XIX Corps H.A.
             19 34th M.G.Battn.
             20 S.C.R.A. 41st Divn.
             21 R.O.R.A. 41st Divn.
             22 War Diary.
        23 - 26 File.

Appendix D

SECRET   COPY No. 8

41st DIVISIONAL ARTILLERY INSTRUCTIONS No. 30.

Reference Map: Sheet 20 S.E.   7th September 1918.
               1/20,000.

1. (a). The 102nd Infantry Brigade are relieving troops of the 123rd Infantry Brigade, 41st Division on that portion of the Corps Front between the present Northern Divisional Boundary and the new Northern Divisional Boundary, as described in para. 2 below, on the night of 7th/8th September.

    (b). The 101st Infantry Brigade are relieving troops of the 102nd Infantry Brigade on that portion of the Divisional Front between the present Inter-Brigade Boundary and the new Inter-Brigade Boundary, as described in para. 2 below, on the night of 7th/8th September.

2. (a). The new Divisional Northern Boundary runs as follows:-

    N.1.central - N.13.d.0.5. - O.13.d.2.2. - O.2.d.3.1. and will be the northern boundary of the Left Group.

    (b). The new Inter-Brigade and Inter-Group Boundary runs as follows:-

    BEAVER CORNER (N.15.c.5.5.) - Road Junction N.23.a.0.2. - Road Junction N.24.d.0.2.

3.   The O.C. 24th Bn. M.G.Corps is arranging to relieve any Machine Guns of 41st Division in the new area to be taken over, and for the adjustment of the Machine Gun Defence between Coys. in accordance with the new Inter-Brigade Boundary.

4.   All Artillery adjustments necessitated by the above will be completed by 5 a.m. on the morning of September 8th.

5.   GROUPS ACKNOWLEDGE.

                                              H. Hopkins
                                              Captain R.F.A.
                                              Brigade Major,
Issued at 10.30 a.m.   41st Divisional Artillery.

       Copy No. 1   Right Group.
               2   Left
               3   41st D.T.M.O.
               4   34th D.A.
               5   80th D.A.
               6   24th Divn. G.
               7   XX Corps R.A.
               8   War Diary.
               9   File.

Appendix E.

SECRET.   Copy No. 13

41st DIVISIONAL ARTILLERY INSTRUCTIONS No. 33.

7th September 1918.

1. 85th Battery R.F.A. and D/11 Battery R.F.A. will withdraw after dusk on 8th inst. to 2nd Position Wagon Lines.

2. S.C.R.A. 41st Division will notify locations of wagon lines to be occupied to Left Group.

3. No restrictions as to route.

4. All ammunition in the vacated battery positions will be taken on charge by Left Group.

5. From 6 p.m. 8th inst. D/152 Battery will come under the orders of O.C. Left Group.

6. Groups will submit proposed S.O.S. tasks as from 6 p.m. 8th inst. to this office.

7. ACKNOWLEDGE.

A. S. Cotter B.G.
Captain R.F.A.
Brigade Major,
Issued at :- 6.45 p.m.   41st Divisional Artillery

```
Copy No. 1    Right Group.
        2    Left    "
        3    34th Divn. G.
        4    101st Infy. Bde.
        5    102nd   "    "
        6    103rd   "    "
        7    XIX Corps R.A.
        8    S.C.R.A. 41st Divn.
        9    34th Divl. Arty.
       10    30th    "    "
       11    11th Army Bde. R.F.A.
       12    41st D.A.C.
       13    War Diary.
       14)
       15)   File.
       16)
```

War Diary Appendix F

NOT TO BE TAKEN BEYOND MAIN BATTERY POSITIONS.

SECRET.   Copy No. 29.

PROVISIONAL DICKEBUSCH SECTOR ARTILLERY DEFENCE SCHEME.

Reference Maps:- 28 N.W. 3 & 4) 1/10,000.   13th September 1918.
                 28 S.W. 1 & 2)

1. Pending the issue of a Defence Scheme for the sector now held by this Division the following is issued for guidance

GENERAL POLICY.

2. Though the position now held is to be consolidated, the closest touch is to be kept with the enemy and any further withdrawal on his part is to be vigorously and closely followed. Batteries must therefore be prepared to move at short notice, and thorough reconnaissance must be made of forward area with a view to occupation of advanced positions. Attention should be specially directed to the matter of routes of advance.

SYSTEMS OF DEFENCE.

3. The systems of defence in the Divisional Area are:-

(a). The Front System.
(b). The VIERSTRAAT System.
(c). The SCHERPENBERG - DICKEBUSCH System.

METHOD OF HOLDING THE LINE.

4. The Divisional Front is held as follows:-

One Infantry Brigade plus one Battalion in the line.

One Infantry Brigade less one Battalion in support.

One Infantry Brigade in Divisional Reserve.

The Front System is divided into two subsectors each held by one Battalion distributed in depth.
The two remaining Battalions of the Brigade in the line are in Brigade Support.

5. In case of hostile attack on the Divisional Front:-

(a). The First line of the Front System will be held to the last. Local reserves are detailed to counter-attack and recover any portion of the Front System which may be lost.

(b). The two Support Battalions of Brigade in the line will occupy and hold the VIERSTRAAT System.

(c). The Brigade in Support (less one Battalion attached to Brigade in the Line) will occupy the SCHERPENBERG - DICKEBUSCH Line ready to:-
    (i). Replace either or both of the Support Battalions of Front Brigade in the VIERSTRAAT Line.
    (ii). Reinforce the VIERSTRAAT Line.
    (iii). Counter-attack and recapture any portion of the VIERSTRAAT Line

(d). The role of the Brigade in Reserve will be laid down later.

(e). Working parties engaged in work forward of the VIERSTRAAT System will man the trenches nearest the spot where they are working, the Officer or N.C.O. in charge of the party reporting for orders to the nearest Company Commander.

ARTILLERY DISPOSITIONS. 6. The Divisional Artillery is divided into two Groups, each covering one of the Battalions in the Line.

Groups are as follows:-

(a). <u>Right Group</u>: 187th Brigade R.F.A.
Lieut. Col. C.D.G. LYON, D.S.O., R.F.A., Comdg.

(b). <u>Left Group</u>: 190th Brigade R.F.A.
Lieut. Col. G.A. CARDEW, C.M.G., D.S.O., R.F.A. Commanding.

Positions of Group Headquarters and Batteries are given in Appendix A, which will be replaced from time to time by periodical Location Statements.

HEAVY ARTILLERY. 7. The Heavy Artillery covering the Divisional Sector consists of the 4th Brigade R.G.A., of the following strength:- (H.Q.G.23.b.5.4.)

9.2" Hows.	1 Battery.
8" Hows.	1 Battery.
6" Hows.	2 Batteries.
60 Pdrs.	2 Batteries.

A direct line exists between this Brigade and 41st D.A.H.Q.

DISTRIBUTION IN DEPTH. 8. As soon as necessary reconnaissances can be made and positions prepared Batteries are to be arranged on the principle of distribution in depth. Each Battery will have a Forward Section for purposes of Harassing Fire. The remainder of the Battery will be silent except in case of S.O.S., a Counter Preparation or of special Operations.

ARTILLERY ZONES. 9. The Inner Zone for purposes of Harassing Fire etc. by Field Artillery is the Zone between our Front line and a line parallel with it at a distance of 1500 yds.
Southern and Northern Boundaries of the Zone are lines drawn due East from N.18.d.1.1. and O.1.b.3.3. Dividing line between Groups will be a line drawn due East from N.12.d.15.85.

S.O.S. PROCEDURE. 10. S.O.S. lines are as shewn in Appendix B.
The usual S.O.S. procedure will be followed.
The S.O.S. Signal at present in use is a rifle grenade bursting into RED over RED over RED.

MUTUAL SUPPORT. 11. Arrangements made with neighbouring Divisions for Mutual Support are set out in Appendix C.

HARASSING FIRE. 12. Harassing fire is to be carried out on the usual system and will be arranged by Group Commanders. Any attempt by the enemy to wire his present front line is to be frustrated.
The allotment of ammunition for harassing fire at night is at present as follows:-

18-pdrs. 150 rounds per Battery.
4.5" Hows. 120 " " "

Gas Shoots are carried out on alternate nights by the two Groups when weather conditions are suitable. 200 rounds of 4.5" How. Chemical shell are allotted nightly for this purpose.

O.P's. 13. Each Group will man an O.P. day and night. A supply of S.O.S. Signals with rifle and ammunition necessary for firing these will be kept at this O.P.

Group O.P's manned day and night are as follows:-

Right Group   N.11.b.0.3.
Left Group   H.35.d.3.3.

In addition O.P's should be reconnoitred and constructed as opportunity permits on the following lines:-

(a). One O.P. per battery for the VIERSTRAAT Line.
(b). One O.P. per battery for close defence of forward sections.
(c). One O.P. per battery for close defence of main battery position.

Visual signalling will be established at all O.P's as early as possible.

The Divisional Observers have established O.P's at N.11.c.15.87 and H.30.c.52.40. When wire permits these should be joined up to Group O.P's with a view to vigorous and prompt engagement of fleeting targets.

AMMUNITION. 14. The following dumps of ammunition will be maintained at Battery positions:-

18-pdrs.   400 rds. per gun (50% A & AX or AXX)
4.5" Hows. 300   "   "   " (BX or BXX).

Ammunition to cover normal daily expenditure should be kept at Battery positions in addition to the above amounts, which should always be on hand.

LIAISON. 15. Each Group finds a Liaison Officer with the Battalion in the line which it supports.
In addition, Groups will take it in turn to find a Liaison Officer at Headquarters of Brigade in the line.
Groups will each carry out this duty for eight days at a time, Left Group relieving Liaison Officer of Right Group at 10 a.m. on the 14th instant. Tour of duty for a Brigade Liaison Officer will be at least 48 hours.

LEWIS GUNS. 16. Each Battery will keep one of its Lewis Guns with its forward section and at least one at its main battery position.
The guns will be mounted for A.A. Defence. Their siting for close defence of positions is to be carefully carried out in conjunction with the wiring in of positions.
2,000 rounds S.A.A. per Lewis Gun will be maintained at each Lewis Gun Emplacement. A small proportion of this should be tracer ammunition. 16 drums will be kept with each gun.

17. ACKNOWLEDGE.

Major, R.F.A.
A/Brigade Major,
41st Divisional Artillery.

Issued at:- 2 p.m.
Distribution over.

DISTRIBUTION.

```
Copy No. 1 - 5   187th Brigade R.F.A.
         6 - 10  190th       "      "
             11  41st Divn. G.
             12  41st Divn. Q.
             13  R.A. XIXth Corps.
             14  XIX Corps H.A.
             15  XIX Corps C.B.S.O.
             16  41st D.A.C.
             17  41st D.T.M.O.
             18  41st Battn. M.G.Corps.
             19  122nd Infy. Bde.
             20  123rd   "    "
             21  124th   "    "
             22  C.R.E. 41st Divn.
             23  4th Brigade R.G.A.
             24  34th Divl. Arty.
             25  35th   "    "
             26  S.C.R.A. 41st Divn.
             27  41st D.A.Signals Officer.
             28  R.O.R.A. 41st Divn.
        29 - 35  War Diary & File.
```

APPENDIX A

To DICKEBUSCH Sector Provisional Artillery Defence Scheme.

ARTILLERY DISPOSITIONS. 13th September 1918.

	Position in action.	Wagon Lines
Headquarters, 41st D.A.	L.14.a.20.00. DOUGLAS CAMP.	L.13.d.90.90.

RIGHT GROUP:-

H.Q. 187th Brigade R.F.A.		H.32.b.55.65.	G.22.b.70.70.
A/187th Brigade R.F.A.	(6 guns)	N. 8.a.60.90.	G.22.a.10.40.
B/187th " "	(6 guns)	N. 3.b.50.00.	G.28.b.40.40.
C/187th " "	(6 guns)	H.32.c.90.20.	G.22.d.20.00.
D/187th " "	(6 hows)	N. 3.b.00.80.	G.22.c.60.60.

LEFT GROUP:-

H.Q. 190th Brigade R.F.A.		H.27.b.70.70.	H. 8.c.65.10.
A/190th Brigade R.F.A.	(6 guns)	H.28.b.45.85.	G.16.b.40.90.
B/190th " "	(2 guns)	H.35.a.33.82.	) G.10.c.70.20.
	(4 guns)	H.23.c.10.35.	)
C/190th " "	(4 guns)	H.23.d.65.76.	G.16.d.45.80.
	(2 guns)	H.28.a.40.40.	(ELGIN FARM).
D/190th " "	(4 hows)	H.28.d.20.60.	G.11.a.70.70.
	(2 hows)	H.28.c.70.70.	(QUERY FARM).

41st DIVISIONAL AMMUNITION COLUMN:-

Headquarters	L.23.a.90.70.	L.23.a.90.70.
No. 1 Section	-	L.22.b.40.80.
No. 2 Section	-	L.16.d.50.80.
No. 3 (S.A.A.) Section.	-	G.19.b.80.70.
41st A.R.P.	G.24.d.40.40. (CORDOVA)	-

APPENDIX B.

To VIERSTRAAT Sector Provisional Artillery Defence Scheme.

<u>S. O. S. LINES.</u>   18th September 1918.

<u>RIGHT GROUP.</u>

1	18-pdr. battery	N.18.d.18.70. – N.18.d.35.98.
1	" "	N.18.b.70.20. – N.18.b.97.50.
1	" "	O. 7.c.37.38. – O. 7.c.49.74.
1	4.5" How. "	on following points:-

                                  N.18.d.14.43.
                                  N.18.d.40.50.
                                  N.18.b.45.13.
                                  O.13.a.00.49.
                                  O.13.a.20.72.
                                  O. 7.c.22.29.

<u>LEFT GROUP.</u>

1	18-pdr. battery	O.7.c.45.85. – O.7.a.70.10.
1	" "	O.1.d.60.09. – O.1.d.89.32.
1	" "	O.2.c.68.95. – O.2.a.87.25.
1	4.5" How. "	on following points:-

                                  O.7.a.85.19.
                                  O.7.b.00.27.
                                  O.7.b.40.75.
                                  O.7.b.53.95.
                                  O.2.c.23.45.
                                  O.2.c.55.80.

<u>S.O.S.Signal</u>
        Rifle grenade breaking into GREEN over GREEN over RED.

<u>S.O.S. Rates of fire</u>
        First 10 minutes   <u>Intense</u>

        Subsequently   <u>Rapid</u>

<u>Ammunition</u>
        18-pdrs. 50% A, 50% AX and AXX

        4.5" Hows. BXX when available, BX when not.

This Appendix takes the place of Appendix B dated 13th instant, which should be destroyed.

SECRET

APPENDIX C.

To VIERSTRAAT Sector Provisional Artillery Defence Scheme.

18th September 1918.

MUTUAL SUPPORT.

Serial No.	Situation.	Code Call.	Support given by	To	Action taken
1.	Attack on Division on our Left, no attack on 41st Divn.	HELP CANAL.	Right Group, 41st D.A.	Division on our Left.	Two 18-pdr. batteries barrage O.2.b.00.10. - O.2.a.00.10.
2.	Attack on 41st Divn. no attack on Divn. on our Left.	HELP DICKEBUSCH.	35th Divl. Arty.	41st Division.	One 18-pdr. battery barrages O.7.b.8.8. - O.2.c.1.1. Four 4.5" Hows. search large ST.ELOI crater (O.2.d.1.6.) for M.Gs. and T.Ms.
3.	Attack on 41st Divn., no attack on Division on our Right.	HELP DICKEBUSCH.	34th Divl. Arty.	41st Division.	One 18-pdr. battery barrages O.13.c.45.75. - O.13.a.00.05. One 18-pdr. battery barrages O.13.a.30.72. - O.13.a.46.96.
4.	Attack on Division on our Right, no attack on 41st Divn.	HELP PETIT BOIS.	Left Group. 41st Divl. Arty.	Division on our Right.	One 18-pdr. battery barrages N.24.c.8.8. - N.24.central. One 18-pdr. battery barrages N.24.a.9.6. - N.18.c.9.0.

This Appendix takes the place of Appendix C dated the 13th Instant, which should be destroyed.

SECRET Copy No. 34

Appendix G.

41st DIVISIONAL ARTILLERY INSTRUCTIONS No. 35.

Reference Maps:- 1/10,000 28 N.W.4.
                  "   28 S.W.2.   26th September 1918.
                  "   28 N.E.3.
                  "   28 S.E.1.

1. These instructions supersede 41st D.A. Instructions No.34 dated the 23rd instant.

GENERAL SCHEME. 2. An attack by the XIXth Corps will shortly take place with the object of gaining, as a first objective, the following line:-

ST. ELOI CRATERS (inclusive) EIKHOF FARM – WHITE CHATEAU – TRIANGULAR BLUFF along the YPRES – COMINES CANAL to O.6.a. – KLEIN ZILLEBEKE – GREENJACKET RIDE (J.19.b.2.5.).

The attack will be carried out by the 14th Division on the Right and the 35th Division on the Left, with the 41st Division in Corps Reserve.

Orders for the attack up to this objective have been issued to all concerned.

ROLE OF 41st DIVISION. 3. Should this operation proceed as planned the role of the 41st Division will be to exploit the success obtained, by operating on the right of the 35th Division either East of, or astride of, or West of the YPRES – COMINES CANAL.

It is not possible to lay down the task of the Division definitely in advance, but its primary function will probably be an advance from the BATTLE WOOD area along the line of the Canal through HOUTHEM to COMINES, with responsibility for safeguarding its own right flank.

ROLE OF 41st DIVISIONAL ARTILLERY. 4. The 187th and 190th Brigades R.F.A., which will support the 35th and 14th Divisions in the attack on the first objective, will revert to control of C.R.A. 41st Division immediately they have completed their tasks in that operation and will support the 41st Division in the performance of the task described in para.3.
They will be reinforced on the second day of the operations by the 46th Brigade R.F.A. (14th Division).

The first task of the 187th and 190th Brigades will probably be to support an attack by the 124th Infantry Brigade from a line O.6.a.0.6. – I.36.central, in a S.E. direction roughly as far as the line P.13.central – P.9.central. Areas allotted for battery positions are set out below.

It is possible that the 46th Brigade R.F.A. may be called upon to advance to positions S.E. of VOORMEZEELE to support an advance along the Western bank of the Canal. But this Brigade should be prepared to operate in the same way as the other two on the Eastern bank in support of the advance along that bank.

1.

AFFILIATION OF ARTILLERY TO INFANTRY.	5.	One Artillery Brigade will be affiliated to each Infantry Brigade.
190th, 187th and 46th Artillery Brigades will be affiliated, provisionally, to 124th, 123rd and 122nd Infantry Brigades respectively and will provide Liaison Officers with them.
The Liaison Officer with an Infantry Brigade will, however, be prepared to act as the representative of whatever Artillery Brigade or Brigades are covering his Infantry Brigade for the time being.
ARTILLERY SUPPORT.	6.	The nature of Artillery Support required by the Infantry will vary with the situation. It is probable, however, that it will take the form of bombardment of strong points and localities rather than a creeping barrage. Brigade Commanders must be prepared to give the closest possible support to advancing Infantry and, if opportunity offers, to push up sections or single guns boldly; they will always act on their own initiative.
F.O.Os.	7.	One F.O.O's party per Brigade will be detailed under Brigade arrangements and will establish a Brigade O.P. at the earliest possible moment with visual signalling back to batteries.
Every possible method of communication between O.Ps and batteries must be developed: telephone, visual, pigeon, mounted or cycle orderly and runners.
INTELLIGENCE.		It is of the utmost importance that information, even of a negative character, be sent back without delay to D.A.H.Q. and that the latter be kept informed of the situation and of the position of Brigade Headquarters. Situation reports will be sent by Brigades to D.A.H.Q. at each even-numbered clock hour, and in addition whenever there is anything of interest to report.
LIAISON.	8.	Infantry Brigade Headquarters will be established at SWAN CHATEAU (I.19.c.7.8.).
These headquarters will be occupied in succession by each of the Infantry Brigades, in the following order:- 124th Infantry Brigade, 123rd Infantry Brigade, 122nd Infantry Brigade.
Liaison Officers provided by 190th and 187th Brigades will report at 1 hour after zero at the Infantry Brigade Headquarters referred to, and will join their Infantry Brigades as these arrive.
Liaison Officer provided by 46th Brigade R.F.A. will report at Advanced D.A. Signal Station at I.25.b.9.7. as soon as that Brigade is put at disposal of C.R.A. 41st Division, and will be directed from there to 122nd Infantry Brigade Headquarters.
Liaison Officers will remain with their Infantry Brigades throughout the course of operations.
ARTILLERY AREAS.	9.	Forward of our present front line the Right Brigade area of the 35th Division has been allotted to 41st Divisional Artillery for battery positions. The area is that between the Canal and a line I.28.c.1.9. - I.28.d.9.0. along light railway to I.35.b.0.4.

The following areas are allotted for battery positions:

190th Brigade:- LA CHAPELLE FARM (inclusive) - I.28.c.
1.9. - I.28.d.0.0.

187th Brigade:- Area between Canal and line LA CHAPELLE
FARM (exclusive) - I.28.d.0.0.

(see Notes on Reconnaissance of Battery area below).

LANKHOF FARM is allotted to 190th Brigade and LOCK 7
to 187th Brigade for Brigade Headquarters if required.

ROUTES OF ADVANCE. 10. Cross country tracks have been prepared as follows:-

Route A. KRUISSTRAATHOEK - IRON BRIDGE (I.26.c.2.6.) -
BEDFORD HOUSE - SANDBAG TRACK (I.26.b.8.6.).

Route B. CHATEAU SEGARD (H.30.b.0.7.) - BELLEGOED FARM -
Light Railway crossing at I.25.b.8.9. - BEDFORD
HOUSE - SANDBAG TRACK, (I.26.b.8.6.).

Troops of 41st Division will have priority over all
other troops on these routes.
Artillery will have priority over all other arms on
these routes.
Infantry must be prepared, if moving concurrently with
columns of transport, to leave the tracks and move across
country.

These routes will be used and kept up until Brigades
have advanced as follows:-
Route A by 190th Brigade, Route B by 187th Brigade;
until 187th Brigade advance both routes may be used by
190th Brigade.

PREPARATION OF ROUTES. 11. Forward of the point where these routes meet SANDBAG
TRACK no prepared track exists (see note to para.9). To
assist in preparation of the necessary approach from this
point to MIDDLESEX ROAD, one Section R.E. and ½ company
Middlesex Pioneers will report to each of 187th and 190th
Brigade Headquarters on the afternoon before Zero day.
It is essential that tracks should be prepared with
the greatest possible speed so as to get the guns forward
without delay. With this in view Brigade Commanders
will send forward as many men per battery as possible
under one or more Officers per Brigade in addition to
the working party of R.E. and Pioneers, as soon as their
tasks under 14th and 35th Divisions have been completed.
A mounted or cycle orderly per battery should also go
forward in order that progress may be reported periodically to Brigade Headquarters.
A supply of fascines and trench bridges has been
deposited at I.26.c.5.8.
Working parties going forward will move in small
parties.
R.E. and Pioneers should be sent forward at Zero hour
with an R.A.Officer conversant with the tracks required.

MAIN ROADS.		It is expected that existing metalled and timbered roads will be fit for use within present enemy lines on the day after Zero day.
ORDER OF ADVANCE.	12.	Batteries will move forward under orders of Brigade Commanders and moves will be so arranged that a proportion of guns is always in action and that rear batteries are first to move.
		Orders for Brigades to commence to advance will be issued from D.A.H.Q.
AMMUNITION.	13.	On arrival at forward positions the following ammunition will be dumped:-

18-pdrs. 176 rounds per gun.
4.5" Hows. 108 " " how.

Echelons of 187th Brigade will be refilled by D.A.C.; 190th Brigade will refill from vacated positions.

WAGON LINES.	14.	Two hours after Zero battery wagon lines will be moved to and arrive in areas allotted in 41st D.A. Administrative Instructions No.14.
CALLS FROM THE AIR.	15.	One battery of 18-pdrs. per Brigade will be superimposed over Brigade front in order that it may be available to answer calls from the air.

"L.L", "G.F", and "N.F" calls will be answered as set out in XIXth Corps No. R.A./G/36/188 of 3-8-18, sent to Brigades on 4-8-18.

A Contact aeroplane will fly along the front of attack about one hour after Zero and thereafter every clock hour.

A Counter-attack aeroplane will patrol the front from Zero plus 40 minutes onwards and will signal the development of an enemy counter-attack by firing a RED parachute flare.

LIGHT SIGNALS.	16.	The S.O.S. Signal remains a Rifle Grenade breaking into RED over RED over GREEN. GREEN over GREEN over RED
		No other light Signal will be used by the 41st Division 41st Divn. Nos. G.833 (67/5) of 22-9-18 and G.872 (67/5 of 25-9-18 are cancelled.
HEAVY ARTILLERY.	17.	4th Brigade R.G.A. is affiliated to the 41st Division and will have a Liaison Officer at 41st D.A.H.Q.

Pinpoints or bearings of located hostile batteries may be sent direct from Artillery Brigades to this Officer, who will transmit the information to Counter Battery Group with the minimum of delay.

F.O.Os should make special efforts to exploit direct observation of enemy battery areas to the full.

COMMUNICA- TIONS.	18.	Communications are dealt with in Appendix "A" and will be as shewn in diagram attached thereto.
		In order to avoid congestion of telephone lines written messages should be used in preference to conversations whenever possible.
ADMINISTRA- TIVE.	19.	Arrangements for ammunition supply and Administrative matter are set out in 41st D.A. Administrative Instructions No.14 dated 25th instant.

CORPS LIAISON PATROLS.	20.	A Platoon of XIX Corps Cyclists will be attack to the Division. Men employed on Corps Liaison Patrol Work will be furnished with a pass and will wear a yellow and white shoulder strap. They should be given any information whixh they ask for and should receive all possible assistance.
TRAPS.	21.	All ranks will be warned against entering dugouts, pill boxes or shelters until these have been inspected by the 184th Tunnelling Company R.E. Dugouts labelled "unsafe" will in no circumstances be entered. Dugouts marked "examined" will only be entered in the event of enemy shelling and will be vacated immediately the shelling ceases. It should be impressed on all ranks that with the carefully concealed fuzes which the enemy is using it is possible that, even after a dugout has been examined by experts, an explosion might occur.
MOUNTED PATROL.	22.	A mounted patrol of 12 O.R. under two Officers of Royal West Kents will be furnished by 41st D.A.C. and will report at Advanced Wagon Line of A/190 R.F.A. at two hours after Zero, sending a mounted orderly to await orders at Advanced Div. Signal Exchange at H.27.d.8.6.

DAYS AND HOURS.	23.	For describing days and hours the following code will be used:-
		    J = day of attack.
		    H = Zero hour.
		Any particular day before or after the attack will be shewn as "J minus or plus ---- days".
		Any particular time before or after Zero will be shown as "H minus or plus ---- hours ---- minutes".
		Time will be synchronized throughout the Division under arrangements made by O.C. Divisional Signal Company on J minus I and J days.

LOCATIONS.	24.	Positions of Headquarters etc. will be as follows:-
		
		41st Div. H.Q.)
		                    ) MERSEY CAMP, G.23.c.9.3.
		41st D.A.H.Q.)
		
		124th Infy. Bde.H.Q.)
		                    ) In succession at SWAN
		123rd " " ")
		                    ) CHATEAU I.19.c.7.8.
		122nd " " ")
		
		Advanced Div. Signal Exchange. H.27.d.8.6.
		
		Advanced D.A. Signal Exchange. I.25.b.9.7.

187th Bde. H.Q.	(?) LOCK 7	I.32.b.7.3.
190th " "	(?) LANKHOF FARM	I.26.d.0.0.
41st D.A.C.	G.28.d.85.50.	
A.R.P.	ROBSON DUMP G.29.d.0.6.	
4th Bde. R.G.A.	G.23.b.5.4.	
	with advanced Signal Exchange at BEDFORD HOUSE.	

25.   A C K N O W L E D G E.

E R Roper

Major,
Brigade Major,
41st Divisional Artillery.

Issued at :- 11.45 p.m.

Note on Reconnaissance of Battery area

From a reconnaissance carried out on morning of 20th instant from CHESTER FARM it appears that two 18-pdr. batteries in echelon could obtain sufficient cover from the Right about I.33.d.3.8., one 4.5" How. battery in ravine or dip about I.33.d.9.9, and one 18-pdr. battery on northern slope about I. 34.a.5.7. (Major J.A.MacDonald R.F.A., of B/187 R.F.A. can give any further information required).

From I.26.b.8.6. an old track runs along the Northern edge of SANDBAG TRACK which, with but little work, is quite practicable for guns. A few boggy portions will require fascines. The country is open and is pitted with a certain number of shell holes, but even off the track is practicable and the going mostly good.

There are no trenches to be crossed; bridges will therefore not be required as far as MIDDLESEX ROAD. There are several belts of wire which will have to be cut.

DISTRIBUTION:-

Copy No. 1 - 5   187th Bde. R.F.A.
         6 - 10 190th   "   "
        11 - 15 46th   "   "
        16   41st D.A.C.
        17   41st Divn. G.
        18   41st Divn. Q.
        19   R.A. XIXth Corps.
        20   R.A. 14th Divn.
        21   R.A. 35th Divn.
        22   H.A. XIX Corps.
        23   4th Brigade R.G.A.
        24   122nd Infantry Bde.
        25   123rd   "   "
        26   124th   "   "
        27   C.R.E. 41st Divn.
        28   41st Battn. M.G.Corps.
        29   S.C.R.A. 41st Divn.
        30   R.O.R.A. 41st Divn.
        31   41st D.A. Signal Officer.
        32 - 36 War Diary and File.

AMENDMENT

Reference paras. 9 and 24 above.
HOME FARM (I.26.a.3.2.) LOCK 7 (I.32.b.7.3) and LANKHOF FARM (I.26.d.0.0.) are allotted to 190th, 187th and 46th Brigades R.F.A. for Brigade Headquarters if required.

APPENDIX "A".
Issued with 41st D.A. Instructions No. 35

SIGNALLING ARRANGEMENTS.

In the first phase of operations, communication with 190th Brigade Headquarters will be by a direct line from the Advanced Divisional Exchange at H.27.d.8.6.; with 187th Brigade and 46th Brigade via 35th and 14th Divisions respectively.
41st D.A.C. and A.R.P. will be connected with Divisional Headquarters exchange direct.

Direct lines from the Divisional Headquarters exchange also go to 35th Division, 14th Division, Corps Heavy Artillery, the three Infantry Brigades of the Division and 3 lines to the Advanced Divisional Exchange.

An R.A.Exchange will be established in a dugout in the eastern bank of the Canal at I.25.b.9.7. This will be connected by a cable line with the Advanced Div. Exchange at H.27.d.8.6. The Exchange will be marked by a blue and white signal flag which will be erected on top of the Signal Dugout, and it will be the Headquarters of the 41st D.A. Signals Officer. A line will also run from this exchange to the Infantry Brigades Exchange at SWAN CHATEAU.

As the Artillery Brigades move their Headquarters forward they will send an orderly to the R.A.Exchange who knows the new Brigade Headquarters. He will direct the cable wagon to the Brigade Headquarters and will remain at the R.A.Exchange to deliver messages to the R.A.Brigades in case the lines are cut.

The cable wagon will remain at the R.A.Exchange ready to lay lines further forward and form an Advanced R.A.Exchange should the situation demand it. The location of that exchange will be notified to all concerned as soon as it is fixed.

A C.W.Wireless set will be erected at the R.A.Exchange and will work back to R.A.Headquarters direct. A N.C.O. is attached to this set and will do all encoding and decoding of messages as required.

A forward Signal Dump containing cable, telephones and message rockets will be established on night before Zero day about H.27.d.9.6., from which Artillery can draw after Zero hour on the signature of a Signals Officer.

A diagram of communications is attached.

26-9-18.

P.T.O

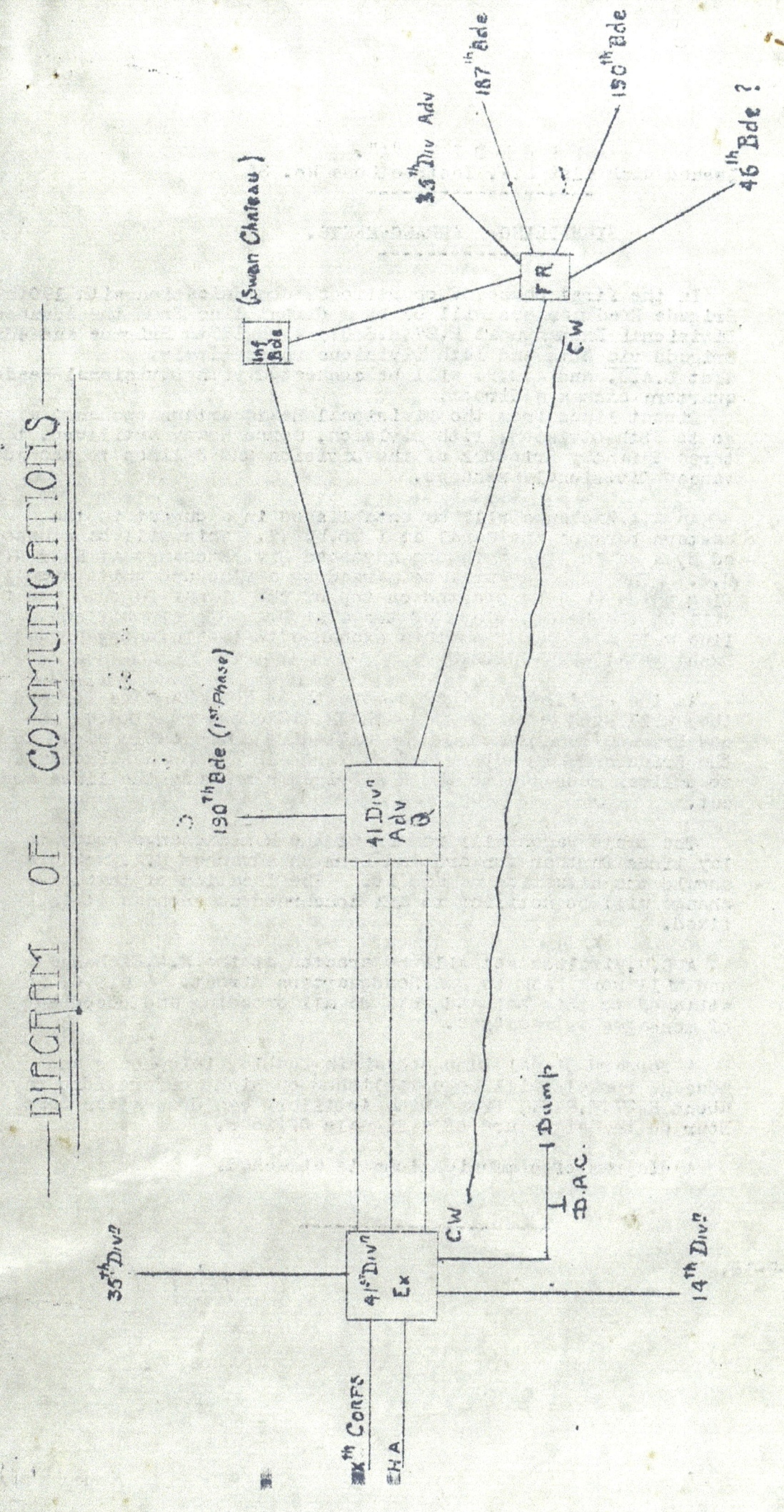

WD Appendix "H"

SECRET 41st D.A. No. S.117.

187th Bde. R.F.A. (5 cos).
190th   "   "   " (5 ").
124th Infy. Bde.   (4 ")
4th Bde. R.G.A.   (5 ")
41st Divn. G.

The areas enclosed in circles will be engaged by heavy and Field Artillery within the zones shewn at the times stated, but Heavy Artillery will be one zone ahead of Field Artillery; i.e. when Field Artillery are shooting on Zone (a) from P to P plus 15 H.A. will be shooting on zone (b) and so on. 60-pdrs. will search all approaches.

H.A. will remain on zone (d) for the double period (c) and (d) less 15 minutes when they will lift 200 yards clear of S.O.S. line.

No fire is to be N. of the zones after the time given to lift, unless observed fire from forward guns.

All fire will cease at P plus 90.

H.A. will bombard selected targets in area from 1 p.m. to P minus 15 minutes, when they will conform to time table.

P will probably be 2 p.m., and is calculated as being approximately the time loading waves of 124th Infantry Bde. reach the Canal bend in O.6.a.

G.O.C. 124th Infy. Bde. will finally fix "P" time and inform "G" and C.R.A. as soon as possible.

ACKNOWLEDGE BY WIRE.

E R Roper

Major,
Brigade Major,
41st Divisional Artillery.

Issued at:- 11 a.m.
28-9-18.

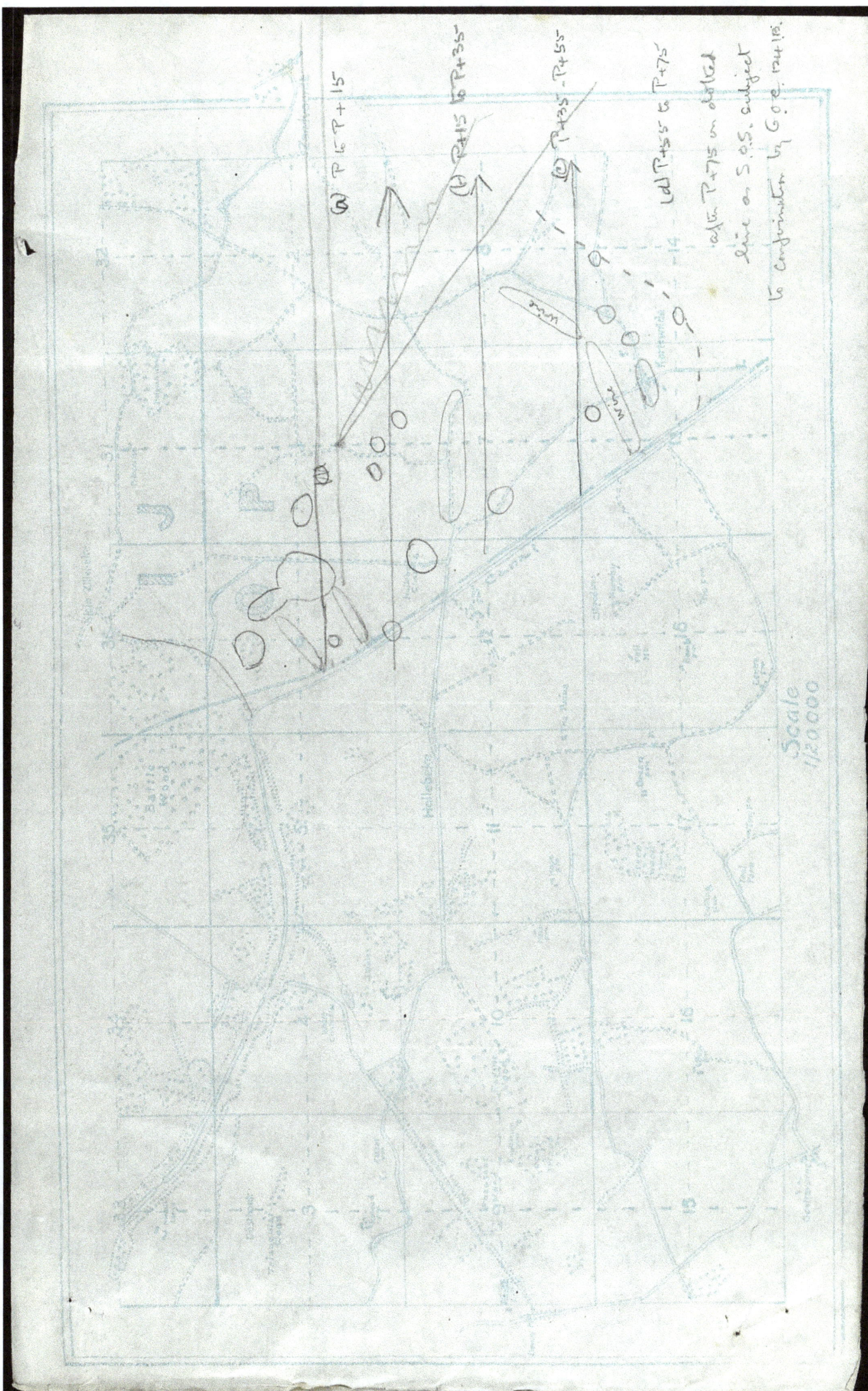

S E C R E T   41st D.A. No. S.122.

Headquarters,
   187th Bde. R.F.A. (5 cos).
   190th   "   "   "
   4th Bde. R.G.A.
   123rd Infy. Bde. (4 cos).
   124th   "   "   "
   35th Divl. Arty.
   41st Divn. G.

1. The advance will be continued tomorrow.
35th Division will advance on TENBRIELEN and if the situation admits, to WERVICQ; 41st Division along East side of the YPRES - COMINES Canal as far as the line P.33.b.5.8. - P.29.central; all crossings of the Canal from the West to this line will be secured.

15th Corps will advance via WARNETON on COMINES.

10th Corps will clear the area W. of the Canal.

2. In accordance with the above 124th Infantry Brigade will advance from their present line to a line through P.20.a.4.0-P.15.central which line they will reach by 7.30 a.m.
Their approach from present line to this will be covered by 190th Brigade R.F.A. under arrangements to be made direct by O.C. 190th Brigade R.F.A. with G.O.C. 124th Infantry Bde.

3. On arrival of 124th Infantry Brigade at this line 123rd Infantry Brigade will pass through the former to further objectives and their advance will be covered by 41st Divl. Arty. and Heavy Artillery as shewn on attached map.

187th Brigade will push forward by sections at daybreak into positions reconnoitred today and take up the Artillery programme from the time guns arrive in action.

4. The areas enclosed in circles will be engaged by heavy and Field Artillery within the Zones shewn at the times stated, but H.A. will be one zone ahead of Field Artillery, i.e. when Field Artillery are shooting on zone (a) from 7.30 - 7.50, Heavy Artillery will be shooting on zone (b) and so on.
Heavy Artillery will remain on Zone (e) from 8.30 - 9.5 when they will lift on to the line of the railway.

5. No fire is to be North of the Zones after the time given to lift unless observed fire from forward guns.

6. Bursts of fire will be put down on the line of railway and West of COMINES until 9.30 a.m. when fire will cease unless called for.
The line of railway will be the S.O.S. line for all guns, subject to confirmation by G.O.C. 123rd Infantry Brigade.

7. An advanced D.A. Signal Exchange will be established in O.6.a. near the bend in the Canal at 5.30 a.m. by the D.A. Signals Officer. Brigades will take steps to find this and notify the D.A. Signals Officer of location of their Headquarters.

P. T. O.

8.   Headquarters of Infantry Brigades are as follows:-

   123rd Infantry Brigade   I.36.b.0.3.
                                            2.4
   124th   "   "   P.1.c.75.75.

   Headquarters of 123rd Infantry Brigade are being moved
shortly before the advance begins to P.1.c.75.75.
                                            2.4

9.   ACKNOWLEDGE BY WIRE.

                              E R Roper
                              Major,
   28th Sept. 1918.   Brigade Major,
   Issued at:- 11.55 p.m.   41st Divisional Artillery.

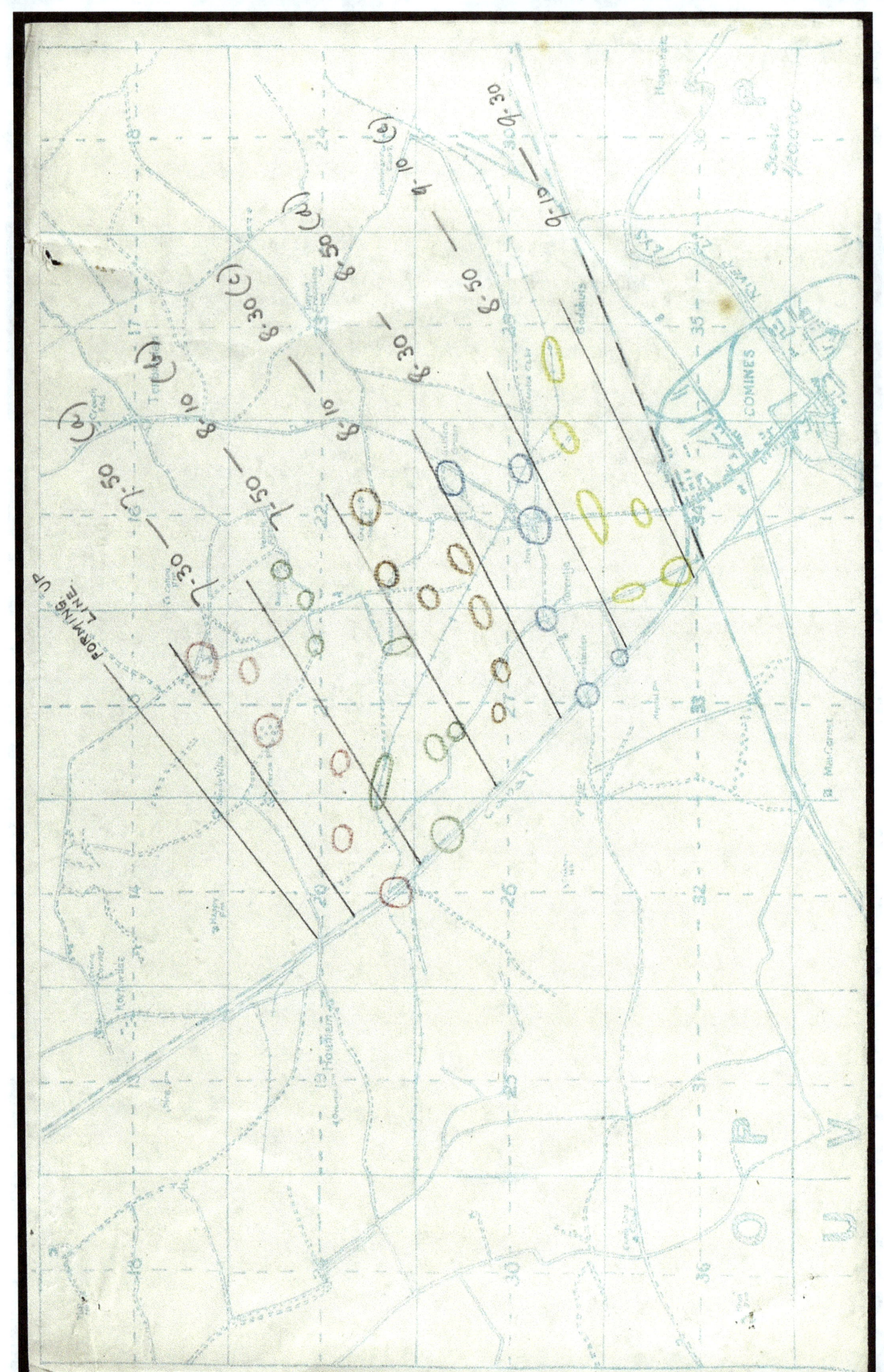

Index..............................

SUBJECT.

No.	Contents.	Date.

41st D.A
Oct 18

(41,365). Wt.9392—94. 2000. 6/19. **Gp.164.** A.&E.W.
(44,173).   ,,   21,613—105. 500. 10/19.   ,,   ,,

Index

Army Form C. 2118.

WAR DIARY
OF
INTELLIGENCE-SUMMARY

(Erase heading not required.)

Headquarters, 41st. Divisional Artillery.

Instructions regarding War Diaries and Intelligence Summaries are contained in F. S. Regs., Part II. and the Staff Manual respectively. Title Pages will be prepared in manuscript.

Place	Date	Hour	Summary of Events and Information	Remarks and references to Appendices
BELGIUM LANKHOF FARM (YPRES-COMINES CANAL)	1918 Octr. 1st.		Brigades moved in Infantry Brigade groups in an advance on the LYS from MENIN to WEVELGHEM (both inclusive). 187th.Brigade were in 123rd.Infantry Brigade Group, 190th.Brigade in 122nd. Infantry Brigade group. Resistance was encountered on the way and both Brigades R.F.A. dropped into action near AMERICA in order to support an attack by 123rd.Infantry Brigade on GHELUWE switch.	
-do-	" 2nd.		122nd. Infantry Brigade, in conjunction with Divisions on each side, attacked GHELUWE and TERHAND Line at 07.00 hrs. The latter line was reached by 122nd.Infantry Brigade but not taken, and flanks being in the air, our line was withdrawn to S.E. of GHELUWE. During night 2/3rd. 190th.Brigade moved to neighbourhood of KRUISECKE.	
-do-	" 3rd.		Lieut.Colonel C.D.G.LYON, D.S.O., Commanding 187th.Brigade, R.F.A., proceeded to England on Senior Officers Course. Major J.A.MACDONALD, R.M.A., assumed command of the Brigade in his absence. Lieut. H.E.McKIE, M.C., R.F.A., Reconnaissance Officer, 41st.Divisional Artillery, admitted to D.R.S., sick.; Duties being performed temporarily by Captain L.S.COKE, R.G.A., Liaison Officer for XIXth.Corps Heavy Artillery. 34th.Division took over front of 41st.Division including Command of artillery. Infantry of 41st.Division relieved infantry of 29th.Division on sector immediately N. of GHELUWE. One section per battery 187th.Brigade moved to positions occupied by 17th.Brigade, R.F.A., (29th.Divisional Artillery) in order to cover new Divisional front.	
GHELUVELT & FORT GARRY.	" 4th.		Command of Sector N. of GHELUWE, including Command of Artillery, passed from G.O.C.,29th. Division to G.O.C.,41st.Division at 06.00 hrs. 190th.Brigade, R.F.A., covered new divisional front from existing positions from 06.00 hrs. onwards. 187th.Brigade,R.F.A., relieved remainder of 17th.Brigade, R.F.A. 41st.D.A., H.Q., with Divisional Headquarters, moved to GHELUVELT; later to FORT GARRY (J.14.a.30.30.-- Sheet 28 1/40,000).	
FORT GARRY.	" 5th.		11th (Army) Brigade, R.F.A., came under Command of C.R.A., 41st.Division, and remained in Wagon Lines in BRANDHOEK Area.	

-1-

Army Form C. 2118.

WAR DIARY
INTELLIGENCE SUMMARY.
(Erase heading not required.) Headquarters, 41st. Divisional Artillery

Instructions regarding War Diaries and Intelligence Summaries are contained in F.S. Regs., Part II and the Staff Manual respectively. Title pages will be prepared in manuscript.

Place	Date	Hour	Summary of Events and Information	Remarks and references to Appendices
BELGIUM	1918			
FORT GARRY.	Oct. 6th.		11th (Army) Brigade R.F.A., moved to HAGEBAERT Area, subsequently to VOORMEZEELE Area. Forward Sections of 187th. and 190th. Brigades, R.F.A., were moved up for wire-cutting. Orders issued for forthcoming attack (41st.D.A.,Preliminary Instructions No.36 - App: "A")	App: "A"
-do-	"	7th.)	Wirecutting and Harassing fire.	
-do-	"	8th.)	Great difficulty was experienced in cutting wire owing to want of good observation. O.Ps	
-do-	"	9th.)	were established for the purpose, 200 yards in front of our line of posts. Enemy carried out certain amount of counter-preparation during nights.	
-do-	"	10th.	Wirecutting and Harassing fire. Three sections of 187th.Brigade, R.F.A.,withdrawn from action, were attached to 124th.Infantry Brigade for training in close support of Infantry Battalions. The training took place in ABEELE Area.	
-do-	"	11th.	(Army) Brigade R.F.A., put 1 section per battery into silent positions in K.32.,N.W. of gHELUWE. 187th.Brigade,R.F.A., put 1 section per battery in forward positions in K.33. Wirecutting continued. Enemy continued counter-preparations.	
-do-	"	12th.	11th(Army)Brigade,R.F.A., put 1 further section per battery in action. 187th.Brigade, R.F.A. put half-batteries in positions previously prepared for attack.	
-do-	"	13th.	187th.Brigade, R.F.A., and 11th (Army) Brigade, R.F.A., put remainder of batteries in action. Sections of 187th.Brigade, R.F.A., training with 124th.Infantry Brigade returned to units.	
-do-	"	14th.	The Division attacked at 05.35 hrs., final objective being high ground overlooking high ground the LYS from N.E. of MENIN to N. N.W. of WEVELGHEM. Little resistance was encountered, but there was a very heavy ground mist which was intensified by the smoke of the barrage, and which greatly hampered the movements of the Artillery, especially of the forward sections attached to battalions.	

Army Form C. 2118.

WAR DIARY
or
INTELLIGENCE-SUMMARY.

(Erase heading not required.) Headquarters 41st. Divisional Artillery

Instructions regarding War Diaries and Intelligence Summaries are contained in F. S. Regs., Part II. and the Staff Manual respectively. Title pages will be prepared in manuscript.

Place	Date	Hour	Summary of Events and Information	Remarks and references to Appendices
BELGIUM FORT GARRY	Oct. 14th (contd.)		At 07.00 hrs. satisfactory progress was reported, and 190th.Brigade,R.F.A.,were ordered to advance. The Brigade went into action in K.30.c. and d. At 08.40 hrs., further satisfactory progress having been reported, 187th.Brigade were ordered to advance. While the Brigade was on the road the mist broke, and fire was opened on its advance party by a nest of enemy machine guns and field guns in 35th.Divisional area, which had been passed by the advancing infantry, who, at this time, were about 2,000 yards beyond the locality. Major J.A.MACDONALD, R.F.A., and Captain J.C.HUNTER, R.F.A., were both seriously wounded by a round from a 7.7cm. gun. Major F.P.KINDELL, D.S.O., M.C., R.F.A., D/187, assumed command of the Brigade, which eventually went into action in L.31.a. and b. The nest of field guns and machine guns referred to above was engaged by Officer Commanding A/190, R.F.A., several casualties being caused among the gun detachments, which left their guns, and were probably captured later, the guns being taken by Infantry of 35th.Division. At 11.15hrs. 4th.Brigade, R.G.A., reported that it had received orders from XIXth.Corps H.A., to advance to L.34. and were doing so immediately. At 16.00 hrs. a report was received from O.C., C/190, R.F.A., that personal reconnaissance shewed our Infantry on their final objective across whole Divisional front, with posts about 200 yards beyond it. At 20.30 hrs., orders were received from 41st.Division H.Q., that 124th.Infantry Brigade were to be relieved by Infantry of 34th.Division, and Divisional Artillery by 34th.Divisional Artillery on the night 15/16th.instant.	
-do-	Oct. 15th.		187th.Brigade, R.F.A., less 1 18pdr. Battery, were withdrawn to Wagon lines. 1 18pdr. battery 190th.Brigade, R.F.A., was withdrawn to wagon lines. Orders were received for Divisional Artillery to relieve 36th.Divisional Artillery on left of 35th.Division in COURTRAI Sector. Orders were issued for 11th (Army) Brigade, and 187th.Brigades, R.F.A., to march to new Divisional Area on morning of 16th., in order to relieve batteries of 36th.Divl:Artillery in afternoon of that day.(App:"B")	App:"B"
ASHMORE FM. MOORSEELE Area.	" 16th.		11th. and 187th.Brigades, R.F.A., marched to new area and relieved 153rd. and 173rd.Brigades R.F.A., (36th.D.A.) which withdrew to Wagon lines. Command of new Sector including artillery, passed to G.O.C.,41st.Division at 18.00 hrs. 2/Lieut. F.PROUD, M.C.,R.F.A.,No.1 Section, 41st.D.A.C.,assumed duties as Acting Reconnaissance Officer vice Lieut. H.E.McKIE, M.C., R.F.A., granted Special Leave to United Kingdom. Orders were issued that there was to be no firing on COURTRAI, owing to number of civilians in the town.	

Army Form C. 2118.

WAR DIARY
or
INTELLIGENCE-SUMMARY.
(Erase heading not required.)

Headquarters, 41st.Divisional Artillery

Instructions regarding War Diaries and Intelligence Summaries are contained in F.S. Regs., Part II. and the Staff Manual respectively. Title pages will be prepared in manuscript.

Place	Date	Hour	Summary of Events and Information	Remarks and references to Appendices
BELGIUM 1918 ASHMORE FARM MOORSEELE Area.	Octr. 17th.		Remainder of Divisional Artillery moved to new area. 190th.Brigade, R.F.A., were not put into action but remained in Wagon lines. Hostile Artillery quiet; but COURTRAI, S.of the LYS, was shelled and gassed by the enemy though none of our troops were in it. Artillery F.O.Os reported M.G. fire from warehouse windows on S.side of Canal.	
--do--	"	18th.	Our artillery remained inactive.	
--do--	"	19th.	Orders received to march with Infantry Brigade groups across LYS to Area south of COURTRAI.	
POESELHOEK (nr.GULLE-GHEM)	"	20th.	March commenced (41st. D.A.,Order No.17 - App: "G") 41st.D.A.,Headquarters, moved to POESELHOEK (GULLEGHEM Area)	App:"G"
T'HOOGHE (nr.COURTRAI)	"	21st.	March continued to SCHELDT. Held up by machine guns on high ground N.E. of KNOKKE. 190th. Brigade, R.F.A., dropped into action S. of SWEVEGHEM and engaged machine guns; 187th. Brigade,R.F.A., in N.29, engaged enemy who were holding up advance at Canal tunnel S.E., of KNOKKE. 11th.(army) Brigade in reserve T'HOOGHE Area, S. of COURTRAI. Good work was performed by forward guns attached to Battalions, engaging machine gun nests at close range which were holding up Infantry. (App: "K") 41st.D.A.,Headquarters moved to T'HOOGHE (COURTRAI Area)	App:"K"
--do--	"	22nd.	Position the same. Machine guns offered strong resistance. 11th (Army) Brigade, R.F.A., went into action with 124th.Infantry Brigade N.E. of ST. GENOIS.	App:"D"
--do--	"	23rd.	Bursts of fire on machine guns. 187th.Brigade, R.F.A., moved in evening N.W. of SWEVEGHEM relieving Brigade of 29th. Division, and being relieved by Brigade of 34th.Division (41st. D.A., Order No.18 - App: "E") Infantry advanced a little during night –Artillery assisting by Area shoots. (41st.D.A., Order No.19 - App:"F")	App:"E" App:"F"
--do--	"	24th.	11th (Army) Brigade, R.F.A., moved into action N.E. of KNOKKE; 119th.(Army) Brigade, R.F.A., in action W. of KNOKKE; 190th.Brigade,R.F.A. S.W. of KNOKKE.	

WAR DIARY
INTELLIGENCE SUMMARY

(Erase heading not required.) Headquarters, 41st. Divisional Artillery

Army Form C. 2118.

Place	Date	Hour	Summary of Events and Information	Remarks and references to Appendices
BELGIUM 1918 T'HOOGHE (Near COURTRAI)	Oct. 25th.		Advance on L'ESCAUT continued; progress satisfactory on right flank. 190th.Brigade,R.F.A. moved forward in afternoon to O.35 and O.29, South of KEIBURG; 119th.(Army) Brigade,R.F.A., moved westward to O.17.a., and 11th.(Army) Brigade,R.F.A. to N.W., of HEESTERT. On left of Divisional Front machine gun fire was troublesome, and objectives were not gained. (41st. D.A., Order No.20 - App: "G") (App: "K")	App:G App:K
-do-	26th.		Artillery support was organised to clear the front of enemy, but Infantry patrols moving forward found enemy had retired to South bank of L'ESCAUT. (41st.D.A.,Order No.21 - App:"H") At night Division was relieved by 35th. Division; batteries moved into areas S. of COURTRAI to rest and re-fit.	App:H
-do-	29th.		Lieut.Col: C.D.G.LYON, D.S.O., returned from Course & rejoined 187th.Brigade,R.F.A. At night half batteries moved up to positions in action (41st.D.A., Order No.22 - App: "I")	App:I
-do-	30th.		Remainder of batteries moved into action.	
-do-	31st		41st.Divisional Artillery put down good smoke barrage along ESCAUT, whilst 35th.Division advanced and captured its objectives. At night 187th.Brigade,R.F.A., moved into positions to cover our front, which infantry took over from 35th.Division. (41st.D.A.,No.S.266 - App: "J"	App:J

3rd.Nov.1918.

Brigadier-General,
Commanding 41st.Divisional Artillery.

W D app 'A'

For personal information of recipients only and for necessary action.

SECRET Copy No. 34

41st DIVISIONAL ARTILLERY PRELIMINARY INSTRUCTIONS No. 36.

(With reference to para. 7 of 41st Divn. Order No. 273).

Reference maps:- 28 N.E. 1/20,000   5th October 1918.
                 29 N.W. 1/20,000
                 28 S.E. 1/20,000
                 29 S.W. 1/20,000

ATTACK. 1. Second Army will attack on a day (J) at an hour (H) which will be intimated later to all concerned.

ORDER OF ATTACK. 2. 41st Division will attack with 34th Division (X Corps) on the right and 35th Division on the Left.
Each Division will attack on a one-Brigade front.
122nd Infantry Brigade will lead, followed by 124th Infantry Brigade.
123rd Infantry Brigade will be in Divisional Reserve.
All preparations are to be completed by midnight 10/11th October, except that silent batteries will not put guns in position until ordered.

ARTILLERY. 3. The Field Artillery available for support of the Infantry will be the 41st Divisional Artillery reinforced by the 11th Army Brigade R.F.A., which will probably move into action by sections on the three nights before J day.
Artillery Brigades will be affiliated, and will find Liaison Officers, as follows:-

LIAISON.
         187th Brigade R.F.A. with 124th Infantry Brigade.
         190th   "   "   "   122nd   "   "
         11th Army Bde. "   "   123rd   "   "

The Liaison Officer with an Infantry Brigade will be prepared to act as the representative of whatever Artillery is covering his Infantry Brigade for the time being.
Liaison Officers will report at Headquarters of their Infantry Brigades at 6 p.m. on the day before (J).

HEAVY ARTILLERY. The 4th Brigade R.G.A. will probably be affiliated to the Division. A Liaison Officer of this Brigade is at D.A.H.Q.

BOUNDARIES. 4. Boundaries of 41st Division are as follows:-

Southern Boundary:- K.33.c.0.0.- K.34.c.0.2.- K.36.c.0.0.- K.36.d.2.0. - K.36.d.7.1. - L.31.d.0.0. - R.3.c.3.2.

Northern Boundary:- K.27.a.0.0. - K.29.central.-K.30.c.8.9. - L.36.a.3.3.

OBJECTIVE. Final objective is high ground between R.3.c.3.2. and L.36.a.3.3.

1.

BOMBARDMENT AND WIRE-CUTTING.

5. Bombardment and wire-cutting will commence forthwith.
There will be no bombardment immediately before (H).
Lanes are to be cut every 50 yards at least through the wire of Front and Support Lines of the GHELUWE SWITCH and TERHAND LINE.
Opposite the Divisional Front lanes 100 yards apart will be cut first, others when these are completed.
Aeroplane co-operation is being arranged.
Brigades will be responsible for cutting as follows:-

<u>190th Brigade</u>:- From Southern Divisional Boundary to East and West Grid line through K.35. central.

<u>187th Brigade</u>:- From grid line as above to Northern Divisional Boundary.

Every effort will be made to locate M.G. and T.M. Posts with a view to their destruction before or neutralization during the attack, by 4.5" Hows.

BARRAGE.

6.(a). The attack will start under a creeping barrage which will move forward at the rate of 100 yards in two minutes and will be continued to the limit of range. There will be a pause of 15 minutes after every 1500 yards. The Barrage will come down two minutes before (H). The first lift and the Infantry Advance will be at (H).

(b). 187th and 190th Brigades will fire the initial barrage from START Line to first pause, supplemented by such batteries of 11th Army Brigade R.F.A. as may be detailed. All available guns of all three Brigades will fire on the first 'pause line'.

(c). The Right and Left Batteries on the Divisional Front will fire a proportion of smoke shell in the barrage as far as first 'pause' to blind enemy and assist Infantry for direction. A proportion of smoke shell will also be fired along the 'pause line' to indicate this to the Infantry.

(d). When the barrage moves forward from the first 'pause line' all Brigades will fire the first lift, after which 190th Brigade R.F.A. will drop out, cease fire, limber up and advance with the least possible delay to forward positions selected. The further barrage will be fired by 187th Brigade R.F.A. and 11th Army Brigade R.F.A. only, a proportion of smoke shell being fired by flank sections of Divisional Artillery to indicate the limits of Divisional front.

(e). On reaching 2nd 'pause line' a proportion of smoke shell will be fired along this.

(f). When the barrage moves forward from 2nd 'pause line', it will be continued to N and S Grid lines between Squares L.32. and L.33, when the barrage will cease; before it ceases a final burst of smoke will be fired to indicate to the Infantry that no further fire will be forthcoming.

Barrage maps and further details will be issued later.

F.O.O's. 13. One F.O.O's. party per Brigade will be detailed under Brigade arrangements and will establish a forward Brigade O.P. at the earliest possible moment with visual signalling back to batteries.
Every possible method of communication between O.P. and batteries must be developed.

INTELLIGENCE. Full and frequent situation reports should be sent back to D.A.H.Q. It is of the greatest importance that the latter be kept fully informed of the progress of events. Even negative information is useful.
Situation reports will be sent by Brigades at every even numbered clock hour and in addition whenever there is anything of interest to report.
In no case will Brigades omit to furnish D.A.H.Q. with their location after a move.

AMMUNITION. 14. The following ammunition will be dumped at original positions:-
18-pdrs.   300 rounds per gun.
4.5" Hows. 200 "   "   how.
On arrival at forward positions the following ammunition will be dumped:-
18-pdrs.   176 rounds per gun.
4.5" Hows. 108 "   "   how.
Wagons and limbers will immediately be refilled at vacated positions. When vacated positions have been cleared Firing Battery Wagons and Gun Limbers will be refilled by D.A.C., while First Line Wagons will remain empty unless orders are issued to the contrary.

TEAMS. 15. Teams will be harnessed and in neighbourhood of battery positions half an hour before probable time of advancing.

CALLS FROM THE AIR. 16. One battery of 18-pdrs. per Brigade will be superimposed over Brigade front in order that it may be available to answer calls from the air.
Brigade wireless sets will be set up at Howitzer battery positions.
"L.L.", "G.F.", and "N.F." calls will be answered as set out in XIX Corps No. R.A. G/36/188 of 3/8/18.
Arrangements reference Contact aeroplanes and Counter-attack aeroplanes will be notified later.

LIGHT SIGNALS. 17. The S.O.S. Signal remains a Rifle Grenade breaking into GREEN over GREEN over RED.
No other light signal will be used by the 41st Division, unless information is issued to the contrary.

TRAPS. 18. All ranks will be warned against entering dugouts, pill-boxes or shelters before these have been inspected by the Company of R.E. detailed for the purpose.
Dugouts labelled "Unsafe" will in no circumstances be entered.
Dugouts marked "Examined" will only be entered in the event of enemy shelling and will be vacated immediately the shelling ceases.

7. 187th Brigade R.F.A. will detach sections to Infantry for close support as follows:-

(a). One Section to accompany Centre Battalion 122nd Infantry Brigade; this will join support Battalion 124th Infantry Brigade when latter passes through after the second 'pause'.

(b). One Section to each of the two leading Battalions 124th Infantry Brigade.

Up to limit of his advance G.O.C. 122nd Infantry Brigade will have one section at his disposal, his advance being covered by the barrage.

After second 'pause' and for the further advance G.O.C. 124th Infantry Brigade will have three Sections at his disposal. They will be pushed forward boldly in close support of the Infantry, and Section Commanders will keep close touch with Battalion Commanders or Company Commanders as may be necessary.

Sections should not advance further East than the line of road R.2.a.3.1., R.2.b.6.3., L.32.d.6.3., L.33.d.2.6., L.34.a.1.6. without a special call from the Infantry Battalions they support.

(Para.16 of Extract from Notes on 3rd Army Front circulated 28/9/18 should be carefully studied, also notes by C.R.A. 29th Division on the working of single guns circulated 28/9/18).

Positions of assembly will be notified later.

METHOD OF ADVANCE.   8. The first order to advance will be given to leading Brigade (190) by D.A.H.Q.; should, however, the situation be obviously favourable and communication be severed, O.C. 190th Brigade will act on his own initiative, informing D.A.H.Q. of his decision.

187th Brigade will advance as soon as its task in the barrage is finished, followed by 11th Army Brigade R.F.A. at a sufficient interval, depending at the discretion of O.C. upon the conditions in front.

The area to which Brigades should advance has been indicated.

ROADS.   9. Roads will be reconnoitred beforehand up to the front line.

The two Artillery Brigades which are first to advance will have parties of R.E. and Pioneers attached to them for the purpose of re-making damaged roads in advance of our present line.

TRENCH MORTARS.   10. Four 6" Newton T.M's are being placed in position for the purpose of cutting wire of the TERHAND LINE in K.29.d. and K.35.b.

11. 41st D.A.C. with 11th Army Brigade A.C. will advance on orders from D.A.H.Q., when the situation permits, to approximate area J.23.c. and d., J.29.a and b. which will be reconnoitred beforehand.

Should the situation permit, the D.A.C. will be established in this area by zero hour J day.

SIGNAL COMMUNICATIONS.   12. A forward D.A.Exchange will be established at a place to be notified later from which communication will be established to Brigades in their advanced positions.

It should be impressed on all ranks that with the
carefully concealed fuzes which the enemy is using,
it is possible that, even after examination by experts,
an explosion might occur in a dugout; also that the
enemy has now had time to prepare for a withdrawal and
to set traps for the incautious.

20. A C K N O W L E D G E.

E R Roper
Major,
Brigade Major,
issued at:-23.00.41st Divisional Artillery.

Distribution:-

Copy No.		
1 - 5	187th Brigade R.F.A.	
6 - 10	190th " "	
11 - 15	11th Army Bde. R.F.A.	
16	41st D.A.C.	
17	41st Divn. G.	
18	41st Divn. Q.	
19	R.A. XIXth Corps.	
20	H.A. XIXth Corps.	
21	R.A. 35th Division.	
22	R.A. 34th Division.	
23	4th Brigade R.G.A.	
24	122nd Infy. Bde.	
25	123rd " "	
26	124th " "	
27	C.R.E. 41st Divn.	
28	41st Battn. M.G.Corps.	
29	S.C.R.A. 41st Divn.	
30	R.O.R.A. 41st Divn.	
31	41st D.A.Signals Officer	
32 - 36	War Diary and File.	
37	D.T.M.O. 41st Divn.	

SECRET   41st D.A. No. S.176.
                                      Copy No. 14

1st ADDENDUM to 41st DIVISIONAL ARTILLERY PRELIMINARY INSTRUCTIONS No.36.

LIAISON.   1.   Reference para.3 of above Instructions.

Battle Headquarters of Infantry Brigades will be as follows:-

	Original H.Q.	H.Q. after Advance.
122nd Infy.Bde.	J.30.d.80.50.	About K.36.a.7.3.
124th " "	K.29.c.30.95.	About K.26.d.4.7.(?)
123rd " "	J.35.c.80.00.	K.26.c.4.3.; subsequently about K.36.a.7.3.

Liaison Officers will report at Original Headquarters set out above.

WIRE CUTTING.   2.   Reference para. 5:

Brigades will inform Infantry Brigades in the line of any gaps cut in enemy wire, in order that arrangements may be made by the latter for patrolling these and keeping them open by Machine and Lewis Gun Fire.

ROADS.   3.   Reference para. 9:

One half Company of 19th Middlesex Regiment (Pioneers) and one section R.E. will report to each of 187th and 190th Brigades R.F.A. at 5 p.m. on second day before J.

AEROPLANES.   4.   Reference para.16:

A Contact aeroplane will fly along the front of attack one hour after Zero and thereafter every clock hour.

A Counter-attack aeroplane will patrol the front from Zero plus 40 minutes onwards and will signal the development of an enemy counter-attack by firing a RED parachute flare..

LIGHT SIGNALS.   5.   Reference para.17:

RED flares will be used by the most advanced attacking troops to intimate their position to Contact Aeroplanes.
    In addition the following signals will be used:-
      Rifle Grenade, BLUE Smoke: "We are here"
      Rifle Grenade, RED Smoke: "We are held up".
The signal denoting "We are here" will be sent up to indicate:-
    (a). That a pre-arranged bound has been completed.
    (b). That a pre-arranged objective has been gained.
    (c). That a locality which offered more resistance than could be dealt with locally has been captured.

P. T. O.

The signal denoting "We are held up" will not be used unless the support of Artillery or of reinforcing Infantry is required.

In every case in which the "We are held up" signal is used, the "We are here" signal will be sent up immediately the enemy's resistance has been overcome.

LOCATIONS. 6. Battle positions of 41st Divisional Artillery are set out in Appendix A hereto.

SIGNALLING 7.
COMMUNICATIONS. The C.W. Wireless set will be attached to Headquarters 190th Brigade R.F.A.

8. ACKNOWLEDGE.

9th October 1918.

Major.
Brigade Major,
41st Divisional Artillery.

Issued to all recipients of 41st D.A. Preliminary Instructions No.36.

APPENDIX A.

41st DIVISIONAL ARTILLERY

	Position.	Wagon Lines
H.Q. 41st Divisional Arty.	J.14.a.3.3.	

11th Army Bde. R.F.A.

	Position.	Wagon Lines
Headquarters.	K.27.c.05.15.	
83rd Battery.	K.34.c.15.10.	
84th Battery.	K.33.a.65.80.	
85th Battery.	K.33.b.25.95.	
D/11 Battery.	K.27.d.70.50.	

187th Brigade R.F.A.

	Position.	Wagon Lines
Headquarters.	J.30.d.70.85.	J.34.d.10.30.
A/187th Battery.	K.33.c.10.50.	J.30.a.30.10.
B/187th Battery.	K.33.c.15.95.	J.22.d.60.20.
C/187th Battery.	K.32.b.80.40.	J.30.b.90.20.
D/187th Battery.	K.33.a.00.85.	J.30.b.30.60.

190th Brigade R.F.A.

	Position.	Wagon Lines
Headquarters.	K.26.c.4.3.	J.34.b.00.50.
A/190th Battery.	K.32.b.30.75.	J.34.b.60.40.
B/190th Battery.	K.31.c.20.70.	J.23.d.90.40.
C/190th Battery.	K.31.a.60.00.	J.23.d.70.50.
D/190th Battery.	K.31.a.80.20.	J.24.d.50.60.

Trench Mortars

Two 6" Newton T.Ms. at each of the following points:-

K.29.c.75.95.
K.29.a.85.00.

Headquarters of 4th Brigade R.G.A., which will probably be affiliated to the Division, are at K.25.c.5.5.

SECRET 41st D.A. No. S.201.

Copy No. 33

SECOND ADDENDUM to 41st D.A. PRELIMINARY INSTRUCTIONS No.36.

1. Reference para. 6 of above Instructions:

BARRAGE MAP.

Barrage Map, as corrected, is attached & shews task allotted to each Artillery Brigade. The Barrage will open at 3 minutes before Zero and the Second Pause will be of 12 extra minutes instead of 15.

The green line on Barrage Map shews boundaries between Right and Left Portions allotted to Brigades.

The dotted red line shows zones for 4.5" How. batteries during the first phase until 190th Brigade drops out. D/187 will take the right zone, D/190 the centre and D/11 the left zone.

After 190th Brigade have dropped out the green line marks the boundary between howitzer batteries of 187th and 11th Brigades.

CREEPING BARRAGE.

Up to First Pause line 18-pdr. batteries of 190th Bde. R.F.A. will fire on Right portion, and 187th Bde. on Left portion of Divisional Front. 82nd and 83rd Batteries (11th Army Bde. R.F.A.)will be superimposed, the former on Right (190th Bde.) portion, the latter on Left (187th Bde.) portion.

On reaching First Pause Line 11th Army Bde. R.F.A. (complete) will shift over to Left Portion and continue on that throughout the remainder of the barrage, 83rd Bty. joining in on its allotted portion of the line. 187th Brigade R.F.A. will shift, by batteries, from Left Portion to Right Portion, the whole shift to be completed 5 minutes before the barrage moves forward.

All batteries will move forward together at H plus 45. At H plus 47 190th Brigade will drop out (vide para 6 (d) of Instructions No.36) and the barrage be fired by 187th Brigade on Right Portion and 11th Army F.A.Brigade on Left Portion.

The above shifts are necessitated by considerations of range.

The barrage will be continued up to 500 yards beyond Second Pause Line, i.e. up to 95 - 97 line (and not as laid down in para.6 (f) of Instructions No.36),when all batteries will cease firing and act as laid down in para.8.

USE OF SMOKE.

The last minute of firing (i.e. plus 96 to plus 97) will be entirely smoke as a signal to the Infantry.

The flank batteries on Divisional front will fire three rounds of smoke per minute per battery throughout the barrage. These batteries will be detailed by Os.C. Artillery Brigades.

On each Pause Line each Battery will fire 2 rounds of smoke per minute per battery for 8 minutes, after which no Smoke will be fired during the Pause except one round from all guns at plus 45 and another at plus 87, which will be the signal to the Infantry that the barrage is moving on.

THERMITE.

The right-hand 18-pdr. on the Divisional front will fire one round of Thermite per minute throughout the barrage in order to assist the Infantry in keeping the correct direction.

PAUSES. During each Pause 50% of the 18-pdrs. will search in bounds up to 500 yards beyond Pause Line.

COMBING BARRAGE. 2. The action of 4.5" Hows. will be as follows (vide Barrage Map).

All farms, strong points and occupied localities in the area allotted to each Howitzer battery will be searched with 106 Fuze to a general depth of 500 yards in advance of the 18-pdr. Creeping Barrage. Howitzers will be employed by Sections on these targets.

Os.C. Brigades will detail targets, with lifts and times, for their howitzer batteries and submit their orders to 41st D.A.Headquarters not later than 12.00 on the 13th instant.

HEAVY ARTILLERY BARRAGE. 3. Heavy Artillery will be similarly employed to a general depth of 700 yards beyond the 4.5" Hows.

4. East of a limit of 5,000 yards from the Infantry starting line fire by Heavy Artillery will be restricted as follows:-
(a). No fire will be delivered W. of a line 5,000 yards (Line A B) from the original Infantry starting line after H.plus 116 minutes.
(b). As above W. of a line 6,000 yards (line C D) after H plus 136 minutes.
(c). As above W. of a line 7,000 yards (line E F) after H plus 156 minutes.
(d). To enable Infantry to exploit, fire by Heavy Artillery beyond 7,000 yards limit will only be placed on the crossings over the River LYS.

The only exception to above orders will be in the case of:- (1) Observed fire; (2) Unobserved fire under direct orders from Divisions; (3) Calls from the air.

RATES OF FIRE. 5. Rates of fire will be as follows:-

18-pdrs: H minus 3 to H.plus 2   4 rds. per gun per min.
         H plus 2 to H plus 28   3 "   "   "   "   "
         H plus 28 to STOP.   2 "   "   "   "   "

4.5" Hows: H minus 3 to H plus 28.   2 rds. per how. per min.
           H.plus 28 to STOP.   1½ "   "   "   "   "

AMMUNITION. 6. Ammunition will be as follows:-

18-pdrs: 30% H.E. delay, 70% Shrapnel.
Should H.E. delay not be available in the necessary quantity shrapnel will be fired. H.E. 106 will not be used in the Creeping Barrage.
Shrapnel fuzes will be so set as to give 50% grazes.
Smoke and Thermite as laid down above.

4.5" Hows: H.E., 106 Fuze where available.
1 round per how. per minute of Smoke during first 8 minutes of each Pause.

SECTIONS ATTACHED TO INFANTRY.	7.	Sections of 187th Brigade R.F.A. attached to Infantry Battalions will rendezvous in vicinity of CHEESEMAN FARM (K.28.c.5.0.) on night before J, where they will bivouac.

Officers in charge of Sections will get into touch with Battalion Commanders, whose Headquarters will be as follows:-

    Centre Battalion, 122 Infy. Bde.)
    (12th E. Surrey Regt.)

    Right Bn. 124th Infantry Bde.) Vicinity of JAPP FARM
    (20th D.L.I.)   ) K.34.a.3.2.

    Left Bn. 124th Infantry Bde.) Farm at K.28.a.50.05.
    (26th Royal Fusiliers).   )

Wagon Limbers will be used as gun limbers and F.B. Wagons only will accompany the guns.

ADVANCED POSITIONS.	8.	190th Bde. R.F.A. will occupy advanced positions in vicinity of K.36.a. and b.; 187th Bde. R.F.A. in L.32.a. and b.; 11th Army Bde. R.F.A. in L.31.a. and b. These areas are indicated as a rough guide.

WAGON LINES.		Wagon Line areas will be as follows:-
		   190th Bde. R.F.A.: K.28.c. and d.
		   187th " " : Vicinity of vacated battery positions in K.33.a. and c.
		   11th Army Bde. R.F.A.: Vicinity of vacated battery positions.

SHELLING OF TOWNS AND VILLAGES.	9.	There is no restriction as to shelling towns and villages which lie in the line of attack.

Other towns and villages will not be bombarded except to engage artillery located in them or concentrations of hostile Infantry.

If considered advisable the entrances and exits to villages and towns may be shelled and gassed.

Bridges and roads in enemy territory are not to be destroyed without authority.

COURTRAI is not to be shelled unless the enemy is known to be concentrated there, but hostile Artillery in COURTRAI will be dealt with by the Artillery.

CAPTURED GUNS.	10.	The B.G.H.A. will arrange for any suitable captured guns or howitzers to be manned and fired on J day.

For this purpose a detachment under an Officer will be detailed by B.G.H.A. to keep touch with each Field Artillery Brigade and receive information as to whereabouts of captured guns.

Officers in charge of these detachments will report at Field Artillery Brigade Headquarters on the afternoon of J minus 1 day in order to be instructed as to movements of F.A. Brigades on J day.

All ranks will be warned of the importance of sending in prompt information as to the whereabouts of captured pieces, and especially of heavy howitzers. F.O.Os. should be specially instructed on this point. Reports sent in should include information as to presence or absence of dial sights, breech blocks and firing pins.

ROADS.	11.	C.R.E. 41st Division will on J day make fit for guns and horse transport the road K.28.a.0.6. - K.34.c.8.4. - K.35.c.1.2. - K.35.c.7.6. - Q.5.a.8.6. - Q.5.b.5.5. - K.36.c.7.0. - L.25.d.6.2. - L.32.c.1.8. - L.32.b.0.2. - L.32.d.6.3. - L.33.d.2.6.

Although work will be concentrated on this road as the main forward route for the Division, all roads and tracks in the Corps area will be used as the tactical situation demands at the moment, and Divisions will not be rigidly restricted to roads in their own areas.

The guiding factor will be the necessity of pushing forward guns as rapidly as possible to support the attack.

Only instantaneous fuzes will be used in the neighbourhood of roads.

(This does not apply to 18-pdrs. in Creeping Barrage).

SIGNAL-
LING
COMMUNICA-
TIONS.   12.   A diagram of Signalling Communications is attached.

13.   Battle Headquarters as given in Para. 1 of First Addendum dated 9th instant should be amended as follows:-

LOCATIONS.

	Original H.Q.	H.Q. after advance.
122nd Infy. Bde.	K.26.c.4.3.	K.36.a.7.3.
124th Infy. Bde.	K.29.c.30.75.	About K.36.a.7.3. subsequently about L.32.b.5.3.
123rd Infy. Bde.	J.35.c.8.0. (In doubt)	K.26.c.4.3.; subsequently about K.36.a.7.3.

14.   A C K N O W L E D G E.

[signature]

Major,
Brigade Major,
41st Divisional Artillery.

12th October 1918.

Issued to all recipients of 41st D.A. Preliminary Instructions No.36.

APPENDIX B.

To 2nd Addendum to 41st D.A. Preliminary Instructions No.36.

COMMUNICATIONS.

12th Octr. 1918.

EXCHANGES. 1. By Zero hour on J day the following exchanges will be in operation:-
    Div. H.Q. Exchange.   J.14.a.3.3.
    GHELUVELT   "   (G.T.) J.22.d.5.0.
    Div. Forward   "   (G.F.) K.29.c.8.8.
All these exchanges will be combined Infantry and Artillery exchanges.

In addition to the above, two linesmens posts will be established. One at J.30.d.8.4. (old A/187 position call V.C.) and one at K.27.d.2.8. (call M.K. Present Battalion Headquarters).
A buzzer unit will be in use at each of these posts and can in emergency be used as an exchange.

LINES.   187th Brigade and 190th Brigade both have a line to V.C. and they will be responsible for connecting this line direct through to their line to G.T. before leaving their present Headquarters.

11th Army Bde. R.F.A. have a line to the Battalion Headquarters (M.K.). They will be responsible for connecting this line direct on to the line to G.T. before leaving their present Headquarters.

In addition to the above there are three lines laid direct from G.T. to G.F. each of them being T'd into and brought in to the linesmens posts at V.C. and M.K.

VISUAL.   A Central Visual Station will be established at K.27.c.9.9. on the 12th instant working to G.T. After the advance it will work to the Infantry Brigades at KNIGHTS and JOHNSON'S Farm. Artillery work by Visual will be through the Infantry Brigades.

WIRELESS.   Each Infantry Bde. in the line will have a trench wireless set (spark) working to the Divisional Directing Station at G.T. This set is also for the use of the Artillery Brigades.

In addition 190th Bde. will be responsible for taking forward with them the C.W. wireless set now working at 187th Bde. Headquarters. This will be erected whenever a halt is made and will call up the D.A. C.W. set at Divisional Headquarters.

In addition to this set 4th Bde. R.G.A. have a C.W. Wireless set which will work to D.A. C.W. set.

D.R's.   4 D.R's will be stationed at Divisional Headquarters to run to G.T.
4 D.R's will be stationed at G.T. to run to G.F. and back to Division, and,
4 D.R's will be stationed at G.F. to run back to G.T. or forward to the Artillery or Infantry Brigades.

When the Artillery Brigades have moved forward and have fixed their advanced Headquarters they will send an orderly back to G.F. to lead a party who will lay a line to the Headquarters in question.

                                      Major,
                    Brigade Major, 41st Divl. Arty.
Issued to all recipients of 41st D.A. Preliminary Instructions No.36.

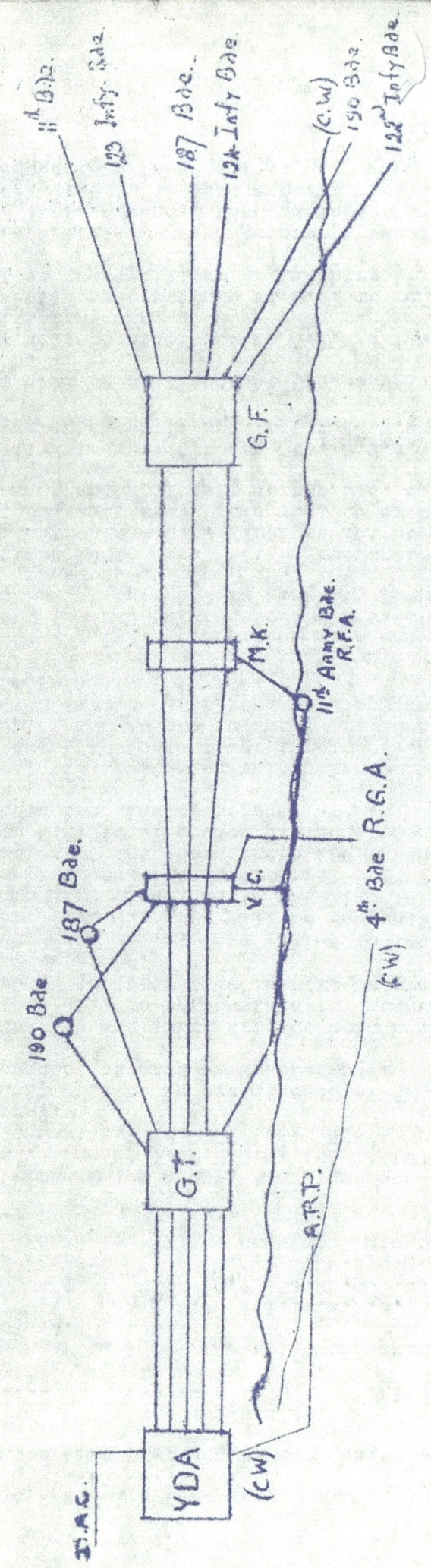

SECRET.

Headquarters,
   122nd Infantry Bde.
   124th   "   "

41st D.A. No. S.203.

Field Artillery Barrage Map and 41st D.A. Instructions are issued down to Battalion Commanders.
   The accompanying explanation is issued for the information of Platoon and Company Commanders.

G.R.Roper
Major,
12-10-18.   Brigade Major, 41st Divisional Arty.

BARRAGE SUMMARY.

   The barrage will open at H minus 3 and move forward at H, at the rate of 100 yards in 2 minutes, to the first 'pause line' 1500 yards from START line, which it reaches at H plus 28 and where it will dwell for 17 minutes.

   It moves forward again at H plus 45 to Second 'pause line', arriving here at H plus 73, where it will dwell for 14 minutes and where 124th Infantry Brigade passes through 122nd Infantry Brigade.

   It moves forward again at H plus 87 for a depth of 500 yards, arriving at H plus 95, where it will STOP at H.plus 97.

   To indicate progress to the Infantry 3 rounds smoke per minute will be fired by flank batteries of the Divisional Artillery, and one round THERMITE per minute by flank guns. At each pause 2 rounds SMOKE per 18-pdr. battery will be fired per minute along PAUSE LINE for 8 minutes, after which no further SMOKE will be fired during the Pause except one round per gun from all guns at plus 45 and plus 87, which will be the signal that the barrage is moving on.
When the barrage has reached its furthest limit, i.e. 3500 yards from START Line (roughly R.2.a.1.5. to L.33.b.7.7.) the last minute of firing, i.e. plus 96 to plus 97 will be entirely SMOKE as a signal to the Infantry that the Barrage is about to CEASE.

   While on the 'Pause Line' 50% of 18-pdrs. will search forward to a depth of 500 yards.
   4.5" Hows. will search all strong points and farms to a depth of 500 yards in front of 18-pdr. creeping barrage line.
   Similarly Heavy Artillery will search to a depth of 700 yards beyond the 4.5" How. area.

S E C R E T.

Copy No. 34

41st D.A. No. S.206.

THIRD ADDENDUM to 41st D.A. INSTRUCTIONS No.36
(in accordance with 41st Divn. Order No.275.

SUPPLEMENTARY INSTRUCTIONS.

1. Should the final objective be reached with very little resistance on the part of the enemy, and it be apparent either that he has little fight in him or that he is retiring, it is the intention of the G.O.C.II Army to secure the crossings of the LYS.
   For this purpose 41st Division will be prepared to capture LAUWE, holding roughly the line M.19.b. - M.21.central. - M.16.a., with 35th Division operating on its left towards MARCKE, the inter-divisional boundary being the road M.3.d. - M.10.a.

2. Para. 8 of 2nd Addendum to 41st D.A. Instructions No.36 will be amended as follows:-

   190th Brigade R.F.A.: No change.

   187th Brigade R.F.A.: Will if possible come into action in L.33.a. or b. instead of L.32.a. or b. with a view to bringing effective fire to bear on WEVELGHEM and LAUWE. The situation must be gauged by O.C. 187th Brigade and he must act at his own discretion.

   11th Army Brigade R.F.A. : will remain in the vicinity of battle positions ready to advance at very short notice and will establish communication with G.O.C. 123rd Infantry Brigade.
   It will not move forward without instructions from D.A.H.Q.

3. Should instructions be received from XIX Corps that the operation referred to above will take place the task of the Artillery will be:-

   (i). to cover the advance of infantry through WEVELGHEM and LAUWE; probably also of R.E. bridging parties.
   (ii). to hold the line established S. of LAUWE, and to cover the Right Flank.

4. 187th Brigade R.F.A. can fulfil task (i) from positions indicated above and will be assisted by 190th Brigade R.F.A. The latter must be prepared to advance to approximately L.27.d. or L.33.b. to carry out this task. Orders on this subject will be issued from this office.

5. It is probable that 123rd Infantry Brigade will be called upon to carry out the crossing of the river. 11th Army Bde. R.F.A. will act in close touch with the G.O.C. this Infantry Brigade and convey his instructions as regards covering fire etc. to 187th and 190th Brigades, keeping his own Brigade intact to cover the line when

/established

P. T. O.

established along M.19.b., M.21.central, M.16.a. When once this has been established 187th and 190th Brigades will reconnoitre positions for closer support to the Infantry.

6. O.C. 11th Army Bde. R.F.A., in selecting his battery positions must bear in mind the fact that reinforcing Artillery (187th and 190th Brigades) will very shortly also be coming into action in his vicinity.

7. A C K N O W L E D G E.

E R Roper
Major,
Brigade Major,
41st Divisional Artillery.

12th October 1918.

Issued to all recipients of 41st D.A. Preliminary Instructions No.36.

S E C R E T   App: B   41st D.A. No. S.584.

Reference Map, Sheet 28 1/40,000.

Units of 41st Divisional Artillery will march to new area tomorrow the 17th instant in accordance with March Table on back hereof.

                                        Major,
                                        Brigade Major,
16-10-18.   41st Divisional Artillery.

Headquarters,
    190th Bde. R.F.A.
    41st D.A.C.
    11th D.A.C.
    41st D.T.M.C.
    41st Divn. E.
    41st Divn. G.
    41st D.A...R.

MARCH TABLE

Unit.	From.	To.	Route.	Remarks.
41st D.A.C.	YPRES R.R. 7.14.a.5.5.	AMBON Rd. L.13.a.9.0.	YPRES – ST JEAN Road to L.6.d.1.0. – L.5.b.0.1. – L.5.b.0.1. – L.21.a.5.5. – L.13.a.9.0.	To be clear of YPRES by 6 a.m.
41st D.A.C. No.1 & 2 Sections 11th D.A.C. 41st T.M.Batteries.	GOLDFISH Chateau.	L.15.b. L.16.b. L.22.d.	- do -	To march under O.C. 41st D.A.C. To be clear of SIEGE KRUISSIKE Cross Roads (J.29.a.1.2.) by 8 a.m.
10th Bde. R.F.A. (H.Q. & 4 batteries)	K.28.central.	L.17.c.5.5.	GWILEM – DAMETLE Road to L.24.a.5.5. – AMBRINE.	Rear of column to pass L.20.d.0.0. not later than 7 a.m.

Usual distances and units to be observed.
Super lines at destination to be reconnoitred in advance.

RDRA
app "C"

S E C R E T.   Copy No. 31

41st DIVISIONAL ARTILLERY ORDER No. 17.

Reference Sheet 29 1/40,000.

1. The Advance will be resumed on the 20th instant.
   The advance of the XIXth Corps will be to the River SCHELDT between Canal Junction at BOSSUYT (V.13.c.) and AVELGHEM (P.34.central).

   Approximate Corps boundaries are as follows:-

   <u>Southern boundary</u>: Straight line from M.10.central to BOSSUYT.

   <u>Northern boundary</u>: COURTRAI - BOSSUYT Canal to O.9.central, thence in a straight line to AVELGHEM.

2. The 35th Division will advance over the whole Corps Front on the 20th instant to the high ground running through O.31., O.27., and O.23, and will push advanced troops forward from this objective when gained.

3. 122nd Infantry Brigade with 2 Field Companies R.E. has been placed at disposal of G.O.C. 35th Division and has already crossed the LYS.
   Remainder of 41st Division will cross the LYS in 35th Divisional area behind that Division on the 20th instant and will concentrate in area S.W. of SWEVEGHEM (O.1.), being prepared to pass through 35th Division on the 21st inst.

4. The Division will advance in Infantry Brigade Groups. Artillery Brigades will march in accordance with march Table annexed and on arrival in concentration area will be grouped as follows:-

   190th Bde. R.F.A. in 122 Inf. Bde. Group
                       (H.Qrs. at G.36.d.15.18.)
   187th Bde. R.F.A. in 124 Inf. Bde. Group
   11th Army Bde R.F.A. in 123 Inf. Bde. Group.

5. 41st D.A.C. with T.M. personnel will march on the 20th inst. to GULLEGHEM area under arrangements which will be notified later and on the 21st inst. to vicinity of M.6.a. & b.

6. A C K N O W L E D G E.

Issued at 23.00.
19-10-18.
                                        Major,
                              Brigade Major, 41st Divl. Arty.

1 - 5	187th Bde.R.F.A.	24	R.A. 35th Divn.
6 - 10	190th " "	25	R.A. 29th "
11 - 15	11th Army Bde.	26	122 Inf. Bde.
16	41st D.A.C.	27	123 " "
17	41st D.T.M.O.	28	124 " "
18	41st Divn. G.	29	C.R.E. 41st Divn.
19	41st Divn. Q.	30	S.C.R.A. 41st Divn.
20	D.A.P.M. 41st Divn.	31	R.O.R.A. 41st Divn.
21	R.A. 19th Corps.	32	41st D.A. Sigs. Officer.
22	H.A. " "	33-36	War Diary & File.
23	4th Bde. R.G.A.		

P.T.O.

MARCH TABLE TO ACCOMPANY 41st DIVISION ORDER NO. 286 dated 19th October, 1918.

Serial	Unit.	From.	To	Route.	Remarks.
1.	190 Bde R.F.A.	MOORSEELE Area.	Area N.W. of SWEVEGHEM in squares H.35.d.&/G.5.a and b. To join 122nd Bde Group.	GULLEGHEM - BISSEGHEM - Bridge M.5.b.7.8. - MARCKE - St.ANNE (N.19.a) N.13.c.05.50 - CHAPEL (N.15.d.8.9) - L'HOOGHE (N.9.central).	To pass BISSEGHEM Church at 09.45. To be clear of this point by 10.30.
2.	124th I.Bde Group 124th I.B. 187 Bde RFA. 1 M.G.Coy. Light Fd.Ambce.	GULLEGHEM Area.	Area composed of squares N.8.b and d, N.9.a.c & d, N.14.b and d, N.15, N.16.a, N.20.b, N.21.a & b.	(a) Dismounted personnel by route to be reconnoitred through G.22.b, G.23.c. & d, G.29 b. and d, G.30.c, to footbridge G.36.a, to road/N.6.a.5.1 POTTELBERG - WALLE N.8.a. (b) Mounted personnel, 187 Bde R.F.A. & "A" Echelon 1st Line Tpt as for Serial No.1.	Both columns to leave GULLEGHEM - HEULE Rd 10.15.
3.	11th (Army) Bde R.F.A.	HEULE Area.	Area in G.36. and M.6. to be allotted by 123 I.Bde.	Via BISSEGHEM and bridge M.5.b.7.8.	To pass BISSEGHEM CHURCH 14.00.
4.	123rd I.Bde Group :- 123rd I.B. 2 M.G.Coys Light Fd.Ambce	Line COURTRAI Sector.	Area in squares G.36. M.6.a and b, including TILE WORKS.	(a) Portion S. of R.LYS by most direct route. (b) Portion N. of River by footbridge H.25.c 6.5. Tpt as for serial No.3.	(b)Not to move S. of GULLEGHEM - HEULE Road before 14.15.

SECRET   Copy No. 33

41st DIVISIONAL ARTILLERY ORDER No. 18.

Reference sheet 29, 1/40 000.

DIVISIONAL SECTOR.	1.	On Night 23rd/24th October 41st Division will hand over to 34th Division that portion of its present front as far North as line N.29.central - O.28 Central - V.9.a. 0.0. On the same night 41st Division will take over from 29th Division that portion of 29th Divisional front as far North as line N.25.d.3.0. - road junction I.31.b.9.8.- I.33.a.0.6. - I.34.a.2.8. (road inclusive) - P.1.c.5.3. (ST. LOUIS inclusive) - P.30.central.
INFANTRY RELIEF.	2.	124th Infantry Bde. will be relieved by 102nd Infantry Bde. (34th Divn.) in the first portion of front above mentioned and will simultaneously relieve 87th Infantry Bde. (29th Divn.) in the second portion above mentioned, command passing in each case on completion of relief.
ARTILLERY RELIEF.	3.	187th Brigade R.F.A. will withdraw from present position at 4 p.m. on the 23rd instant and move at once to positions vacated by 17th Bde. R.F.A. (H.Q. O.3.c.7.4.) relieving batteries of that Brigade immediately on arrival.
	4.	11th Army Bde. R.F.A. will remain in present positions pending issue of further orders.
GROUPING.	5.	187th Bde. R.F.A. will be in 124th Infantry Bde.(Left Brigade) group. 190th Bde. R.F.A. will be in 123rd Infantry Bde. (Right Brigade) Group. 11th Army Bde. R.F.A. will for the present not be grouped with an Infantry Brigade.
BRIGADE BOUNDARIES.	6.	Dividing line between Infantry Brigades will be a straight line from O.9.b.0.0. to P.34.central.
S.O.S. LINES.	7.	S.O.S. lines of 187th and 190th Brigades will be arranged by Brigade Commanders in consultation with Infantry Brigade Commanders. 11th Army Brigade R.F.A. will be superimposed over Right Brigade sector on selected points S.E. of line O.35.b.4.6. - O.30.c.8.2. - P.19.c.8.0. Front line of 29th Division is reported to be as follows:- O.17.d.6.6.-O.18.c.3.8.-O.18.a.5.5.-O.12.d.0.0.-O.12.d.5.6.
	8.	ACKNOWLEDGE.

23rd October 1918.   Major,
Issued at:-1500   Brigade Major,
                                    41st Divisional Artillery.

Distribution over.

```
Copy No.  1 - 5   187th Bde. R.F.A.
          6 -10   190th    "     "
         11 -15   11th Army Bde. R.F.A.
            16    41st D.A.C.
            17    41st D.T.M.O.
            18    41st Divn. G.
            19    41st Divn. Q.
            20    D.A.P.M. 41st Divn.
            21    R.A. 19th Corps.
            22    R.A.    "     "
            23    4th Bde. R.G.A.
            24    R.A. 34th Divn.
            25    R.A. 29th Divn.
            26    122nd Infy. Bde.
            27    123rd    "     "
            28    124th    "     "
            29    C.R.E. 41st Divn.
            30    S.C.R.A. 41st Divn.
            31    R.O.R.A. 41st Divn.
            32    41st D.A. Sigs. Officer.
         33-36    War Diary and File.
```

app 7

S E C R E T   Copy No. 19

41st DIVISIONAL ARTILLERY ORDER No.19.

Reference Sheet 29, 1/40,000.

1. The advance will be continued tonight by 123rd Infantry Brigade; Starting line O.23.d.1.8. - O.23.a.6.7. - O.23.a.7.6. - O.18.c.35.45; Objective Canal Bridge at O.29.c.O.O. - O.30.c.2.4. - O.24.d.99.15. The Right of the Brigade will be on BOSSUYT Canal, Left on KATTESTRAAT - HEESTERT road.

    Right Battalion 124th Infantry Brigade, after relieving Right Battalion 29th Division, will co-operate on left of 123rd Infantry Brigade, pushing forward its right in touch with 123rd Infantry Brigade.

2. Field and Heavy Artillery will assist by bursts of fire on area of attack during afternoon of 23rd and night 23/24th. These have been arranged and are being carried out under verbal orders already issued.

    Artillery preparation of ridge VIERKEERHOEK- P.13.central- OOTEGHEM is being arranged by C.R.A. 29th Division.

3. The advance will begin at 02.15. Field Artillery will co-operate with bursts of fire on selected targets ahead of the advancing troops. Assistance required of 190th Brigade R.F.A. will be arranged on this system by O.C. that Brigade in direct consultation with G.O.C. 123rd Infantry Brigade.

    11th Army Brigade R.F.A. will fire on following targets:-

    Z plus 10 - Z plus 15   (a). Area O.29.b.6.0. - O.29.a.2.0.- O.28.b.9.4.
                                     (b). KEIBERGMOLEN.
                                     (c). Area O.24.a.8.1.
    Z plus 20 - Z plus 25   (d). Area O.29.c.4.9. - O.29.d.1.6.
                                     (e). Area O.29.d.6.9.
                                     (f). Area O.24.d.7.3.
    Z plus 35 - Z plus 40   (g). Area O.29.c.1.1.
                                     (h). Area O.30.c.1.4.
                                     (i). Area O.24.d.9.0.

    Heavy Artillery will fire from Z to Z plus 20 on KLIJTTE, HOSKE and HEESTERT areas in bursts according to amount of ammunition available.

4. Ammunition allotment for whole operation (including preliminary bursts referred to in para.2):-
    18-pdrs. a total of 120 rounds per gun.
    4.5" Hows.   "   "   95   "   "   how.

5. Watches will be synchronized at   23.00 tonight.

6. A C K N O W L E D G E.

23rd October 1918.   Major,
Issued at 13.30.   Brigade Major,
                                                 41st Divisional Artillery.

Distribution over.

```
Copy No.  1      187th Bde. R.F.A.
          2      190th    "    "
          3-7    11th Army Bde. R.F.A.
          8      41st D.A.C.
          9      41st Divn. G.
          10     4th Brigade R.G.A.
          11     H.A. 19th Corps.
          12     R.A. 34th Divn.
          13     122nd Infy. Bde.
          14     123rd   "    "
          15     124th   "    "
          16     S.C.R.A. 41st Divn.
          17     R.O.R.A. 41st Divn.
          18-22  War Diary and File.
```

App E

Reference para. 11 (b) 41st D.A. Order No.20.

O.C. 187th Brigade will turn two Hows. on the following with SMOKE:-

High ground P.8.a. from H.10 to H.21.
"   "   P.8.b. from H.21. to H.40.
"   "   P.9.c. from H.40 to H.51.

Major,
Brigade Major,
41st Divisional Artillery

24-10-18.

187th Bde. R.F.A.
124th Infantry Bde.
41st Divn. G.
R.A. 19th Corps.
H.A. 19th Corps.
R.A. 19th Division.
War Diary.

SECRET   Copy No. 48

41st DIVISIONAL ARTILLERY ORDER No.20.

Reference maps 29 S.E. 1/20,000
                29 S.W. 1/20,000.

ATTACK.   1.   The Division will attack on the 25th instant at an
                     hour to be notified later in conjunction with the divi-
                     sions on either flank.

BOUNDARIES.   Left flank of Division's advance will be ST.LOUIS
                     (incl) - P.1.d.0.0. - P.15.central. - P.30.central;
                     right flank will be the KNOKKE - KEIBERG - MOEN road as
                     far as O.30.c.1.4., thence to V.1.central and V.9.a.0.0.

OBJECTIVES.   First objective is a line P.31.c.0.0. - P.31.central -
                     P.14.central - P.8.d.7.0.
                     Final objective is the line of the SCHELDT between
                     present divisional boundaries.

RIGHT   2.   Infantry of 34th Division will advance over area be-
FLANK.   tween road above referred to and present right divisional
                     boundary. They will be covered over the area in question
                     by Artillery supporting 41st Division.

INFANTRY   3.   41st Division will attack on a two-Brigade front;
DISPOSITIONS.   dividing line between Brigades as at present.
                     Each Brigade will attack on a two-Battalion front. 123rd
                     Infantry Brigade will attack on Right, 124th Infantry
                     Brigade on left; 122nd Infantry Brigade in reserve.

FIELD   4.   Field Artillery available to support the attack will
ARTILLERY.   be 41st Divisional Artillery plus 11th and 119th Army
                     Brigades R.F.A..
                     Battle positions are being occupied by all Brigades today
                     under instructions already issued

LIAISON.   Artillery Brigades will be affiliated, and will find
                     Liaison Officers where necessary, as follows:-
                     187th Bde.R.F.A. with 124th Inf. Bde.(H.Q.I.33.c.1.7.)
                     190th   "   "   " 123rd   "   " (H.Q.O.14.a.6.4.)
                     11th Army Bde.RFA " 122nd   "   " (H.Q.O.14.a.7.7.)
                     The Liaison Officer with an Infantry Brigade will be
                     prepared to act as the representative of whatever
                     Artillery is covering his Infantry Brigade for the time
                     being.
                     Liaison Officers will report at H.Qrs. of their
                     Infantry Brigades not later than 6 p.m. to-day.

HEAVY   5.   Heavy Artillery to support the attack will be as
ARTILLERY.   follows:-
                     4th Bde. R.G.A. 2 batteries 60-pdrs. 2 batteries 6"Hows.
                     10th "   "   "   "   "   "   "   "
                     A Liaison Officer supplied by 4th Bde. R.G.A. is at
                     41st D.A.H.Qrs.

BOMBARD-   6.   Bombardment of the area of attack has already
MENT.   commenced under orders issued verbally to Brigade
                     Commanders. In addition to systematic bombardment
                     by Heavy Artillery and 4.5" Hows. of all known
                                                              points

of resistance and centres of activity within Brigade areas there will be synchronized bursts of fire each of 5 minutes duration, by all available guns of Field and Heavy Artillery at the following hours:-

   1400 24th inst.
   1700 do.
   2100 do.
   2400 do.
   0300 25th inst.
   0500 do.

Rate of Fire NORMAL.
Targets have been communicated verbally to Brigade Commanders.

CLOSE SUPPORT OF INFANTRY.   7.   187th and 190th Brigades will each attach two guns to leading Battalions of 124th and 123rd Infantry Bdes. respectively: one gun under an Officer being attached to each Battalion.

These guns will be pushed forward boldly in close support of the Infantry and Officers detailed for this duty will keep in touch with Battalion or Company Commanders with this object in view.

Where no orders from these are forthcoming, initiative is to be used.

114 rounds will accompany each gun.

Brigade Commanders will arrange with G.Os.C. Infantry Brigades times and places for these guns to report.

BARRAGE.   8.   The attack will start under a creeping Barrage which will move forward at the rate of 100 yards in 2 minutes, and will dwell an extra 5 minutes every 500 yards for the first 1500 yards, after which it will go right through to the PAUSE LINE. The Barrage will come down at 4 minutes before H. The first lift and the Infantry advance will be at H.

The Barrage and its allotment to Brigades are shewn on attached Barrage Map.

Fire will not be evenly distributed over the whole front of a Brigade but will be intensified over probable strong localities and centres of resistance.

The O.C. each Brigade will arrange that any road in his area is dealt with by a whole battery searching down it and the houses on either side. As far as possible all houses and likely M.G. posts will be dealt with as the barrage moves forward.

Special attention will be paid by 119th Army Bde.RFA. to Hill 66, where M.Gs. are reported, and to the HOOGMOLEN area; by 190th Bde. R.F.A. to the locality 0.23.c.3.0. and HOOGMOLEN area within his boundary.

Fire will move forward at the rate of 100 yards in 2 minutes with extra pauses as above to the PAUSE LINE, where it will dwell at SLOW rate for 10 minutes (last 2 minutes entirely SMOKE) and then CEASE, except that fire along the E. and W. grid line between 0.36 and U.6. (i.e. 190th Bde. area) will only dwell for 2 minutes and will cease at H plus 83, after which time no fire will be put down outside the Divisional Boundary except observed fire from forward guns.

4.5" Hows. will move 200 yards beyond 18-pdr. creeping barrage.

THERMITE will be fired down HOOGMOLEN road from 0.23.a.7.3. to 0.29.b.4.2. by 190th Bde.R.F.A.; also down road 0.18.c.4.4. to cross roads 0.24.d.9.1. by 11th Army Bde. R.F.A.

No THERMITE or SMOKE will be fired on START LINE. Thermite as above and 15% Smoke will be fired by 18-pdrs and 4.5" Hows. from the first lift onwards.

Bursts of fire will be put down during the 2 Hour Pause on selected targets within Brigade Boundaries. A burst of smoke will be fired by all guns every half hour from H plus 105 inclusive along the Pause Line to indicate this line.

At H plus 109 the barrage will re-open on the Pause Line for 2 minutes and advance for 1000 yards if guns can range so far, when it will STOP.

After H plus 91 no fire will be placed within 300 yards of the Northern Divisional Boundary except observed fire from forward guns.

RATES OF FIRE. 9. Rates of fire will be as follows:-

18-pdrs.
H minus 4 to H plus 10   3 rounds per gun per minute.
H plus 10 to H plus 30   1½ " " " " "
H plus 30 to H plus 91   1 " " " " "

4.5" Hows. Half above rates.
Except that on arrival at PAUSE LINE all 18-pdrs. will fire ½ round per gun per minute until H plus 91 while 4.5" Hows. will STOP.

Rates of fire during extra pauses referred to in para. 8 will be 1½ rounds per gun per minute.
4.5" Hows. Half the above.

Rate of fire for further barrage beyond PAUSE LINE (H plus 199 to H plus 219) will be:-
18-pdrs.   1½ rounds per gun per minute.
4.5" Hows.   1 " " " " "

AMMUNITION. 10. Ammunition expended will be as follows:-

18-pdrs.   15% Smoke.
         40% H.E. delay.
         45% Shrapnel (50% grazes).

4.5" Hows.   15% Smoke.
          85% H.E. 106 fuze.
No 106 fuze will be fired in the 18-pdr. barrage.

SPECIAL TARGETS. 11. (a). From 6 a.m. until 8.30 a.m. Hill 66 (O.23.b.0.5.) will be bombarded by 4.5" Hows. as follows:-
6 – 6.45 a.m.   D/187)
6.45 – 7.30 a.m.   D/190) 15 rounds per How.
7.30 – 8.0 a.m.   D/119)
8.0 – 8.30 a.m.   D/11.)

(b). O.C. 187th Brigade R.F.A. will be prepared to turn three Hows. with SMOKE on high ground in P.8.a and b. and P.9.c. for a period not exceeding 10 minutes at short notice – rate of fire 2 rounds per how. per minutes.

This may be ordered as the barrage approaches the above area and will not be required once this area is passed.

HEAVY ARTILLERY. 12. Tasks of Heavy Artillery are being arranged by B.G., C.H.A.

METHOD OF ADVANCE.

13. As soon as 190th Brigade R.F.A. has finished its task in the barrage, i.e. at H plus 83, it will limber up, cross the canal and move forward to a position of readiness East of it with a view to advancing to cover the final objective if the situation admits. An Officer with telephists and a mounted orderly will be left at present Brigade H.Q. until new H.Q. have been established, location reported to D.A.H.Q. and C.W. Wireless set put in operation.

187th Bde. R.F.A. will probably follow 190th Brigade R.F.A. on orders from D.A.H.Q.

Theses two Brigades will have teams with Limbers and Wagons in close vicinity of Battery positions half an hour before probable time of advancing.

It is improbable that 11th and 119th Army Brigades will be required to advance before conclusion of the operation, but teams should be ready in Wagon Lines.

SIGNAL COMMUNICATIONS.

14. The C.W. Wireless set will be with 190th Brigade H.Q.

15. A C K N O W L E D G E.

E.R.Roper
Major,
Brigade Major,
41st Divisional Artillery.

24th October 1918.
Issued at 19.45.

LATER:- H will be 0904 on the 25th instant.

Distribution:-
```
Copy No. 1 -  5    187th Bde.R.F.A.
         6 - 10    190th   "    "
        11 - 15    11th Army Bde.R.F.A.
        16 - 20    119th    "    "    "
             21    41st D.A.C.
             22    41st D.T.M.O.
             23    41st Divn. G.
             24    41st Divn. Q.
             25    R.A. 19th Corps.
             26    H.A. 19th Corps.
        27 - 35    4th Brigade R.G.A.
             36    R.A. 34th Divn.
             37    R.A. 9th Divn.
             38    122nd Infy. Bde.
             39    123rd   "    "
             40    124th   "    "
             41    C.R.E. 41st Divn.
             42    D.A.P.M. 41st Divn.
             43    S.C.R.A. 41st Divn.
             44    R.O.R.A. 41st Divn.
             45    41st D.A.Sigs Officer.
        46 - 50    War Diary and File.
             51    41st Bn. M.G.Corps.
```

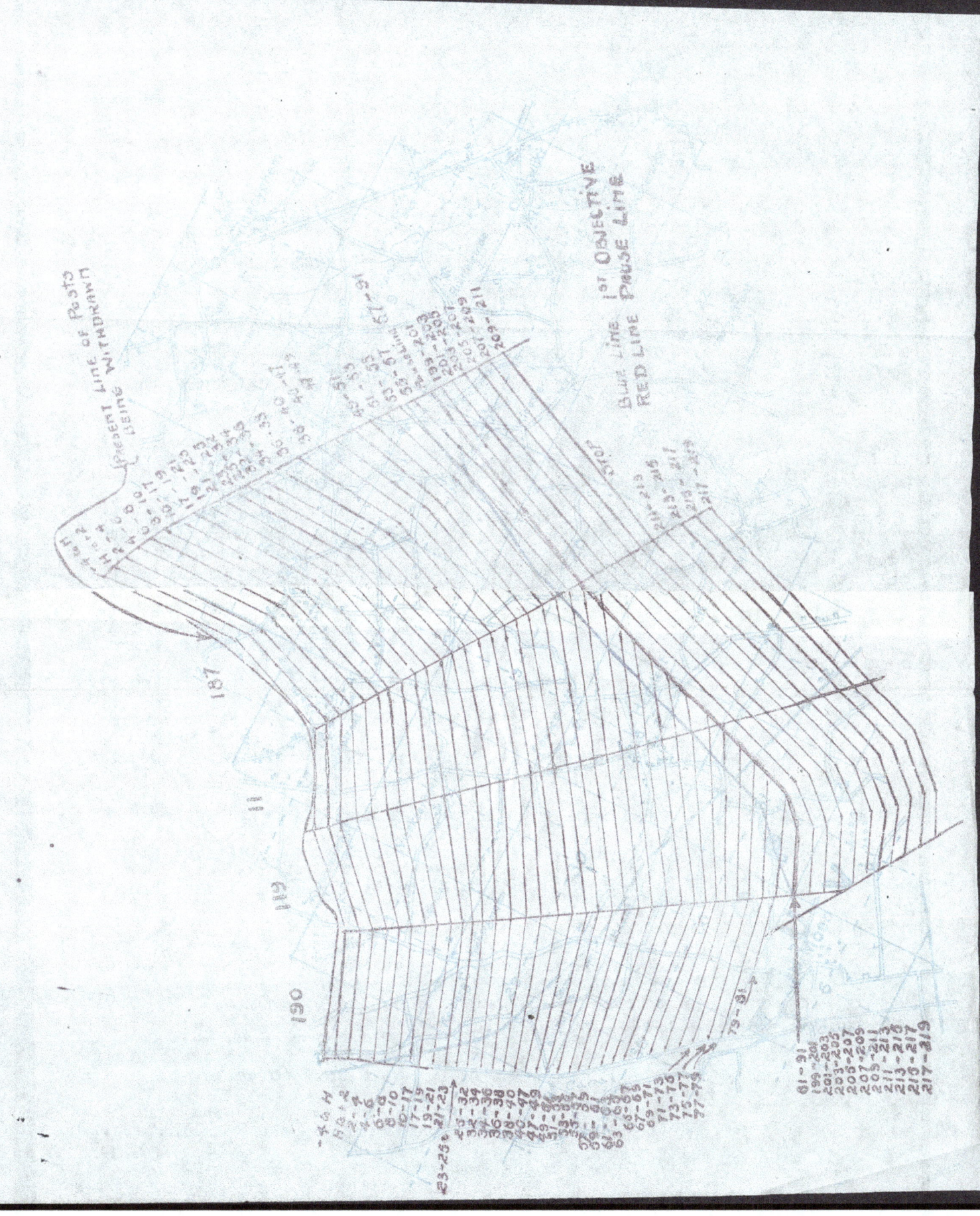

App H

SECRET.   Copy No. 45

41st DIVISIONAL ARTILLERY ORDER No.21.

Reference Sheet 29 1/40,000.

ADVANCE.	1.	The advance will be resumed tomorrow the 26th instant, at an hour (H) to be notified later, with the object of reaching the following line within present divisional boundaries: V.9.a.0.0. along N. bank of SCHELDT to AVELGHEM (incl), thence along road AVELGHEM - KLAPHOEK - P.15.d.7.7.
ARTILLERY SUPPORT.	2.	Detailed orders as to Artillery support for the operation cannot be prepared until present dispositions of the Infantry have been ascertained. It is probable, however, that it will take the form of a preliminary twenty-minute bombardment of area immediately ahead of infantry forming-up line, followed by a lifting bombardment of area over which the attack will proceed.
INFANTRY.	3.	122nd Infantry Brigade will probably be used to reinforce 123rd and 124th Infantry Brigades for the attack.
DETAILS.	4.	Details of the bombardment will be transmitted by telephonic message which will refer to this order, and give the following details under the letters shewn. A. Forming up line. B. Area of preliminary bombardment. C. Successive areas for lifting bombardment. D. Final bombardment line. E. Allotment of zones to various Artillery Brigades. F. Details as to ammunition, rate of fire, etc.
BOMBARDMENT.	5.	The bombardment will be put down by Artillery Brigade Commanders on probable defended areas, strong points, M.G. localities, etc., on lines laid down in para. 8 of 41st D.A. Order No.20.
ZERO HOUR.	6.	Zero hour (H) will be notified by the following code:- X = 12 noon. Variation of Zero hour from noon will be given in minutes Thus "H is X minus 30" will mean that Zero hour is 11.30 a.m.
HEAVY ARTILLERY.	7.	Heavy Artillery will fire on areas 500 yards beyond successive bombardment areas.
ADVANCED POSITIONS.	8.	Advanced positions will be occupied by 11th and 190th Brigades R.F.A. as follows:- 11th Bde.: Area O.30. and P.25.) as already indicat- 190th " : Area O.35. and O.36.) ed verbally. Batteries will be in action, with full echelons dumped, not later than 10.30 a.m. on the 25th instant.
	9.	ACKNOWLEDGE.

25th October 1918
Issued at 22.30

Major,
Brigade Major,
41st Divisional Artillery.

Distribution over.

```
Copy No. 1 - 5    187th Bde. R.F.A.
        6 - 10.   190th   "    "
       11 - 15.   11th Army Bde. R.F.A.
       16 - 20.   119th Army Bde. R.F.A.
            21.   41st Divn. G.
            22.   R.A. 19th Corps.
            23.   H.A. 19th Corps.
       24 - 32.   4th Bde. R.G.A.
            33.   R.A. 34th Divn.
            34.   R.A. 9th Divn.
            35.   122nd Infy. Bde.
            36.   123rd   "    "
            37.   124th   "    "
            38.   41st Bn. M.G. Corps.
            39.   C.R.E. 41st Divn.
            40.   S.C.R.A. 41st Divn.
            41.   R.O.R.A. 41st Divn.
            42.   41st D.A. Sigs. Officer.
       43 - 48.   War Diary and File.
```

SECRET

41st D.A. No. S.242.
Copy No. 45

1. Reference 41st D.A. Order No.21, para.4.

BOMBARDMENT.
B.C.D. and E. are shewn on attached map which gives times of lifts.
Forming-up line will be as close up to START LINE as Infantry can approach with safety.

SPECIAL TASK.
2. 187th Bde. R.F.A. do not take part in lifting bombardment but have a special task which is set out in para.6 below, with all details regarding ammunition and rates of fire.

AMMUNITION.
3. SMOKE will be used as follows:-
18-pdrs.
(a). 10% of rounds fired on START LINE.
(b). 1 round per battery per minute down roads.
Remainder H.E. and Shrapnel in equal proportions, shrapnel being fuzed to burst 50% on graze.

4.5" Hows.
3 rounds per gun per 4 minutes on river bed from V.9.b.8.0. to RUGGE from H minus 30 to H plus 30 (see para. 5 below).
Remainder H.E., 106 fuze if available.

RATES OF FIRE.
4. Rates of fire will be as follows:-
18-pdrs.
   11th Army Bde. R.F.A.
   H minus 10 to H plus 32   1½ rds. per gun per min. = 63
   H plus 32 to H plus 52   3   "   "   "   "   "   = 60
   H plus 52 to H plus 60   1   "   "   "   "   "   = 8

   119th Army Bde. R.F.A.
   H minus 10 to H   1½   "   "   "   "   "   = 15
   H to H plus 26   3   "   "   "   "   "   = 78
   H plus 26 to H plus 60   1   "   "   "   "   "   = 34

   190th Brigade R.F.A.
   H minus 10 to H.   1½   "   "   "   "   "   = 15
   H to H plus 26   1½   "   "   "   "   "   = 39
   H plus 26 to H plus 46   2   "   "   "   "   "   = 40
   H plus 46 to H plus 60   1   "   "   "   "   "   = 14

4.5" Hows. which assist the 18-pdr. barrage will fire a total of 80 rounds per How., rate of fire being varied according to the importance of the target engaged; those engaged in smoking river bed, 3 rounds per gun per 4 minutes.

4.5" HOWS.
5. D/11, D/119 and D/190 will each use one section to smoke river bed from V.9.b.8.0. to RUGGE from H minus 30 to H plus 30, in order to hide from opposite bank movements of infantry to forming up line and in initial stages of attack.
   D/190 will take from V.9.b.8.0. to V.4.a.7.0.
   D/11   "   "   " V.4.a.7.0. to P.34.d.8.9.
   D/119   "   "   " P.34.d.8.9. to RUGGE.
Remainder of hows. of these batteries will search down roads with 106 fuze 300 yards ahead of 18-pdrs., ceasing fire on reaching limits of barrage.

1.

DIVERSION. 6. 187th Bde. R.F.A. will be employed as follows:-

H minus 30 to H plus 30: 18-pdrs. will bombard (a). high ground in P.9.c.; (b). area P.15.c.2.3.; (c). BOSCH (P.21.d.).
 Rate of fire: 1½ rounds per gun per minute.
 Ammunition: 50% H.E., 50% Shrapnel.

4.5" Hows. will fire on P.9.c. and BOSCH (1 section on each).
Rate of fire 1 round per how. per minute.
 Ammunition : on P.9.c. 3 rounds Smoke, 1 round H.E.
  per How. per 4 minutes.
 on BOSCH All H.E.

HEAVY ARTILLERY. 7. Heavy Artillery will be employed as follows:-

H minus 30 to H. on AVELGHEM and MEERSCHSTRAAT with
 106 Fuze if available.

H to H plus 30 on bridges in vicinity of AVELGHEM
 and on cross roads P.28.c.9.7. and
 P.28.c.8.0.

AMENDMENTS. 8. Objective will be Villages of HUTTEGHEM, MEERSCH-STRAAT, AVELGHEM, KNOCK, and DRIESCH, and not as stated in para.1 of Order No.21.

122nd Infantry Brigade will carry out the attack and will not be used as stated in para. 3 of said Order.

Heavy Artillery tasks are as set out in para.7 hereof and not as set out in said Order.

ZERO HOUR. 9. H will be 14.00

SYNCHRONIZA- TION. 10. Watches will be synchronized by telephone from D.A.H.Q. at 9 and 11 a.m.

26-10-18.
Issued at 09.00

E.R.Roper.
Major,
Brigade Major,
41st Divisional Artillery.

To all recipients of 41st D.A. Order No.21.

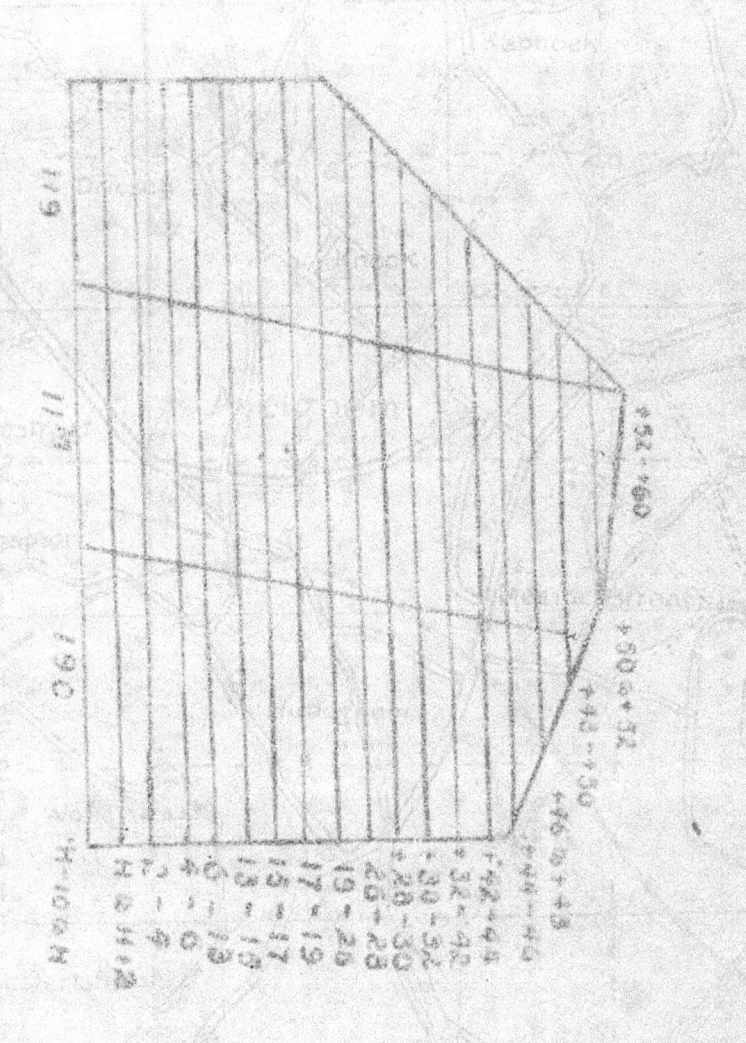

"A" Form.
MESSAGES AND SIGNALS.

Army Form C. 2121.
(In pads of 100.)

TO	TOWA
	LOBO
	41st Divn G (for information).

Sender's Number: S.421. Day of Month: 22. AAA

From 4.25 to 4.30 p.m. today points still offering resistance in Squares O.22.d, O.23.c & d., O.28.b., O.29., & O.30 will be bombarded by all guns of Divisional Artillery AAA Rate of fire 5 rounds per gun and 2 rounds per how. per minute AAA Bombardment of points N of E & W grid line between O.23 and O.29 will be carried out by LOBO after consultation with VUBU AAA Bombardment of points S of this grid line will be carried out by TOWA and JIGA after consultation with JUMU O.C. TOWA making necessary arrangements for division of area AAA Smoke to be used AAA TOWA to communicate these orders to JIGA forthwith AAA

From: POKU

WD

App I

S E C R E T   Copy No. 29

41st DIVISIONAL ARTILLERY ORDER No.22.

Reference Sheet 29 1/40,000.

ATTACK.	1.	The XIXth Corps, in conjunction with IInd Corps on the Left, will resume the attack in a North-Easterly direction on the 31st October.
ROLE OF 41st DIVL. ARTILLERY.	2.	41st Divisional Artillery will be employed under G.O.C.,R.A. XIX Corps, in the masking of high ground on Right Bank of the SCHELDT and in the neutralization of enemy batteries and Machine Guns on Right Bank of the SCHELDT during the attack.
FRONT LINE.	3.	Present front line of 35th Division is as follows:- Along Left Bank of River to P.35.a.1.9. - P.28.d.7.9. - P.22.d.9.2. - P.22.b.5.3. - P.16.d.1.2. - P.16.a.7.0.
OBJECTIVES.	4.	The attack will be delivered by 35th Division on two objectives with a pause between objectives. First Objective:- WAERMAERDE (Q.19.c.) - Chapel at P.12.d.5.0. Final objective:- KERKHOVE (Q.15.central) - HAELENDRIES (Q.9.a.).
FLANKS.		Flanks of advance will be approximately as follows:- Right Flank: P.35.b.6.7. - Q.19.c.8.2. - Q.15.central. Left Flank: P.16.central - P.12.d.7.1. - Q.9.a.0.5.
RATE OF ADVANCE.		The advance will be at the rate of 100 yards in 3 minutes with a pause of two hours on First Objective.
ARTILLERY TASKS.	5.	41st Divisional Artillery, consisting of 187th and 190th Brigades R.F.A. with 11th Army Brigade R.F.A., will be employed as follows:-
SMOKE SCREEN.		50% of 18-pdrs., with all 4.5" Howitzers in action, will put up a Smoke Screen along Left bank of river, screen being placed as near right flank of advance as possible with a view to masking high ground on opposite bank. Barrage maps shewing exact progress of advance will be distributed, if available later. Each Brigade will form a Smoke Screen over its own area as allotted below. Thus, if a North Easterly wind is blowing Brigade allotted C area will require to fire a certain proportion of its Smoke into B area (vide "Notes on the Use of Smoke" S.S.175, p.7.).
NEUTRALIZATION OF M.Gs.		Remainder of 18-pdrs. will search area between right flank of advance and Railway running from V.5.d. to Q.21.c. with H.E. and shrapnel, with the object of neutralizing Machine Guns and Guns, if any, within the area.

1.

P. T. O.

BRIGADE AREAS.	6.	Areas are allotted as follows:-

Area A: 190th Brigade R.F.A.: Q.19.c.8.3. - Q.14.d.2.0. - Q.21.c.4.1. - Q.26.c.1.5.

Area B: 187th Brigade R.F.A.: P.30.c.3.0. - Q.19.c.8.3. - Q.26.c.1.5. - P.36.d.5.6.

Area C: 11th Army Brigade R.F.A.: P.34.d.2.6. - P.30.c.3.0. - P.36.d.5.6. - V.5.d.6.3.

BATTERY POSITIONS. 7. 4.5" How. batteries will occupy positions with 4 Hows. per battery in action only; all of these being put into action tonight.
18-pdr. batteries will put half batteries in action tonight and the balance on night 30th/31st October.
Areas for battery positions have been allotted verbally

AMMUNITION. 8. The following ammunition will be used in the operation:-

4.5" Hows.: 1350 rounds B.S. per Battery.

18-pdrs.: 833 rounds A.S. per Battery.
1350 rounds A and AX per Battery.

18-pdr. batteries will dump full battery echelons at positions tonight.
4.5" How. batteries will dump whatever B.S. is available tonight.
Balance up to above amounts will be dumped tomorrow night under arrangements being made and notified by S.C.R.A.

RATES OF FIRE. 9. Smoke will be fired at an even rate throughout the operation.
A and AX will be fired at an average rate of 1½ rounds per gun per minute; details will be issued later.

ORDERS. 10. Brigades will not be affiliated to Infantry Brigades nor will they find Liaison Officers with them. All orders will be received from 41st D.A.H.Q., which will be established for the duration of the operation at 35th D.A.H.Q. (O.2.c.2.7.).

SIGNAL COMMUNICATIONS. 11. A forward Signal Exchange will be established in vicinity of O.18. and Brigade Headquarters connected with it. Exact location will be notified later.
Brigades will each send an orderly to be at 35th Div. Advanced Exchange (O.19.c.3.5.) at 10 a.m. tomorrow 30th October in order to guide cable-laying party to Brigade Headquarters selected for the operation.

O.Ps. 12. Brigades will establish O.Ps. from which progress of the advance and density of smoke screens can be watched.

F.O.Os. In addition each Brigade will send forward a F.O.O's party in order to locate hostile M.Gs. in bed or on right bank of river within or near its own area.
Situation reports will be sent back to D.A.H.Q. as often as possible.

DEFENCE OF THE LINE.

13. At conclusion of the operation 41st Division will take over from 35th Division present Corps Sector as far North as P.29. Artillery Brigades will then be withdrawn from positions occupied for this operation to positions more suitable for defence of the line.

14. A C K N O W L E D G E.

[signature]
Major,
Brigade Major,
41st Divisional Artillery.

29th October 1918.
Issued at:- 18.00.

```
Copy No. 1 -  5    187th Bde. R.F.A.
         6 - 10    190th   "    "
        11 - 15    11th Army Bde. R.F.A.
        16         41st Divn. G.
        17         41st Divn. Q.
        18         R.A. XIX Corps.
        19         H.A. XIX Corps.
        20         4th Bde. R.G.A.
        21         R.A. 35th Divn.
        22         41st D.A.C.
        23         41st D.T.M.O.
        24         D.A.P.M. 41st Divn.
        25         S.C.R.A. 41st Divn.
        26         R.O.R.A. 41st Divn.
        27         Sigs. Officer 41st D.A.
        28 - 32    War Diary & File.
```

SECRET   41st D.A. No. S.257.

  187th Bde. R.F.A.(5 cos) R.O.R.A. 41st Divn.
  190th " " " Sigs. Officer
  11th Army Bde. R.F.A. "
  R.A. XIXth Corps.
  R.A. 35th Division.
  41st Division G.
  S.C.R.A. 41st Divn.

  Reference 41st D.A. Order No.22, para. 9:-

RATES OF FIRE. 1. Rates of fire for 18-pdrs, will be as follows:-

 <u>Guns firing Shrapnel and H.E.</u>

  <u>Area A. 190th Brigade R.F.A.</u>

Z to plus 50	1 rounds per gun per minute	50
plus 50 to plus 64	1½ " " " " "	21
plus 64 to plus 82	2 " " " " "	36
plus 82 to plus 207	1½ " " " " "	187
plus 207 to plus 243	2 " " " " "	72
plus 243 to plus 273	1 " " " " "	30
		396

  <u>Area B: 187th Brigade R.F.A.</u>

  Z to plus 20 2 rounds per gun per minute 40
  plus 20 to plus 70 2½ " " " " " 125
      (Average rate; each battery
      will fire 3 rounds p.g.p.m.
      for 10 minutes after creep-
      ing barrage has reached its
      sector).
  plus 70 to plus 82 2 rounds per gun per minute. 24
  plus 82 to plus 207 1 " " " " " 125
  plus 207 to plus 273 1½ " " " " " 99
          413

  <u>Area C: 11th Army Bde. R.F.A.</u>

  Z to plus 10 3 rounds per gun per minute. 30
  plus 10 to plus 42 2 " " " " " 64
  plus 42 to plus 82 1½ " " " " " 60
  plus 82 to plus 207 1 " " " " " 125
  plus 207 to plus 273 1½ " " " " " 99
          378

  <u>Guns firing Smoke</u>: 1 round per gun per minute from Z
      to Z plus 278 throughout.
    4.5" Hows. will fire at such a rate
    that the whole of the Smoke available
    is spread evenly over the period Z to
    Z plus 278.

DEFENCE OF THE LINE. 2. On conclusion of the operation batteries of 187th Brigade R.F.A. will withdraw to approximate area O.30. central - P.19.central, and will cover Divisional Front from AUTRYVE (excl.) to AVELGHEM (Excl.)

11th Army Brigade R.F.A. will remain in present area and will cover Divisional front from AVELGHEM (incl). to RUGGE (incl).

190th Brigade R.F.A. will remain in present area as a silent Brigade prepared to cover front from RUGGE (excl eastwards in case 41st Division is ordered to take over this portion of the line.

ZERO HOUR. 3. Zero hour will be 05.25 on the 31st instant.

TARGETS. 4. Attention is directed to list of hostile M.Gs. sent to Brigades under wire from these Headquarters No. R.O.10 of to-day's date; also to Intelligence Map No.109 being issued tonight to Brigades.

Fire will be kept as close to the Western branches of the SCHELDT as is consistent with the safety of the right of the attacking troops.

Para.6 of 41st D.A. Order No.22 will be amended as follows:-

Area C: For P.34.d.2.6. read V.4.a.8.6.

BOUNDARIES. 5. The boundary between XIX and II Corps is now as follows:-
Q.3.d.0.0. - Q.8.central - Q.7.d.5.6.
- P.12.d.0.0.- P.11.c.0.0. - P.16.a.4.0.
- P.15.d.7.7.- thence as before.

SYNCHRONIZATION. 6. Watches will be synchronized by telephone at 23.00 30th instant, and 03.00 31st instant.

7. A C K N O W L E D G E.

30th October 1918.
Issued at:- 19.00

Major,
Brigade Major,
41st Divisional Artillery.

App J.

SECRET.   41st D.A. No. S.266.

187th Bde. R.F.A. (5 cos).	123rd Infy. Bde.
190th " " "	124th " "
11th Army Bde. R.F.A."	4th Bde. R.G.A.
R.A. XIXth Corps.	41st D.A.C.
H.A. XIXth Corps.	41st D.T.M.O.
R.A. 35th Divn.	41st Bn. M.G. Corps.
R.A. 30th "	S.C.R.A. 41st Divn.
41st Divn. G.	R.O.R.A.
41st Divn. Q.	41st D.A. Sigs. Officer.
122nd Infy. Bde.	War Diary and File (5 cos).

Reference 41st D.A. Order No.22, para.13:

RELIEF. 1. On night 31st Oct./1st Nov. 122 Infantry Brigade will relieve 106th Infantry Bde., 35th Division, in the line, taking over XIX Corps front from V.9.a.0.0. to P.30.central.

BOUNDARIES. 2. Divisional boundaries in forward area will be as follows:-
Right Boundary: N.29.central - O.28.central - V.9.a.0.0.
Left Boundary: O.2.b.95.50. - O.9.d.7.0. - O.10.d.35.00.-
                - O.24.b.3.4. - P.26.central - P.30.central.

ARTILLERY DISPOSITIONS. 3. From time of occupation by 187th Brigade R.F.A. of positions in approximate area P.19. the Divisional front will be covered by two Field Artillery Brigades as follows:-
187th Bde. R.F.A.: From V.9.a.0.0. - AVELGHEM CHURCH (P.34.a.7.0.) excl.
11th Army Bde. RFA: From AVELGHEM CHURCH incl. to P.30.cen

S.O.S. LINES. 4. Os.C. 11th Army Bde. and 187th Brigade will arrange their S.O.S. Lines in consultation with G.O.C. 122nd Infantry Brigade.

LIAISON. 5. A Liaison Officer will be found by each Brigade in turn; tour of duty three days, commencing 10 a.m. 31st October. 11th Army Bde. R.F.A. will provide the Officer for first tour of duty. Headquarters of 122nd Infantry Bde. will be at O.36.a.3.4.

190th BDE. R.F.A. 6. 190th Brigade R.F.A. will remain in present positions for time being. Orders as to movements will be issued later.

7. F.A. Brigades A C K N O W L E D G E.

31st October 1918
Issued at:-18.00.

Major,
Brigade Major,
41st Divisional Artillery.

WAR DIARY
INTELLIGENCE-SUMMARY

(Erase heading not required.)

Army Form C. 2118.

Headquarters, 41st. Divisional Artillery.

Place	Date	Hour	Summary of Events and Information	Remarks and references to Appendices
BELGIUM				
T'HOOGE – COURTRAI.	1st. Novr. 1918.		Orders issued for adjustment of artillery to conform with infantry reliefs (App."A") 187th.Brigade,R.F.A., relieved 159th.Brigade,R.F.A., (30th.Divisional Artillery) during night 1/2nd.November. Lieut. H.B.McKIE, M.C.,R.A., Reconnaissance Officer, 41st.D.A., returned from 14 days leave of absence in England.	App:A
ST.LOUIS.	2nd. Novr.		Headquarters, 41st.D.A., moved from T'HOOGE (near COURTRAI) to ST.LOUIS, I.34.d.80.20., where they were established at 14.30 hrs. (Sheet 29 1/40,000)	
"	3rd. Novr.		Conference of C.R.A., and Brigade Commanders held at 187th.Brigade, R.F.A., Headquarters, at 10.00 hours, with reference to operations to be carried out shortly by 41st.Division (App:"B")	App:B
"	4th. Novr.		190th.Brigade, R.F.A., relieved by 157th.Brigade, R.F.A., (30th.Divisional Artillery) during night 4th/5th. On completion of relief 190th.Brigade, R.F.A., withdrew to Wagon Lines.	
"	5th. Novr.		190th.Brigade, R.F.A., moved to DEERLYCK Area. Capt. W.A.Mackenzie, M.C., R.F.A., acting Staff Captain, 41st.D.A., returned to duties of Adjutant, 190th.Brigade, R.F.A., Lieut.H.E.McKIE,M.C., R.A., Reconnaissance Officer, acting as Staff Captain in his place, pending the arrival of Captain T.H.BISCHOFF, M.C., R.A., from Leave.	
"	6th. Novr.		C.R.A., with Captain E.G.R.WADDOW, M.C., R.F.A., Div'l Trench Mortar Officer, 41st.Division, carried out a Reconnaissance of hostile wire in front of BERCHEM and MEERSCHE, this hostile artillery and machine-gun fire, with a view to having this wire cut by 6"Newton T.Ms and 18pdrs R.G.	
VICHTE.	7th. Novr.	18p.m.	41st.D.A., Headquarters, moved to VICHTE. R.G.	
"	8th. Novr.		During the early part of the night patrols of 123rd.Infantry Brigade succeeded in crossing L'ESCAUT without opposition and pushed on. Orders were received by the 11th.(Army) Brigade R.F.A., attached 41st.D.A., during the night to support the advance of the 123rd.Infantry Brigade. Batteries occupied Battle positions until a pontoon had been thrown across the L'ESCAUT.	
"	9th. Novr.		11th.(Army) Brigade, R.F.A., crossed the river during the morning and pushed on to the area of P.22.d. No opposition was met by the Infantry. The enemy had blown up several cross roads and bridges; some difficulty was experienced in advancing. 187th.Brigade,R.F.A.,moved across the river during the day, and pushed on to the NUKERKE Area, where they remained in support of 124th.Infantry Brigade.	
CASTER.	10th. Novr.		41st.D.A., H.Q., moved to CASTER. 41st.D.A.G. moved to the area of TIEGHEM (P.6.d.80.90) (App:"C"). 190th.Brigade,R.F.A., crossed the river in the morning of the 10th. with 122nd. Infantry Brigade, and marched to the SULSIQUE area. *Capt.T.H.Bischoff, M.C., Staff Capt. 41st DA: returned from Leave on 6th Novr.*	App:C

-1-

Army Form C. 2118.

WAR DIARY
or
INTELLIGENCE–SUMMARY.
(Erase heading not required.)

Headquarters, 41st. Divisional Artillery.

Instructions regarding War Diaries and Intelligence Summaries are contained in F. S. Regs. Part II. and the Staff Manual respectively. Title pages will be prepared in manuscript.

Place	Date	Hour	Summary of Events and Information	Remarks and references to Appendices
BELGIUM SCHOORISSE	11th.Novr.		Headquarters, 41st.D.A., moved to area of SCHOORISSE. 187th.Brigade,R.F.A., from NUKERKE Area in 124th.Infantry Brigade Group, to NEDERBRAKEL. 11th.(Army) Brigade,R.F.A., remained with 123rd.Infantry Brigade, in the area of R.22.d. 190th.Brigade,R.F.A., remained with 122nd. Infantry Brigade in the SUISNEUR area. Hostilities ceased at 11.00 hours. 41st.D.A.C. moved to GRISKOORT - BRUGGE Area. (App:"D")	App: D.
NEDERBRAKEL	12th.Novr.		41st.D.A., Headquarters, moved to NEDERBRAKEL to billets vacated by 187th.Brigade, R.F.A., who moved with 124th.Infantry Brigade to GRAMMONT Area. 41st.Division came under IInd.Corps.	
"	13th.Novr.		190th.Brigade, R.F.A., moved with 122nd.Infantry Brigade Group to DEFTINGE.	
"	13th.Novr.		11th.(Army) Brigade, R.F.A., moved to SCHOORISSE Area.	
"	14th.Novr.		11th.(Army) Brigade, R.F.A., moved to NUKERKE.	
"	15th.Novr.		11th.(Army) Brigade, R.F.A., moved to STEENBERG Area. It was decided that 11th.(Army) Brigade R.F.A., should form the artillery of the third Infantry Brigade group (122nd.Infantry Brigade) 190th.Brigade,R.F.A., were now grouped with 123rd.Infantry Brigade. (App:"E" para.2)	App: E
"	16th.Novr.		Conference of Brigade Commanders with C.R.A., with reference to march to the GERMAN Frontier.	
"	17th.Novr.		Thanksgiving Service held in Church of NEDERBRAKEL. Headquarters group, including parties from 41st.D.A.C. and 41st.D.A.,H.Q., inspected by G.O.C., 41st.Division., prior to the Service. The Service was also attended by the Burgomaster and leading townsmen of NEDERBRAKEL.	
SANT BERGEN	18th.Novr.		Headquarters group (41st.Division) marched to SANT BERGEN area. (App:"F")	App: F.
"	19th.Novr.		41st.Division relieved in the out-post line by 9th.Division.	
GRAMMONT	21st.Novr.		41st.D.H.Q., Group marched to GRAMMONT.	
"	24th.Novr.		41st.Division came under Xth.Corps.	
"	26th.Novr.		41st.Division, part of the Xth.Corps, came under the FOURTH Army. G.O.C., 41st.Division presented Medal Ribbons to recipients of decorations in the D.H.Q. Group during the months of October & November 1918. (App:"G")	App: G.
"	30th.Novr.		G.O.C., 41st.Division, inspected Batteries of 187th.Brigade, R.F.A., in their gun parks.	

2nd.Decr.1918.

[signature]
Brigadier-General,
Commanding 41st. Divisional Artillery.

RAXX   Appendix "A"

SECRET.   Copy No. 31

41st DIVISIONAL ARTILLERY ORDER No.23.

Reference Sheet 29   1/40,000.

1. The following reliefs will take place tonight:-
   (a). An Infantry Brigade of 30th Division will relieve 122nd Infantry Brigade on sector now being held by the latter.

   (b). 124th Infantry Brigade will relieve 104th Infantry Brigade (35th Division) in sector now being held by the latter.

2. The new front of 124th Infantry Brigade, which will be the Division front, will be from P.30.d.0.0. to Q.10.central to Q.3.c.0.0. (all approximate).

3. Both present front of 122nd Infantry Brigade and new front of 124th Infantry Brigade will be covered tonight by 41st Divisional Artillery reinforced by 119th Army Brigade R.F.A.
   Sectors are allotted as follows:-

   187th Brigade R.F.A.   V.9.a.0.0. - P.35.b.5.8.

   190th Brigade R.F.A.   P.35.b.5.8. - Q.20.b.2.9.

   119th Army Bde. R.F.A. Q.20.b.2.9. - Q.10.central - Q.3.c.0.0.

4. From 20.00 on 2nd November present front of 122nd Infantry Brigade will be covered by 30th Divisional Artillery and new front of 124th Infantry Brigade will be covered by 41st Divisional Artillery, as follows:-

   190th Brigade R.F.A.   P.30.d.0.0. - Q.19.d.5.8.

   187th Brigade R.F.A.   Q.19.d.5.8. - Q.15.central.

   119th Army Bde.R.F.A.   Q.15.central. - Q.10.central. - Q.3.c.0.0.

5. 30th Divisional Artillery will probably not take over present Headquarters or battery positions of 187th Brigade R.F.A.
   187th Brigade R.F.A. will move to positions at present occupied by 159th Brigade R.F.A. as follows:-
   One section per battery to leave present positions at dusk; one section per battery to leave present positions at 20.00; remainder at one hour after dusk.
   Occupation of new positions will be reported by wire to these Headquarters.

   Wagon Lines of 159th Brigade R.F.A. will be vacated by that Brigade not later than 11.00 on 2nd November, after which hour they are available for occupation by 187th Brigade R.F.A. Advance parties should be sent to take over accommodation.

                    1.   P. T. O.

Locations of 159th Brigade R.F.A. are as follows:-

	Position in action.	Wagon Lines.
Headquarters.	O.12.central.	O.4.c.3.3.
A/159.	P.4.c.5.5.	O.2.b.8.3.
B/159.	P.10.a.70.95.	I.33.d.1.1.
C/159.	P.10.b.2.7.	O.3.d.1.3.
D/159.	P.10.b.6.6.	O.4.c.9.1.

6.   Liaison Officer of 190th Brigade R.F.A. at present with 122nd Infantry Brigade will remain with incoming Infantry Brigade of 30th Division till 11.00 on 2nd November when he will be relieved by an officer of 30th Divisional Artillery.

    119th Army Brigade R.F.A. will find a Liaison Officer with 104th Infantry Brigade (being relieved by 124th Infantry Brigade) until 18.00 2nd November, when he will be relieved by an Officer of 187th Brigade R.F.A. Thereafter 187th and 190th Brigades R.F.A. will find the Liaison Officer in turn; tour of duty three days; next relief to be at 10.00 on 5th November.(Headquarters of 124th Infantry Brigade P.13.c.4.8.).

7.   119th Army Brigade R.F.A. will be withdrawn from action into Corps Reserve at 05.30 on 3rd November. Details will be notified later.

    On withdrawal of 119th Army Brigade R.F.A. Divisional front will be covered by 190th Brigade R.F.A. on Right and 187th Brigade R.F.A. on Left, dividing point between Brigades being Windmill at Q.14.d.8.6.

8.   41st Divisional Artillery Headquarters will remain for the present at N.3.c.1.1. but are probably moving later to ST.LOUIS area.

9.   Brigades R.F.A. to A C K N O W L E D G E.

E.R.Roper.
Major,
Brigade Major,
41st Divisional Artillery.

1st November 1918.
Issued at:- 17.00.

```
Copy No. 1 - 5   187th Bde. R.F.A.
         6 -10   190th   "     "
        11 -15   119th Army Bde.R.F.A.
           16    41st D.A.C.
           17    41st D.T.M.O.
           18    41st D.A.Gas Officer.
           19    XIX Corps R.A.
           20    XIX Corps H.A.
           21    R.A. 35th Divn.
           22    R.A. 30th   "
           23    41st Divn. G.
           24    41st Divn. Q.
           25    122nd Infy. Bde.
           26    123rd   "    "
           27    124th   "    "
           28    41st Bn. M.G.Corps.
           29    D.A.P.M. 41st Divn.
           30    S.C.R.A. 41st Divn.
           31    R.O.R.A. 41st Divn.
           32    41st D.A.Sigs. Officer.
        33 -37   War Diary & File.
```

Q.O.R.a/ Appendix B

For personal information of recipients only.

S E C R E T.   Copy No. 17

41st DIVISIONAL ARTILLERY INSTRUCTIONS No. 37.

Reference Sheet 29 1/40,000.

PASSAGE OF THE SCHELDT.	1.	The XIXth Corps will force the passage of the SCHELDT on a date and at a time to be notified later. Corps front will be from P.30.d.0.0. to Q.10.central. The 35th Division will cross on the Right, from P.30.d.0.0. to Q.20.a.8.8.; the 41st Division on the Left from Q.20.a.8.8. to Q.10.central.
INFANTRY DISPOSITIONS.	2.	41st Division will carry out the operation on a two Brigade Front, with 124th Infantry Brigade on Right and 122nd Infantry Brigade on Left. Each Infantry Brigade will have two Battalions in front line and each Battalion will have two companies in the front line. Infantry Brigade Boundary will be as follows:- J.28.c.0.0. - J.36.a.0.0. - Q.1.central.- Q.15.b.2.3.
SUPPORTING ARTILLERY.	3.	The Infantry of 41st Division will be supported by 41st Divisional Artillery and the 11th Army Brigade R.F.A. Amount of Heavy Artillery available has not yet been notified.
METHOD OF EFFECTING PASSAGE.	4.	The method of effecting the passage will probably be as follows:- Coverin parties of Infantry will cross the River in boats. When covering posts have been established foot bridges for Infantry and pontoon bridges for Field Artillery and horse transport will be thrown across. Infantry will then cross in force and deploy along railway on South eastern bank. When deployment is complete Infantry will advance under a barrage put up by Artillery on N.W. bank to approximate Final Objective W.5.a.0.0. - Q.36.central. - Q.25.d.0.0. The barrage will probably move at the rate of 100 yards in 3 minutes, with halts of varying duration after each 500 yards. For the first 1000 yards of the barrage forward Brigades will fire only H.E. delay action and no shrapnel. The advance to railway and deployment on that line will be known as the First Bound; subsequent advance to Final Objective will be known as Second Bound.
SUPPORTING FIRE.	5.	The passage will be effected under cover of :- (a). The utmost possible Artillery support, including the use of Smoke shell. (b). The concentrated fire of Medium T.Ms., Stokes T.Ms and Machine Guns. (c). Smoke Screens put up by captured German Smoke Generators provided the wind is favourable and by our own Field Artillery.

1.

ARTILLERY ARRANGEMENTS.	6.	All Artillery arrangements for the passage will be co-ordinated by G.O.C.,R.A. XIXth Corps.

Tasks of Artillery supporting 41st Division will be as follows:-

187th and 190th Brigades R.F.A. will occupy positions along road running through Q.19. and Q.14. in order to put up creeping barrage up to attainment of Final Objective.

11th Army Brigade R.F.A. will occupy positions approximately in Q.7. and Q.8. in order to cover Infantry up to conclusion of First Bound and possibly for portion of Second Bound. In addition, this Brigade will have detached sections to enfilade River in Q.15. and Q.21. and will detach four forward guns to push across River at earliest possible moment for close support of battalions.

Remainder of Brigade will follow across River when possible for support of Infantry in final stages of the operation.

Six Medium Trench Mortars will be in action in positions suitable for bombardment of BERCHEM and MEERSCHE.

Four Mobile M.T.Ms will cross in boats at earliest possible moment after covering party has crossed and will support covering posts when established.

BATTLE POSITIONS.	7.	Reconnaissance of battle positions is being carried out under verbal instructions. The following areas have been allotted:-

<u>187th Brigade R.F.A.</u>: Q.14.c.4.2. to Q.15.a.6.8.

<u>190th Brigade R.F.A.</u>: Q.15.a.6.8. to Q.10.a.6.6.

<u>11th Army Bde.R.F.A.</u>: Area S. of road through P.7.a.& b. and P.8.a. and N. of line Q.13.b. 4.0. - Q.3.d.5.1.
Enfilade sections in approximate areas P.16.central and K.34.b. or K.28.d.

T.M. positions will be reconnoitred as close up as possible for bombardment of BERCHEM, GRIJKOORT and MEERSCHE.

Positions selected will be reported as early as possible to D.A.H.Q. in order that necessary arrangements may be made for resection, insertion of bearing posts, etc.

Battle positions will not be occupied until a date to be notified later. In the meantime, work will proceed on gun platforms and slit trenches.

Arrangements for dumping ammunition will be notified by S.C.R.A.

Concealment of work is all-important and the most careful camouflage should be undertaken in advance.

INTERIM POLICY. HARASSING FIRE.	8.	Pending occupation of battle positions systematic harassing fire will be carried out on observed targets opposite the whole of the front now held by this Division. Dividing point between 187th and 190th Brigades R.F.A. for this purpose as well as for purposes of defence of the line will be Q.20.a.8.8. The principal object of this harassing fire will be the destruction of hostile Machine Guns in houses and along Railway Line on the South Eastern bank of the River. In addition the enemy's <u>moral</u> will as far as possible be destroyed by infliction of casualties and suppression of movement. O.Ps. will

/be

be established as far forward as possible with a view to close observation of fire effect and of movement. Artillery Officers will keep the closest possible touch with Infantry in the Line and will take every opportunity of locating M.Gs., T.Ms, and posts with their assistance.

The Harassing Fire will be carried out by forward sections. Main battery positions will remain silent except in case of S.O.S. or of Counter Preparation ordered by C.R.A.

REHEARSALS. There will probably be rehearsals of the Artillery programme for three or four nights before the day of passage. These will be carried out from present positions and not from Battle positions.

SECRECY. 9. Preparations for the operation will not be discussed by telephone.

10. A C K N O W L E D G E.

E.R.Roper
Major,
Brigade Major,
41st Divisional Artillery.

4th November 1918
Issued at:-23.30.

Copy No.	
1	187th Bde. R.F.A.
2	190th " "
3	11th Army Bde. R.F.A.
4	41st D.A.C.
5	41st D.T.M.O.
6	XIXth Corps R.A.
7	XIXth Corps H.A.
8	R.A. 35th Divn.
9	41st Divn. G.
10	41st Divn. Q.
11	122nd Infy. Bde.
12	123rd " "
13	124th " "
14	41st Bn. M.G.Corps.
15	O.C. A.C.D.41 (Francais).
16	S.C.R.A. 41st Divn.
17	R.O.R.A. 41st Divn.
18	41st D.A.Sigs. Officer.
19-23	War Diary & File.

SECRET   Appendix C9

61st DIVISIONAL ARTILLERY ORDER No.55.

Reference Sheet 29 1/40,000.

1. Headquarters and Nos. 1 and 2 Sections 61st D.A.C. will march tomorrow the 10th November to Headquarters and Wagon Lines being vacated by 107th Brigade R.F.A., as follows:-

Headquarters	F.6.c.8.9.
A/107 Wagon Line.	F.4.c.6.4.
B/107 " "	F.4.c.8.0.
C/107 " "	F.6.b.4.0.
D/107 " "	F.11.b.9.8.

   Route DESSLIN - VICHTE - INGOYGHEM; Head of column to pass DESSLIN at 8 a.m.

2. Advance party will be sent to take over Billets and Lines, to reach 107th Brigade Headquarters not later than 7 a.m.

3. D.A.C. will take over all ammunition left behind at above positions; particulars will be given by 107th Brigade to Advance party at 7 a.m.

4. A.R.P. will be moved to WAEREGHEM area; exact spot to be reconnoitred by Officer i/c A.R.P. early on 10th instant.

5. Officer i/c A.R.P. will collect dumps left at vacated battle positions in WAEREGHEM - SEMHOVE area before issuing from A.R.P.

6. Surplus T.M. and F.H. ammunition now lying in SEMHOVE area will be dumped by 61st D.T.M.O. beside road at G.15.a.4.4. and G.15.a.b.8. where they will be picked up subsequently by Officer i/c A.R.P., T.M. being returned to D.A.D.O.S. and ammunition being taken on charge of A.R.P.

7. Mobile T.M.Sections will march with 107th Brigade R.F.A. tomorrow 10th instant; to report at 107th Brigade Headquarters at 7 a.m.

8. D.A.C. and D.T.M.O. ACKNOWLEDGE.

                                        Major,
9th November 1918   Brigade Major,
Issued at 23.30.   61st Divisional Artillery

Copy No. 1 61st D.A.C.
        2 61st D.T.M.O.
        3 107th Bde. R.F.A.
        4 108th
        5 11th Army Bde. R.F.A.
        6 61st Divn. G.
        7 61st D.A.D.O.S.
        8 61st D.A.Signal Officer.
        9-10 File, & War Diary.

SECRET

Appendix "S"

Copy No. 7

41st DIVISIONAL ARTILLERY ORDER No. 25.

Reference Sheets 29 and 30   1/40,000.

1. Headquarters and Nos. 1 and 2 Sections 41st D.A.C. will march on the 11th instant to area GRIJKOORT - REUNEN at hour to be determined by O.C. D.A.C. and communicated by him to D.A.F.M. 41st Division. Locations will be reported to D.A.H.Q. as early as possible after move.

2. Before completing this move D.A.C. will transfer to A.R.P. at G.15.a.6.9. the ammunition handed over this morning by 187th Brigade R.F.A. in accordance with 41st D.A. Order No. 25.

3. All Boxed ammunition will be dumped at A.R.P. and G.B. Wagons in which it has been carried will be at disposal of O.C. Divisional Train for purpose of carrying rations from Lorry Head (RENAIX) across SCHELDT to Supply Refilling Point at KRUISSTRAAT (N.22.b.).

4. G.B. Wagons referred to will report at Lorry Head at 3 p.m. on 11th. Attention of O.C., D.A.C. is directed to 41st Divn. No. G.15/99 of to-day's date.

5. Orders verbally issued to D.A.C. for transfer of ammunition from A.R.P. at I.31.c.1.1. to A.R.P. at G.15.a.6.9. are cancelled.

6. 41st D.A.H.Q. will close at CASTER at 09.00 11th instant and re-open at same hour at SCHOORISSE (N.11.c.).

7. D.A.C. A C K N O W L E D G E.

[signature]

Major,
Brigade Major,
41st Divisional Artillery.

10-11-18.
Issued at :- 21.50.

Copy No. 1 41st D.A.C.
       2   107th Bde. R.F.A.
       3   190th   "   "
       4   11th Army Bde. R.F.A.
       5   41st Divn. Q.
       6   41st Divisional Train.
       7   41st D.A. Signal Officer.
       8   D.A.F.M. 41st Division.
       9)
      10)   War Diary & File.

SECRET

Appendix "E"

SECRET   Copy No. 9

41st DIVISIONAL ARTILLERY ORDER No. 127.

Reference Sheet 29 & 36 1/40,000.

1. On 13th November 41st Division will take over outpost line on whole XIX Corps Front. Northern boundary will be as at present. Southern boundary - Diagonal line from 30/T.7.c.5.0. to 29/X.25.d.0.7. 123rd Infantry Brigade will be on right, 124th Infantry Brigade on left, 122nd Infantry Brigade in Divisional Reserve.
   Inter Brigade boundary. N and S grid line between 30/R.26.d.5.5. and 30/R.26.c.0.0.

2. 10th Brigade R.F.A. will cover right Brigade and be grouped in 123rd Infantry Brigade Group, moving on 13th November to destination shown on March Table annexed and thence to positions from whence the outpost line on right Brigade front can be covered.

3. 11th Army Brigade R.F.A. will move ~~to~~ on 13th inst. again times and billets vacated by 190th Brigade R.F.A., and will probably be withdrawn into Corps Reserve. Orders on ~~this~~ latter point will be issued later.

4. 123rd Infantry Brigade Headquarters will be located in MARIEMBOURG Area (30/L.10.a.o b.), where O.C. 190th Brigade R.F.A. will get into touch with G.O.C. Brigade.

5. 41st D.A.H.Q. moved on 12th instant to 30/L.10.a.0.5.

6. ACKNOWLEDGE.

                                              [signature]
                                              Major,
12th November 1918   Brigade Major,
Issued at:- 18.15.   41st Divisional Artillery.

Copy No. 1   187th Bde. R.F.A.
     "   2   190th   "
     "   3   11th Army Bde. R.F.A.
     "   4   41st D.A.C.
     "   5   41st Divn. G.
     "   6   41st Divn. Q.
     "   7   41st D.A. Sigs. Officer.
     "   8   D.D.M.S. 41st Divn.
     9-10   War Diary & File.

R A N G E   T A B L E.

UNIT.	FROM	TO	REMARKS.
A.etc. & Batteries 105th Inf. Bde. R.F.A.	EUSTON 6rm.	30/O.2b, 2b; 34, 35;	No restrictions as to rate. Load R.32a.d. - h.69.b. - FTE.Guns - Batton - HONORSTOWN - G.34.d. - SUTTEES - NORMANHALL is known to be good.
R.etc. & Batteries 115th Army Bde. R.F.A.	SUTTEES area.	SUTTEES area.	As above. Location of 115th Brigade are approximately as follows:- R.etc. R.23.a.7.6. A/115. R.21.c.4.0. B/115. R.22.d.4.3. C/115. R.28.c.6.10. D/115. R.29.b.6.0.

Usual distances and halts will be observed.

Appendix "F"

Copy No. 24

41st DIVISIONAL ARTILLERY ORDER No.28.

17th November 1918.

Reference Map:- TOURNAI. 1/100,000.

MARCH.	1.	In accordance with 41st Division Order No.284 dated 16th instant. Headquarters Group will march to the SANTBERGEN - GRAMMONT area on 18th instant in accordance with March table attached.
D.H.Q. UNITS.	2. (i).	Divisional Headquarters personnel will march in the following order:- (a). Div. H.Q. (b). Divl. Arty. H.Q. (c). Hd.Qrs. R.E. (d). No.1 Sect. Divl. Sig. Coy.
	(ii).	First line transport of above will march in rear of personnel in same order.
DISTANCES.	3.	Distances will be as laid down in Field Service Regulations, Part I; Halts as in 41st Div. Administrative Instructions No.1.
SYNCHRONIZ-ATION.	4.	Watches will be synchronized by D.R. during afternoon of 17th instant.
BILLETS.	5. (a).	Billeting parties composed as laid down in Appendix 'A' of 41st Division Administrative Instructions No.1 will meet the Staff Captain R.A. at GRAMMONT Railway Station at 08.00.
	(b).	Supply Rendezvous on Novr. 18th will be GRAMMONT Railway Station at 12.00.
11th A.F.A. B.A.C.	6.	The 11th Army Brigade A.C. will move under orders of O.C. 41st D.A.C.
D.A.H.Q.	7.	41st Divisional Artillery Headquarters will close at NEDERBRAKEL at 11.00 on November 18th and open at SANTBERGEN at same hour. Completion of move and locations of Headquarters will be notified to Divisional Artillery Headquarters on arrival in new area.

Major,
Brigade Major,
41st Divisional Artillery.

Issued at 14.30.

Copy No.1	41st Divn. G.
2	41st Divn. Q.
3	Camp Commandant.
4	C.R.E. 41 Divn.
5	41st Div. Sig. Officer.
6-10	19th Middlesex Regt.(P).
11-13	41st Bn. M.G.Corps.
14-17	41st D.A.C.
18	11th A.F.A.B.A.C.
19-20	H.Q.41 Divl. Train.
21	52 Mobile Vety. Sect.
22	D.A.P.M. 41st Divn.
23	S.C.R.A. 41st Divn.
24	R.O.R.A. 41st Divn.
25	41st D.A. Sigs. Officer.

P.T.O.

MARCH TABLE.

Unit.	From.	To.	Starting Point.	Time.	Route	Remarks.
1. H.Qrs.& No.1 Coy.Divl.Train.	NEDERBRAKEL.	SANTBERGEN -GRAMMONT area.	Cross Roads 450ˣ E of L in NEDERBRAKEL	08.30	Main Rd.NEDERBRAKEL -X Roads ½ mile W. of OPHASSELT - X Roads 1000ˣ S of TRIPPEN -IDEGEM.	
2. Div.H.Q.& First Line Transport.	do.	do.	Road Junction at K of NEDERBRAKEL head of column in rear of No.1 Coy. Divl. Train.	08.30	do.	
3. 52nd Mobile Vet. Section.	do.	do.	NEDERBRAKEL Church; column formed up on road running N.W. from church.	08.30.	do.	
4. 41st I.A.C.& 11th F.A.B.A.C.	ROOVORST area.	do.	Cross Roads 150ˣ S.W. of NEDERBRAKEL Church.	08.30.	do.	Approach to starting point to be so timed that there in no halt in the Village.
5. 19th Middlesex Regt. (Pioneers) with First Line Transport.	OPBRAKEL.	do.	Road Junction 100ˣ S.E. of L in OPBRAKEL.	08.50.	do.	To follow 41st D.A.C. and 11th A.F.A. B.A.C.
6. 41st Bn. M.G.C. less 3 Companies.	PARICKE area.	do.	X Roads 400ˣ W. of NEDERBRAKEL Station.	09.00	do.	To follow 19th Middlesex Regt. One Company to march independently from SARIAR- DINGE to destination.

Units will proceed to billeting areas independently after reaching Cross Roads 700ˣ N.W. of IDEGEM Railway Station.

Appendix G

41st.D.A. No.H/1/55/3.

PRESENTATION OF MEDAL RIBBONS.

1. The G.O.C., 41st. Division will present Medal Ribbons in the Courtyard, SANTBERGEN Chateau, at 11.30.a.m. on Tuesday, 26th. November 1918.

2. The following will parade in addition to Officers and men to be decorated:-

   Not less than 30 men per Section 41st. D. A. C. and per 11th. B. A. C.
   Detachment of 200 men of 19th.Battn. MIDDLESEX Regt.(With Band)
   Detachment of 100 men 41st. Bn. M.G.C.

   Lieut:Col: A. W. TATE, 41st.Bn.M.G.C. will command the parade.

3. The programme will be as follows:-

   11.10.a.m. – Officers and men to be decorated report to Staff Captain R.A.41st.Divn. at SANTBERGEN Chateau.

   11.15 " – Markers.

   11.20 " – Troops march on to their markers.

   11.30. " – G.O.C. arrives on parade and is received with the General Salute.
   Presentation of Medal Ribbons.
   March Past.

4. All Officers and men to be decorated will prior to the parade, remove the ribbons with which they are subsequently to be presented In the case of recipients of the M.M., new Medal Ribbon will be provided.
   In the case of all other decorations, recipients will arrange to have their own ribbons mounted on a stiff card, with a pin at right angles (see illustration). These will be handed to the Staff Capt.R.A. before the

DRESS.   Drill Order.   Box Respirators will be carried.   of the G.R.A. on the is unit

services in respect of which ... have earned their awards.

5. On the conclusion of the presentation of Medal Ribbons, the Officers and men who have been decorated will fall in in rear of the G. O. C. at the saluting point. The troops will then march past. After passing the saluting point, units will return to their billets independently.

6. A C K N O W L E D G E.

                                        Captain,
25th.Novr.1918.   Staff Captain,41st. Divisional Artillery.

Distribution:-   41st. D. A. C.   (4)   No.1 Coy.41st.Div.Train(1
                 11th. B. A. C.   (1)   Camp Comdt.41 Div. (1)
                 41st.Div:Sig:Coy.R.E.(2)   41st.Divn. 'G' (For inform
                 19th.Bn.Middlesex Regt.(4) 52 M. V. S.   (1)
                 41st.Bn. M. G. C. (4)   D.A.P.M.41st.Divn. (1)
                 41st.D.T.M.O. through D.A.C

Appendix G

41st.D.A. No.H/1/55/3.

PRESENTATION OF MEDAL RIBBONS.

1. The G.O.C., 41st. Division will present Medal Ribbons in the Courtyard, SANTBERGEN Chateau, at 11.30.a.m. on Tuesday, 26th. November 1918.

2. The following will parade in addition to Officers and men to be decorated:-

   Not less than 30 men per Section 41st. D.A.C. and per 11th. B.A.C.
   Detachment of 200 men of 19th.Battn. MIDDLESEX Regt.(With Band)
   Detachment of 100 men 41st. Bn. M.G.C.

   Lieut:Col: A. W. TATE, 41st.Bn.M.G.C. will command the parade.

3. The programme will be as follows:-

   11.10.a.m. - Officers and men to be decorated report to Staff Captain R.A.41st.Divn. at SANTBERGEN Chateau.

   11.15 " - Markers.

   11.20 " - Troops march on to their markers.

   11.30. " - G.O.C. arrives on parade and is received with the General Salute.
   Presentation of Medal Ribbons.
   March Past.

4. All Officers and men to be decorated will prior to the parade, remove the ribbons with which they are subsequently to be presented In the case of recipients of the M.M., new Medal Ribbon will be provided.

   In the case of all other decorations, recipients will arrange to have their own ribbons mounted on a stiff card, with a pin at right angles (see illustration). These will be handed to the Staff Capt.R.A. before the parade and will subsequently be presented by the G.O.C.

   The Senior recipient of a decoration from each unit of the H.Q.Group (other than 41st.D.A.C.) will hand to the S.C.R.A. on parade a short statement (Preferably type-written) of the services in respect of which the Officers and men of his unit have earned their awards.

5. On the conclusion of the presentation of Medal Ribbons, the Officers and men who have been decorated will fall in in rear of the G.O.C. at the saluting point. The troops will then march past. After passing the saluting point, units will return to their billets independently.

6. A C K N O W L E D G E.

25th.Novr.1918.   Staff Captain,41st. Divisional Artillery.
Captain,

Distribution:-   41st. D. A. C.   (4)   No.1 Coy.41st.Div.Train(1
                 11th. B. A. C.   (1)   Camp Comdt.41 Div. (1)
                 41st.Div:Sig:Coy.R.E.(2)   41st.Divn. 'Q' (For inform
                 19th.Bn.Middlesex Regt.(4)   52 M. V. S.   (1)
                 41st.Bn. M. G. C. (4)   D.A.P.M.41st.Divn. (1)
                 41st.D.T.M.O. through D.A.C

WAR DIARY
or
INTELLIGENCE-SUMMARY. Headquarters, 41st.Divisional Artillery

Army Form C. 2118.

Place	Date	Hour	Summary of Events and Information	Remarks and references to Appendices
BELGIUM GRAMMONT	1918 Dec. 1st.		G.O.C.,41st.Division inspected Batteries of 190th.Brigade, R.F.A., in their Gun Parks.	
-do-	" 4th.		G.O.C., 41st.Division inspected Batteries of 11th (Army) Brigade, R.F.A., in their gun parks.	
-do-	" 9th.		G.O.C.,41st.Division, presented Croix de Guerres to recipients of this decoration in 41st. Divisional - Brigadier-General A.S.COTTON, D.S.O., C.R.A.,41st.Division, and Major E.R.ROPER D.S.O.,M.C.,Brigade Major, 41st.Divl. Artillery, were among the recipients.	App "A"
-do-	" 10th		Orders issued for March of the 41st.Divisional Artillery Group to Area N.E. of NAMUR (App:"A")	
TUBIZE	" 12th.		41st.D.A.,H.Q.,marched from GRAMMONT to TUBIZE.	
BRAINE- LE CHATEAU.	" 13th.		41st.D.A.,H.Q.,marched to BRAINE-le-CHATEAU.	
MONT ST.JEAN.	" 15th.		41st.D.A.,H.Q.,marched to MONT ST.JEAN.	
SART-DAME- AVELINES.	" 16th.		41st.D.A.,H.Q.,marched to SART-DAME-AVELINES.	
ST.MARTIN	" 17th.		41st.D.A.,H.Q.,marched to ST.MARTIN.	
NOVILLE-LES- BOIS.	" 18th.		41st.D.A.,H.Q.,marched to NOVILLE-LES-BOIS	
OTEPPE	" 19th.		41st.D.A.,H.Q.,marched to its final destination at OTEPPE	
-do-	" 20th		G.O.C., 41st.Division proceeded on one month's leave to England - Brigadier General A.S.COTTON D.S.O., C.R.A., 41st.Division, acted as Divisional Commander in his absence.	

-1-

Army Form C. 2118.

WAR DIARY
or
INTELLIGENCE-SUMMARY.

(Erase heading not required.) Headquarters, 41st. Divisional Artillery

Place	Date	Hour	Summary of Events and Information	Remarks and references to Appendices
BELGIUM OTEPPE	1918 Dec. 31st		The dispositions of Units of 41st.Divisional Artillery on completion of move were as follows:-	
			H.Q., R.A. — OTEPPE	
			H.Q., 11th.Army Bde., R.F.A. — LAMONTZEE	
			H.Q., 187th.Brigade, R.F.A. — MARNEFFE	
			H.Q., 190th.Brigade, R.F.A. — VIEUX WALEFFE	
			H.Q., 41st.D.A.C. — BURDINNE	
			11.1.1919.	
			Brigadier-general, Commanding 41st.Divisional Artillery.	

Appendix "A"

Copy No.

41st DIVISIONAL ARTILLERY ORDER No.28.

Reference Maps 1/100,000 TOURNAI & BRUSSELS.

1. R.A. Group will move from present area in accordance with attached March Table.

2. "A" Day will be 11th December 1918.
   March Tables for days subsequent to "D" day will be issued later.

3. R.A. Group will consist of following Units:-

   1. Headquarters R.A.
   2. 11th Army Bde. R.F.A.
   3. 187th Brigade R.F.A.
   4. 190th Brigade R.F.A.
   5. 41st D.A.C. with 11th Army Bde. A.C.
   6. No.1 Coy. Divisional Train.

   11th B.A.C. will march under orders of O.C. 41st D.A.C.

4. Throughout the March the following distances will be maintained:-

   100 yards in rear of Batteries, B.A.C. and Sections D.A.C.

   500 yards in rear of Brigades and equivalent units.

   500 yards in rear of Infantry Brigade Groups.

5. 41st D.A.H.Qrs. will close on each marching day 30 minutes before time shewn for it to pass Starting Point. It will re-open on arrival at new destination.

6. Location of Headquarters at conclusion of each day's march will be reported to R.A.H.Qrs. by orderly immediately on arrival.

7. Usual halts at 10 minutes to each clock hour will be observed.

8. Administrative Instructions have been issued to all concerned.

9. A C K N O W L E D G E.

Issued at 2.30 p.m.
10th Decr. 1918.

Major,
Brigade Major,
41st Divisional Artillery.

Copy No. 1 - 5   11th Army Bde. R.F.A.
         6 - 10 187th Bde. R.F.A.
        11 - 15 190th   "   "
        16 - 20 41st D.A.C.
             21 No.1 Coy Divl. Train.
             22 41st Divn. G.
             23 41st Divn. Q.

Copy No. 24 122nd Infy. Bde.
         25 123rd   "   "
         26 124th   "   "
         27 D.A.P.M. 41 Divn.
         28 H.Q. 41st Div. Trn.
         29 R.A. Xth Corps.
         30 S.C.R.A. 41 Divn.
         31 R.O.R.A.   "   "
      32 - 35 Spare.

P.T.O.

MARCH TABLE to accompany 41st D.A. Order No. 28.

Serial No.	Lay.	Unit.	From	To	Starting Point.	Time.	Route.	Remarks.
1.	B	11th Army Bde. R.F.A.	OVERBOUL-AERE.	VIANE.	Road Junction ½ mile S. of I of IDEGEM	10.00	Via LES DEUX ACREN.	Not to enter LES DEUX ACREN before 10.00
2.	B	41st D.A.C. & 11th B.A.C.	SCHENDEL-BEKE.	MOERBEKE.	SANTBERGEN Church.	10.30.	Via ONKER-ZEELE.	
3.	B	No.1 Coy. Divl. Train.	LUST.	VIANE.	Rd. Junction on VIANE-ENGHIEN Road ½ mile E. of I of HERNHOUT	09.00	ENGHIEN-HAL Road	
4.	C	187th Bde. R.F.A.	BIEVENE & VIANE.	TUBIZE area.	VIANE Church.	08.20	do.	
5.	C	11th Army Bde. R.F.A.	VIANE.	do.	Road Junction 1/3 mile N.W. of V of VIANE.	08.30	do.	
6.	C	190th Bde. R.F.A.	LES DEUX ACREN.	do.	Windmill ½ mile S. of MOERBEKE Railway crossing.	08.55	do.	
7.	C.	41st D.A.C. & 11th B.A.C.	MOERBEKE.	do.	VIANE Church.	09.40	ENGHIEN-HAL Road.	
8.	C	No.1 Coy. Divl. Train.	VIANE.	TUBIZE area.	Cross Roads ½ mile N. of O in GRAMMONT.	09.00	do.	
9.	G.	R.A.H.Qrs.	GRAMMONT.	do.	CLABECQ Church.	10.55		
10.	D.	R.A.H.Qrs.	TUBIZE area.	BRAINE-LE-CHATEAU Area.		11.00		
11.	D.	187th Bde.	do.	do.	Rd.Junction ½ mile N.E. of E in TUBIZE	10.45.		
12.	D.	11th Army Bde. R.F.A.	do.	do.	do.	11.10.		
13.	D	190th Bde. R.F.A.	do.	do.	do.	11.35.		
14.	D.	41st D.A.C. & 11th B.A.C.	do.	do.	do.	12.15.		
15.	D.	No.1 Coy. Divl. Train.	do.	do.	do.			

41st D.A. No. S.465.

To all recipients of 41st D.A. Order No.28.

1. Reference March Table accompanying above order:

    One hour will be added to times laid down for passing Starting Point for Serial numbers 4 to 8 (only).
    Thirty minutes will be added to times laid down for passing Starting Point for Serial Numbers 12 to 15 (only).

2. Heavy Draught Transport will be brigaded and march in rear of each Brigade (or D.A.C.) under command of an Officer.

3. An ambulance will march each day at rear of Column in order to carry men medically unfit to march.
    Such men will be provided with a M.O's certificate of unfitness to march and will parade at Starting Point of their unit, where they will be picked up.

11th Decr. 1918.

Major,
Brigade Major,
41st Divisional Artillery.

Copy to O.C. 138th Field Ambulance.

41st D.A. No. S.485.

11th Army Bde.R.F.A. (6 cos).   D.A.P.M. 41st Dvn.
187th Bde. R.F.A.   (6 cos).   H.Q. 41st Divl. Train.
190th "   R.F.A.   (6 cos).   S.C.R.A. 41st Dvn.
41st D.A.C.   (6 cos).   R.O.R.A. 41st Dvn.
No. 1 Coy. Train.
41st Dvn. G.
41st Dvn. Q.

Reference 41st D.A. Order No.26 of the 10th inst. March Table for D day will be as under and not as set out in that order.
Advance parties and Transport may be sent in advance; Not to pass GLABECQ Church before 11.00

Serial	Day.	Unit.	From	To	Starting Point.	Time.	Route. Remarks.
11.	D	187th Bde.R.F.A.	GLABECQ	OPHAIN	GLABECQ Church	13.00	
12.	D	11th Army Bde.R.F.A.	TUBIZE	BRAINE LE CHATEAU.	Road Junction 300ˣ E of E of TUBIZE	13.15.	
13.	D	190th Bde. R.F.A.	do.	do.	do.	13.40	To leave road clear till 11th A.F.A.Bde has passed S.P.
14.	D	41st D.A.C. and 11th A.F.A.B.A.C.	do.	do.	Road Junction ½ mile N.E. of E in TUBIZE	14.05.	
15.	D	No. 1 Coy. DvI. Train.	do.	do.	Road Junction 300ˣ E of E of TUBIZE.	14.50	To leave road clear till D.A.C. has passed S.P.

13-12-18.

Major,
Brigade Major,
41st Divisional Artillery.

41st D.A. No. S.527.

MARCH TABLE to accompany 41st D.A. Order No.28.

Serial No.	Day.	Unit.	From	To	Starting Point.	Time.	Route.	Remarks.
27	H.	R.A.H.Qrs.	SART-DAME-AVELINES Area.	ST.MARTIN Area.	Cross Rds at Kilo 37 v/a NIVELLES-NAMUR Road.	09.25.	Cross Rds. at Kilo 41 - BRYE - LIGNY-BOIGNEE.	To be clear of cross roads at Kilo 41 by 10.40.
28	H.	190th Bde. R.F.A.	do.	do.	do.	09.30	do.	To be clear of above cross Rds by 10.45.
29	H.	11th A.F.A. Bde.	do.	BALATRE area.	Cross Rds 200x E. of Kilo 36 on above road.	09.40	do.	To be clear of above cross Rds by 11.10.
30	H.	187th Bde. R.F.A.	do.	BOIGNEE area.	do.	10.25	do.	To be clear of above cross Rds by 11.35.
31	H.	41st D.A.C. 11th B.A.C.	QUATRE BRAS area.	LIGNY area.	QUATRE BRAS Cross Roads.	10.00.	do.	To be clear of above Cross Rds by 12.20.
32	H.	No.1 Gov. Mv1.Train.	do.	ST.MARTIN	do.	11.10.	do.	To be clear of cross Rds at Kilo 41 by 12.25
33	I.	R.A.H.Qrs.	ST.MARTIN	HAURET area.	Cross Roads at Kilo 17 on NAMUR Road.	06.30	Cross Rds at Kilo 11-ST DENIS-LONG-CHAMPS.	To be clear of cross Rds at Kilo 11 by 07.45.
34	I.	190th Bde. R.F.A.	do.	do.	do.	06.40	do.	To be clear of above cross Rds by 08.10.
35	I.	11th A.F.A. Bde.	BALATRE area.	do.	Western Outskirts of ST.MARTIN village.	06.45.	do.	To be clear of above cross Rds by 08.40.
36	I.	187th Bde. R.F.A.	BOIGNEE area.	do.	Road Jn.500x E. of Kilo 18 on NAMUR Road.	07.25.	do.	To be clear of above cross Rds by 09.05.

P.T.O

Serial No.	Lay.	Unit.	From.	To.	Starting Point.	Time.	Route.	Remarks.
37	I	41st D.A.C.& 11th B.A.C.	LIGNY Area.	HAURET Area.	Cross Rds. 500x E. of Kilo 20 on NAMUR Road.	07.30	Cross Rds at Kilo 11-ST.DENIS -LONGCHAMPS.	To be clear of above cross Rds by 09.50.
38.	I.	No.3 Coy. D.A. Train.	ST.MARTIN area.	do.	As for Serial No.33	08.45	do.	To be clear of Cross Rds at Kilo 11 by 10.05.
39.	J.	R.A.H.Qrs.	HAURET area.	OTEPPE Area.	Road Jn.100x N. of E. of HAMERAINE.	07.40	BIERWART- BURDINNE.	To be clear of BIER- WAART by 09.35.
40.	J.	190th Bde. R.F.A.	do.	do.	do.	07.45.	do.	To be clear of BIER- WAART by 09.40.
41.	J.	11th A.W.A. Bde.	do.	do.	Road Jn. 600x N.E. of T of HAURET.	08.00.	do.	To be clear of BIER- WAART by 10.10.
42.	J.	187th Bde. R.F.A.	do.	do.	do.	08.25.	do.	To be clear of BIER- WAART by 10.35.
43.	J.	41st D.A.C.& 11th B.A.C.	do.	do.	Cross Roads 700x N. of U. of HAURET.	08.45.	do.	To be clear of BIER- WAART by 11.20.
44.	J.	No.1 Coy. Divl. Train.	do.	do.	do.	09.30.	do.	To be clear of BIER- WAART by 11.30.

Usual billeting parties will meet the S.G.R.A. on H day at X roads BOIGNEE at 9 a.m. and on I day at X roads L'ANGLE at 10.0 a.m.

R.A.H.Qrs. will close each day half-an-hour before starting time and re-open on arrival at destination.

On I day all units will water and feed where they are at 11.50, resuming march at 12.30.

A Motor Cyclist D.R. will march on I day with 41st D.A.C. H.Qrs. and may be used by units for communicating with I.A.H.Qrs.

Usual halts will be observed at 10 minutes to each clock hour.

17-12-18.

Major,
Brigade Major,
41st Divisional Artillery.

… Army Form C. 2118.

WAR DIARY
INTELLIGENCE-SUMMARY.

(Erase heading not required.)

Headquarters, 41st. Divisional Artillery.

Instructions regarding War Diaries and Intelligence Summaries are contained in F. S. Regs., Part II. and the Staff Manual respectively. Title pages will be prepared in manuscript.

Place	Date	Hour	Summary of Events and Information	Remarks and references to Appendices
BELGIUM OTEPPE	1919 5th Jan.		Warning Order received from 41st.Division reference to move of 41st.Division to COLOGNE BRIDGEHEAD (GERMANY) to relieve 1st.Canadian Division (App: "A").	App: "A"
"	10th Jan.		Orders regarding entrainment issued (App:"B").	App: "B"
"	11th Jan.		Order received from Xth.Corps R.A. that 11th.(Army) Brigade, R.F.A., would not proceed to COLOGNE BRIDGEHEAD with 41st.Divisional Artillery (App: "C").	App: "C"
"	12th Jan.		41st.D.A., Headquarters entrained at ANDENNES (BELGIUM).	
GERMANY COLOGNE (BAYEN THAL)	13th Jan.		41st.D.A.,Headquarters detrained at WAHN (GERMANY) and marched to COLOGNE where they were established at No.144, OBERLANDER UFER, BAYEN THAL.	
"	14th Jan.		"A" Battery, "B" Battery, 190th.Brigade,R.F.A., "A" Battery 187th.Brigade, R.F.A., and portions of Nos. 1 and 2 Sections, 41st.D.A.C., detrained and marched to billets vacated by units of 1st.Canadian Divisional Artillery which they were relieving.	
"	15th Jan.		"C" Battery, "D" Battery, 190th.Brigade, R.F.A., "B" Battery, 187th.Brigade, R.F.A., remainder of No.2 Section, and portion of No.1 Section, 41st.D.A.C., detrained at WAHN.	
"	16th Jan.		Headquarters, 190th.Brigade, R.F.A., Headquarters, 187th.Brigade, R.F.A., "C" Battery, and "D" Battery, 187th.Brigade, R.F.A., and remainder of No.1 Section, 41st.D.A.C. detrained at WAHN.	
"	17th Jan.		126th (Army) Brigade, R.F.A., which had come to replace 11th (Army) Brigade, R.F.A., detrained at WAHN.	
"	20th Jan.		Disposition of Units of 41st.Divisional Artillery was as follows:— 187th.Brigade, R.F.A., grouped with 124th.Infantry Brigade which was in outpost line, had one battery in forward area, the others being in the vicinity of DEUTZ on the right bank of the RHINE, East of COLOGNE. 1.	

Army Form C. 2118.

WAR DIARY
or
INTELLIGENCE-SUMMARY.
(Erase heading not required.)

Headquarters, 41st. DIVISIONAL ARTILLERY.

Instructions regarding War Diaries and Intelligence Summaries are contained in F.S. Regs., Part II. and the Staff Manual respectively. Title pages will be prepared in manuscript.

Place	Date	Hour	Summary of Events and Information	Remarks and references to Appendices
GERMANY	1919			
COLOGNE (BAYENTHAL)	20th Jan.		190th. Brigade, R.F.A. grouped with 123rd. Infantry Brigade, which was in Divisional Reserve, had all batteries at WAHN Artillery Barracks. 126th (Army) Brigade, R.F.A., grouped with 122nd. Infantry Brigade, which was in the outpost line, had one battery in forward area, the others being in the vicinity of PORZ, on the right bank of the RHINE S.E. of COLOGNE.	
"	22nd Jan.		187th. Brigade, R.F.A., and 126th (Army) Brigade, R.F.A., arranged to change the battery in the outpost line area under Brigade arrangements. Orders issued regarding Inter-Battery and Inter-section D.A.C. Competition in the Divisional Artillery (App: "D")	App:"D"
"	28th Jan.		Owing to 5 4th.Divisional Artillery taking over a portion of the 41st.Divisional Artillery at an early date, orders were issued for relief of 190th.Brigade, R.F.A., by 113 th.Brigade, R.F.A., 34th.Divisional Artillery. (Appendix "E")	App:"E"
	5th.March 1919.			

R. S. Otton
Brigadier General,
Commanding 41st.Divisional Artillery.

Army Form C. 2118.

WAR DIARY
or
INTELLIGENCE SUMMARY.
(Erase heading not required.)

Headquarters, 41st. Divisional Artillery

Instructions regarding War Diaries and Intelligence Summaries are contained in F. S. Regs., Part II. and the Staff Manual respectively. Title pages will be prepared in manuscript.

Place	Date	Hour	Summary of Events and Information	Remarks and reference to Appendices
GERMANY 1919 BAYENTHAL, COLOGNE	Feb. 1st.		Brigadier-General A.S.COTTON, C.M.G., D.S.O., C.R.A.,41st.Division proceeded on one month's leave of absence to England; Lieut.Colonel G.A.CARDEW, C.M.G., D.S.O., Commanding 190th. Brigade, R.F.A., acting as C.R.A. in his absence.	
			No.1 Section 41st.D.A.C. beat 138th.Field Ambulance, R.A.M.C.,(41st.Division) in Semi-Final of Divisional Association Football Competition (Appendix "A")	App:A
-do-	Feb. 2nd.		190th.Brigade, R.F.A., moved from WAHN BARRACKS to POLL Area (Appendix "B")	App:B
-do-	" 3rd		Lecture of "The Work of the Navy" given by Commander Viscount BROOME, R.M., at PORZ (126th. (Army) Brigade R.F.A.) to units of 41st.Divisional Artillery.	
-do-	" 6th		No.1 Section, 41st.D.A.C., beaten by "D" Company, 20th.Durham Light Infantry in the Final of Divisional Association Football Competition.	
-do-	" 8th		Capt. E.C.R.HADDOW, M.C., R.F.A., D.T.M.O.,41st.Division proceeded to England for demobilization (Z.15a.).	
-do-	" 16th		a/C.R.A., and Brigade Major carried out reconnaissances of Out-post Area with a view to choosing positions for artillery.	
-do-	" 24th		Lecture given at PORZ by Bishop FRODSHAM to units of 41st.Divl:Artillery on "Imperialism". G.O.C., 41st.Division presented medals to winners and runners-up in the Divisional Boxing Competition; Dvr. MORRIS, 190th.Brigade, R.F.A. was among the recipients. (app: "C")	App:C
-do-	" 26th		41st.Divl: Artillery Defence Scheme for Artillery of the Left Sector Xth.Corps issued.	App:D
-do-	" 28th		Lecture on "Industrial Unrest" given by Archdeacon Wakefield to all units of 41st.Divl:Arty.	

A.S.Cotton
Brigadier-General,
Commanding 41st.Divisional Artillery.

Army Form C. 2118.

WAR DIARY
INTELLIGENCE SUMMARY.
(Erase heading not required.)

Headquarters, London (late 41st) Divl: Arty.

Instructions regarding War Diaries and Intelligence Summaries are contained in F.S. Regs., Part II. and the Staff Manual respectively. Title pages will be prepared in manuscript.

Place	Date	Hour	Summary of Events and Information	Remarks and references to Appendices
GERMANY	1919			
BAYENTHAL (COLOGNE)	Mar. 1st.		Major E.R.ROPER, D.S.O., M.C., Brigade Major, 41st.Divl: Artillery, proceeded on 14 days leave of absence to England; Major R.N.RASHLEIGH, D.S.O.,M.C.,187th.Brigade,R.F.A. acted as Brigade Major, in his absence.	
-do-	" 4th.		Brigadier General A.S.COTTON, C.M.G., D.S.O., returned from leave; Lieut.Colonel G.A.CARDEW C.M.G.,D.S.O., returned to 190th.Brigade,R.F.A. Lecture given by D.T.HOLMES Esq., on "INDUSTRIAL PEACE" at 126th (Army) Brigade, R.F.A., PORZ.	
-do-	" 5th.		C.R.A. carried out reconnaissance of Out-post area of Bridgehead.	
-do-	" 8th.		D.T.M.O. asked to submit a statement showing his proposals as to establishment of Mobile 6" Newton Trench Mortar Batteries.	
-do-	" 10th.		Lieut. H.S.A.WHITE, 41st.D.A.C., Education Officer, 41st.Divisional Artillery H.Q.,proceeded to England for demobilization.	
-do-	" 13th.		C.R.A. carried out inspection of 190th.Brigade,R.F.A.	
-do-	" 15th.		Major E.R.ROPER, D.S.O., M.C., Brigade Major,London Divisional Artillery, returned from leave in England; Major R.N.RASHLEIGH, D.S.O.,M.C., re-joined 187th.Brigade, R.F.A. Nomenclature of Divisions in Second Army changed:- 41st.Division becomes "London Division."	
-do-	" 24th.		Brigadier General L.C.L.OLDFIELD, C.M.G., D.S.O., took over Command of London Divisional Artillery, vice Brigadier General A.S.COTTON, C.M.G., D.S.O.	
-do-	" 25th		Orders issued as to relief of 124th.Infantry Brigade by 123rd.Infantry Brigade on 28th. On completion F.A. Brigades affiliated as under:- 187th.Brigade, R.F.A. to 123rd.Infantry Brigade, 190th.Brigade, R.F.A. to 124th.Infantry Brigade, (Appendix "A") Lieut H.E.McKIE, M.C.,Reconnaissance Officer, London Divisional Artillery, proceeded to England w.e.f. demobilization.	App: "A"

WAR DIARY
or
INTELLIGENCE-SUMMARY.

(Erase heading not required.)

Army Form C. 2118.

Headquarters, London (41st) Divisional Artillery (Late)

Place	Date	Hour	Summary of Events and Information	Remarks and references to Appendices
GERMANY BAYENTHAL (COLOGNE)	1919 Mar. 26th		Lieut. F.C.GEORGE, M.C., R.F.A., 104th.(Army) Brigade, R.F.A., appointed Staff Captain, London Divisional Artillery, and assumed duties of Staff Captain on 27.3.1919.	
-do-	Mar. 28th		Major H.W.L.WALLER, D.S.O., M.C., R.A., 12th.Divisional Artillery, joined London Divisional Artillery, as Brigade Major, vice T/Major E.R.ROPER, D.S.O., M.C., R.A., assuming duties on 1.4.1919.	
-do-	Mar. 30th		Orders issued as to transfer of 126th (Army) Brigade, R.F.A., to IInd.Corps area; B/190 5th. Brigade, R.F.A., to relieve 2 B.Battery, H.A.C., in forward area (OVERATH) on 31st. (App."B")	App:B.
-do-	" 31st		Relief carried out. (App:"B")	App:B.
	7.4.19.		Brigadier General, Commanding London Divisional Artillery.	

www.ingramcontent.com/pod-product-compliance
Lightning Source LLC
Chambersburg PA
CBHW080837010526
44114CB00017B/2323